SUPERVISION

Principles of
Professional
Management

SECOND EDITION

Robert M. Fulmer
Stephen G. Franklin

Emory University

SUPER

VISION

Principles of Professional Management

Macmillan Publishing Co., Inc.
New York

Collier Macmillan Publishers
London

Macmillan Publishing Co., Inc.
866 Third Avenue, New York, New York 10022

Collier Macmillan Canada, Ltd.

Library of Congress Cataloging in Publication Data

Fulmer, Robert M.
  Supervision.

  Includes bibliographical references and index.
  1. Supervision of employees. 2. Personnel
management. I. Franklin, Stephen G. II. Title.
HF5549.F83   1982   658.3'02   81–1704
ISBN 0–02–479660–3   AACR2

Printing: 1 2 3 4 5 6 7 8   Year: 2 3 4 5 6 7 8

Preface

For too long, the first-line supervisor has been a forgotten person in industry and academic programs. Despite the fact that the basic supervisory role is a vital one, involving more people than any other managerial category and serving as a gateway to higher positions in government and industry, many colleges continue to prepare their students to head General Motors or IBM. Some schools, however, are recognizing that there is a tremendous need for practical, down-to-earth supervisory courses for the countless students who wish to do a better job in their part-time positions and then move on to full-time supervisory roles immediately after graduation. Other students have already achieved full-time positions of responsibility by their own efforts and initiative and wish to sharpen their skills by part-time academic programs. This book is written primarily for these special programs and these special people.

In preparing the manuscript, we have drawn heavily on our own business experience and exposure to supervisory training programs in business, government, and trade associations. The book should be equally useful to the student wishing to learn about supervision and to supervisors hoping to better their performance on their current job and improve their future prospects. All the material has been reviewed by teachers and supervisors with extensive experience in practicing and teaching basic management skills.

The book begins by acknowledging that the most fundamental challenge of supervision is *self-mastery*. Part One considers the supervisor in terms of his or her role in the organization and the crucial responsibility as a catalyst for outstanding performance. It also considers the need to practice good communications and creativity in the work environment.

Part Two discusses the *administrative skills* that ensure competent organization of a project. Such functions as planning, staffing, and control are introduced in connection with the challenges of decision making and problem solving. The management of time and information is also stressed as a practical component of supervisory responsibility.

Part Three focuses on the *human relations skills* that ensure the competent supervision of workers. Whereas previous chapters have stressed logic, rationality, and accurate decisions, this section recognizes that even the best ideas must be accepted and implemented by people. Leadership, group dynamics, motivation, and resistance to changes are among the topics covered here in Part Four, in addition to the complex and controversial issues of labor relations, and the future.

Each chapter in the book is supplemented by specific learning objectives, key terms, review questions, exercises, and cases derived from our teaching and consulting experiences. This material is designed to supplement and reinforce the text materials. Typically, the student is asked to apply supervisory concepts in a test situation before trying them on the job. We believe that this process will improve recollection of, and confidence in, the essentials of supervision.

Without the insight, assistance, and encouragement of many people, this book would not have survived the problems associated with gestation and birth. In preparing the original edition, the senior author was especially fortunate to have enjoyed a consulting relationship with the Joint Task Force on Certification from the National Management Association and the International Management Council during the project. By working with leaders from the two largest groups of first-line managers in the United States, many new insights were gained about the emerging needs of the practicing manager. Because of their suggestions, this book would be helpful to individuals who wish to prepare themselves for examinations associated with the Institute of Certified Professional Managers. We would also like to thank the Macmillan Publishing Company for granting permission to use various selections from *The New Management,* 2nd ed., 1978. Donna Wood of Vanderbilt University made countless valuable suggestions concerning content and end-of-chapter materials. Betty Ullman was most helpful in securing permissions and typing major portions of the original manuscript. We are especially grateful for the suggestions of such distinguished reviewers as Joseph L. Massie of the University of Kentucky and James P. O'Grady, Jr., of Florissant Valley Community College, who read the entire manuscript and made many recommendations for improving the book.

In the second edition of this book, the senior author was fortunate to have Stephen G. Franklin of Emory University join him as co-author. His participation brings extensive practical experience as a manager and a consultant for business firms. He has been extremely helpful in coordinating and executing the many changes and details associated with this new edition. We would like to thank Philip Alan Cecchettini for his contributions as developmental editor on the new edition, Joyce Konigsberg for her many constructive suggestions, and Margie Langston for her swift and errorless typing of the manuscript.

R. M. F.
S. G. F.

Contents

PART FOUR
The Supervisor's Environment

SUPERVISION

Principles of
Professional
Management

PART

ONE

Developing Supervisory Skills

CHAPTER 1
An Overview of Supervisory Management

Good supervision is merely common sense mixed with the golden rule. The problem is, common sense just isn't very common these days.

Anonymous

Learning Objectives

- To describe the supervisor's role and functions.
- To see supervision as an art, a talent, and a skill.
- To differentiate the roles that supervisors must assume and the kinds of knowledge they must master to fill each of those roles.
- To understand the demands of supervision and the challenge of coordinating varied activities to reach a predetermined goal.
- To recognize the varied job possibilities for a supervisor and to decide which type of position might best fulfill your own needs.

The quality of an organization's leaders, from first-line supervisor to president, is the prime ingredient for its success. Experience tells us that effective supervision is of the utmost importance in all organizations—whether government, church, university, or corporation. An example is the government's attempt, after World War II, to aid poor countries by providing billions of dollars for recovery and development programs; the money served its purpose only in those nations where the programs were capably supervised. Business magazines, too, often hold up good supervision as a crucial factor in a company's success.

Except in single-owner businesses or partnerships, where the owners do everything and have no employees, a firm without supervisors would have to depend on an unusually compatible group of people. An informal group of sales representatives, accountants, or factory workers would have trouble organizing a successful business and management operation until they put someone in charge. The need for supervision applies in small and large businesses alike.

Most writers make a distinction between managers and supervisors. Typically, a supervisor is an individual who directs subordinates with no administrative responsibilities. Managers, by contrast, are those who direct the activities of supervisors or other managers. Throughout this book, however, the terms are used more or less interchangeably; thus, while it is written primarily for first- and second-level managers, most of the concepts also apply to supervisors throughout an organization. In thinking about the supervisor, then, we have not visualized an unimportant overseer but a highly skilled person who aspires to *professional management*—a person who is a vital, essential part of the management team.

With these points in mind we can formulate a simple definition of a manager or supervisor: *someone who is responsible for directing the performance of one or more workers so that organizational goals are accomplished.*

The Need for Supervisors

As a business grows and increases its staff with more people than an owner or chief executive can possibly handle, a second level of supervisors is added. If it grows even more, still another level of supervisors will be necessary. In very large corporations there might be ten or more levels of supervisors between the workers on the bottom rung and the president or top worker.

In fact, it is hard to imagine any kind of organized operation that does not group its workers under supervisors. From government agencies to schools, hospitals, churches, businesses, clubs, and sports, every human organization uses supervisors. Thus there is a great need for qualified supervisors; approximately one-eighth of all employed persons serve in a supervisory capacity.

Where do you find professional management? Unlike the hardware of production, supervisors are not readily available from a supply house. They do not come catalogued in the various price ranges and quality levels. There is no way a company can submit a purchase order and receive exactly the manager it wants. Neither can the assumption be made that good supervision will result from the process of moving the best workers up the organizational chart.

What Is a Supervisor's Job?

It is not enough to say simply that supervisors are responsible for the work of a group of people. They are also responsible for creating and maintaining an environment in which individuals can work effectively and efficiently together toward desired goals. They must be able to get their staff working and keep them working productively. In addition, they must work *with* and *for* various people, making sure that they have the information and materials necessary to do their jobs. Communicating a profit objective to line workers requires the finest communication skills and the clearest managerial understanding. A supervisor whose workers know their individual goals, the company's overall goals, and the relation between the two is truly a professional manager.

Supervisors as creators of surroundings. All too often supervisors are thought of as steely eyed individuals who methodically punch buttons, write letters, and boss people around. At the same time a supervisor is often expected to be a company psychiatrist, directing the workers' lives, actions, and personalities. But the supervisor's main job is to help individual workers achieve the organization's goal by showing them how to get the job done with the least amount of wasted effort. The supervisor should also communicate the great amount of personal satisfaction that can be obtained by doing that job well.

So it is all up to the supervisor to develop surroundings in which people will feel like working at their top potential. Of course, some workers are only interested in picking up their paychecks, but most people would like to get something more out of their jobs. The supervisor must help these workers get as much satisfaction as they can.

The wise use of authority is a large part of any supervisor's job. Authority is the right to command or request people to do something; however, a smart supervisor should think of it more as the opportunity to use and demonstrate good judgment. Above all, the decisions that a supervisor makes should help workers do their jobs better and get satisfaction from them.

Also, supervisors must keep in mind the limitations on their power of judgment. As the president of the United States must be guided by the Constitution, so the first-line supervisor is bound by organizational policy.

How environment can influence performance. The supervisor is responsible for many aspects of the workers' environment that will encourage maximum accomplishment. Some of these contributions are particularly important:

1. A worker's environment must include definable goals to work toward. These objectives must be carefully outlined and explained so that they are clearly understood by everyone involved. One of the biggest reasons for poor performance in organizations is that workers do not know what is specifically expected from them. A person simply cannot work toward an end that is not understood.

2. Surroundings should give workers a definite, clear idea of their roles in the organization.

3. The supervisor should try to remove any obstacles that might stand in the way of a worker's effective performance. If a supervisor cannot solve critical problems, he or she should ask for help from an immediate superior.

4. Ideally, the working environment should encourage personnel to do their jobs as the supervisors want them to. It must be clear both that certain procedures are preferred and that these procedures will be most effective.

5. The worker should not be made to feel like a cog in a huge machine. The supervisor must always be aware that subordinates are people with needs and desires to be considered.

6. The supervisor should realize that some workers may have useful ideas for solutions to current problems. The work environment should stimulate workers to express these ideas so that more answers can be found and more people participate in making decisions.

The supervisor as a catalyst. In the science of chemistry a catalyst is a substance that starts a chemical reaction. When certain materials are combined and a catalyst is introduced, things begin to happen. The similarity between a chemical catalyst and an able supervisor should be apparent.

A supervisor is the agent that makes a company department operate effectively. The successful performance of a group proves that its supervisor has catalytic qualities. Poor management, by contrast, represents what chemists would call an anticatalyst, an element that freezes activity instead of generating it. Thus a supervisor who has poor judgment, or does not know the job, or is clumsy in dealing with workers, can undermine the productivity of the entire department.

The catalytic supervisor moves calmly and methodically about the task of making the business move evenly and systematically without personally doing the workers' jobs. Supervisors at Goodyear may know how to build tires, but they do not actually do the work. Instead, they direct the efforts of workers at each stage of the process. The supervisor's real objective is to get things done by seeing that others do whatever is required for success.

Walking through the noise and activity of an assembly line, it is easy to assume that the real work is happening on the factory floor. Still, it should not take long to realize that the quiet, catalytic actions of the supervisor also make the factory go.

The supervisor as the person in the middle. The supervisor, whose job is by its nature in the middle of everything, may sometimes appear to be "neither fish nor fowl." While frequently in direct contact with the labor force, the supervisor is not "one of them." At the same time, supervisors must represent the company and enforce its policies, procedures, and rules. Yet they are not part of top management.

Labor and top management are often suspicious of each other. The supervisor is the key to overcoming this suspicion and making each group realize that it is totally dependent upon the efforts and success of the other. Without management, laborers would not have jobs to complain about. Without labor, top management would not have the profit picture to worry about. In fact, representatives of both groups might find themselves unemployed if the supervisor fails to do an effective job of balancing the needs, interests, and concerns of each group.

The Supervisor's Goals

Business profits, of course, do not include all the money made in sales but only what is left after company expenses are paid. When a supervised group of people has turned out products or services that will sell, and production costs are low enough so that extra dollars remain after overhead, the business will be a profitable one.

These extra dollars are called surplus, and creation of this surplus is a major goal of every practical supervisor, no matter what type of organization is served. Thus the supervisor will try to make certain that subordinates clearly understand the department's objectives. When workers know what their specific goals are, surplus is much easier to strive for and obtain.

The central business goal of supervisors in a private enterprise system is profit. To obtain this, there are additional goals that a successful supervisor must achieve. The efficient and effective use of human and physical resources is a goal that comes with creative implementation of skills acquired through on-the-job experience and other learning activities. Maintaining smooth operations is a necessary goal contributing to the profit picture. Coaching and developing employees into hard-to-replace, productive assets is a critical goal for the perceptive supervisor who wants to advance in the organization. Clear, concise communication to and from subordinates is a perpetual, challenging goal for the effective supervisor.

The Supervisor's Skills

Managing workers is an art that demands certain special talents and abilities—as do medicine, architecture, music, writing, engineering, and football. Each profession, however, is also a craft. A person in any of these fields will do a better job by acquiring a basic knowledge of the principles involved and learning how to apply those principles to daily problems.

At this point, science becomes an art. The best supervisor is most likely the one who combines a flair for supervision with a scientific approach to the skills involved. Although few workers think of their bosses in this way, an unskilled supervisor can quickly make a mess of any department.

Knowledge of skills alone does not ensure that a person can perform them well. A tennis fan may know the proper way to hold a racquet and still be unable to hit the ball over the net. Likewise, a supervisor may know a number of theories about supervision without being able to handle the staff. To become a supervisor, then, a worker should understand the science of supervision and know how to apply it on the job.

The skills of supervision are many and complex. Given the varying attitudes, desires, and backgrounds of different human beings, a successful supervisor must have considerable knowledge and understanding of human behavior. Furthermore, the supervisor of each department must mesh personal activities with those of the company's other supervisors, which may cover a broad range of functions and objectives. Fulfilling this task means performing as both coordinator and diplomat. New supervisors, polled for a research study, expressed the following feelings as they began new careers:

- 90 percent wanted more knowledge of human relations.
- 60 percent needed better communications techniques.
- 40 percent felt deficient in personnel procedures and record keeping.
- 40 percent needed help in production planning.
- Nearly 30 percent wanted better methods of improvement training.
- 15 percent did not understand quality control and inspection procedure as well as they felt they should.
- 6 percent wanted better material-handling knowledge.[1]

Not that most supervisors identified specific needs in areas where the knowledge could not be supplied relatively simply and easily. The overwhelming problem for most new managers, it appears, is learning the most effective methods for dealing with people. The acquisition of good skills in human relations, communication, and personnel is a less tangible objective than the mastery of good quality control and material-handling techniques. The latter goal may be achieved through training and education, but experience in managing subordinates is the only valid route to the former. Nevertheless, the qualified supervisor must learn to wear all these hats in helping workers toward organizational goals.

Aside from any specialized knowledge, however, most supervisors could make better use of the knowledge they already have. We can get a better idea of the knowledge needed by effective supervisors in pointing out that they must serve as historian, psychologist, sociologist, professional decision maker, forecaster, and management scientist.[2]

The supervisor is a historian. Supervisors can learn by studying their own and other supervisors' past experiences and failures, concentrating on the basic reasons some projects went smoothly and other projects went wrong. Using this approach, supervisors can predict the likely outcome of future undertakings.

Experience, however, must be weighed carefully, for it can prove a very strict and expensive teacher. For example, the person who believes that something can be done even though it has never been done before is a valuable asset in business. Approaches that failed before may suddenly work in the face of different circumstances.

Because supervisors cannot experience all of the knowledge necessary for their jobs, the wise supervisor draws conclusions from others' experiences. Most supervisors learn from the people they have worked for. An individual guided by capable, enlightened bosses has a real advantage over the person who can only see how things should not be done. Supervisors with real potential, however, can learn from bad experiences as well as good and apply these lessons to other situations they face today and anticipate tomorrow.

The supervisor is a psychologist. The effective supervisor also pays great attention to the personal characteristics of subordinates. There is no need to be a practicing amateur psychiatrist, but a manager should understand what makes people behave as they do. The supervisor's job is not to manipulate workers but to combine new theories about human behavior with a common

---

[1] Quoted by Lester Bittel, *What Every Supervisor Should Know,* 3rd ed. (New York: McGraw-Hill, 1974), p. 18.

[2] Based on Harold Koontz, "Making Sense of Management Theory," *Harvard Business Review,* July/August 1962, pp. 24 ff.

sense understanding of people. When a supervisor listens, selects, and uses psychological information about people with care and wisdom, heightened morale and productivity should result. The supervisor motivates people most effectively by understanding their importance and the underlying causes of their behavior.

The supervisor is a sociologist. Supervisors are even more interested in groups of people than in individuals. They know that people working together develop certain attitudes and patterns of actions. For example, your own attitude toward anything—money, politics, school—is primarily a pattern of feelings developed in responding to your family, your school, your neighborhood, or your job.

The supervisor deals with many groups: subordinates, other company departments, customers, suppliers, buyers, and so on. At the same time, everybody in business is influenced by memberships in many other groups, oriented toward family, church, school, social life, and ethnic background.

The supervisor is also a professional decision maker. A supervisor can become more effective in dealing with others by learning some basic behavioral science, but management is more than sociology or psychology. Supervisors must decide major issues, such as what to buy, what to sell, how much inventory to stock, whom to hire, and many other things. So each supervisor is a *professional* decision maker, not just a casual decision maker. Managers are paid more than subordinates because they are expected to make better and more responsible decisions.

Supervisors must be able both to forecast and face changes. For example, if a manufacturer of women's clothing waited until after styles had changed before redesigning its own line of clothes, it would be hard pressed to catch up with competitors who had foreseen new clothing styles.

Supervisors must react positively and efficiently to new policies, procedures, techniques, and bosses. Moreover, they must be successful in selling change to other people. Sometimes supervisors will ask subordinates to accept changes that they have developed, but, more frequently, they must get subordinates to accept changes someone else has developed. Considerable loyalty and ingenuity are required to meet this challenge successfully.

Supervisors rely heavily on forecasts in many different areas—economic, political, social, technological—because they must manage for the future.

The supervisor is a scientific manager. The supervisor must be a virtual scientist to do the job well. This requires the ability to devise and test new answers to old problems. It also requires an extensive understanding of the underlying factors that cause problems and make solutions work.

Still, knowledge is not enough. The supervisor's most important and challenging duty is to apply this knowledge to everyday problems in supervision.

Demands of the Supervisor's Job

Both the company president and first-line supervisor hold highly demanding jobs. Each must adopt and promote the company's and department's goals. They must be concerned with the buyers of the company's product as well as the suppliers of raw materials. They must be aware of the governmental regulations and laws under which they operate. In addition, they are required to observe what goes on inside the organization while constantly interpreting the present and peering into the future.

But that is not all. Because people are the most important single concern for supervisors, they must interact skillfully with the people who report to them, those they work with in other departments, and those to whom they report. For example, a worker's outside interests and personal goals usually take precedence over company or department goals. Thus these personal goals must be carefully considered by every supervisor who wishes to motivate the staff effectively.

Supervisors must also make sure their workers have the necessary tools, machines, and materials to perform their jobs. They need to inform subordinates clearly about the goals their jobs are designed to achieve. Every supervisor assumes a multitude of duties. They must make certain that workers know what their jobs are, how much freedom and authority they can exercise, how their jobs relate to others, for what and to whom they are responsible, when and where they work, how much they are to be paid, what policy they should follow, how well they are doing, and how to make their performances more beneficial to themselves and the company. In short, the supervisor's job is a composite of many demanding tasks.

Coordination: The Essence of Supervision

Coordination involves making all of the parts of a department or organization operate in harmony with each other. Many details must be integrated in order for goals to be successfully reached. The goal of coordination is to achieve a unified effort in the planning and execution of every operation. Coordination involves identifying, planning, and monitoring the various activities, objectives, resources, and systems that must come together for an organization to function effectively.

Logic and knowledge help in planning for coordinated activities, yet they are not enough. The effective supervisor must gain the cooperation of subordinates in order for the pieces to fit together in a smooth, efficient manner. This requires human relations skills. The willingness of employees to cooperate will depend upon positive leadership techniques, and motivation will be required to stimulate cooperative effort. The supervisor must have an understanding of techniques for overcoming resistance to change in order to gain cooperation for new ventures. Each of these skills will be discussed in much greater detail later in this book. For now, we can say that coordination is the essence of a supervisor's administrative skills and leadership is the essence of his or her human relations skills.

Coordination becomes important as soon as business involves more than one person. It becomes crucial when the efforts of dozens, hundreds, or thousands of people must fit neatly together. Although effective organization may appear as merely one of the supervisor's many jobs, coordination of people and their various skills is actually the essence of supervision.

Because each individual comprehends a group's goals differently, and each tries to reach those goals in a unique way, coordination is rarely easy. A coordinator must keep everyone on the same track. At the same time, the supervisor must draw out individual strengths and desires. A group's work should show a balanced combination of each member's strengths. Thus the supervisor's central task is to resolve major differences between workers and to harmonize company and individual goals.

Understanding Supervisory Functions

If the success of an organization depends on the caliber of supervision, we should try to formulate a clear picture of exactly what goes into the job of supervision by examining the major functions involved, analyzing typical responsibilities, and reviewing key problem areas. This text will explore these areas in succeeding chapters on planning, organizing, directing, and controlling.

Planning has been called the primary supervisory function. Before any effective supervision can be exercised, some planning has to take place. This involves developing a program of action to achieve personal, departmental, and organizational goals through the use of procedures and policies.

Organization involves determining the jobs to be performed and creating a framework of authority and responsibility to help workers perform their jobs. At the highest levels of a corporation, organization involves setting up divisions or departments. The first-line supervisor's role may have less scope but is equally as vital. This challenge will focus on involving the best combination of people and resources in a cooperative effort to achieve goals that have been previously determined. Organization involves the allocation of personal and subordinate effort in the most effective manner. "Getting your own act organized" may be one of your most difficult supervisory tasks.

The control function involves seeing that things happen as they were planned and identifying the activities that are not meeting expectations. Control efforts include attempts to prevent problems from arising by diagnosing their causes and implementing corrective measures.

As used here, the term *directing* is the human side of the control function. It involves the challenges of stimulating productive work through good human relations utilized in the pursuit of the organizational goals.

As will be seen, the supervisor as planner works to design the basis of supervision. As organizer the supervisor sets up a structure of positions in which workers may perform. Leadership will *start* the department working. Then, because all supervisors want to know whether or not their plans *are* working, they must apply measurements and controls.

Supervision's Many Facets

Supervisory challenges, opportunities, and environments differ according to organizations, but supervisors appear in almost all organized activity. Some readers, for example, will doubtless serve as supervisors in government at local, state, or federal levels. Others will work for businesses—perhaps a discount store, restaurant, insurance company, or manufacturing firm. A few of you, after gaining experience and knowledge, will choose to start your own business.

Of course, going into business is not a simple matter. The majority of new businesses fail. Those that succeed must cope with extensive regulations and rigorous competition. Nevertheless, supervision may be more rewarding, both financially and emotionally if you are supervising your own operation.

Small Businesses

Many students think of business only in terms of large companies such as General Motors or IBM. Actually, the majority of goods and services are produced by firms considered "small." The Small Business Administration defines *small business* as a manufacturing company with 250 or fewer employees, and any retailing or service business with a million dollars or less in annual sales.

According to the National Federation of Independent Business, these smaller firms supply jobs to 34 million Americans. The 500 largest corporations in the country employ over 21.6 million people. Obviously, there is considerable opportunity to be found outside corporate giants.

In small companies, talented supervisors can usually command salary and fringe benefits comparable to those offered by a larger company. They are much closer to the top of the organization and are likely to possess a wide range of authority and responsibility. Their decisions may be more critical in directly affecting the bottom-line profitability of the firm. A small business supervisor probably will not have the luxury of a personnel or training department, and will have to be capable of hiring, training, and developing employees to their full potential. A supervisor may gain much broader experience in a small business than would be possible in a specialized area of a large firm.

Large Companies

Of course, there are valid reasons why many people decide to pursue a career with one of the nation's larger firms. These companies offer the prestige associated with working for a well-known organization. Associates are often impressed to learn that one is working for a prominent firm.

There is also a greater degree of security in working for a large firm. Industrial giants are not likely to fail. Bad decisions will have less impact on a mammoth organization than they would on a smaller one. This does not mean that large companies are completely immune to problems and instability. Penn Central, Lockheed Aircraft, Chrysler Corporation, and others have suffered serious cutbacks in personnel and have been threatened with bankruptcy and extinction. But, in general, large corporations have a much stronger survival rate and a more secure base than smaller companies.

Larger organizations also offer more extensive training and development programs and can provide a greater variety of opportunities to work in several types of operations and in many geographical locations. Of course, factors one person sees as advantages may appear as disadvantages to a person with a different point of view.

Other Opportunities

An individual with skills in supervision will find that these talents are in demand in every type of organization. Religious groups, military units, educational institutions, welfare agencies, athletic teams, social clubs, and even families require the skills that every supervisor must employ. This book, then, is for every individual who plans to work with other people in order to get things accomplished.

Summary

Well-developed supervisory skills are the most important ingredient for successful business. Supervisors are necessary to all organized groups in which people work together to accomplish common goals.

We can easily define a supervisor as someone who is responsible for directing the performance of one or more persons toward the achievement of goals. But to understand the extent and variety of these tasks, we must say more. Supervisors are also responsible for creating and maintaining a working environment in which staff members can efficiently attain desired goals. Their main objective should be to help the workers achieve company goals with the least amount of wasted effort while encouraging employees to seek personal satisfaction and pleasure through their work. Although supervisors have the authority to direct and control workers, they must remember that authority is also wise, creative judgment in helping others perform to the best of their ability.

Important elements in creating an effective working environment include:

1. Goals that are clearly understood by all employees and adequate work plans to accomplish these goals.
2. Meaningful explanations of workers' positions in the department so that they understand their part in the total operation and their relation to other people.
3. Removal of as many obstructions to departmental operation as possible.
4. Motivating workers to accomplish company goals, both because they want to and because they know the importance of the goals.
5. Recognition and understanding of workers' personal needs.
6. Realization that many workers have their own ideas about solutions to departmental and company problems, and establishment of an atmosphere that will encourage expression of those ideas.

As supervisors create a good working environment, they must strive for surplus. They must help their department achieve goals with the minimum amount of materials and money as well as the maximum amount of worker efficiency and satisfaction.

To do their jobs best, supervisors need sound knowledge of the nature of supervision and the techniques and approaches which underlie it. This is not to say that supervising is strictly a science; it is more an art. But, like all arts, supervision must be practiced until the knowledge gained can be quickly applied to everyday problems.

The knowledge required of supervisors is great and varied. They should be historians who understand the lessons of experience. To deal effectively with people, they must understand basic psychology. Since they direct groups of people who are shaped by all kinds of outside influences, the supervisor should also understand sociology. At the same time, the supervisor must remain a professional in terms of decision-making ability. Because these decisions will influence the future, the supervisor must also be a forecaster. In conclusion, the successful supervisor must be a scientist, artist, and practitioner.

To convey better the vast knowledge a supervisor must have, the chapters that follow will explore the four major functions: planning, organizing, directing, and controlling.

Key Terms

Authority. The limited power of a supervisor to use personal judgment.

Catalyst. An agent that acts within a static situation to trigger an interaction between forces, or that encourages conflicting forces to achieve a resolution in balance with each other.

Coordination. Organizing group members as a foundation for increasing supervisory skills.

Human Behavior. Patterns of action that people develop in working with and reacting to one another.

Sociologist. One who studies the how and why of group behavior, as opposed to the psychologist or psychiatrist who studies individual behavior.

Supervisor. A person responsible for directing the performance of one or more workers toward the achievement of goals.

Review Questions

1. What is a supervisor?
2. What is the major concern of a supervisor?
3. It is said that a supervisor is like a catalyst in a chemical reaction. What does this mean and what does it imply?
4. How can a supervisor use past experience in creating the present working environment?
5. Describe the ways in which a supervisor can become a wiser and more effective decision maker.
6. What is a supervisor's main purpose when dealing with workers in a department? How can a supervisor best achieve this purpose?
7. Describe or give examples of several supervisory goals and purposes in informing workers about their jobs.
8. What is the proper use of authority in managing people in a department?
9. What information should a supervisor give workers to make them work harder?
10. It is said that a supervisor should create a work environment that minimizes waste in time and materials, and provides workers with maximum personal

and professional rewards. What does this mean and how can it be accomplished?

11. What is more important to a supervisor than in-depth technical knowledge?

12. Practically speaking, what is the financial goal of a supervisor? Is this the same goal of most workers?

13. Why is it often difficult to coordinate activities within a department?

14. To maintain effectiveness, how should a supervisor view the future?

Exercise

Discover Your Supervisory Skills

A. Write a paragraph discussing the relationships between authority and responsibility as they affect the supervisor's job.

B. Describe briefly any experience you have that qualifies you to be a supervisor. Rather than list your actual work experience, consider skills you have acquired in administration, dealing with people, and managing yourself. List all your special skills and qualities that would prove useful in supervisory work. Do you have the basic skills and abilities you would need? If you do not, can you get them? How do you measure up as a potential supervisor?

Case 1 • Harriet Brown

After four years with the Lakewood Assembly Plant, Harriet Brown has been promoted to supervisor. Prior to Lakewood she attended one year at a community college and worked three years at another manufacturing plant. Her employment record at both plants was excellent as was her rapport with fellow employees. Nevertheless, Harriet is apprehensive about her new role. In her new position she will have six subordinates: three are older than she, two have been employed at Lakewood longer, and two are men.

Harriet worries that her subordinates as well as friends in other departments of the plant may resent her new position and authority. She is an extremely close friend of two of her subordinates and wonders if she can continue social activities with them. She is also worried about reactions of the men to supervision by a woman and of those who have been with the company longer. Although concerned about the future, Harriet is determined to be a first-rate supervisor and plans to read a number of books on supervision she has secured from the library. She says, "I need to find out how to act as a supervisor. I have been pretty successful as a worker, but I'll have to develop a new personality and start treating my friends differently if I am to succeed in this new job."

1. Evaluate Harriet's attitude. Do you agree that she has to develop a new personality and begin treating her friends differently?

2. Can you make any suggestions that would reduce the chances of resentment by her subordinates?

3. In what ways should her behavior change as she assumes her supervisory responsibilities?

An Overview of Supervisory Management • **17**

CHAPTER 2

First, Manage Yourself

Would the power some giftie give us, to see ourselves as others see us, it would from many a blunder free us.

Robert Burns

Learning Objectives

- To discover the key to self-understanding, which will help you understand other people.
- To identify the various approaches to self-knowledge and to select the one that best applies to you.
- To assess personal skills and abilities and decide which need improvement and which are strengths.
- To relate the importance of accepting yourself to the job of changing the behavior of others.
- To learn to apply concepts of self-management to every area of personal and professional life.

Throughout the ages people have sought a magic key capable of unlocking their own hidden gifts and utilizing the full potential of other human beings.

If there is such a magic key, it lies in first achieving self-understanding. For the supervisor or anyone constantly involved with other people, the adage "know thyself" may serve as a helpful reminder that any knowledge and understanding of individual attitudes and motivations begin at home.

In all the world you are unique—yet you share many characteristics with other people. Although no one has your exact combination of physical appearance, personality, feelings, knowledge, and experience, you and other humans have many things in common. Thus understanding yourself—what makes you tick, what you want from life, and how to go about obtaining it—can help you to understand those around you.

Understanding Your Human Needs

In the course of his long and distinguished clinical practice, the psychologist Abraham Maslow discovered that all people feel certain needs which they seek to meet. From his observations Maslow formulated his "humanistic" philosophy based on the ways in which human needs govern behavior.

The human needs approach is very positive. It views the individual's drives as good, not evil, and considers people to be continually seeking health, happiness, and accomplishment. In the past many people felt that basic drives forced them toward failure and self-destruction. Maslow's human needs theory reversed this approach and, correct or not, provided a more positive way to view and motivate human beings.

Maslow identified five levels of needs and arranged them on an ascending scale.[1] He believed that people attempt to satisfy a higher-level need only after satisfying at least some of the needs on the ladder's preceding lower levels (see Figure 2-1).

The following levels of human needs have been described by Maslow:

1. Physiological needs. The needs for air, water, food, and shelter are basic to physical survival and so rank as the first human needs to be satisfied. Unfortunately, many people in the world have not been able to satisfy these needs even minimally.

2. Safety and security needs. For many people these are difficult needs to satisfy. People who live in earthquake or hurricane zones or in politically explosive areas can never satisfy their needs for safety and security. Additionally, many people are trapped in life-endangering jobs such as coal and ore mining. All workers want to come to work each day without the fear of being fired or laid off.

3. Love and belonging needs. In our society, where most people's lower-need levels are at least minimally satisfied, many people spend their lives seeking to love and be loved. People are social animals and are rarely happy unless they have contact with and are accepted by other people.

4. Self-esteem needs. Needs near the top of Maslow's ladder are very difficult to satisfy. Because the need for self-respect underlies most accomplishments, individuals need to know and like themselves in order to know and like other people. Fulfilling these self-esteem needs involves understanding your

[1] See Abraham Maslow, *Toward a Psychology of Being,* 2nd ed. (New York: Van Nostrand Reinhold, 1968). One of the first business writers to apply Maslow's ideas to supervision was Douglas McGregor in *The Human Side of Enterprise* (New York: McGraw-Hill, 1960).

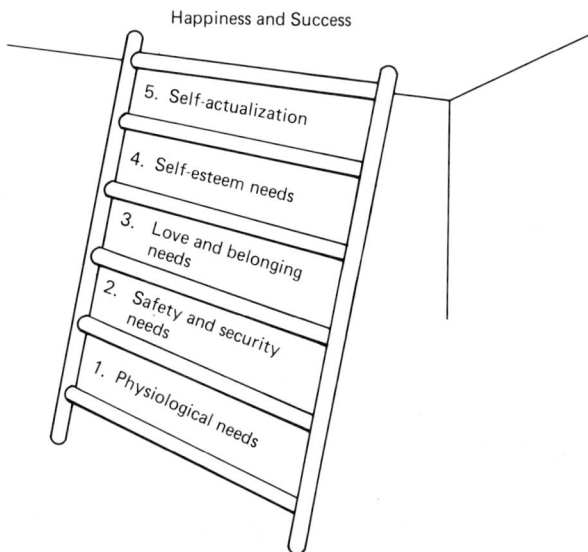

Happiness and Success

5. Self-actualization

4. Self-esteem needs

3. Love and belonging needs

2. Safety and security needs

1. Physiological needs

Figure 2-1. Maslow's Ladder of Needs.

own talents and limitations, knowing the value of your experiences, and being able to relate well to others. Lack of self-esteem can remain a basic individual problem in a society that has enabled people to meet most of their lower-order needs.

5. Self-actualization needs. The height of human achievement, according to the human needs approach, lies in an individual's understanding and respecting personal merits, recognizing the potential of these unique talents, and proceeding to develop them. The self-actualized person is sometimes referred to as being "fulfilled." This person can accept reality, is not afraid of growing close to others, is a good judge of character and situations, is creative and appreciative of others' help, and has a personal set of values which guide daily actions. Finally, the self-actualized individual is willing to learn from anyone.

What do these needs have to do with the supervisor's job? Each supervisor seeks to meet these needs through work as well as through relationships with other people. The supervisor will earn enough to provide the basic physical needs for food, clothes, and shelter. The job will probably be relatively safe from physically dangerous surroundings and secure from employee cutbacks.

But what about higher-level needs? In seeking love and affection or social acceptance and stability, some supervisors overlook their responsibility to manage and direct their workers effectively. The saying, "You can't be loved by everyone," is nowhere more true than in supervision. A supervisor's authority alone is sometimes enough to trigger workers' dislike. Although every supervisor must remember that the job is not to win the love of workers, supervisors are usually more successful if they are liked in spite of the authority that goes with the job.

Both supervisors' and workers' self-esteem needs can be met in a supervisory setting. If a supervisor has self-respect, he or she will understand others' needs for respect as well. People cooperate more fully under the direction of a person who respects them. Workers are no exception to this rule. When this cooperation helps a supervisor perform the job competently and with understanding, there is a strong foundation for self-esteem.

Can the supervisor be a self-actualized person? A review of the characteristics enjoyed by the self-actualized individual suggests that such a person would be tolerant, decisive, understanding, efficient, realistic, innovative, eager to learn—in short, a remarkable human being.

Assessing Your Skills

From time to time, companies offer programs designed to help their supervisors do a better job of managing. Most of these programs are valuable to some extent but in the final analysis their success depends upon the dedication and determination of each supervisor and manager. Whether through a company-sponsored program or an individual's burning of the midnight oil, improvement of managerial skills is largely a matter of self-development.

Nobody else in the world is as concerned as you are about the way you are going to live your life. Nobody else will maintain the same closeness to your desires and ambitions. The popularity of Robert Ringer's book, *Looking Out for #1*, reinforces the notion that if anyone is going to open the doors of improvement, it will be old number one. The organization can make things easier. But in the long run it is up to you.

Your personal skills are tools in developing your supervisory ability. Your ability to plan, obtain information, solve problems, and make decisions, as well as your work attitudes and methods, will affect everything you do.

So many skills are involved in a supervisor's day-to-day activities that most of this book will describe the necessary skills to supervise effectively and explain how you can begin to develop them. Using Figure 2-2, you can rate yourself on a number of basic supervisory skills. If you have already worked in a supervisory situation, you should have an accurate basis for judging yourself on these skills. If you have not yet begun to work, try to anticipate the level of your skills in each area.

Rating Yourself

In completing the following Skills Rating Chart, circle the dot that corresponds to your estimate of your level of ability in each skill area. If you are very proficient at judging people, for instance, rank yourself "high." If you have some problems in this area, you might rank "medium," and if you have often been proven wrong as a judge of character, you should rank yourself "low" as a judge of people.

If you are too harsh or too lenient in estimating your skills, the assessment of your skill development level will be inaccurate and will not provide a basis for analysis and improvement. Try to picture different situations in which each skill has been applied, then set those images aside so that your rating of one skill will not color your judgment of another.

When you have completed the chart, draw lines connecting the dots you circled. You now have a picture of your estimated abilities in several key supervisory areas.

	Low	Medium	High
1. *Using the expert*—getting information, opinions, ideas from well-informed people inside or outside your company.	•	•	•
2. *Building a reputation*—making yourself known; developing a favorable name for yourself in the company.	•	•	•
3. *Activating*—getting people to understand and follow your instructions.	•	•	•
4. *Imparting information*—making yourself understood by subordinates or superiors.	•	•	•
5. *Judging people*—gauging individuals so as to be able to establish good relations and mutually increase job satisfaction.	•	•	•
6. *Working with subordinates*—establishing cordial and effective relationships with those who work for you.	•	•	•
7. *Interviewing*—talking with people face to face.	•	•	•
8. *Listening*—learning from the words of others how they think and feel.	•	•	•
9. *Getting cooperation*—motivating people to join you in accomplishing departmental goals.	•	•	•
10. *Maintaining good relations with your superior*—being both friendly and businesslike in your dealings up the line.	•	•	•
11. *Using working time effectively*—being able to get sixty minutes of work out of every hour.	•	•	•
12. *Decision making*—arriving at a logical conclusion and sticking to it.	•	•	•
13. *Planning*—developing a course of action to accomplish a definite objective.	•	•	•
14. *Controlling paper work*—maintaining the flow of interoffice communications and reports, and maintaining communication with business associates outside your company.	•	•	•
15. *Getting information*—uncovering the facts you need to advance your work.	•	•	•
16. *Delegation*—making subordinates responsible for some of your activities while retaining control.	•	•	•
17. *Problem solving*—licking the tough situations that interfere with efficiency.	•	•	•
18. *Pacing your energy expenditures*—conserving your energy so that you can complete the day without undue fatigue.	•	•	•
19. *Concentration*—being able to stick with a complex or difficult task until you reach completion or find a workable solution.	•	•	•
20. *Memory*—remembering events, incidents, ideas, plans, and promises.	•	•	•
21. *Budgeting your time*—accomplishing the objectives of your job by efficient allotment of your time.	•	•	•

Figure 2-2. Skills Rating Chart. (With permission of the Research Institute of America.)

As you may notice, these skill areas reflect the major sections of this book. They also reflect the major areas involved in the certification program for managers developed by the National Institute of Certified Professional Managers. If you plan to seek certification or wish to improve your abilities in management, you may want to sum up your rankings in each category. If you ranked yourself high in human relations skills, your sensitivity to others will be reflected in both your ability to supervise and your manner of supervision. If you find yourself weak in this area, you will want to focus your attention on developing these skills to become a more effective supervisor.

Comparing Your Results

If your skills profile resembles a straight line continuing the length of the chart, you have probably not judged yourself honestly. Experts at the Research Institute of America suggest a good balance between "high," "medium," and "low" is an indication that the rater has been fair in estimating skills. Compare your profile with Figure 2–3, an "average" ranking. How do you compare?

Do not be discouraged if you rank below average in general; however, you need to start improving your skills or you may retire from the same department—and at the same rank—in which you started out!

If you are above average, however, you cannot rest on your laurels. Acquiring supervisory skills and increasing your ability to use them well involve constant work.

Naturally, your rating cannot be considered "good" or "bad" based on a comparison with the "average" profile. It is more important to realize and understand your own areas of strength and weakness than to compare favorably with an "average" supervisor. Besides, our goal is to help you develop above-average supervisory skills.

Figure 2-3. Average Skills Profile. (With permission from the Research Institute of America.)

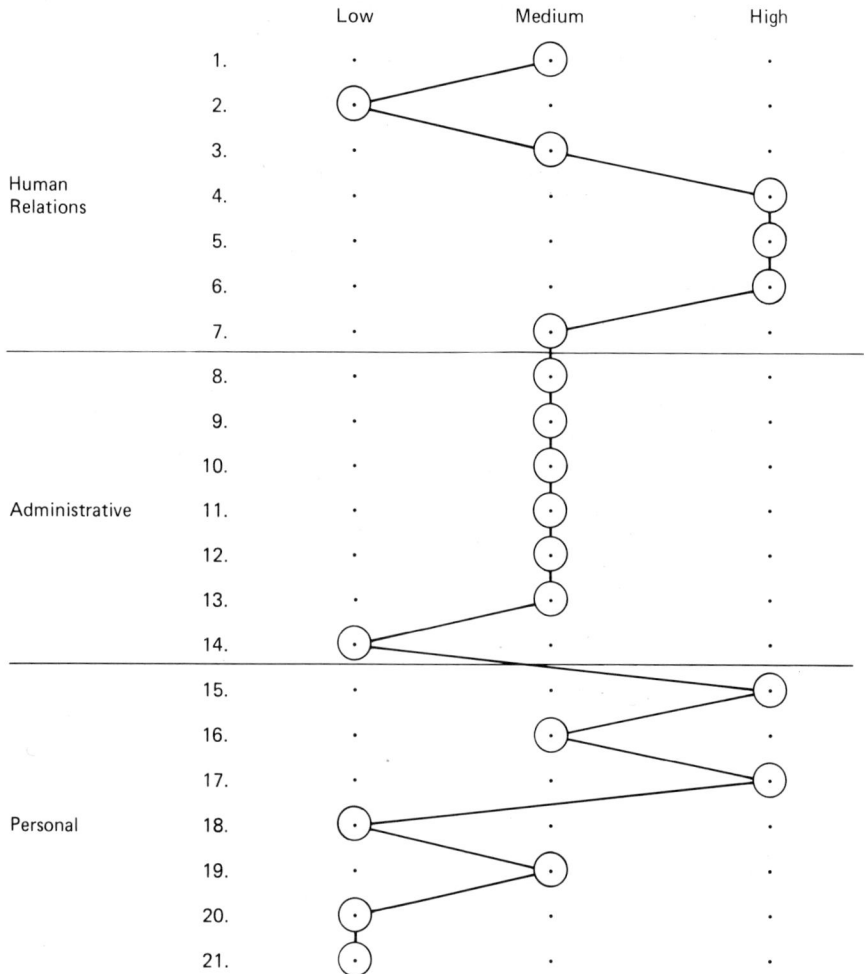

Three Types of Skills

While ranking yourself, you may have noticed that the skills in the profile can be grouped into three categories:

1. *Human relations skills* include "getting cooperation" and "working with subordinates."
2. *Administrative skills* are gauged by "planning" and "controlling paperwork."
3. *Personal skills* are those of "concentration" and "budgeting your time."

Which Skills Rate Extra Effort?

After assessing your abilities, you probably feel the next logical step is to concentrate on improving your weak points. It may prove most rewarding, however, to further develop *all* these skills—even those in which you ranked high. Paying attention to all your skills, regardless of your ratings, can bring impressive rewards.

Skills rated *high* are your natural strong points. If you are at first inclined to pass over these areas and avoid further improvement, consider this: Only a little more effort in these areas could upgrade your natural talents to outstanding skills. Becoming highly proficient in a limited area gives you an advantage in building a reputation as a specialist. Achieving a top-notch reputation as a troubleshooter or negotiator in labor disputes, for example, should improve your chances for success in most organizations.

Skills rated *medium* may be trouble areas. You probably have enough competence in these areas to deal with related problems, but you are not yet fully effective in utilizing these skills. Tackling situations that require greater sophistication than your skill level can delay and even prevent you from finding a workable solution. Skills you ranked "medium" may require considerable time and effort to develop, but your reward in perfecting them will be well worth the effort.

Skills ranked *low* probably represent areas in which you have little natural ability. Consequently, these skills will be difficult to develop. Improvement in these skills will be an uphill battle. You may have to work very hard for only a small gain. But if these skills represent important avenues to achieving your goals, you should be willing to spend the extra effort required to master them. Your answers to the following questions will help you determine which skills deserve that extra effort: Which do you most often employ in completing your job effectively? Which will best help you achieve your personal and departmental objectives?

If you decide that formal training is the best approach to building your areas of weakness, look around your community for some of the outstanding growth opportunities that often go unnoticed. Local colleges and universities probably offer specific courses in most areas that interest you. In addition, many high schools and social centers are now involved with community education. If you live in or near a city, you may also have access to the excellent self-development programs sponsored by associations for supervisors such as the National Management Association, International Management Council, Society for Advancement of Management, and American Management Association.

Your training may focus on the basics—writing business letters, speed reading, and so on—or you may wish to sign up for highly technical courses that relate to your managerial speciality. These advanced subjects may require completion of a prerequisite course, but everything you learn contributes to your development of a confident, self-actualized identity.

Remember that the way you pursue this program of self-development will reveal the kind of problem solver and decision maker you are. For example, suppose your major self-development need cannot be dealt with in an educational framework anywhere near your home. What will you do? Give up? If you are made of the managerial stuff you want to be, you will make the study opportunity for yourself. *Somebody* knows how to handle the area you are weak in. Find that person and arrange a special tutoring situation. You are sure to learn a lot and, what's more, you will be taking aggressive action—meeting a managerial problem head on and overcoming it.

Plan some reading for yourself. Subscribe to newspapers that will broaden your general understanding and journals that will deepen your knowledge of your specialty. Do not read just to get through—try out some of the new ideas you encounter.

Accepting Yourself

A trip to your local bookstore may convince you that the secret of success lies in writing a book about how to be successful! Self-help guides promise to reveal their secret formulas for living longer, looking younger, and acquiring a fortune through encyclopedia sales. Almost all these books are based on the same philosophy—you can achieve success by changing your attitudes about yourself. Positive attitudes can promote the development of skill, experience, and understanding in almost every area, from politics to athletics to your personal life.

Although coaches would agree that all-star players with negative attitudes rarely win championships, a good self-image is only part of the success formula. People with healthy self-images know their strengths and weaknesses and do not gear themselves up to expect the impossible. Although these people rely heavily on their talents, they are willing to try new methods and face possible failures. Because they attack problems instead of people, they gain insights from both good and bad experiences and profit from everyone's contributions.

Does this sound like Maslow's self-actualized individual? Naturally, we all fall short of that top-level behavior pattern once in a while. We are sometimes hesitant, stubborn, or closed-minded. But if our self-image is positive, we will be achievement-oriented and eager to get on with life. The key lies in not being afraid to try and to learn.

Research has shown that a person's self-image can affect thinking.[2] People who do not like themselves usually solve problems only with great difficulty. They think in rigid patterns and are rarely creative in seeking solutions. They categorize everything as black or white, recognizing no shades in between. They are often completely unable to deal with complex or poorly defined problem situations.

[2] See Charles Taylor and Arthur Combs, "Self-Acceptance and Adjustment," *Journal of Consulting Psychology,* 1954, pp. 89–91.

On the other hand, individuals who like and respect themselves have difficulty in these areas. They can understand complex relationships, con hend ambiguous situations, and break out of a mold to experiment with creative solutions.

Motivation and Self-Image

One writer has concluded that motivational needs can be grouped into three categories.[3] Because evidence indicates that these motivational needs can affect our concepts about ourselves, they are described briefly below.

1. *The need for achievement* is the drive for success—a personal goal defined in each individual's own terms. For some, success is $30,000 a year and a vacation cottage. For others, success lies in creating a masterful sculpture. Successful people know that each accomplishment along the way is just as important as reaching their final objective. Achieving success, however, is an accomplishment not limited to ultimate goals. Learning to play the guitar, reading all of Mark Twain's works, or reorganizing the factory can all be defined as success. Because of these built-in desires to achieve, most of us need to be successful in some area.

2. *The need for affiliation* makes us seek out other individuals and form close personal relationships. Affiliation needs are quite similar to the love and affection needs outlined in Maslow's human needs approach. Not only do we need to be loved, we also need to be liked. You can see that informal relationships are also important to most people. We require friendly relationships at many levels in our lives—deep family love, affection from our close friends, and the casual friendships of those we know in passing.

3. *The need for power* involves our desire to change events, either directly or through people who are able to exert direct influence. People with strong needs for power are usually more concerned with being promoted, getting to the top of the heap, or being recognized as the best. Fortunately, we can all learn to harness this drive for power by exerting control over small areas as well as large ones. You may not be able to influence the course of national politics, but you can control activities in your own department.

Building an Accurate Self-Image

The maxim, "know thyself," looks good on paper. But if you have tried it, you know that one of the greatest hurdles is being able to see yourself objectively. We all have built-in biases about who and what we are, and these biases can color our self-images until we really cannot weigh our own abilities. It is very difficult to see ourselves as others see us. In the same way, we often cannot be objective about our emotional selves because we have built up defenses that hinder accurate self-evaluations.

Our "insights" about ourselves usually contain a number of convenient blind spots. The self-actualized individual, who can speak freely and honestly about personal faults and abilities, is rare.

[3] See David McClelland et al., *The Achievement Motive* (New York: Appleton, 1953).

Many writers on success encourage us to exert a "110 percent" effort in everything we do. Of course, this is unrealistic, but it is not unrealistic to set up a goal of exerting 10 percent more effort than you thought you could. When people "outdo themselves," they have exceeded their own expectations. With a little more effort most of us can exceed even our most optimistic expectations.

Many people tend to be too humble about their talents and activities. We have a strong cultural taboo against bragging, and most of us are fearful of appearing too self-confident and self-assured. We need to realize that diminishing our own talents can be as socially and psychologically damaging as overconfidence. Dizzy Dean said, "If you've done it, it ain't bragging!"

Several years ago Frankie Szymanski, Notre Dame's star center, gained a reputation for humility. Although he was outstanding in both defense and offense and had been named to most of the All-America teams, he was never heard to brag or to speak highly of his own abilities in football. One day Frankie appeared in court as a witness. The attorney asked if he was on Notre Dame's football team and Frankie replied that he was. Next, the attorney asked the young man what position he played. "Center," answered Frankie without looking up.

"How good a center are you?" demanded the attorney. The shy young man squirmed a little but answered confidently, "Sir, I am the best center in the history of Notre Dame."

Coach Frank Leahy, who was in the courtroom, was shocked by such a statement from the usually modest boy. Afterward the coach asked Frankie why he had spoken as he did.

Szymanski blushed and responded, "I hated to do it, Coach, but after all, *I was under oath!*"

The Notre Dame star center knew his ability and had tested it on the field. Though physical abilities are often easy to test, it is those elusive inner strengths that are difficult to probe. Each of us must discover who we really are, and we must learn to like what we find. But how can we overcome both the natural and the social barriers to self-objectivity?

Psychological tests can point out certain personality characteristics, both strengths and weaknesses. Because they are designed for mass testing, however, they cannot give us all the answers. Unique individuals have unique qualities and combinations of qualities. Despite these difficulties it is imperative that all of us seek to know ourselves and to discover our strengths, weaknesses, and talents. An accurate view of ourselves coupled with a positive attitude can help us make the best of ourselves and our opportunities.

Now Manage Yourself

If you cannot supervise yourself, how can you expect to successfully supervise the actions of others? It is naïve to believe that you can realize your full potential as a supervisor without systematic planning and goal setting on a day-to-day basis. Can you imagine Coach Bear Bryant responding to a question of how he has had so many championship football teams by replying, "Oh, we just throw a ball out to our boys and tell them to have fun, run fast, hit hard, and make touchdowns—that's all!"? In Chapter 9 more will be said about planning, but it must be emphasized that personal planning and goal setting are essential factors in successfully managing yourself.

In addition to planning, one top management consultant has provided sound advice regarding this first important task of supervision by identifying five areas in which any supervisor can learn to govern personal behavior effectively.[4]

1. Focus your effort on fewer tasks. Some people are happiest when they have fifty projects going at one time, but only a few of these people are able to do a good job on most of their projects. Most of us would be torn in many different directions and find ourselves unable to complete any one project to our satisfaction. Everyone knows someone like this. He or she is always rushing to meetings, organizing a wide variety of affairs, doing volunteer work, taking on major tasks on the job, pursuing a number of different hobbies, and sandwiching in just enough food and sleep to maintain this exhausting pace.

Most people cannot handle the pressure of too many tasks. When they take on too much, they become so disorganized that nothing gets done. A wise individual will understand personal limitations and concentrate on doing a few tasks well.

2. Eliminate tools that are obsolete. Working with old, outdated habits can be as difficult and time-consuming as working with old, worn out equipment. It is useful to take inventory now and then. Study the materials and equipment you work with, the procedures you use, and your own personal habits. Determine what should be replaced by newer, more efficient methods or fresher attitudes.

3. Discover where you are wasting time. How much time do you spend each day wondering what you should be doing, wishing you were somewhere else, or asking yourself where the time has gone? A twenty-four-hour day is sufficient *if* you know how to use your time effectively.

Sometimes wasters are external, such as telephone interruptions or a crisis situation over which you have limited control. However, most wasters are habits you have developed such as a cluttered desk, procrastination, the inability to say "no," or not delegating authority.

Try this simple exercise tomorrow: Carry a small notebook, and try to jot down everything you do, noting how long each activity takes. You will find you can accomplish a great number of things in a single day when you are time-conscious! Next draw up a time budget for yourself. If there are projects you want to undertake in the coming week, list them and estimate how long each will take. Leave room for essentials, such as eating, sleeping, and relaxing, in setting up your schedule for the week. Chances are that you will find you can accomplish more than if you had proceeded in a less-organized fashion.

4. Learn to weigh your decisions in terms of your goals. Decisions that do not carry you closer to your objectives waste departmental time, money, and effort. Learn to anticipate the end result of your decisions. If making a particular decision will help you achieve your goals, then choose your answer with care. If the decision is incidental to your main objective, do not waste much time making a choice.

5. Do not be afraid to test new ideas. Remember, however, that new

---

[4] Peter F. Drucker, quoted by T. W. Engstrom and R. A. MacKenzie, *Managing Your Time* (Grand Rapids, Mich.: Zondervan Books, 1967), p. 35.

methods require trial periods. Certainly, it would be foolish to re-equip your production plant totally with untested machinery.

Your personal job of managing yourself includes testing new ideas. As a mature individual who is constantly growing, learning, and changing, you may wish to consider new ideas on a trial basis to see if they will fit in smoothly with your current values and beliefs. Sometimes new ideas force us to recognize that those values and beliefs should be changed.

In the opening sentence of this section we paraphrased the French novelist, François Rabelais, who said, "How shall I be able to rule over others if I have not full power and command of myself?" Though we can never be sure of successfully controlling the actions of others, we can always seek better control of the most difficult subordinates—ourselves. Learn to manage yourself and you will discover how to supervise others.

Summary

The key to understanding other people lies in first understanding yourself. A human needs approach may help you to understand what drives motivate you and others around you. Needs are ranked in their order of importance, but needs at higher levels will be sacrificed in most cases if lower-level needs are not being met. All people seek to satisfy the same needs: physiological, safety and security, love and belonging, self-esteem, and self-actualization.

You can assess your supervisory skills by using the skills profile in this chapter. The questions it poses reveal strengths and weaknesses in human relations, your administrative and personal skills. Skills in which you rate high represent your natural strong points; those in which you rate medium may present trouble spots; and those in which you rate low are probably your areas of least natural ability.

Self-image can affect the way a person thinks and determine personal motivation. In turn, a person's self-image can define the needs for achievement, affiliation, and power. Often the only difference between success and failure is a realistic, positive self-image with the courage to say, "I can do it!"

Building an accurate self-image requires objectivity about your abilities and weaknesses. Too much humility can be as damaging—socially and psychologically—as overconfidence. Psychological tests can help by pointing out certain characteristics, strengths, and weaknesses.

The task of self-management includes five key areas. To supervise yourself more effectively, you can (1) focus your effort on fewer tasks, (2) eliminate obsolete tools, (3) discover where you are wasting time, (4) learn to weigh your decisions in terms of your goals, and (5) be willing to test new ideas.

Key Terms

Achievement Need. The individual's drive to reach desired goals.
Administrative Skills. Those supervisory skills used in mastering paperwork demands and the routine supervision of everyday activities.

Affiliation Needs. The drive to seek out other individuals and form close personal relationships.

Human Needs Approach. An approach to understanding human behavior developed by psychiatrist Abraham Maslow. The approach includes the following needs, arranged in order of priority: physiological, safety and security, love and belonging, self-esteem, and self-actualization.

Human Relations Skills. Skills in dealing with people, including the ability to communicate, to understand, and to facilitate group members' interrelationships in the work environment.

Need of Power. The desire to control events, either directly or through people who can apply direct influence.

Personal Skills. Skills in managing oneself, including an accurate self-image, a positive attitude, the proper use of time, knowledge of one's strengths and weaknesses, and the ability to use those strengths wisely while improving the weaknesses.

Self-Image. The personal picture one holds of oneself.

Skills Profile. A checklist that aids in rating each supervisor in assessing personal strengths, talents, and weaknesses.

Review Questions

1. Should a supervisor be expected to adhere to the maxim, "Know thyself"? Why or why not?

2. List and give examples of the five levels in the human needs approach of Abraham Maslow.

3. List several characteristics of a self-actualized individual.

4. Describe and give examples of areas of life requiring supervisory skills.

5. Why should a supervisor or anyone work at improving skills in areas where they are strong? Wouldn't this be a waste of time?

6. How would you describe individuals who know just enough about a problem so that if they try to handle the situation, they only make it worse?

7. Why should a supervisor or anyone else work at improving skills in an area where he or she has been shown to have little or no natural ability?

8. Can people be successful in changing attitudes about themselves? Do you think you could change an attitude you now hold about yourself?

9. What are some ways we can improve our ability to "see ourselves as others see us"?

10. What are the dangers of taking on too many projects at one time?

11. What does self-management mean?

12. How can psychological testing be useful in gaining self-understanding?

13. It is said that a person's self-image is related to the basic needs for achievement, affiliation, and power. What does this mean and what does it imply?

Exercises

I. Using The Skills Profile

A. Look at the skills profile you completed. Rate the skills on the chart in order of importance to you, then in order of your abilities—your highest skill to your lowest. How do the two rankings compare?

B. List the skills you would most like to improve and draw up a plan for improving them. Check yourself in two weeks to see if you have improved.

II. Quiz: Are You Supervisory Material?

A. Choose the answer that comes closest to your actual behavior attitude.

1. Are you completely familiar with all the aspects of your job?
   (a) No.
   (b) Not yet.
   (c) I shall learn it as I go along.
   (d) Yes, of course.

2. Do you look for better ways of doing your job?
   (a) It is not really worth the trouble.
   (b) Sometimes.
   (c) Usually.
   (d) Almost always.

3. Do you ask for increased responsibility?
   (a) Why ask for trouble?
   (b) If it comes along, I shall take it.
   (c) Yes, now and then.
   (d) Yes, whenever I can handle it.

4. Do you put in extra time and effort to get a job finished?
   (a) When quitting time comes, I am through.
   (b) Not very often.
   (c) Fairly often.
   (d) Whenever it is necessary.

5. Are you willing to take the time to learn?
   (a) I know my job well enough already.
   (b) If I learn something, I learn it, but I do not go out of my way.
   (c) I pick up new things fairly often.
   (d) I am always ready to learn something new.

6. How much do you "sell" your company?
   (a) After hours, what I say about the company is my business.
   (b) I probably would not gripe about it in public.
   (c) I am satisfied and let people know about it.
   (d) I think my company is terrific and all my friends think so too.

7. Do you keep close track of the time you spend at work?
   (a) I watch every minute.
   (b) Sometimes the days drag.
   (c) Usually the time goes fairly fast.
   (d) I never know where the day has gone when it is over.

8. How well do you accept criticism?
   (a) Know-it-alls are always trying to tell me how to do my job.
   (b) Sometimes I get irked when people criticise me.
   (c) I can listen to criticism but do not always like it.
   (d) I try to separate personal emotions from criticisms of my work and take the best advice I can get.

9. Do you like and perform well in a competitive working situation?

(a) Nobody would want my job, so I am not worried.

(b) I do not like it, but I try to do a good job.

(c) I can compete with anybody for my job.

(d) I compete with myself to try to do a better job.

10. How much do you share your experience and knowledge with other supervisors and subordinates?

(a) They should get it for themselves.

(b) I never give advice unless asked.

(c) Some things I share freely; others I would rather keep to myself.

(d) If I have knowledge that someone else does not have and needs, I will almost always make suggestions or give information.

B. Now score your quiz, using this scale to figure your total points: for each (a) answer, 4 points; for each (b) answer, 6 points; for each (c) answer, 8 points; and for each (d) answer, 10 points. If you scored 94–100, there is no doubt about it—you are supervisory material. If you rank somewhere between 80–94, keep working and you will make it. If you scored 70–80, and you try hard to improve those areas in which you are weak, you should have few problems. From 65–70, you will really have to fight to overcome the weaknesses that hold you back. Below 65, you will have to exert considerable effort to make it as a supervisor.

C. If you are trying to improve your skills and attitudes, save your responses to this quiz and test yourself again in six months. You should then be able to tell if you are progressing toward your goal.

Case 2 • Archie Bradshaw

After graduating from Orange Blossom Community College, Archie Bradshaw was hired by Shelby Publishing Company and worked for eighteen months as route coordinator for the circulation department. In college Archie was a good student, managing mostly A and B grades in a business program. He was involved in numerous campus activities, including the business fraternity, campus politics, and the varsity baseball team. He married a woman he met in college.

Archie gets along well with people and is a relaxed person in most social situations. At work he feels that he is doing an excellent job of dealing with the various demands placed on him and is proud of the extra hours he spends reading business publications and attending continuing education courses that relate to his work. Archie believes that he has a good understanding of the people who work for him in the circulation department and that they benefit as employees because he is their supervisor. He meets with individual employees on a regular basis and makes certain that they understand their jobs and are informed of ways of improving their performance through discussion of the new ideas he is exposed to in his classes. Archie feels that he gets the performance from his employees that is essential and that he has to be "hard-nosed" on occasion to get the results he expects.

Although the performance of his department and employees is excellent, the turnover rate is almost double the company average. Archie has overheard more than one of his subordinates refer to him as a "slave driver." One person's comment was dismissed as "innocent" due to an unusually demanding work schedule on the day the comment was made. Archie explained another person's criticism as jealousy of his energy and ambition. Archie believes that turnover is to be expected and a high turnover rate means only that "average" employees are unwilling to take the challenge of his department.

1. From what you know of Archie's performance as a supervisor, evaluate his managerial skills. What are his strengths and weaknesses?

2. Suppose you were asked to advise Archie on ways to improve his performance. What would you recommend?

CHAPTER 3
Communication: The Key to Understanding

Nature has given to men one tongue, but two ears, that we may hear from others twice as much as we speak.

Epictetus

One of the best ways to persuade others is with your ears—by listening to them.

Dean Rusk

Learning Objectives

- To learn why good communication skills are the key to successful supervision.
- To analyze the various methods by which people communicate.
- To apply the basic styles of communication to the supervisor's task.
- To contrast effective communication techniques with poor ones.

Defining communication is as difficult as efficiently performing the function. Making a speech or writing a memo does not mean that communication has taken place. There are many ways to define the communication process. However, in this chapter, we will define communication as *the process of transferring information from the mind of one individual to the mind of one or more other individuals.* As such, communication is something that one person cannot do alone. There must be a sender and a receiver. Though the active party or sender may have a greater responsibility, everyone who is a party to a communication effort must work to see that communication is successful.

Communication may take place, but desired results may not be obtained. In other words, the communication process appears to work effectively but incorrect or incomplete information has been transmitted. Similarly, an individual may receive a communication message but not be motivated to respond as the sender intended. In this case, however, the problem may be motivation rather than communication.

The supervisor who learns to handle communication problems by asking a few simple questions is well on the way to bettering rapport with subordinates. Each communication experience is unique: two individuals are interacting, but each represents different life experiences, attitudes, and expectations. Even so, you can apply these basic questions to any communication situation. Asking these questions before you send an idea out can help avoid misunderstandings and bad feelings and can ensure the results you seek.

1. What is the idea to be communicated?
2. Who is supposed to receive the idea?
3. How can I most effectively communicate this message to that other person?
4. How could my message undergo changes along the way?
5. How can I prevent these distortions?
6. How can I tell if that person has received the right message?

The Communication Process

Communication is a complicated process, but it can be reduced to a fairly simple diagram (see Figure 3-1). This diagram is only a rudimentary model, but it highlights the major components of the communication process and helps us understand it.

Someone originates an idea (1) and decides to share it with someone else. First comes the coding of the idea (2) into written, spoken, or otherwise communicable form, which can be transmitted (3) through symbols, sounds, or expressions. For the message to be correctly transmitted, it must jump a noise hurdle (4). The direct line between communicator and receiver is always interrupted by various types of interferences. Actual environmental noise, competing messages, and conflicting interpretations are all types of noise that can garble the original message beyond recognition.

The message is received (5) through the eyes, ears, or other physical sensors of the receiver. The message then travels to the receiver's brain, which decodes the message (6) and interprets the meaning of the words or gestures received. The result is an idea received (7). The idea is rarely received exactly as it was transmitted. If we consider all the possibilities for misinterpretation and confusion along the way, it is surprising that we communicate with each other as well as we do.

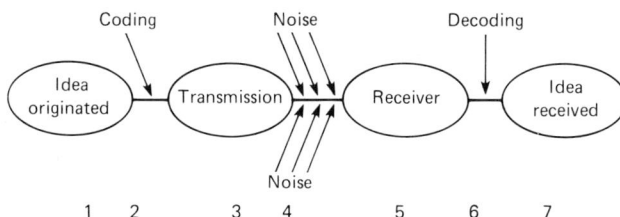

Figure 3-1. Basic Communications Model.

A communication is considered successful if the transmitted idea (1) is like the received idea (7). If the idea received is exactly the same as the idea sent, we may be sure that two skillful communicators joined in the process. Either person, as well as noise (4), can distort the message in various ways, causing a communication breakdown. Each person involved is responsible for effective communication—teacher and student, supervisor and worker, husband and wife. The sender must code the message carefully, and the receiver must decode it with perception and understanding. Therefore, communication is really an *exchange* of meanings and not just one-way processes of sending and receiving ideas.

The seven-step communication diagram quickly becomes complex when we consider that two people rarely, if ever, communicate with each other in only one way. In a single exchange of ideas between a supervisor and an employee, for example, the supervisor may hand the employee a written message, interpret it verbally, and use gestures and facial expressions to convey the full meaning of the message. The employee reads the message, hears the supervisor's words, asks questions, interprets the gestures and expressions of the supervisor, and responds to the message in a way the employee considers appropriate.

This process, which includes many types of communication, represents an outline of most information exchanges. In the classroom, for instance, you *listen* to and *watch* the instructor, *write* notes, *read* what you have written, *react* mentally to the ideas presented (communicating with yourself), and *respond* physically by smiling, frowning, nodding, or shifting position. Are there other ways in which you communicate in a classroom situation?

Roadblocks to Communication

Danger lurks at every step when we attempt communication with other people. Because correct communication is vital to each supervisor's job, you should be aware of the many areas in which mishaps occur.

A common roadblock to effective communications is the assumption that a message was received because one was sent. Have you ever given someone a piece of information, then been asked, "What did you just tell me?" Imagine how this situation would worsen if your listener does not even require you to repeat it! Whenever we proceed on the illusion that a message sent is a message received, we multiply the possibilities for misunderstanding and inappropriate action.

A good general would never send troops to battle without preparing them for a fight. In the same way, a supervisor should never send a message without arming it against the interference and possible misinterpretations it will encounter along the way. You should prepare your messages to overcome the dangers of inaccurate coding and transmission on your part, additions and deletions caused by competing or conflicting messages, and the possibilities of inaccurate decoding at the receiving end.

To understand how easily the process can go awry, consider that at least six messages can result from one attempt to communicate with another person. They are illustrated in this incident involving a supervisor and his most promising subordinate. As long as the first four messages are fairly similar, no problems arise. But as the incident suggests, the original message can undergo a series of dramatic transformations by the time it reaches stage four.

1. First there is the message you intend to send. Imagine the supervisor (we shall call him Harry) sitting at his desk reviewing the production records of his employees in the manufacturing division. He has noticed that for some time John Adams ranked as his department's best producer. Filled with supervisory pride, Harry decides to call John in and tell him what a great job he has done.

2. Sometimes the message we actually send is not the one we intended to send. Harry has always had trouble with direct expressions of praise, so he smiles broadly at John and says, "You haven't been doing a bad job."

3. Even when we transmit our message correctly, however, the message the other person hears is often not the one we intended him or her to receive. John, angry at being called away from his job and tired after a full day's work, is in no mood for chitchat. Because John's machine runs at a deafening roar, he sometimes has trouble hearing what people say to him.

4. The other person's interpretation of the message can completely change its original meaning. John begins to glare and shift from foot to foot as he begins to realize the implications of what he thinks he has heard.

5. The productive employee vents his anger. "Yeah?" he says, "and you're a fat slob yourself." This is the fifth type of message implicit in the communication process—the receiver's response. As in this example, this phase of the process presents additional communication problems.

6. The sender will compare the response received with the message he believes was sent. If the response varies widely from expectations, the sender must consider this unexpected response and redirect behavior in an appropriate manner. Harry is shocked. He orders John back to his machine, puts his feet up on the desk, and scratches his head in bewilderment as he tries to figure out what went wrong.

What does this story tell us? Whenever we try to communicate with another person, we must express ourselves so that our receiver will choose to hear our particular message, and we must consider the responses in terms of the receiver's background. We must try to see our message through new eyes and hear it with new ears.

If the seven-step diagram showed the complete process of communication, exchanging ideas successfully would be very simple. Messages could be received exactly as they were intended, and we would not have to consider so many possibilities for error. In real life, however, communication depends on constant feedback at all stages of the process because both transmitter and receiver interpret and reinterpret the meanings of the message. Perhaps it is a good thing that communication is such a complex process. If it were simple and straightforward, such things as conversation, discussion, and education could not facilitate complex idea exchanges between people. It is the two-way flow of communication that enables us to share individual viewpoints and skills in achieving common goals.

How We Communicate

Think about the variety of ways people communicate with each other. How many of these methods can you list? Begin with the easy ones, speaking and writing, and then add as many types of communication as you can.

1. Thinking. This is the method of communication most often overlooked when people list ways we communicate. It is such an obvious method—and one that we use more than any other—that it is easy to ignore. This internal means of communication participates in all the other modes of communication. Of course, each of us can probably think of an exception to this rule—a teacher, student, supervisor, or worker who makes a habit of speaking before thinking!

Even though thinking is a necessary part of all other methods of communication, it remains a vital means of communicating when used alone. Psychiatrists have told us that we should communicate more often and more effectively with ourselves. Meditation can not only introduce us to ourselves, but also can help shape goals and guide our actions in reaching them.

2. Action. For many years, Ted Williams claimed the distinction of having paid the largest fine ever levied against a professional baseball player for arguing with an umpire. Williams never said a word to the umpire; his intent was communicated with a single gesture.

A single action can supersede a thousand words. It provides a clear, easily understood message that no office memo can match. Can you imagine what confusion the minutemen would have suffered if Paul Revere had received the following message on the night of his famous ride:

> Through the machinations of our emissaries in the noble military circle, we have learned conclusively that His Majesty's battalions will be arriving at approximately mid–afternoon, having synchronized their operating mechanisms and commandeering a large vessel of unknown carrying capacity. Considering heuristic functional scenarios, however, the British have decided that optional monitored flexibility would provide for better logistical contingency. In view of this new information, the previous data becomes inoperative and we must plan for increased reciprocal capability.

Were the British coming? If they were, was it by sea or by land? We owe a large debt to the creative communicator who placed the lantern in the steeple of Boston's Old North Church.

Action is such a powerful mode of communication that we must use care in exercising it. Wherever a gesture, expression, or deed will convey our message best, we should act without hesitation. When our actions could portray a more powerful meaning than we had in mind, however, we must control our activity and rely more on words.

3. Observation. It is common knowledge that we all practice selective perception to some degree. We hear only what we want to hear and see only what we want to see whenever we encounter situations that make us uncomfortable. Emotional maturity is required for a person to see and hear things that are very personal, embarrassing, or offensive. When we block out too much, however, we may act inappropriately because we lack full information.

Ignoring or refusing to see or hear certain things is not the only reason why people fail to observe correctly. Sometimes things happen too fast for us to comprehend the full scope of events or the situation is so confusing that thirty witnesses will have thirty different versions of what occurred. Honest witnesses will give conflicting testimony about the same event because each has perceived that event in a slightly different way.

A law professor was having trouble convincing his students that witnesses could be honestly mistaken. He struck upon a plan to communicate his message. The next day, during his lecture, a stranger suddenly stepped into the classroom, pointed a pistol at the professor, and fired three blanks. The professor clutched his chest and fell to the floor. The gunman escaped in the confusion that followed.

The professor stood up, and after the witnesses (students) recovered from the shock, he asked them to write an exact description of the assailant. The class decided that the professor had been shot by a man who was between five feet seven and six feet two, weighing between 140 and 195 pounds, and having either red, brown, blond, or black hair that was quite curly, or straight.

4. Speaking. The average person speaks at the rate of 125 words per minute, though some can reach 200 words per minute. If the objective is to see who can produce the most words in a minute, a high rate is useful. If, however, the objective is to communicate, fewer words can almost always do a better job. Using fewer words to get your message across not only saves time but allows less opportunity for confusion. Almost everyone knows someone who cannot give a brief answer to any question.

5. Listening. This is the more important side of the speaking mode of communication. Even if a supervisor is able to get the message across briefly and clearly, he or she must still listen to the ideas and problems of subordinates. This means being able to hear them when they indicate that they do not understand instructions. Ten commandments for good listening are listed in Figure 3-2.

6. Writing. Writing takes up only about 10 percent of our total communication time. But the fact that writing makes our messages permanent elevates this method to one of the most important modes of communicating. A spoken message can always be immediately clarified by using a few more words if the listener does not understand. But a written message must usually stand on its own.

For some reason, many business writers have difficulty using ordinary language and a simple writing style. The Gettysburg Address contains 266 words;

Figure 3-2. Ten Commandments for Good Listening.

1. Stop talking. You cannot listen if you are talking.
2. Put the talker at ease. Help him or her to feel free to talk.
3. Show the talker that you want to listen. Look and act interested. Do not read your mail or perform other paperwork chores while the person is talking. Listen to understand rather than to oppose.
4. Remove distractions. Do not doodle, tap, or shuffle papers. It might be quieter if you shut the door.
5. Empathize with the talker. Try to put yourself in his or her place so that you can see that point of view.
6. Be patient. Allow plenty of time. Do not interrupt. Do not start for the door or walk away.
7. Hold your temper. An angry person gets the wrong meaning from words.
8. Go easy on argument and criticism. The talker may clam up or get angry. Do not argue; even if you win, you lose.
9. Ask questions. This encourages discussion and shows that you are listening. It helps to develop points further.
10. Stop talking. This is first and last because all other commandments depend on it. You just cannot do a good listening job while you are talking.

the Ten Commandments has only 297. Yet a government order to reduce the price of cabbage required 26,911 words.[1] When you know what to say, it does not take many words to say it. Supervisors must cope with this problem twice. They must interpret messages from higher management and pass those messages along to subordinates in language the subordinates can understand. The supervisor who can accomplish this clearly and effectively in writing understands the sender and reader as well as the subject.

7. Reading. This is a crucial communication skill. Reading remains the best method of staying informed. You will read reports, memos, documents, purchase orders, and a wide variety of other material in connection with your job. In addition, you may read books, magazines, newspapers, street signs, and even breakfast cereal boxes.

What characteristics qualify reading as an important method of communication? Once someone writes down some ideas, it is up to each reader to interpret those ideas, compare them with past experience, and form a judgment. Although no one can remember everything, it is important to implement those particular written messages which fit into the pattern formed by your experiences and your expectations. Anything you read that does not fit should be questioned, reinterpreted, and re-evaluated before being accepted or tossed out.

Every type of communication has two basic problems: (1) saying more than we mean to say, and (2) saying less than we intend. We all know how to think, act, observe, speak, read, and write, but we need to learn how to do them more effectively. Careful attention to the information coming in and going out can help avoid problems caused by poor communication.

Supervisory Communication Styles

The way we communicate with other people usually depends on what we think of them and what we think of ourselves. It also depends on the situation. In a close friendship, for example, you might *tell* your girlfriend what to do, *ask* for advice, *relate* an amusing or upsetting incident, *listen* to what she has to say, *watch* her actions, *advise* her on a course of action, or utilize various other styles of communication.

Most of us use four basic styles of communication in different situations and with different people. It is a rare person who adopts one style of communicating and uses it consistently in every situation. Understanding these styles may help us to comprehend better the reactions we receive at different times.

The Developmental Communicator

This communicator is not concerned with always being right. He or she is willing to give advice and to listen to other people's opinions, and does not attempt to force ideas on others. Instead, this type tries to develop a joint understanding of the problem or issue and lead the discussion toward a mutual conclusion.

[1] Quoted in Dennis Murphy, *Better Business Communication* (New York: McGraw-Hill, 1957), p. 15.

Developmental communicators understand the two-way process of communication. They explore, experiment, and look for new approaches. They respect the other person's thoughts and ideas and firmly believe that two heads are better than one. With this type of communicator, one plus one can add up to a lot more than two.

A supervisor need not give up control over the situation to be a developmental communicator. Despite asking employees' advice in a particular situation, he or she retains the final decision-making power. This communicator recognizes the responsibility to arrive at solutions and knows the importance of help in making an informed decision.

The Controlling Communicator

This style uses a high-pressure approach to communication. The controller is convinced that his or her idea is the only right one, and, further, that no one else could add to it or find fault with it. This type never experiments or considers alternatives because there are no alternatives. This type of communicator sees two-way communication as a waste of time; he or she knows all the answers, and needs only to tell people what to do.

As a supervisor, you may encounter this style of communication when dealing with bosses. Many managers are strong, controlling communicators. They consider their memos the last—and only—word. Their attitude prevents a supervisor from seeking clarification or additional information. When you must deal with a controlling communicator and pass messages along to your own subordinates, remember that without your assistance, the manager's "pearls of wisdom" may be meaningless to your workers.

Of course, there are situations in which the controlling approach to communication is appropriate. No discussion is necessary to clear a building after a fire is discovered. If you have special knowledge that your workers do not share, the controlling approach may provide the best path to speedy, efficient action. Even in some noncrisis situations the controlling approach can be best. If the plant workers are being given two weeks' paid vacation this year instead of the traditional one week, there is likely to be no resistance to your one-way communication. On the other hand, the controlling communicator is not usually effective in situations where resistance to change is high.

The Relinquishing Communicator

These people insist that others should take the lead in decision making and discussions. Humble and unsure, such individuals believe they can offer no worthwhile contribution. When someone else presents a new idea or solution, the relinquisher is happy to accept it. But these communicators will not actively participate in discussions or problem-solving sessions. They are quite content to let someone else do the thinking, guide the discussion, or vocalize a group decision.

Relinquishing communicators usually get along very well with controlling communicators. Unfortunately, this pair can never rise above the potential of the controlling communicator, for the relinquisher never contributes any fresh concepts, unusual solutions, or communication skills.

A controlling supervisor demands that workers respond to directions by relinquishing. Workers may try to initiate discussions, but they rarely accomplish their purpose. Whether a top manager or a first-level supervisor, the controlling communicator seeks a position of greater power and authority in order to set and maintain the tone of the communication.

Sometimes responding in a relinquishing style is appropriate if the other person possesses more knowledge, experience, or expertise. Laymen should not try to tell a doctor how to perform an operation or a lawyer how to pursue a court case. People who have special information are valuable resources and should be treated with respect. If you have an employee who knows everything about a particular job, you can assume a relinquishing role in some dealings with this person. In some situations, you need only be kept informed of an individual's progress.

The Withdrawn Communicator

Of all the styles of communication, this type usually involves the least amount of actual communication. Withdrawn communicators like to keep things on an even keel. New ideas and problems to be solved only upset the pattern; they would much rather not be involved. They assume that nothing can improve a situation and that plenty is sure to go wrong if anyone meddles with it.

Withdrawn communicators do not ask for or give advice. They never offer ideas or listen to anyone else's and they avoid interaction of any type. Naturally, a supervisor cannot direct or guide workers as a withdrawn communicator. When asked to give reasons for a decision, this individual is likely to respond, "We have always done it that way. Stop bothering me with details."

Comparing the Communicators

All these styles of communication are used every day. Some choose only one style and stick with it. Others realize that different methods are appropriate in different situations. Perhaps the easiest way to understand the different approaches is to visualize them in a circle, remembering that these types of communicators must interact with each other daily and must respond to each other's style.

Keeping the Channels Clear

If you were to diagram the communication patterns of an effective supervisor, you would have arrows going in every direction. Typically, most communication will be with subordinates, but this does not merely mean communication *at* them. You must be receiving regular information from the people around you in the organization. An open-door policy is one way of encouraging people to communicate. If you are too busy for your subordinates, they will soon find that they have little time for you. If a supervisor fails to provide outlets for workers' concerns, they will probably communicate their concerns though the grievance or complaint system. Just as a reporter must protect sources, a supervisor must be careful not to betray confidences and candor shared by subordinates.

Most organizations have formal channels for communication, and in most instances, the chain of command should be followed. It is usually a mistake to bypass a superior and go to his or her superior with a request. In the same way, you would probably resent someone in another department coming to you and making demands without clearing the matter with his or her superior. However, there are emergencies, for example, when your superior is not available and you must get advice or assistance from a higher authority. In such cases it is a good idea to inform your superior at the earliest opportunity.

Formal channels seldom exist for horizontal communication. Yet, you will want to know what is happening in other departments in your organization. This type of information will usually be revealed in informal communication. For example, you may talk at lunch or on breaks with people who have similar jobs. Well-managed companies have meetings to discuss problems and share information. A good rule to remember is that if you ever cross formal channels of communication, make certain that your superior knows what you are doing and why. Bosses tend to resent employees who go behind their backs.

It should be clear that there are formal and informal approaches to communication. Formal communication usually follows the approved channels identified by the organization, such as written communiqués. Written material may become part of the formal record of an organization and must be reviewed carefully. Meetings, conferences, and appointments with individuals also constitute formal communication. Minutes to meetings are the record, and usually the only valid source available to resolve misunderstandings. In certain instances, even a telephone conversation may constitute formal communication. If the call is strictly business, it should be treated as a formal activity that deserves careful attention. It is good practice to make notes of telephone conversations; you may need to document a particular conversation.[2]

Informal communication exists when people come together without formal planning or purpose. It includes a variety of social situations on the proverbial grapevine. Much of this informal communication contains worthwhile, accurate information that can be valuable to a supervisor. Much is worthless, however, but is a necessary part of the needs of employees. A supervisor should not attempt to discount information from the grapevine, but should attempt to understand how it works and what its messages mean. They are often accurate and helpful in making wise decisions.

The Five C's of Communication

Whenever you must relay information, ask yourself these five questions: Is it clear? Is it complete? Is it concise? Is it concrete? Is it correct? If your message brings positive responses to all five, it is likely to be successful.

1. Be clear. Use simple words and few ideas in each sentence. When Murphy's Law ("If anything can go wrong, it will.") is applied to communications, it becomes, "If there is any way your message can be misunderstood,

---

[2] See Jud Monroe, *Effective Research and Report Writing in Government* (New York: McGraw-Hill, 1980).

it will be." If your message is not straightforward and logical, it will almost certainly be misinterpreted. Trying to put too many thoughts into one sentence makes messages unclear.

2. Be complete. Use all the words and thoughts necessary to convey the message you are attempting to deliver. Clarity will not help others understand your message if you have omitted important information. To prevent this, pretend you are the person receiving the message. Given the information in your message, should the recipient be able to interpret it correctly and respond appropriately?

An incomplete message can be dangerous because when we do not have all the facts, we are more likely to act incorrectly and trigger a chain of misunderstandings. The following incident illustrates the havoc an incomplete message can cause:

> Sol Herk, a Danish pilot, heard a radio message that said, "Herk, your plane is on fire!" The pilot reacted instantaneously to this limited information. He bailed out of his plane, which then crashed into a mountainside. As the explosion subsided and Herk drifted gently toward the earth, he saw that he was going to come down on the runway of a small airport.
>
> From his parachute vantage point, Sol Herk watched airport personnel putting out a minor fire in the tail section of a small private plane that belonged to John Herk.

3. Be concise. Brevity is beautiful. Use the fewest words possible to convey your message. Sir Winston Churchill was asked by a college student to deliver a brief, ten-minute talk at the graduation ceremony one week away. Sir Winston replied, "Young man, if you had asked me to speak for several hours you could have asked me the day before graduation. If you desired that I speak only an hour, you should have asked me three months ago. But for ten minutes, you should have asked a year ago!"

Brief, effective communication takes thought and preparation. Most of us use too many words to convey our messages. One president of a large detergent manufacturing company solved this problem by refusing to read any memo more than one page long. He insisted there was nothing anyone could say about soap that should take more than a page.

4. Be concrete. Use specific words and terms rather than generalities. When people are unsure about what they want to say, it seems easier to use abstract terms and broad generalizations while avoiding concrete facts. Consider this example: Ralph Martin has discovered that several of his employees have been coming in late and leaving early every day, while other employees have been illegally punching them in and out at the proper time. Martin pinpointed the culprits, wrote the following memo, and posted it on the employee bulletin board: "Everyone must be responsible for punching his or her own time card." Given Martin's concrete knowledge of the situation, was his message too abstract? Will Martin's employees interpret the message properly and correct the problem? How would you handle this situation?

5. Be correct. Make sure your message is true, accurate, properly researched, and documented. If the message is not correct, it does not matter how well it is worded or how concise it is. Like the boy who cried "Wolf!" we may achieve short-term goals by sending incorrect messages, but in the long run, such messages will always backfire. In an incorrect message, we may exaggerate, tell a lie, mislead, or exclude important information. Can you think of other ways in which a message could be incorrect?

Inaccurate information is a major barrier to good communication. Several years ago, a multimillion-dollar satellite had to be destroyed in space because of a minor miscalculation. The error was traced to a single apostrophe that had been omitted from several detailed pages of computer instructions. Little things do mean a lot.

You're O.K., but What About Me?

In Chapter 2, we discussed the importance of attitudes about ourselves and other people—attitudes that shape our ways of communicating, responding, and acting. In an effort to categorize human behavior patterns, psychiatrist Tom Harris developed his theory of transactional analysis,[3] which groups various styles of behavior according to these attitudes. The transactional analysis theory can help us understand why we communicate as we do and why we behave differently with different people.

Everyone, Harris suggests, reacts to others in one of three basic ways. Sometimes we act like a *child,* sometimes like a *parent,* and in other situations we respond like an *adult.* These behavior patterns do not refer to our actual roles as children, parents, or adults. Rather, they describe the ways we respond to other people.

The child in each of us contains the collection of experiences and emotions stored in our brains when we were small. These include feelings such as frustration and satisfaction, inadequacy and curiosity, helplessness and imagination, and anger and joy. Because a child's reaction is governed largely by emotions, it is often said the child represents the "felt concept of life." The child in you is asserting itself whenever you throw a tantrum, mope or sulk, experience joy or pleasure, or suffer from feelings of inadequacy.

When you were a child, you observed your parents and learned what they considered right and wrong. You watched your teachers and other adults about you to learn correct behavior patterns. You may also have learned that if you did not act appropriately, you would be punished. All these experiences join to form the parent part of you—your conscience. When you were little, you assumed that all those big people were "right." So, the parent in each of us embodies the "taught concept of life." Your parent is the part of your mind that reminds you what is right and wrong, lays down the law, and lectures you whenever you stray from doing the right thing.

When you gather information and relate it to past experiences, then make a decision based on facts, your adult is acting. There is a strong similarity between the adult in each of us and the developmental communicator. In this mode of behavior you calculate risks, estimate probabilities, and make decisions based on only factual evidence. You can easily see why the adult is usually called the "thought concept of life." When you explain with sound reasons why you acted as you did, or when you suggest alternatives rather than react emotionally, your adult is in command.

When you can identify the child, parent, and adult in yourself, it becomes easier to spot these types of behavior in other people. Depending on whether the child, parent, or adult in each of us controls situations most of the time, we hold various *life positions* that guide the way we react to other people.

[3] Tom Harris, *I'm O.K., You're O.K.* (New York: Harper, 1969).

Who Is O.K.?

These life positions can be classified into four categories:

1. I'm O.K. and you're O.K.   Persons who have taken this life position have made a rational, adult choice. They understand that they have gained valuable knowledge from past experiences and that other people also have valuable information to share.

2. I'm O.K. and you're not O.K.   These people are distrustful of others. The parent is most often in command. They feel that their ideas present the best possible solution to any problem. They will attempt to control and dominate discussions. If other people are "not O.K.," why should they have to listen to them? This person is like the controlling communicator.

3. I'm not O.K. and you're O.K.   The child has taken control in this situation, and the person responds to others as though they were parents. They expect to be told what to do and feel incapable of contributing anything of value to a discussion. These people are the relinquishing communicators who must seek advice but never give it.

4. I'm not O.K. and you're not O.K.   This negative person views all people as children. Conversation is often sprinkled with phrases like "No," "I can't," "Don't bother me," and "Who cares?" This person is withdrawn and assumes nothing can be done because no one is competent enough to do it. (See Figure 3-3.)

Once we are able to spot a parent or child reaction in ourselves and in others, we can better steer the discussion back to the adult level. For instance, the supervisor who tells subordinates that they must improve production and stop goofing off (parent action) is likely to see anger, guilt, mistrust, or anxiety in the workers (child reaction). On the other hand, if they get involved in a discussion to find new ways to improve production, both supervisor and workers can respond to each other as problem-solving adults.

	I'm OK	I'm Not OK
You're OK	We can do it. 1.	You can do it. 3.
You're Not OK	I can do it. 2.	Nobody can do it. 4.

Figure 3-3. Comparison of Parent, Child, and Adult Relationships.

Summary

Everything we do in life involves the process of communication. The quality of our communication is often responsible for whether we succeed or fail. There is no single cure for communication problems, but we can learn techniques to increase the effectiveness of our communication skills. The first step in developing these skills is to grow aware of communication processes at work in ourselves and in others.

If you want to make sure that your ideas will take root, you must continually develop an awareness of (1) the communication process of coding-transmitting-decoding, (2) the roadblocks that exist at each step in the process, (3) the methods we use to communicate, (4) the four types of communicators, (5) how to keep communication channels open, and (6) our concepts of ourselves and of others.

The "Five C's" of communication help us evaluate the messages we send and receive. There are no guarantees of successful communication, but if our messages are clear, complete, concise, concrete, and correct, they will more likely result in effective and meaningful interchanges with others.

Key Terms

Controlling communicator. An individual who communicates by command. This person rarely gets any feedback and thus never knows if the message has been received and translated correctly.

Developmental communicator. An individual who seeks to apply the two-way process of communication to achieve joint understanding and joint decisions.

Feedback. A return message that tells the sender whether or not a message has been received and decoded correctly.

Noise. Outside interference or distortion in the sending-receiving process of communication. Noise may be tangible—radio static, loud machinery, intervening comments by other people—or intangible—gestures and expressions by others or the mental "roadblocks" they have erected that obstruct incoming messages

Relinquishing communicator. An individual who does not actively participate in the communication process. This person will never take the lead in discussions, problem solving, or decision making, but is willing to go along with others' ideas.

Transactional analysis. A theory that categorizes various styles of behavior according to the concepts we hold of ourselves and other people. The basic modes of behavior, or concepts of life, are child, parent, and adult.

Withdrawn communicator. An individual who rarely participates in human interaction. This person does not ask for or offer advice, ideas, or suggestions.

Review Questions

1. In what ways has the "information explosion" changed our communication processes?
2. Diagram and describe the seven-step process of communication.
3. How can the message you send to another person become confused, distorted, or misleading?
4. People communicate in a wide variety of ways. Which type of communication is most valuable to the supervisor?
5. Describe the four styles of communication for supervisors. Describe a

situation in which each style would be most appropriate. Which style is generally the most appropriate for a supervisor? Why?

6. In a problem-solving situation, which type of communicator would you prefer to work with? Why are the others inadequate in problem solving?

7. It would probably be unwise for a supervisor to refer directly to a subordinate as a parent, a child, or an adult. If you were addressing a subordinate and one of these labels from transactional analysis applied, how would you put into words the meaning of each?

8. Give an example of a parent, child, and adult reaction to the remark, "You're late for work again!"

9. List and describe the "Five C's" of communication. Discuss the importance of each to the communication process.

10. If everyone communicated through mental telepathy, how would the communication process be altered?

Exercises

I. Writing Skills

Imagine that you arrived at work and found an analysis of the future job market on your desk. You have been instructed to extract the key information from the article and present it in readable form to your employees. Rewrite the following paragraph from the article so that the information it presents is conveyed simply and concisely.

There is a remote possibility that in the future there may be somewhat more jobs available. It is estimated that quite a lot of the improvement may be attributed to some of the more important industries and trades which normally become increasingly more active with the onset of warmer weather. In other words, it will be due mainly to the seasonal factors that always cause the over-all basis of the rise and fall in the nation's economic activity, and even though there has been no noticeable strengthening of basic conditions, the general business situation is by far considerably better than most of the pessimistic economic forecasters have expected. According to extensive records compiled by the Bureau of Labor Statistics, the unemployment total in April was substantially below the 4½ million mark reached during March and the recent trend of applicants for jobless benefits suggests that the total of national unemployment is possibly now somewhat below 3 million employable persons who are available for work.

II. Controlling Verbal Communications

A. Everyone is familiar with the childhood game of whispering a message to one's neighbor and sending it around a room of people. Try this experiment with a group of six to ten classmates or work associates.

1. Devise a fairly complex but easy to understand message, something like the following:

The final exam will be held on Friday, unless the following Monday is a holiday, in which case the exam will be on Wednesday after the holiday. In any event, the exam will be in Room 640 and will cover the last half of the book and all the outside readings.

The initial sender whispers the message to his neighbor, who whispers it to the next person, and so on until every member of the group has received the message. The final member to hear the message tells what he or she heard to the rest of the group.

2. Discuss the following questions as a group: Was the final message distorted? Was any important information left out? Was any information added that was not included in the original message? How did the message change in the process of being transferred from one person to another?

B. Try the following experiment at your job. Each time you give someone verbal instructions, ask that person to repeat the instructions to you. In each instance, pay careful attention to the following:

1. The accuracy of the instructions repeated.

2. The accuracy of the person's interpretation of your instructions.

3. The person's reaction to your request to repeat information (parent, child, adult).

4. Your reaction to the accuracy or misinterpretation of your instructions as they are repeated to you.

Case 3 • Les Roe

Les Roe is a supervisor in a regional office of a nationwide computer service company. He has been with the company for six years and is proud of his record. Recently, he has had problems with one of his subordinates, Tim Clark. Tim has a remarkable record after only three years with the company, and it appears that he will be promoted to supervisor within the year. However, Tim is required to have weekly reports to Les by noon on Tuesday. It is now two o'clock Wednesday and Les has not received the weekly report. This is the third time in two months that Tim has been late, so Les decides to approach Tim with the problem.

"Tim, you're late again!" yells Les. "You're going to have to stop goofing off and get on the ball!"

"I'm sorry, Mr. Roe," responds Tim. "George and Phyllis haven't turned in their figures, which I need to finish the report. And why are you always picking on me? Ben hasn't turned in his report either."

"I'm not picking on you," says Les. "But this is the third time in two months that you have been late with the weekly report and I am not going to tolerate it anymore. If you're late again, you will be subject to review. I cannot tolerate incompetence in my office. Have the report to me by five o'clock today."

"Yes, sir," Tim responds. Les abruptly returns to his office. Tim then decides to call George and Phyllis together.

"George, you and Phyllis still have not supplied me with the weekly figures I need, and, as you know, they were due yesterday morning. This has happened before and the result is that I am in hot water with Les. In fact, my job may be on the line if I don't get the report to him by the end of the workday. Now what seems to be the problem from your end?"

Phyllis replies, "The central processing center just isn't generating the basic figures to us in time to analyze them by the deadline. As you can imagine, this puts other employees in the same position you find yourself, Tim."

George suggests, "Why don't we simply ask the processing center to have field personnel submit their reports earlier, so they can be prepared in time for us to prepare our reports for you."

"Okay," replies Tim. "That sounds like a good idea for the future, but can you get me what I need today?" Both replied that they could.

"Good," says Tim, "I'll mention this to Les and see what we can do to implement your suggestion."

1. Analyze the participants in this dialogue from the viewpoint of transactional analysis. What ego states are represented by each participant?

2. Directly under the present dialogue, rewrite the conversation between Les and Tim to show how you would have handled the problem.

CHAPTER 4
Creativity on the Job

Creativity is ten percent inspiration and ninety percent perspiration.

Thomas Edison

Learning Objectives

- To help each supervisor recognize and develop his or her own creative skills.
- To learn the process of creativity by examining its major aspects.
- To become aware of negative factors that stifle creativity on and off the job.
- To identify the potential of creative groups and various ways of releasing that potential.
- To utilize creative techniques in problem-solving situations.

The concept of creativity confuses many people who feel they are not particularly creative. We often think of creativity as something vague and out of reach, a grand ability to do important things that no one else has thought of doing. In fact, though, every person has creative abilities. The supervisor who constantly seeks better ways to solve problems on the job is a creative individual. Memos by these managers may never hang in an art gallery, but their creative approaches to everyday challenges will be rewarded.

The first chapters of the Old Testament use a special Hebrew word for the act of creation attributed to God. Literally translated, the word means "to make from nothing." In the books that follow, a more humble word is used to indicate creation, meaning "to make, to assemble, to build." It is in this sense that human beings create. Though creativity indicates an important talent in our language, the Hebrew distinction is important to remember. Creativity is not a mystical spark some have and most do not. Given the right circumstances, creativity can be created and nurtured in anyone. Do not dismiss your own potential by saying, "Oh, I'm just not creative." To be more correct, you should probably say, "Unfortunately, I have never received much praise for my initial efforts at creativity, so I have decided it is safer and more secure not to pursue the ideas that occur to me."

Shortsighted Overseers

In earlier days, supervisors served merely as overseers. The factory owner could not personally direct all the simple and unvarying processes that were continuously performed throughout the plant. To help, the owner hired a person to keep things moving and report any problems. Naturally, under the factory owner's heavy thumb, the supervisor often found that any attempted creativity was met with instant disapproval and often dismissal. The entrepreneur or inventive genius usually owned the business; the supervisor had little chance to exercise personal talents for creativity.

Many supervisors have remained highly paid overseers, especially in more tightly structured operations where they are not allowed to threaten the status quo. In these situations supervisors are often given a title which clearly indicates that they simply pass papers and orders between the people above and below them. They truly become safe, comfortable, and noncreative paper shufflers.

A supervisor must develop true leadership abilities in order to uncover creative talents and encourage creativity in subordinates. Because creativity is tightly bound to the subject of change, a new idea represents a challenge and a threat to everyone who did not originate the concept. Innovators soon realize the dangerous and unstable position occupied by anyone who breaks with tradition. They must be willing to endure the jibes of narrow-minded, insecure subordinates and bosses who naturally shy away from the untried. When the heat is on, more than motivation is needed to keep an innovator going. Inventors, explorers, and leaders who have brought about great and praiseworthy changes have almost always done it by fighting the tide of popular opinion.

Creativity is often viewed in terms of verbal or artistic skills. Creative managers, too, must guard against using the term *creativity* to mask bad habits. Some people hide behind the word as an excuse for over spending budgets, delivering past deadline, and never being available when wanted.

What Does It Take to Be Creative?

To better understand creativity, we shall look briefly at four aspects of it: innovation, synthesis, extension, and duplication.

Innovation refers to the originality of a product or a method of doing things. Innovative creativity results in a new combination of familiar parts. Fantasy and dreaming play an important part in innovation, but an inquisitive mind is required to investigate these new thought combinations. Of course, those who march to the beat of a different drummer must recognize that others will probably just consider them out of step.

A creative supervisor will be on the lookout for new ideas, people, machinery, or technology, and be thinking of ways to combine existing resources into more productive means. One young man we know went to work as a first-line supervisor for a large textile mill immediately after college. The first year, he suggested a new production idea utilizing existing machinery and people that saved the company $1 million!

Synthesis involves the absorbent, spongelike nature of creative persons. They draw ideas from almost any source and can recognize interrelationships and parallels, which they then transfer to their jobs or other areas of life. Creative association can combine things that appear totally unrelated. James Watt's whistling tea kettle suggested the steam engine, and a falling apple helped Newton uncover the law of gravity.

Each supervisor must develop the ability to synthesize in order to attain creativity. You have many resources at your disposal, including material goods and the people you supervise. It is important that you understand the unique contributions which each of these makes to the smooth operation of the whole. You must combine the highly varied talents of people with other resources to produce a unique product or interrelationship of smoothly functioning skills in your department.

The founder of a small construction business supervised several office and field personnel. Prior to holding the first company meeting of all personnel, she asked each employee to bring a money-saving or problem-solving idea to the meeting. The office personnel came up with a suggestion of reusing job notebooks that instantly saved $1000. They also proposed a new office layout to solve traffic flow in the office and guarantee contract secrecy.

Extension is almost impossible to separate from synthesis, for without extension, synthesis becomes meaningless data collection. The creative person's desire to understand everything is mobilized by an ability to extend knowledge and understanding to problems that must be solved. This quality allows application of new-found relationships and recognizes new implications of discoveries. For example, Einstein's single discovery of the theory of relativity enabled other scientists to continue their advances in various scientific areas.

In the construction company example above, the reuse of job notebooks led to the idea of reusing other items in the office and on job sites. The use of petroleum jelly on door jambs and thresholds prevented concrete splatter damage and led to its use on other objects for protection.

Duplication is an important aspect of creativity. Many creative activities got under way through intentional duplication of someone else's discovery.

Just as it would be foolish for every machine maker to reinvent the wheel, taking advantage of others' creative acts can provide a spark to the creative supervisor. Of course, if the copier loses sight of the original purposes in copying, the duplication becomes an end in itself and is no longer applicable to the situation at hand. Duplication then ceases to be a creative act and becomes thoughtless acceptance. The creative supervisor takes the best ideas of other creative individuals and adjusts them to current job requirements and problem-solving needs.

Ted Levitt, of the Harvard Business School, has asserted that many managers, especially in small organizations, would fare better utilizing "innovative imitations" than attempting to create a unique idea. Excessive development costs and the high risk of failure in introducing new products make "original" creativity too expensive for many companies. Your ability to find a more efficient application for an existing idea can constitute a profitable form of creativity. Supervisors who solve new problems by drawing on past experiences or adopting techniques they have seen applied somewhere else deserve gold stars for creativity. Our creative construction extensions were later developed into construction policies for use on all future buildings—saving the company time and money, and increasing profitability.

Characteristics of Creative Managers

In a classic treatment, Carl E. Gregory[1] has developed a list of characteristics often found in creative persons. These traits are not always positive indicators of creativity. Some individuals who display one or more of them may simply have chosen to play the creative role. Creative persons will not necessarily score 100 percent on the list because that would be uncharacteristic of such independent people. They will, however, score higher than those who suppress their creativity.

Personality traits that can indicate creativity

1. Highly creative:
   Believes nothing is impossible.
   Believes that truth, as people understand it, is relative.
   Can think in terms of abstract figures, designs, and constructs.
   Has a keen awareness of self and environment.
   Has a high sensitivity in isolating problems.
   Uses written and spoken language fluently.
   Has the ability to elaborate on concepts, plans, and inventions.
   Is able to tolerate ambiguity while looking for connections and combinations.
   Is adaptive to change in events and circumstances.
   Is flexible and adaptive in making changes to achieve goals.
   Is highly original in conceptual output.
   Is open-minded.
   Is frequently presenting new and constructive suggestions.
   Plays with combinations of concepts, ideas, facts, and objects.
   Vacillates from periods of creativity to periods of judging personal capabilities.

[1] Carl E. Gregory, *The Management of Intelligence* (New York: McGraw-Hill, 1967), pp. 188–90.

2. Enthusiastic:
    Does not contemplate failures.
    Does not permit frustration to lower motivational drive.
    Gets a tremendous emotional charge from discovery.
    Is highly motivated.
    Often rides on "cloud nine."
    Is optimistic.
    Is quick-witted.
    Is sometimes impulsive.
    Thinks positively.

3. Self-actualized:
    Accepts himself or herself and reality as they are.
    May appear to be egoistic.
    Constantly reviews personal beliefs.
    Is critical of any restriction on knowledge sharing.
    Is critical of falsehoods.
    Is critical of pretenders.
    Does not want to be the "life of the party."
    Engages in goal seeking.
    Engages in independent thinking.
    Has a sense of self-fulfillment.
    Has a sense of personal worth.
    Has an independent set of values.
    Has social boldness.
    Is highly selective of associates and friends.
    Maintains independent judgments.
    Is more self-sufficient than most.
    Has motives that are often misunderstood by others.
    Is self-assured in the conceptual field.
    Is open to new ideas.
    Is self-motivated.
    Speaks his or her mind to the degree of being considered outspoken.
    Survives failure and criticism.

4. Strong-willed:
    Dislikes policing.
    Dislikes rigid authority structures.
    Does not compromise personal beliefs easily.
    Does not follow administrative rules well.
    Does not accept defeat.
    Learns from mistakes and failures.
    Is often in danger of being estranged from other people.
    Is often unpredictable.

5. Broadly experienced:
    Profits from new experiences in such areas as friends, recreation, dining,
        and other activities.
    Maintains contact with all types of people.
    Reads extensively.
    Searches out different environments.

6. Activist:
    Expends enormous energy.

Experiments with serious issues.
Has tremendous drive.
Initiates action.
Is very active.
Is self-starting.
Works on many problems at the same time.

7. Has periodic outbursts of creativity (illumination).
Has longer creative periods than most people.
Is more creative at certain hours of the day than at others.

8. Goal-oriented:
Innovates in different directions.
Expresses ideas in different ways.
Often budgets and focuses time, energy, and creativity.
Is not consistently creative in all aspects of life.

9. Generally:
Is a poor speller.
Works in a state of apparent disorganization.
Moves from conceptual disorganization to organization.

Creative Groups

Attributes and characteristics associated with creative individuals can apply to creative groups as well. In fact, a creative group's talents will exceed the sum of the skills of all its members. For example, if one creative person can produce five ideas per minute, five creative people should provide more than twenty-five new ideas in that same minute. The creative potential of any group, however, is largely determined by that group's supervisor or leader. If the supervisor recognizes the necessity of freedom, the group can rise to creative peaks that will outweigh the risks of making some mistakes. Supervisors who feel insecure working within flexible environments and trial-and-error philosophies are likely to control their people so tightly that they kill all creative urges.

To lead a creative group of workers, a supervisor must understand the difference between a loose, seemingly unstructured atmosphere that is actually disciplined and productive, and the loose atmosphere of a bull session. There is nothing mechanical about the creative process, but the truly creative superviser must run a controlled shop that provides some goal orientation while allowing the group enough freedom and flexibility to recognize and satisfy needs of individual members. If all members understand the goals and the rules, they can produce record numbers of innovative ideas. The challenge faced by supervisors in creative groups is to establish the atmosphere for generating new ideas: a combination of mutual respect, security to be open in exchanging ideas, and an underlying firmness and sense of direction.

The Creative Leader

Former President John F. Kennedy is often viewed as the epitome of the creative leader working effectively with a creative group. He exemplified the pattern of a highly creative person who magnetizes and activates a small nucleus of creative people. Groups like this can be found in art, science, military history, and almost any area of life. Areas of endeavor do not define creative groups—it is the group leader's special guiding abilities that make the difference.

This leader must serve as a rallying point, a source of support for every group exploration. No matter how far from the beaten path members may roam, each recognizes the leader and knows exactly where the mutual goal lies and exactly how all the pieces will fit together.

Because creative leaders accept the responsibility for implanting and nurturing confidence, self-assurance, and security in subordinates, they are always wary of negativism among group members, and are generous in rewarding people for their creative efforts. By letting them know that they are important and capable, the supervisor communicates confidence, the essential fuel of creativity.

Interaction, output, success, growth, purpose, and more success also fuel creative groups. With proper care, a creative group need never know real failure. Mistakes will occur, but a creative group working in a supportive atmosphere can engender a steady cycle of success. A company may pay a premium salary to hire creative supervisors, but it is not the salary that makes them creative. No company can make its people creative, but a company can arrange the circumstances that allow people to be creative. Each supervisor should serve as the facilitator in the work environment, subtly directing the show by letting people build the confidence and freedom they need to be innovators.

The following checklist may be helpful in evaluating the creative climate surrounding any work group.

Testing the Creative Climate

The creative organization

- Has open communication among members.
- Has open communication with the outside.
- Has a large variety of personality types.
- Allows members to be themselves.
- Approaches tasks objectively and is able to see both sides.
- Is not afraid of change.
- Is not enamored of change for its own sake.
- Enjoys experimenting with new ideas.
- Wants to know about everything.
- Can tolerate flexible scheduling.
- Is committed to defining goals and achieving them.
- Enjoys its work.
- Makes decisions without concern for repercussions.
- Cannot be charted by time and motion studies.

After reviewing this list, check the items controlled largely by the supervisor. Clearly, supervisor quality is the key to creativity in groups.

How to Create Creativity

The increasing need for creative approaches to problem solving has triggered a growing demand for techniques to help people discover and utilize their creative abilities. Systems, procedures, and techniques that have enabled a particular group to produce large quantities of new ideas have been eagerly sought and copied. The warning issued earlier in this chapter concerning the dangers of duplication should be remembered: *something that works in one creative situation may bring disaster to another.* However, the search continues for successful recipes and methods by which creative individuals can increase their capabilities by joining groups. Many professional meetings include techniques for creating creativity in their programs. Readers of this text may be guided by noting the general characteristics of the methods discussed below. Try different techniques and combinations of these characteristics within your own groups.

Techniques for creating creativity can be grouped under three headings: *analytical* (the logical attack), *free association* (the blue sky techniques), and *forced relationships* (the systems approach). A fourth category exists, but it is more difficult to describe: *eclectic techniques* (combinations and adaptations of the other three groups).

The Logical Attack

Basically, analytical approaches to stimulating creativity use our human ability to focus logically on a sequence of problem solutions while we give free reign to our imaginations. Two major analytical approaches follow.

Attribute listing was developed by Robert Crawford, a pioneer in recognizing creativity as a basic force. His approach[2] is quite simple but is extremely effective in breaking the ice and sparking creative thought processes. The first step is to rapidly list the major characteristics of a product, an object, an idea, or a problem. Next, the group discusses each attribute in detail, writing down or tape recording all of their observations. No idea is scoffed at or rejected—the sky is the limit. When the group has come up with all possible ideas, they are evaluated one by one until it becomes obvious what the most advantageous next move is. Attribute listing is extremely useful in initiating creativity. The creative supervisor can use this technique to synthesize, extend, and evaluate solutions to all kinds of problems, whether the topic under discussion is a new marketing strategy, a more convenient display arrangement, or a system of sales incentives.

Input-output is a technique developed by General Electric specifically for working with problems involving energy uses. The major advantage of this approach is that the goal is clearly identified and described at the outset—the desired output is defined. Once this is accomplished, all possible inputs or combinations of ideas which could lead to the desired output are listed. At this point, agreement among group members as to the "proper" input is unnecessary and probably undesirable. When all inputs have been listed, they

---

[2] Robert P. Crawford, *The Technique of Creative Thinking* (Englewood Cliffs, N. J.: Prentice-Hall, 1954).

are discussed and gradually listed in order of priority by considering the elements of time, resources, practicality, and expected returns. Eventually, one input clearly emerges as the preferred method of achieving the stated goal.

The Blue Sky

This technique demands that the group members extend their imaginations to the limit in developing relationships, seeing connections, and anticipating problem solutions. The goal may or may not be known; the important issue in free association is to initiate ideas, however "far out" they may be.

Brainstorming is a popular method for initiating as many of these ideas as possible. In ordinary conversation and discussion, a group often gets sidetracked into discussions unrelated to the original idea or problem. In brainstorming, the group is given a particular topic or problem and encouraged to associate ideas freely for a period of time. During the brainstorming session, members reserve critical evaluation until all the ideas are laid on the table. No negative responses are allowed while the group is brainstorming. The generation of ideas is the main goal of this method. Evaluation of ideas is not allowed until actual plans or problem solutions are finalized later. Brainstorming represents the most familiar and widely accepted technique for encouraging creativity. The method can be so overused and misused that some people call every commonplace discussion a brainstorming session. When this happens, the chairperson has failed to control the meeting and keep the ideas flowing until all the alternatives are on paper. Only then should the productive and necessary step of discussing the merits of alternatives be introduced.

A variation on brainstorming known as the *Gordon technique* was developed by W. J. Gordon of the Arthur D. Little Company, a research and consulting firm.[3] Gordon's revision was to keep the specific problem in question under wraps during the brainstorming session. He felt that traditional brainstorming had a tendency to lose its participants early in the discussion. If participants knew what the problem was, they often suggested the first solution that occurred to them and then sat back and let things glide. Gordon realized that if group members are making statements about a general subject area, they may tend to be more creative—even accidentally—than if they had already contributed the "obvious answer" to a specific question.

Success in using the Gordon technique requires a highly skilled group leader. Only the leader knows the problem and is responsible for keeping all options open. Thus, as discussion moves into smaller circles, focusing more directly on the actual problem, group members must be kept open-minded and ready to shift gears as the topic changes character. Imagine being part of such a group and hearing the leader open with, "Let's talk about taking a trip." What would be your first response? And how could the discussion be guided from there to a consideration of solutions for a particular problem?

The *Phillips 66 buzz session* was developed by Donald Phillips while he was president of Hillsdale College in Hillsdale, Michigan.[4] This system is particularly effective when large groups must participate in the brainstorming process. The group is divided into a number of smaller groups containing five to eight

[3] William J. Gordon, *Synectics* (New York: Harper, 1951).
[4] Op. cit., p. 200.

persons each. Every group picks a leader and brainstorms about the same idea. Each leader then summarizes the group's conversation and presents the ideas generated to the group as a whole for discussion. Originally, a large group was divided into six subgroups of six members, which met for six minutes (thus the name "six-six") to discuss only a single aspect of a problem or a topic. Each small group's contribution was then presented to the total group by each leader. The method has all the assets and liabilities of regular small-group brainstorming with the advantage of increased input because of the much larger number of participants. As in every other form of creativity stimulation, the success of this technique depends largely upon the group leader's skill and creativity.

The *collective notebook* method makes use of time, a dimension usually neglected in brainstorming. In this method each member of the group is given a notebook. The problem is stated on the first page, and other necessary information given. Working at their own pace, participants note in the book any thoughts on the problem for a full month, or some appropriate length of time. When the time is up, the notebooks are turned in along with a concise statement of each participant's best solution to the problem. This information is then consolidated and coordinated by the supervisor or some other competent coordinator. A final creative discussion of the question is then held to wrap up any loose ends to allow participants to see the results of their efforts.

Forced Relationship Approaches

These techniques are systematic inquiries into the vast number of relationships that may occur between any two objects or ideas. They are especially useful for the generation of ideas on a broad, general scale, such as future directions for company expansion or projections about the market situation in twenty years. They are less useful for specific problem solving.

The *catalog technique* is probably the most popular approach. Two words or ideas are randomly selected from a dictionary or other source, and a creative discussion of the possible relationships between the two is encouraged. Of course, the control of the word selection source will be very important in determining just how broad the discussion must be. For instance, it may not be especially helpful for a group seeking new ways to stimulate employee productivity to choose a gourmet cookbook as their word selection source!

The *listing technique* allows the group to deal with a problem or an idea by listing any number of objects, ideas, or relationships that come to mind in connection with a specific subject or problem. After they are listed, each item is assigned a number, and its relationship to the original topic is discussed. The process continues until all the items have been discussed and an emerging consensus can be detected.

Eclectic Approaches

Eclectic approaches are those which use the best or most appropriate parts of many different techniques. Such approaches are as varied as the people who utilize them. As mentioned earlier, a creative leader is unlikely to be content with a wholesale, flippant adoption of someone else's approach to creativity.

These different methods provide a creative supervisor a variety of tools, but a combination of techniques which works well for one group may lead to a dead end for another. In choosing an approach, the creative supervisor must always remember that as a group leader he or she must consider the talents and abilities of people as well as the goal to be met. The methods described in this chapter are intended only to stimulate the creative supervision of creativity.

Creative Blockbusting—Working Yourself and Your Group Out of a Hole

Most groups occasionally find themselves blocked, unable to get on with their task. They find themselves returning to the same old ideas. When this happens, these techniques can crack the block to creativity.

1. Isolate the problem. It is easy to be distracted by symptoms and forget the real problem causing them. Try to focus the group's attention on identifying and specifying the problem under discussion. When the group is headed in the right direction, it will spin its wheels less.

2. Do not narrow the question too much. This warning presents the hazard involved in distinguishing the symptoms from the problem. If the group leader steers the group toward too narrow a topic, members may arrive too quickly at the "right" answer. They may then stop innovating, since the "new" problem is so specific that it eliminates many avenues for creativity.

3. Define your terms. If your group members are using the same words to mean different things, the communication process is stymied and innovation cannot occur. Similarly, everyone may be repeating the same thing in different words. Take a moment to clarify and define the concepts being used so everyone understands where the group is headed.

4. Observe the problem from every conceivable angle. Make every effort to view the problem or topic from many different perspectives. Use all your senses and all your faculties to see the situation's pros and cons, and examine these favorable and unfavorable characteristics from several viewpoints. This technique will insure that your group does not adopt one particular way of looking at things, which then automatically emerges as the right way.

5. Start working from the back. Start considering the problem from the perspective of a possible solution and work your way back, watching carefully for snags and missed connections. Try to see remote relationships. Consider every possible alternative, no matter how ridiculous it may seem.

6. Investigate what is obvious. The process of observing and investigating the obvious has led to some remarkable discoveries. When considering a problem or a situation in a creative way, make every effort to see familiar aspects as though you were observing them for the first time.

7. Do not worry about conforming to the adopted pattern. Remember how the pattern came to be adopted—somebody decided that it was the right way and went out on a limb to be innovative. As conditions change, new methods may have to be adopted. There is no reason why the original way of doing things should always be considered the best way.

8. Do not worry about practicality and economy until after all the possibilities have been considered. Seemingly impractical means of accomplishing some goal may actually be the best and most economical. After you have established what ought to be done, you can then consider elements of practicality and economy.

9. Do not try to invent what has already been invented. If you spend creative time reinventing the wheel, you have wasted efforts that could better be applied to creating new methods of using the wheel. Some things have to be accepted.

10. Do not worry about being polite if it means you must sacrifice creativity. People with negative attitudes can undercut progress if you are not aware of their games and are overconcerned with niceties of social interaction.

11. Ask someone who is not an expert. When the pace of progress has slowed and the task is getting old, call in someone who knows nothing about the question or the solution, explain the group's progress, and ask for reactions. Feedback is a critical part of the communication process in creative activity, and an outsider can provide just the perspective you need to get back on the right track.

Summary

Creativity is a highly desirable qualification for almost every job. Though the qualifications may be stated in other words, every task is best done by the person who can observe, evaluate, and approach it with objectivity and innovation. The term *creativity* tends to be a catchall for almost all accomplishment. In addition, a deceptive stereotype has convinced many of us that the truly creative person possesses odd clothes, long hair, or eccentric habits. Real creativity and independent action are likely to exist in places where they are least expected. We are surprised by the seeming contradiction of the term *creative supervisor* applied to anyone but the head of R&D. Yet, significant creative action is needed in policy-making and need-assessing positions as well. Creativity is not determined by the kind of work but by the kind of approach taken to any job. People, not jobs, are creative.

There are creative people and order-fillers at every level of endeavor. All people possess the potential to be creative. The deciding factor is whether or not an environment can be created that favors and reinforces creative effort. In most cases, it is the supervisor who must make sure that conditions *allow,* rather than force or hinder, creativity.

Four aspects of creativity have been isolated: *innovation,* the originality of the product or service; *synthesis,* the tendency of a creative person to absorb information from every surrounding source; *extension,* the ability to put divergent bits of information and experience together and form other concepts; and *duplication,* which can serve as a starting point to further creativity.

Experts have occasionally listed attributes of the creative personality. As with most generalizations, these must be read wisely because truly creative persons are notoriously poor at displaying traits found on the attribute lists.

Creative groups also have personalities but depend more than anything else upon the skill and creativity of their leaders.

Several techniques for creating creativity have been reviewed: the *analytical approaches*—attribute testing and input-output; *free-association techniques*—brainstorming, the Gordon technique, the Phillips 66 buzz session, and the collective notebook; *forced relationships techniques*—catalog techniques and listing techniques; and *eclectic approaches*, which utilize parts of several other techniques.

It is important to remember that reading a chapter on creativity is not going to make you a creative individual. Your creative application of the techniques discussed and an understanding of the issues involved will be crucial to your development as a creative supervisor.

Key Terms

Attribute Listing. A logical approach to creativity. A group rapidly lists the major characteristics of a product, object, idea, or problem. Each attribute is discussed in detail and evaluated to identify the next, most appropriate move in problem solving.

Brainstorming. A technique where members of a group use free association to come up with as many ideas as possible relating to a particular problem. Criticism and evaluation are reserved until all possible ideas have been recorded.

Catalog Technique. Random discussion of all possible relationships between two words or ideas.

Collective Notebook Approach. Each member of the group receives a notebook stating the problem on the first page. During a specified period of time, each individual writes down ideas and thoughts about the problem. The notebooks are then collected and consolidated, and the information and ideas obtained are used in a final problem-solving session.

Creativity. The ability to bring something new into existence by rearranging existing ideas in new relationships.

Duplication. Adaptation of an existing idea, product, or process to another situation or set of circumstances.

Eclectic Techniques. Combinations of two or more techniques for releasing creativity (such as brainstorming before and after keeping a collective notebook). Eclectic approaches to creativity are many and varied as supervisors adapt techniques to their own needs.

Extension. In the creative process, the ability to extend knowledge, understanding, or ideas to problem areas.

Gordon Technique. A type of brainstorming in which the group members do not know the specific problem to be discussed but join in throwing out ideas about a general subject area.

Innovation. A product, method, process, or idea that is new or original.

Innovative Imitation. The ability to take a new idea and find a more efficient or effective application for it.

Input-Output Technique. A method of creative problem solving in which the desired goal is stated as "desired output" and all possible inputs, or combinations of ideas that could lead to the desired output, are listed.

Listing Techniques. A group approach to creativity in which members are given a subject or problem to consider and then list every object, idea, or relationship that comes to mind. The relationship of each item to the topic is then discussed.

Phillips' 66 Buzz Session. A creative technique for large groups. The large group is divided into smaller groups with five to eight members. The small groups brainstorm on the same subject, then report their ideas to the group as a whole, which then discusses these ideas.

Synthesis. The ability to draw ideas from any source and to recognize relationships and parallels which can then be applied to specific problem-solving situations.

Review Questions

1. Describe a creative supervisor.

2. It is suggested that creativity is a dangerous talent for supervisors. How can this be possible?

3. List and describe the importance of the four aspects of creativity discussed in the chapter.

4. Why are supervisors often afraid to praise their subordinates on the job?

5. Rate yourself and a good friend using the list of personality traits attributed to creative people. How do you compare? Do your results have anything to do with why you are friends?

6. Why is the role of leader so important in groups?

7. What do logical attack and blue sky creativity techniques have in common?

8. Why is feedback so important in the creative process?

9. How important do you think it is for a supervisor to be creative? What does taking a creative approach to a job mean to you?

10. What kinds of work are more creative than others?

11. Where can a supervisor obtain input to synthesize and capitalize upon his or her creative potential?

Exercises

I. Using a Collective Notebook Approach

You have been given the following problem: "How could a class on supervision be more interesting, enjoyable, and informative?" Put the problem statement in the front of a small notebook and spend a week jotting down your ideas and thoughts about effective classroom procedures. At the end of the week, compare your ideas with those of your associates and discuss these questions:

1. Were most of the ideas similar?

2. Did anyone come up with a particularly creative solution?

3. Were most of the comments negative or positive?

4. How could your ideas be implemented?

II. Learning to Brainstorm by Yourself

You have just learned that research scientists have been able to train great apes successfully to do simple manual labor and follow verbal instructions. Given this information, list your ideas on how this new source of "mammal power" might be utilized. Consider also the implications such a development could have for business. How could trained apes be used in your own business? What aspects of the creative process are you applying in this task?

Case 4 • Ned Collins

Ned Collins is the regional sales manager for a national publishing firm that sells advertising space for more than twenty magazines. Three sales representatives work for him, each covering several states with specific magazines. Brit Holmes is twenty-five years old and has worked for Ned the longest—four years. He directs his sales to manufacturing companies and has established a regular travel schedule that has him on the road and in the office on alternating weeks. Tena Moran is thirty-eight years old, had a sales career with two similar companies, and has been working with Ned for three years. Her earnings have progressed consistently each year, and she has solid relationships with her clients. Jim Richly is thirty-one years old and is the newest sales representative working for Ned—he has yet to complete six months. He is single, loves the travel aspect of the job, and is very enthusiastic about working in all or part of the region with any of the magazines.

Ned's staff is producing at a good level, but he is concerned that no new major accounts have been opened in the last year and that the competition appears to be getting more aggressive. In hiring Jim, he hoped to have the "missing link" he needed to improve sales; he could restructure the territories, assign new magazines to each sales representative, and create a new spirit of aggressiveness among them that would lead to higher sales totals for the division.

Ned has called a meeting of the three sales representatives and has shared with them his view of the new possibilities for increased sales with Jim on the staff. This conversation followed his opening remarks:

"I don't like it," said Tena. "I've worked hard to establish good relationships with my clients. I am a good friend to many of them, and if I am in a real bind for a sale, there are several I could call and they would give me an order just for friendship's sake. Besides, this office is doing well and all of us are making a good buck!"

"I agree with Tena," said Brit. "I have a good travel schedule established now, and I know my people and magazines. I don't really want any new magazines or territory. Besides, specialization is best in this business anyway."

Somewhat confused by the intensity of these comments, Ned interjected, "But what about the fact that our competition is growing faster than we are? They are turning up new business that we should be finding first. I think change would be good for all of us, and I am including my own territory and magazines in this too. How much new business can I expect from each of you under the status quo?"

"Please," Tena replied. "I don't want to start keeping more records of new accounts called—that's for the order-takers, not professional representatives."

"I don't think we can say exactly how much new business we could expect," said Brit. "Let's face it—new business depends a lot on luck. I propose just shooting for increased sales with our established clients."

Ned closed the meeting after suggesting that they all think this matter over for a few days, but he was frustrated for lack of a creative solution to the challenge before him.

1. What basic concepts of creativity have been overlooked at this situation?
2. If you were Ned, what would you do to help solve the problem?

CHAPTER 5

Managing Time, The Scarcest Resource

Dost thou love life? Then do not squander time, for that is the stuff life is made of.

Poor Richard's Almanac

Learning Objectives

- To start treating time as a resource.
- To identify major time wasters and learn how to plug personal time leaks.
- To discover time orientations and perceptions, compare the relationship between time and achievement needs, and dispel some myths about time and work.
- To solve time problems by building more efficient habits, using a time log, and keeping in touch with your personal concepts of time.

If asked whether you have enough time as a supervisor, would your answer be yes? If so, you are in the very small minority of supervisors—and people in general. Each of us has exactly the same amount of time, yet few of us ever seem to have enough.

Supervisors Need More Time

There never seem to be enough hours in the day to handle all the tasks, problems, administrative details, routine work, and crises that occur. Most of us probably wish for a time extension each day, just to catch up on the other facets of life we are missing!

One researcher found that out of thousands of supervisors, only one in one hundred admitted to having enough time.[1] One in ten would like 10 percent more time, four out of ten wish for 25 percent more time, and the remaining 50 percent of supervisors need another twelve hours in each day!

Since no one has any more time than anyone else, using it well is of utmost importance. Although we all have different personalities, talents, and skills, there is one thing each of us has in exactly the same amount, and that is time. When we notice that a person seems to accomplish more in a day than three average people, we begin to realize that the problem does not lie with the actual number of hours we have available. Rather, the problem lies in how well we utilize the time we have.

Our Most Valuable Resource

Resources are things to be used wisely. Everyone would agree that time is a resource and a unique one. We cannot save it for a rainy day, or accumulate it like raw materials. Machines can be turned off and people can be replaced, but time continues its march at a fixed rate. Time, unlike many other resources, can never be replaced.

Fortunately, we can exercise a degree of control over how we use our time resources. Raw materials, energy, and other resources can be managed wisely or misused, and time is not different. R. Alec MacKenzie, a consultant on time management, has remarked, "Time is the scarcest resource. Unless it is managed, nothing else *can* be managed."[2]

Most people agree that time is not only every individual's most valuable resource, it is also a business's most valuable resource. There are many situations in which return on time provides a more useful criterion for action than return on capital invested. In the future, we may see corporations begin to ask staff members with experience in time studies to help supervisors and managers spend their hours more wisely. "Scientific management" began when such people as Frederick W. Taylor and Frank B. Gilbreth helped workers with time management. Obviously, supervisors need this kind of assistance as well.

Time management has often been ignored as a skill to be developed in supervisory training. For all our emphasis on planning, we often fail to plan the use of our most valuable and scarce resource. Although "managing time" is not an accurate phrase—the clock's minute hand will ignore our rules, regulations, and office directives—we can learn to manage ourselves in relation to time. Once we understand this principle, we are on our way to solving a wide variety of problems.

[1] Quoted by Ross A. Webber, *Time and Management* (New York: Van Nostrand, 1972), p. 15.

[2] R. Alec MacKenzie, *The Time Trap* (New York: McGraw-Hill, 1975).

How Supervisors Lose Time

Each of us likes to feel that his or her problems are unique. There are numerous similarities, however, in the problems associated with managing time at all levels of supervision. One study asked six different groups of high-level supervisors in several parts of the world to draw up lists of their major time wasters.

Table 5-1. Time Wasters of Four Groups of Top Managers. (Adapted from R. Alec MacKenzie, *Managing Time at the Top* (New York: The Presidents Association, 1970.)

Group A	Group B
Unclear objectives	Scheduled meetings
Poor information	Unscheduled meetings
Postponed decisions	Lack of priorities
Procrastination	Failure to delegate
Lack of information	Interruptions
Lack of feedback	Unavailability of people
Routine work	Junk mail
Too much reading	Lack of planning
Interruptions	Outside (civic) demands
Telephone	Poor filing system
No time planning	Fatigue
Meetings	Procrastination
Beautiful secretaries	Telephone
Lack of competent	Questionnaires
personnel	Lack of procedure for
Lack of delegation	routine matters
Lack of self-discipline	
Visitors	**Group D**
Training new staff	Attempting too much at
Lack of priorities	once
Management by crisis	Lack of delegation
	Talking too much
	Inconsistent actions
Group C	No priorities
Trash mail	Span of control
Socializing	Usurped authority
Unnecessary meetings	Cannot say no
Lack of concentration	Lack of planning
Lack of managerial tools	Snap decisions
Peer demands on time	Procrastination
Incompetent subordinates	Low morale
Coffee breaks	Mistakes
Crisis management	Disorganized secretaries
Unintelligible	Poor communication
communications	Overoptimism
Procrastination	Responsibility without
Lack of clerical staff	authority
Poor physical fitness	
Red tape	
Pet projects	
Lack of priorities	

When compared, the lists were almost identical! Army colonels, college presidents, public school superintendents, corporation chief executives, insurance salesmen, and religious leaders all have similar problems in managing time.[3]

Table 5-1 presents lists of time wasters by noted military officers, religious leaders, college presidents, and managers. Can you identify the list compiled by each group? The answers can be found on the last page of this chapter.

The problem of time management is universal. Management consultant Peter F. Drucker has prepared a film demonstrating the misuse of supervisory time.[4] In the film, Drucker is visiting with a busy corporation president who, during the day, commits almost every possible error in time management. Before this film is shown to a group, the members of the audience are asked to draw up a list of their major time wasters. They then view the film and are asked to make up a second list. Each time these two lists are compared, an interesting difference appears. The first list is usually composed of ways in which *other people* waste the supervisor's time, while the second list focuses on how the *supervisor* wastes his or her own time. To illustrate this point, compare Lists A and B in Table 5-2. A group of electrical contracting executives made up the first list before seeing the Drucker film and the second list after.

Most people blame others for their poor use of time. Outside causes are usually blamed for inappropriate time management until we are reminded that we have the most control over each day's hours (see Table 5-2). Knowledge of our own ineffectiveness is a painful and difficult insight, but one we must all grasp if we are to overcome our time-wasting habits. Pogo, the famous cartoon character, once remarked sadly and wisely, "We has met the enemy, and they is us."

Table 5-2. Executive Time Wasters, External and Internal. (Adapted from R. Alec MacKenzie, *Managing Time at the Top* (New York: The Presidents Association, 1970.)

List A	List B
1. Incomplete information presented for solutions to problems	1. Attempting too much at once
2. Employees with problems	2. Unrealistic time estimates
3. Lack of delegation	3. Procrastinating
4. Telephone	4. Lack of organization
5. Routine tasks	5. Failure to listen
6. Lunch	6. Doing it myself
7. Interruptions	7. Unable to say no
8. Meetings	8. Refusal to let others do the job
9. Lack of priorities	9. Delegating responsibility without authority
10. Management by crisis	10. Involving everyone
11. Personal attention to people	11. Bypassing the chain of command
12. Outside activities	12. Snap decisions
13. Poor communication	13. Blaming others
14. Mistakes	14. Personal and outside activities

[3] R. Alec MacKenzie, "How to Manage Your Time," *Association Management,* May 1974, pp. 30–37.
[4] "The Effective Executive," Bureau of National Affairs Film Series, Washington, D. C.

How Do You Waste Time?

You have seen several lists of time wasters drawn up by many different kinds of supervisors and managers. Now take a little time to draw up your own list of major time wasters. When you have listed all you can think of, rank them in order of priority. Do not limit yourself to those time wasters shown in the lists—try to identify every way in which *you* use time ineffectively. Your own time wasters may include handling crises rather than problems, disorganization, uncertain responsibilities, failure to motivate your employees, lack of coordination, waiting for decisions to be handed down, failure to apply standards, lack of control or evaluation procedures, too much control, too much communication, and focusing on problems rather than on opportunities for improvement.

Now look closely at your list. Which of your major time wasters are caused by *you*? Which are caused by other people or outside events? Of the last group, which time wasters could you avoid or control better? When you have answered these questions carefully, would you agree that you are responsible for both your major time wasters and finding solutions to your problems?

Working Smart

The everyday tasks of supervision take a lot of time. As a supervisor, you may work very long hours. You may recognize, however, that many of the tedious jobs which must be done could easily be handled by an assistant, a work-group leader, or employees themselves. Do you ever take time to think and plan? As a first-line manager, you have closest contact with many aspects of the business which could be improved, remodeled, redesigned, or restructured to operate more efficiently and effectively. Time spent in creative thinking can result in saving valuable hours later on.

If supervisors or executives talk about how hard they work, how they have not taken a vacation in five years, and how seldom they see their family, you can be almost certain that such persons will not succeed in the aspects of business that demand creativity and produce high profits. The "workaholic" is common in our society. Overdedication, compulsive task completion, and pushing oneself to the limit are errors not confined solely to supervisors. These impulses also afflict housewives, volunteer workers, students, and just about everybody. It is no accident that heart attacks frequently strike supervisory and managerial personnel.

Is the workaholic dedicated and competent or merely a poor user of time? Consider these characteristics and decide for yourself. The workaholic can never get a desk in order, chokes down a quick sandwich at lunch, directs employees so that they are constantly running here and there, carries piles of work home, panics over every emergency (and seems to have many of them), never takes a vacation, and cannot seem to meet a deadline. If you can see yourself in this profile, perhaps you should reconsider the number of hours you have in a day, determine which tasks must be accomplished, and discover how you can best control your time.

The Myth of Working Hard

Some people equate hard work with long hours. In the words of the popular musical *Porgy and Bess,* "It ain't necessarily so." What are some of the dangers in working too many hours?

Personal efficiency usually drops rapidly after eight hours of work. Long hours also encourage supervisors to put off doing what should be done in a normal work day. "After all," they reason, "I can always do that tonight." It is easy to see how eight hours of work can stretch into twelve hours. Under these conditions, employees add to their supervisor's time-wasting method of operation by reasoning, "I can do that just as easily tomorrow."

Working too many hours can also have serious effects on the supervisor's family life. If supervisors are willing to neglect family for jobs, they must also be willing to pay the price. If your small son asks for an appointment to see you, you have some important business to take care of away from your job. Supervisors who sacrifice their families for their work inevitably suffer from drastically lower production capabilities and make very inefficient use of their time.

Realizing the price a workaholic can exact from self, employees, and the employer, some companies require all employees to take vacations. By preventing the accumulation of vacation time, they force supervisors and other employees to take time off. The military's "rest and relaxation" for combat troops should strike a familiar note to supervisors on the firing line.

"The Harder I Work, the More I Get Done"

This is another popular myth about time and work, but it would be more correct to paraphrase the old maxim, "The faster I go, the behinder I get."

This phenomenon is commonly known as the "buckets-of-sweat syndrome." Some people seem to believe their results are directly proportionate to the buckets of sweat they generate. In fact, there is no direct relationship between hard work and positive results. Many intervening factors make this relationship a false one.

People experienced in time management know an hour spent in planning could save several hours' work. With this in mind, it might be better to plan how to accomplish objectives than rush into the field with no battle strategy in mind. Planning does take time, but it is time well spent when it saves valuable hours in efficient execution.

The Activity Trap

A fallacy which can interfere with effective time use is the notion that the most active person always gets the best results. If you observe carefully, you will notice many people who seem busy and important have lost sight of their goals and are vigorously pursuing a path that leads nowhere. Instead of getting the *best* results, the active individual with no objectives and no plan may frequently get *no* results.

People differ in their abilities to concentrate and perform. Individuals also perform differently during various parts of the day. Some of us are bright-eyed, wide awake, and ready to tackle tough problems at the crack of dawn. Others have difficulty crawling out of bed before noon, but perform quite efficiently after lunch. If you worked only during your peak hours, could you accomplish as much as you normally do in a full day? Chances are that you could. Unfortunately, most companies have not yet discarded the idea that time expended, and not results achieved, is the critical factor in performance evaluation.

Testing Your Time Perspective

Does everyone operate on the same time clock? Does time have the same meaning for all people? In many Oriental and Middle Eastern countries if people show up for an appointment within three hours of the agreed-upon time, they are not considered late. It is apparent that different cultures, and different individuals within those cultures, attach different meanings to time. Concepts of time are integral parts of one's personality and culture. To discover some of the meanings you attach to time, answer the following questions.

Metaphors. Which image of time do you like best?

1. A calm, quiet lake.
2. A speeding jet.

Descriptions. Choose two of the following words that best describe your idea of time:

acute, lively, hollow, calming, exciting, depressing, distinct, icy, bottomless.

History. Without asking anyone or consulting any references, list the dates (month and year) on which the following events occurred.

1. Beginning of the Korean War.
2. The first moon landing by man.
3. The Supreme Court's first major ruling on school desegregation (*Brown* v. *Board of Education*).
4. President Richard M. Nixon's resignation.
5. Martin Luther King's assassination.

Now check the correct dates, listed at the end of the chapter exercises. For each event, determine if you were correct, too early, or too late.

Looking at your watch. This simple test may show you how your concept of time affects your behavior. Write down the time on your watch or clock. Now check the correct time by telephone or radio.

Time shown on watch or clock: _____.

Radio or phone time: _____.

Your watch or clock is: accurate _____, fast _____, or slow _____.

When you checked your watch with the correct time, was your watch fast? If so, you show another characteristic of a high need for achievement. This is a little game that people with high achievement needs play with themselves—setting their watches a little ahead seems to give them a little extra time.

Perception of time. For this experiment, you need another person. Arrange for your partner to call you within a specified range of time (approximately fifteen minutes to an hour). Go into a quiet room where you will not be interrupted, and remove your wristwatch and all clocks in the room. You should not have anything to read, work to do, or television to watch. You may listen to quiet radio music, but make certain that the program does not announce the time.

After arranging to be called at a time your partner decides upon, enter this room and tune everything out. Meditate, think, dream, or just sit. Do whatever you want to do, but do not work or watch television.

When you are called, estimate how much time passed before he tells you the correct time.

Your estimate: _____ minutes.

Correct time: _____ minutes.

Your estimate was accurate _____, under _____, over _____.

High achievers tend to be accurate or to overestimate the amount of time they spent sitting alone in the room waiting for their partner to arrive. People with lower achievement needs will usually underestimate the time—possibly because they are normally less active, less impatient, less bothered about lost time, or because they become passively absorbed in their thoughts.

As you can see, the concepts you hold about time are closely related to your needs for successful achievement and thus to your orientation to supervision as a career. Will you handle things one deliberate step at a time or will you become involved in many projects and plans at once? Will you be able to manage your time effectively to get the most out of each day or will the days more or less drift into one another?

What Do the Tests Mean?

These simple experiments are useful in determining an individual's achievement orientation. People with a certain perspective on time have a high need for achievement and tend to go into achievement-oriented careers such as management.

Some people strive constantly for successful completion of projects, fulfillment of goals, and rewards gained from their own efforts to reach perfect conclusions. The *process* of achieving gives the achiever a satisfaction beyond any material rewards that may be gained. People with high needs to achieve get immense satisfaction from (1) meeting high standards and performing their jobs well, (2) working hard to overcome difficult barriers, (3) trying out new methods of doing things, and (4) reaching creative problem solutions. Worthwhile, difficult tasks command emotional commitment from high-need achievers.

These individuals shy away from no-risk ventures. They are attracted to supervision because of challenges that can be successfully met through hard work, planning, and creativity. Although material rewards often follow the person with high achievement needs and the dedication to meet those needs, the internal satisfaction of coping successfully with challenges is often the greater reward.

On the first time perspective test, an individual with high achievement needs will choose a metaphor that projects motion, direction, and value. He or she prefers the "speeding jet" to the "calm, quiet lake."

In choosing words to describe time, the high-need achiever will select words like "acute, lively, exciting, distinct" rather than "hollow, calming, depressing, icy, bottomless." The latter set of words is more likely to be picked by persons low in achievement needs.

People with a high need for achievement tend to underestimate the amount of time that has passed since the occurrence of important events. The historical events in the test's third part will be recalled as nearer the present by these people.

Inventory Your Most Valuable Resource

Most of our habits are so deeply ingrained they are difficult to change. Our uses of time are no different. Before you can begin to use your time more effectively, you must know how you use it now. Keeping a time log or inventory is a useful device for cataloging your activities and discovering what is wasting your time.

When you begin to log your time, you may have some surprises in store. Whether you are a student or are now working in supervision, you will face many of the same time habits and time wasters. Trying to log a "typical" week is useless, for there is no "typical" week. Every week brings something new—assignments, objectives, problems—and the supervisor must learn to plan for the nonroutine events that will continually occur.

You may also be surprised at your lack of free or uncommitted time. This is time that is essential to planning, thinking, mulling over problem solutions, and just relaxing from the strains of the day. Many supervisors find that, at best, they have less than an hour of such discretionary time in each day.

Using the Time Log

Figure 5-1 shows a sample time log that can be adapted to your own needs. The time log can be a simple but valuable tool if you follow these steps:

1. Set up time categories.   Decide upon broad, general categories of time-consuming activities. For the student, these might include studying, class time, preparing future assignments, other activities, and, of course, wasted time. The supervisor might use categories similar to these: inspection, job assignment, paperwork, problem solving, correspondence, telephoning, and the inevitable wasted time. Now decide what percentage of your day you wish to devote to each of these activities. Place the categories and your estimate percentages in the "allocation" column.

2. Set goals for each day.   Before leaving work in the afternoon, list the goals you wish to accomplish the following day and arrange them in order of priority. Write your goals down, making sure they are in order of importance.

3. Keep a record of your time.   Using fifteen-minute intervals, record what

Daily Goals	Mon. 1. 2. 3. 4. 5.	Category	Tues. 1. 2. 3. 4. 5.	Category	Wed. 1. 2. 3. 4. 5.	Category	Thurs. 1. 2. 3. 4. 5.	Category	Fri. 1. 2. 3. 4. 5.	Category	Sat. 1. 2. 3. 4. 5.	Category	
9:00													
9:30													
10:00													
10:30													
11:00													
11:30													
3:00													
3:30													
4:00													
4:30													
5:00													

Allocation Category	%	Time Spent	% of Day	Time Spent	% of Day	Time Spent	% of Day	Time Spent	% of Day	Time Spent	% of Day	Time Spent	% of Day	Summary Total Time Spent	% of Week
1.															
2.															
3.															
4.															
5.															
6.															
7.															
8.															
Estimate of Effectiveness															

Figure 5-1. Time Inventory Form. [Adapted from R. Alec MacKenzie, *Managing Time at the Top* (New York: The Presidents Association, 1970).]

you do during the day. If you wait until the end of the day to fill in the time log, you will deceive yourself, for time memories of daily events are very short. You may wish to use the numbers assigned to your allocation categories to save time in recording. For instance, if you inspected the packaging assembly line at 1 P.M., write "assembly" in the large box and "1" in the small box.

4. Keep records for at least a week and summarize. After a week, add up the total number of hours spent in each category and figure the percentage of your time actually spent in these activities. If you can keep records for at least two weeks, you will have a more accurate indication of your time usage.

5. Compare percentage estimates with actual time percentages. To see how effective you have been at meeting your daily and weekly goals, compare your estimates of time spent in each category with the actual amount of time spent. If you have devoted more than 30 percent of your "ideal estimated time" in meeting your chosen goals, you have exceeded the estimated national average.

6. Evaluate your use of time. In which areas are you most effective in your use of time? Where are you least effective? Determine which areas need improvement in time management and draw up a strategy for using your time in these areas more effectively. Begin to put your strategy into operation immediately.

After monitoring their time for a number of weeks, many supervisors find that much of their time was spent in routine work which could be delegated to someone else. You may find that you talk frequently with the same people about the same subjects, or that many of your phone calls and visits are not that important. After finishing your chart, did you find that you had any time for thinking or planning?

One of the authors was asked by an automobile repair shopowner to help with his business. "I'm working 12 hours a day, 5½ days a week, but I'm still not turning out enough work or making enough money," was the owner's summary of the dilemma. A time log was prepared with fifteen-minute intervals that included categories such as talking on the phone, talking with customers, actual repair work, running errands, eating, and so on. After one week of time logging, the owner discovered he was actually working on cars a maximum of four hours a day. Eight hours a day was being spent in other activities, and many were completely unproductive.

Building Efficient Habits

As we discussed earlier in this chapter, many of our time wasters are internal— the result of habit. Changing behavior is often a matter of breaking out of old habits and developing new ones. Breaking old habits takes practice, determination, and constant attention. Following these steps in acquiring new time-use habits may make the task easier.

1. Begin a strong campaign against the old habit. Start a routine that sharply contrasts with the old one. Remind yourself continually of your intentions to change. Tell your friends about your new routine. Give yourself every support you can to prevent immediate backsliding. Every day you successfully apply the new routine makes it more difficult for the old habit to recur.

2. Do not tolerate exceptions until your new habit is firmly established. It is much easier to maintain control from the start than to recover control once it is lost. If you slip at the beginning, you may become immediately discouraged. But if you never give in to your old desires, they will die quickly and honorably.

3. Begin changing your behavior as soon as you resolve to change. Do not wait until next week to begin restructuring your time. If you have identified your major time leaks and have resolved to plug them, begin to do so right away. Your resolutions to "do better" will be worthless if you continuously resolve but never act.

Popular Time-Wasting Habits

Getting started seems to be a very difficult task for many people. Can you recognize yourself in the following scene?

Harry has been asked to check over production schedules for the week. As he begins to look at the forms, the sales manager calls to complain that an important customer has not received his order. On his way to the front office to pull the customer's file, Harry stops to pick up his mail and begins reading it along the way. On the top of the stack is a memo from the union local regarding a grievance. Harry decides to stop along the way to talk with the union's employee representative about the problem but sidetracks to buy a cup of coffee from the cafeteria. What has Harry accomplished during his busy morning? Absolutely nothing.

Harry is one of those individuals who drift aimlessly from one cue to another. Instead of concentrating on one simple task long enough to complete it, Harry is constantly sidetracked by problems that pop up. He is always "getting ready" to do something. Harry certainly keeps active and busy, but he never gets started. He promises himself that tomorrow will be different, but tomorrow is all too often a repetition of today.

Procrastination is a long word for avoiding unpleasant tasks. Many supervisors rank procrastination near the top of their time-waster lists. Procrastinators are easy to spot—they are always open for interruptions and diversions. It is not surprising that they can never seem to meet a deadline because "there isn't enough time." There is even a national society of procrastinators who have yet to hold an annual meeting because they keep putting it off. Visitors, meetings, phone calls, routine mail, idle chats, and a host of other things keep the procrastinator from doing what should be done.

Decision by committee is a time-wasting habit developed by some supervisors. These individuals are reluctant to take the offensive in decision making. They would rather get a variety of opinions and then take a vote. Although there are certainly occasions for participatory decision-making, routine matters do not qualify.

Not following through is another habit that wastes time. What is the use of planning, preparing, and delegating if results are not checked? You will find that it takes more time to correct an error than to make sure the work is properly done in the first place.

Breaking bad habits is not easy. But persistence and determination can produce dramatic results that will be well worth the effort. You cannot remind yourself too often that time is your most valuable resource and that you can learn to use that resource wisely.

Removing Time Leaks

Once you have spotted your major time wasters and have resolved to do a better job of managing your time, what is the best way to accomplish this goal? The following list of time wasters, possible causes, and potential solutions may serve as a guide for analysis and action. While time wasters are universal, causes and solutions are personal. Causes must be identified within the supervisor's own situation, and solutions must spring from his or her own abilities and responsibilities, as Figure 5-2 suggests.

Time Waster	Possible Causes	Solutions
Lack of planning	Failure to see the benefit of planning	Recognize that planning takes time but saves time in the long run.
	Orientation toward action.	Emphasize results, not activity.
	Success without planning.	Recognize that success is often in spite of, not because of, lack of planning.
Lack of priorities	Lack of goals and objectives	List goals and objectives. Discuss priorities with employees.
Overcommitment	Too broad interests	Learn to say no.
	Misplaced priorities	Put first things first.
	Failure to set priorities.	Develop a personal philosophy of time. Relate priorities to a schedule of events.
Management by crisis	Lack of planning	Use the same solutions as for lack of planning.
	Unrealistic time estimates	Allow more time. Allow for interruptions.
	Problem orientation	Look for opportunities.
	Reluctance of subordinates	Encourage rapid communication to ensure fast correction of errors.
Haste	Impatience with routine.	Take time to do it right. Do not waste time doing it over.

Figure 5-2. Troubleshooting Chart for Time Wasters. [Adapted from R. Alec MacKenzie, *Managing Time at the Top* (New York: The Presidents Association, 1970), pp. 36–37.]

Summary

Some people accomplish more than others, yet each person has exactly as much time as anyone else. The problem lies not in the actual number of hours available but in how well we use our time. Time is a unique and valuable resource. It can be managed wisely or misused because every individual enjoys control over personal use of time.

The problem of time management is universal. Though most people tend to blame others for their poor use of time, most time wasters should blame themselves. Knowledge of your own ineffectiveness in managing time is a difficult but crucial insight. The supervisor should make a list of major time wasters to prepare for accepting responsibility of time control.

People who manage time poorly are often "workaholics." They usually believe one of the following myths about time and work: (1) tremendous energy generates top results, (2) the harder I work, the more I get done, or (3) most activity equals best results.

Some simple tests can help give you a perspective on your own concepts about time. Frequently, time perceptions are related to achievement needs. People with high needs to achieve perceive time as having motion, direction, and value. They underestimate the time that has passed since major historical events and overestimate the time they spend alone or without activity. Their watches may be set slightly ahead of correct time.

Time Waster	Possible Causes	Solutions
	Dealing with the urgent	Learn the difference between urgent and important.
	Lack of planning ahead	Take time to plan. It will be well worth the effort.
	Trying to do too much in too little time	Attempt less. Delegate more.
Paperwork and reading	Information overload	Read selectively. Learn to speed read.
	Failure to screen	Delegate reading to subordinates.
Routine and unimportant detail	Lack of priorities	Set goals and stick with them. Delegate nonessential tasks.
	Oversupervision of subordinates	Delegate; then give subordinates responsibility. Expect results not particular methods.
	Inability to delegate; feeling of greater security dealing with trivial routine	Recognize that without delegation it is impossible to get anything done through others.
Visitors	Enjoyment of socializing	Do it somewhere else. Meet visitors outside your office. Go to lunch if necessary. Hold on-the-spot conferences.
	Inability to say no	Screen visitors. Say no. Be unavailable.
Telephone	Lack of self-discipline	Screen and group calls. Do not talk long.
	Desire to be informed and involved	Stay uninvolved with all but essentials.

Figure 5-2. *(continued).*

A time log can be a useful tool in determining how your time is spent and where most of your time leaks occur. Time for thinking and planning is frequently not available during the day.

Many time wasters are the result of bad habits. Habits can be broken and behavior changed by following these rules: (1) campaign strongly for the new habit, (2) do not tolerate exceptions, (3) begin changing your behavior as soon as you resolve to change. Some popular time-wasting habits are not getting started, procrastination, decision by committee, and not following through.

Plugging time leaks is often a matter of identifying the time wasters, recognizing their causes, and developing solutions. Twelve major time wasters are lack of planning, lack of priorities, overcommitment, management by crisis, haste, paperwork and reading, routine and unimportant detail, visitors, telephone, meetings, indecision, and lack of delegation. While possible causes and solutions were suggested, actual causes and solutions depend on each supervisor's personal skills and unique situation.

Key Terms

Decision by Committee. The method of decision making chosen by indecisive supervisors. Participatory decision making can be valuable but not in routine matters.

Time Waster	Possible Causes	Solutions
Meetings	Fear of responsibility for decisions	Make decisions without meetings.
	Indecision	Make decisions even if some facts are missing.
	Overcommunication	Do not plan or attend unnecessary meetings.
	Poor leadership	Stick to the subject. Prepare minutes immediately afterward.
Indecision	Lack of confidence in the facts	Improve information-gathering procedures.
	Insistence on getting all the facts	Accept some risks. Decide without all the facts.
	Fear of the consequences of a mistake	Delegate the right to be wrong. Use mistakes as a learning process.
	Lack of a workable decision-making process	Get facts, set goals, investigate alternative actions and consequences, make the decision, and put it into operation.
Lack of delegation	Fear of subordinates' inadequacy	Train them well. Allow mistakes. Replace if necessary.
	Fear of subordinates' competence.	Delegate fully. Give credit.
	Work overload on subordinates	Balance the workload. Create new positions. Set priorities in the proper order.

Figure 5-2. *(concluded).*

External Time Wasters.   Time-wasting activities that the supervisor does not generate. Incoming phone calls, visitors, and managerial meetings are examples.

Internal Time Wasters.   Time-wasting activities the supervisor initiates, which should be avoided. Procrastination, failure to get started, and lack of concentration are examples.

Need to Achieve.   A need that constantly drives some individuals toward successful completion of projects and fulfillment of goals. The individual with a high achievement need will derive more satisfaction from the process of achievement than the material rewards of success.

Procrastination.   A tendency to put things off. Procrastinators may put off unpleasant tasks, routine detail work, and even urgent and important duties.

Resource.   A means of accomplishing something; personnel, funds, or materials that can be used to meet a goal or fulfill a need. Time is our most valuable resource.

Time Log.   Device for recording the supervisor's actual use of time, which indicates the percentage of time allotted to various activities. A time log is a useful tool in recognizing major time wasters and planning for a more efficient use of time.

Workaholic.   A compulsive worker who insists on completing tasks at the expense of everything else. The workaholic often becomes so overloaded with busywork and routine, so exhausted physically and mentally, that he or she is a less valuable employee than more relaxed colleagues.

Review Questions

1. How would you make use of an additional two hours in each day?

2. Why is time considered a resource?

3. Make a list of your internal and external time wasters. How would you go about achieving greater control over them? Would you use the same approach for both types of time wasters?

4. Why is a "workaholic" likely to be ineffective at work? How can you keep yourself from developing the symptoms of "workaholism"?

5. The chapter explored a number of myths about time and work. Can you think of any myths that were not discussed?

6. Describe the concept of "personal time zones." Does everyone operate on the same internal clock?

7. Explain the relationship between time and personality. What role does culture play in shaping this relationship?

8. A person with a high need for achievement is usually drawn to certain types of work. What are some of these and why do they attract the achiever?

9. If time is valuable, how can filling in a time log be considered a valuable use of time? Explain.

10. Review the lists of popular time-wasting habits in the chapter. Make a list of at least ten additional ones.

11. Once an individual has compiled a list of personal time-wasters, what is the next step toward the goal of effectively using time?

Exercise

I. Budgeting Your Time

A. Make a list of everything you would like to accomplish in the next week. Estimate the amount of time it will take to accomplish each goal. Now increase your total estimate by 40 percent to allow for unforeseen problems, interruptions, and other time wasters. Add time for routine work, sleep, meals, recreation, club meetings, and so on. You may want to use a chart similar to the one on the following page.

1. Write your goals for each day in the large column under each day.

2. Place your time estimate for accomplishing each goal in the small column to the right of the goal.

3. Add your time estimates for each day and place this figure in Row A at the bottom of the page.

4. Multiply your estimated time needs by 40 percent and place the product in Row B for each day.

5. Subtract the smaller figure in Row B or C from the other, and place this figure in Row D. If your time estimate exceeds the time available, the figure in Row D will have a minus sign. If you have time left over in a day, place a plus sign before the figure in Row D.

B. Now look at your time figures in Row D for each day and answer the following questions:

GOALS FOR NEXT WEEK													
Mon.		Tues.		Wed.		Thurs.		Fri.		Sat.		Sun.	
Goal	Est. Time	Goal	Est. Time	Goal	Est. Time	Goal	Est. Time	Goal	Est. Time	Goal	Est. Time	Goal	Est. Time
A. Total est. time													
B. (Realistic estimate) Increase est. 40%													
C. Time available	24 hr		24 hr		24 hr		24 hr		24 hr		24 hr		24 hr
D. Time left over/ time needed													

1. Did you set too many or too few goals?
2. Do you need more time than twenty-four hours in a day? How much more?
3. How could you cut down some of your time-wasting activities to gain more time?
4. If you have time left over, how will you use it?

II. Answers to Quiz on Dates

1. June 1950.
2. July 1969.
3. May 1954.
4. August 1974.
5. April 1968.

III. Answers to Quiz on Manager Groups

Group A. Managers.
Group B. College Presidents.
Group C. Military Officers.
Group D. Religious Leaders.

Case 5 • Rex Harris

Rex Harris is a manager at K. D. Nickel Company, a toy manufacturer. He has the responsibility of selecting a new supervisor for the order processing department. The position involves supervision of ten employees who process orders from the company's retail and catalog stores throughout the nation. After reviewing the performance records of a large number of employees and conducting several screening interviews, Rex has narrowed his choice to two candidates.

One candidate is Harry Higgins, who has the reputation at Nickel as the hardest-working person in his department. He generally arrives at work thirty minutes early and is often the last one to leave. He has been known to work on weekends for a few hours in order to get in some extra work. He rarely takes breaks during the day because he refuses to rest or interrupt his work until he completes an assignment. In the interview, he mentions that if he does not know the answer to a problem, he will spend hours if necessary figuring it out on his own. He is proud of the fact that he has never been "stumped" or had to ask for help in solving problems or getting answers to questions. Harry is impressed by his individuality and tireless approach to problem solving, but is troubled by the insistence that his work will be of greater quality if he handles every aspect of it himself.

The other finalist for the position is Lisa Little. She is the opposite of Harry in many ways. She is not known to arrive early to work or to stay beyond working hours and she has never worked on weekends. However, Lisa is widely regarded at Nickel as a sociable person and is very popular. When a problem develops, she is the first to recommend that everyone relax and discuss the problem together. She is not as experienced as Harry but her work is equal in quality.

1. Based on the information and impressions Rex has of the two candidates, which employee would you recommend he hire? Why?

2. Would it be fair to describe Harry as a "workaholic?" How do you distinguish between someone who is a "workaholic" and someone who simply works hard?

PART

TWO

The Administrative Challenge

CHAPTER 6

Ethics and the Supervisor

Ideals are like stars. You will not succeed in touching them with your hands, but, like the seafarer, you may choose them as your guides, and following them, you reach your destiny.

Carl Shulz

Learning Objectives

• To learn what a code of ethics is and determine how these codes apply to managers and supervisors.

• To compare different theories about the rationales for ethical choices.

• To analyze the background of organizational ethics.

• To investigate the importance of maintaining high ethical standards in supervisory management.

• To analyze the supervisory relationship where ethics are essential.

Newspapers report almost daily that the world is having trouble with ethics. Although seldom expressed in exactly those terms, that is the cumulative message of the news. Some observers suggest that human nature remains the same from generation to generation. Others believe that evil is hitting an all-time high or low.

As we listen to the fears of the concerned and observe that much of our behavior falls in a gray area between right and wrong, we must admit that ethics is a problem. It is not so much that we lack moral convictions as that we have never quite identified them. We may display great verbal concern for "ethical" behavior, while the pressures of the daily grind encourage us to ignore that concern in our actions.

Like many philosophical concepts, "ethics" is often most easily understood when weak or absent. In our time the popular catchall phrase to account for almost everything that goes wrong is "the country's moral and ethical breakdown."

Some of us think human society has moved along at approximately the same clip over the centuries, while others are convinced that we are going downhill fast and this era is about the worst ever:

> Statements announcing that a given product is preferred by leading authorities without saying what it is preferred to, statements claiming a product's superiority to unspecified competitors, statements implying that a given characteristic belongs uniquely to the product in question when in fact it belongs to its rivals as well all serve to blur the distinction between truth and falsehood in a fog of plausability. Such claims are "true" yet radically misleading. President Nixon's press secretary, Ron Ziegler, once demonstrated the political use of these techniques when he admitted that his previous statements on Watergate had become "inoperative." Many commentators assumed that Ziegler was groping for a euphemistic way of saying that he had lied. What he meant, however, was that his earlier statements were no longer believable. Not their falsity but their inability to command assent rendered them "inoperative." The question of whether they were true or not was beside the point.[1]

Should the average manager be troubled with ethical concerns or emphasize a hard-driving, nose-to-the-grindstone attitude with the sole objective of making a dollar? In today's world, obviously, a manager not only should but must give thought to ethics. Supervisors who fail to evaluate and refine the ideals and principles upon which their actions are based will be little more than robots. They must question their motivations and methods, consciously establish beliefs which they intend to maintain, and follow that stated code of ethics. A person without a clear-cut, purposeful ethical stance is like a ship with neither sail nor anchor.

What Is Ethics?

In simplest terms, we can define ethics as "a system of moral principles." More broadly, our definition might expand to "that branch of philosophy dealing with values relating to human conduct, with respect to rightness or wrongness of certain actions and to the goodness or badness of the motives and ends of such actions."[2]

As this definition suggests, our code of ethics is really that "still, small voice"

---

[1] Christopher Lasch, *The Culture of Narcissism* (New York: Warner, 1979); p. 141.
[2] Marvin Hurley, "Ethical Problems for the Association Executive" *Study Guide for the Institutes of Organization Management* (Washington, D. C.: Chamber of Commerce of the United States, 1972), p. 2.

that points out the difference between right and wrong. The truth is that our ethics describe our aspirations more often than our behavior. We are rarely as concerned about *doing* right as we are about knowing what *is* right. Some advocates of the "new morality" suggest that instead of the old double standard (saying one thing and doing another), it would be more ethical simply to admit that circumstances will not always permit us to do the "right" thing.

From a manager's point of view, ethics may be described as "the rules or standards governing the moral conduct of the members of the organization management profession."[3] Ethical questions, for the manager, are real life concerns. They are not ivory tower affairs. The supervisor is involved in a daily struggle to consolidate, understand, and give intellectual coherence to the motives and impulses that characterize behavior.

Before they can function consistently, supervisors must know what to expect from organizations, other individuals, and themselves. Thus organizational policies and codes of professional ethics are essential. They are like the draftsman's working lines, which provide a starting point and a reference point for all subsequent lines. Ethics allow us the luxury of standardizing our expectations and our performance.

How Do We Define Ethical Standards?

Developing a code of life rules is not an easy task. It is almost never a matter of choosing between the obvious, clear-cut good and the obvious, clear-cut evil. We could accomplish that without any special help. The difficulty with ethical considerations is that the alternatives usually do not present such a black-and-white choice.

For example, some forms of warfare are commonly viewed as unethical. We may agree to disagree with bullets, while nuclear weapons—with the potential for demolishing the human race—are kept under wraps. What about napalm and poison gas, however? During the Vietnam War, the military firmly asserted that chemical weapons were the only effective response to the Viet Cong guerrillas, but our government's use of such tactics, rejected by all other nations since World War I, drew sharp criticism from humanitarians and environmentalists alike.

In the same way, some management practices that appear justifiable in one sense may also be denounced as unethical from another viewpoint. Lying to a potential employee about his or her chances for promotion may seem an easy way to hire a good worker, but no ethical supervisor would try this trick, which cheats the employee and, in the long run, management as well. Similarly, the temptation to pad an expense account or work so-called "banker's hours" can easily be rationalized—"I'm underpaid anyway," or "I worked plenty of overtime two months ago." But in terms of ethics these practices are inexcusable. This time, the manager is lying and cheating the company.

By now you have probably recognized that there is a subtle difference between *unethical* actions and *illegal* actions. It is quite possible that behavior we consider unethical would be entirely legal, which makes the temptation to ignore ethics even stronger in some instances. The supervisor's legal responsi-

[3] Ibid.

bilities are discussed at greater length in Chapter 7. For our purposes here, however, you should keep this simple distinction in mind: an *unethical* action is one that does not conform to accepted social or professional standards of conduct, while an *illegal* action is one that is specifically prohibited by an official statute or law.

The purpose of laws is to keep society on an even keel by protecting its members from antisocial or inhumane actions by others. The purpose of ethics is to ensure an element of trust in business and personal relationships *above and beyond* that provided by the legal structure. We can be fairly certain that the manager of our bank will not embezzle millions of dollars because the likely result would be a lengthy prison sentence. We can also expect that the banker will try to treat employees fairly because any other approach would lead to a reputation as an unethical manager, and the bank would likely suffer accordingly.

Over the years, philosophers have suggested four alternative approaches to reaching a decision on what is right and what is wrong, what is ethical and what is not. Most discussions of ethics combine these theories to some extent, but we have defined them separately for the sake of clarity.

Empirical theory holds that all knowledge must derive from what can be seen, quantified, and measured. Empiricists accept the idea that deeds *can* be right or wrong, but require actual verification—visible or personally experienced proof—before they will agree that a particular action *is* right or wrong. What the empiricist must do, then, is *translate* an ordinary value judgment about right or wrong into tangible terms, so a person can deal with it on a factual basis. Clearly, this is not always easy or even possible because observable reality is not necessarily the best source of ethical guidance. Often we must look beyond our own self-knowledge or experience to make an ethical decision—"a man's reach should exceed his grasp," as English poet Robert Browning has so eloquently written.

Rational theory holds that we can use our reasoning powers to determine what is right and what is wrong. These logical determinations will not necessarily conform to real-life experience, however, because it is rare for any of us to be entirely rational in our thoughts or actions. And the rational approach can be twisted and used for distinctly unethical purposes. Often, a seemingly logical argument can be applied to propaganda, brainwashing, or prejudice, and the listener must be very alert to determine whether the appeal to "reason" is not actually an appeal to emotions. Similarly, all of us, at one time or another, have indulged in rationalizing or wishful thinking—another example of the rational approach used for the wrong purpose.

Intuitive theory, in reaction against the cool logic of rational theory, asserts that we do not need to go through any logical or experiential process to discover what is right or wrong because we are all born with a basic understanding of ethical truths. Our native intuition should tell us when something is wrong, but this "natural moral law" has been corrupted by such outside influences as bad environments, poor political institutions, inadequate education, and misguided religious training. According to this theory, if we all lived healthy lives in pleasant surroundings none of us would ever feel any wish to do something "wrong."

Revelation theory derives from religion. The idea is that the divine perspective on right and wrong is the one we were intended to follow; we could not possibly duplicate the perfection of the Bible's ethical dictates on our own.

Until the middle of this century, most people devoutly believed that the Bible offered the ultimate in ethical guidance, but today many people are less confident that religious rules are infallible.

Philosophers may debate the individual merits of these various approaches to deciding what is right or wrong, but in everyday life situations that require an ethical choice we probably use elements of several approaches simultaneously. In terms of business ethics, the role of empirical, rational, intuitive, and revelation theories on any given issue has evolved over the years into a group of unwritten standards—a series of assumptions regarding ethical behavior that reflects both the moral traditions of history and the economic demands of the free enterprise system.

For example, companies are expected to provide a fair product or service for a fair price. Employers are expected to pay employees an honest wage for honest work. Employees are expected not to pilfer merchandise or pad expense accounts. Thus each of the four theories described above in some way influences the ethical choices of American business today.

What Is So Special About Managerial Ethics?

Modern business ethics represent a compromise between two extreme positions: (1) that business does not and should not do anything but maximize profits, and (2) that business should forget all about profit motives and the profit measure and dedicate itself to improving the general welfare of society. Although the former position certainly prevailed in this country through the early twentieth century, in recent years business has come to acknowledge the interdependence of the two views: profits are necessary to pay for services, but the profits will not last long if our social well-being is ignored.

Clearly, then, balance must be sought. Business executives must decide exactly what they are aiming to do with their business. Managers are in leadership positions which define their responsibility as that of mediator. Like it or not, they must bring the two factions to deliberation. This is no intellectual calisthenic, no topic meant just to fill the agenda of some convention. The obvious fact is that unless a supervisor knows why a job is being done, it is probably being done poorly and someone is not likely to be doing it long. Nothing is quite so critical to a journey as a clear understanding of the destination.

Deciding ethical questions is not simple. Supervisors must think about their responsibilities to several players on the stage of business activities. Although the standards for managerial ethics are not carved in stone, they do reflect the opinions and experience of several managers in the National Management Association and the International Management Council. Anyone certified as a manager by these associations is expected to adhere to these standards, which are also valid objectives for people in any supervisory position and, indeed, for business in general.

Responsibility to Self

The first right and obligation of all supervisors, as for all human beings, is to act in accordance with their sense of self. Everyone has the right to expect that the way he or she spends the day will not ruin one's sleep at night.

Personal values have often been subverted in the eager search for success. What is expected of us and what we expect of ourselves often become confused. Society's demands are usually expressed clearly and with cool assurance. Our own inner voices often whisper and sometimes tremble. But misplaced values cripple effectiveness. We are at our best only when we believe that the result of our actions is worthy of our best.

Responsibility to Employer

Serving company purposes is a condition of employment. An employee implies his or her willingness to work toward the company's goals simply by accepting a job offer. If we agree that deception is unethical, then employees must try to be truthful with both themselves and their employers. Blatant, intentional lying is dangerous as well as unethical. Employees who lie are usually punished severely, and lies are notoriously transparent. A supervisor must be entirely truthful with superiors and workers alike. This position is particularly vulnerable as spokesperson and interpreter for two groups whose interests often conflict. Misunderstandings can arise in spite of truthful dealings with each side.

Responsibility to Workers

"Company people" often practice one-sided ethics. Loyalty and truthfulness toward the company is the highest priority for this kind of supervisor. Meanwhile, the supervisor pressures workers to achieve company goals and keep quiet. These managers want no rumblings from below to jeopardize their standing above. They placate workers as a group but ignore the individual motives and goals of their team members. A supervisor of this type usually is seen not as a representative but as an overseer of the group. Such a stance will certainly cost the supervisor the respect of the workers, who will feel that they have no advocate in, and no access to, management. This supervisor is also likely to lose the respect of superiors. These people, while not entirely useless, are seldom respected. Finally, a supervisor who practices one-sided ethics will likely forfeit self-respect as well.

Unquestioned upward loyalty of managers is required by some companies, but this policy is most unwise. Disregard for workers erodes productivity. Workers become bitter and resistant. A supervisor who behaves responsibly toward workers knows and considers workers individually and personally. This supervisor helps workers perform in the safest, least expensive and most effective way possible to achieve the quality and quantity of production desired by the company. The supervisor who takes responsibility to workers seriously may find the following guidelines helpful:

1. Consider employees as individuals, important human beings at all times and respect them. Know each worker personally and speak to each by name whenever possible. Know something about the person each worker is during the *other* sixteen hours of each day.

2. Represent your employees to top management with straightforwardness and understanding. *Listen* carefully to employees as a group and individually, then

organize and communicate what you have heard so that management gets the same message.

3. Make every effort to interpret and explain company policy accurately to subordinates at all times. Never withhold information that employees need to know. Ask yourself, and your superiors if necessary, and then try to clarify for employees the *why* behind company policies. Try to define the specific contributions your workers will make to company goals.

4. Be an example to your workers both at work and at play. Forthrightness and fair play are always worthy of your attention no matter what your activities. Keep your sense of humor. Be prepared to laugh at yourself from time to time.

5. Go out of your way to pat an employee on the back when he or she does a job well. When necessary, reprimand, but in *private*. Always remember, "Praise in public and reprimand in private."

6. Let your workers know that you are giving them every opportunity to develop and improve their skills and earnings. Encourage questions and reply with concise, straightforward answers. Freely share what you know. Allow workers to assist with work that may be routine to you but will teach them new and useful skills.

7. Always evaluate performances and potentials carefully and objectively. Never permit individual personalities or prejudices to cloud your objective opinion of any employee as an employee. Remember, your judgments must be based on only those aspects of personality which directly affect work performance.

8. Always try to improve worker confidence in you by being considerate, firm, and fair in your individual dealings with all employees under your supervision. Never play favorites and never allow personality differences to cause you to abuse a worker.

9. Always place a worker on a job according to his or her present skill, ability, and attitude. Never try to break in new employees by putting them on the toughest job in your area. Whenever possible, do not assign workers jobs for which they are so overqualified that they will feel bored and unchallenged.

10. Never pass the buck if something goes wrong in your department. Always assume the responsibility for the action or the job done by employees under your supervision. Such an example will encourage workers to take responsibility for themselves, but final responsibility for your department stays with you.

11. Learn how your workers relate individually to their jobs. Learn as much as you can about their individual interests, likes, and dislikes. Try to find out what each enjoys and dislikes about his or her job. Be alert to small changes that might make big differences in how workers view their jobs.

12. Always take time to give proper and adequate instructions to new job applicants and make them feel at home through proper job orientation. Be patient. Every new employee, every worker doing a new job for the first time is anxious about his or her performance.

13. Always be alert to keeping your work area safe and clean. Be mindful of the importance of good, clean, and safe working conditions. Encourage worker suggestions on how to make the work area a more pleasant place.

14. Managers are responsible for communicating correctly the feelings and attitudes of workers to top management. Similarly, managers are responsible for conveying to workers the plans, intentions, and expectations of top management in a manner that will build team spirit, high morale, job satisfaction, and harmony on both sides.

Responsibility to Associates

Competition between supervisors at the same organizational level is often fierce. Few want to remain at their current level, and the number of managerial positions drops with each ascending level. Managerial competition produces better work from individual managers and often from the workers they supervise. However, each manager must recognize that the difference between friendly competition and paralyzing in-fighting is the difference between progress and failure. Supervisors at a particular management level form a team just as the supervisors and the workers they supervise. Teams must work together or they will not work very well. An attitude of professionalism toward fellow managers can assure effective teamwork. Professionalism in management implies a willingness to be courteous, fair, supportive, and straight in dealing with all colleagues in the organization. A few guidelines for dealing with associates follow. Their aim is to assure a strong, unified organization.

1. Cooperate. Always put cooperation before competition.
2. Exchange ideas for improvements in all areas of company policy that can benefit all concerned. Share insights rather than hoard information for personal gain. Plans contributed by several are often more useful than the initial scheme that set the minds in motion.
3. Show courtesy, respect, understanding, and tolerance to other managers at all times. Treat fellow managers just as you wish to be treated by them.
4. Try to help fellow supervisors with their personal problems if invited to do so. Building friendships with them will ease working relations, and small misunderstandings will pose less of a threat.
5. Make every effort to set a good example with the helpful cooperation of other managers.
6. Never belittle a fellow supervisor in front of subordinates for any reason. Grievances you have with your fellow supervisor are a private matter.
7. Always show confidence in and respect for fellow supervisors in the presence of subordinates. No supervisor has the right to gamble with the respect shared by a fellow supervisor and the workers he or she supervises.
8. Be fair, patient, understanding, and helpful to all fellow supervisors at all times. You know how difficult your job can be. Your associates' tasks are no less demanding.

Responsibility to Immediate Superior

Understanding this responsibility becomes simple as a person begins to manage. When the difficulties and trials involved in directing a group of individuals toward a single common objective are experienced firsthand, it is easy to understand what obligations a manager owes to his or her superior. The superior wants from a manager just what the manager wants from subordinates: cooperation, obedience, courtesy, respect, and regular reports. Most of us, as managers, would expect those who work for us to do their best and be ready and willing to accept full responsibility for their actions. Our superiors expect no less from us. Regular attention to the following guidelines can insure that the duties owed a manager's immediate superior are fulfilled:

1. Cooperate with your immediate superior.

2. Obey your superior's orders and execute his or her instructions in detail. Inform your superior of all changes in working conditions and other phases of production. You must take responsibility to insure that job instructions and day-to-day orders are clearly understood by subordinates.

3. Prepare yourself for greater responsibility by training with your superior to be the back-up person. At the same time, you should be training your own subordinate to do much of your routine work. Such practice increases empathy and understanding for the persons at both the level above and the level below your own.

4. Report the outcome of any important phase of the production or service operation fully, simply, and accurately to your immediate superior when requested to do so. Actually, alert and effective managers usually recognize information that is essential for the superior to know even if they have not been specifically asked for such a report.

5. Display courtesy and respect to your immediate superior at all times.

6. Look for better ways of doing things and offer ideas and suggestions for improvements to your immediate superior. Because your supervisor sees the activities of the company as a whole—and especially the activities of the department you supervise—from a perspective different from your own, he or she will probably appreciate the insights that your particular viewpoint offers.

7. Make every effort to relieve the immediate superior of job details or routine work functions whenever possible. Taking on such duties will provide you with useful experience and perhaps lead to your early promotion. Your superior will appreciate the opportunity to spend his or her time and energies on more demanding matters.

8. Always assume full responsibility for work assigned to you and your subordinates. Never attempt to pass the buck when answering to your superior for work done or undone. If you are unwilling to take the blame for shortcomings, you should not expect to take the credit for jobs well done. The responsibility is yours, and attempts to shirk that responsibility can only lead to loss of respect on all sides.

Responsibility to the Public

The question of public responsibility is a controversial issue in business today. Minimum social responsibility for American businesses is defined only through government guidelines in such areas as civil rights and antitrust legislation (discussed in Chapter 7). The appropriate extent of a corporation's social accountability has been expressed in two mutually exclusive theories, but no consensus between the opposing camps has been achieved as yet. One of these theories proclaims that the corporation can recognize no responsibilities except legal ones. The unions take care of the worker; the corporation must take care of itself. The other approach emphasizes that the company has the same rights and duties as a citizen and endeavors to get business involved in many types of benevolent social and cultural projects. The future of business definitely depends upon which of these two theories is allowed to guide its growth in the next few decades.

Fortunately, it appears that the latter theory is rapidly taking precedence over the former. A 1975 newspaper article reported that although business contributions to solving key social problems remain tiny compared to actions by government agencies, "corporate executives feel a major responsibility to help fight poverty, pollution, and racial discrimination."[4] According to the executive vice president of Arco Petroleum Products Company, "Government can't do it all; business has to help. We have the management ability and the money, plus a large pool of employees—many of them willing and eager to help." In the same vein, AT&T president Robert W. Kleinert asserts that his company operates "for the public, as part of the overall community. We certainly can't disregard what's going on. The community's problems are our problems."

This new understanding has led corporations to develop a wide range of programs under the social responsibility heading, aimed at reducing poverty, racial discrimination, and pollution, or improving the quality of life in general. Though some of these activities are specifically mandated by federal legislation, others have originated with business itself. These include buying supplies from black-owned firms, building employee recreation centers, mounting consumer information programs, supporting public television, or appointing consumer representatives to boards of directors. Another widespread practice is to encourage company employees to volunteer for full-time community service work, keeping them on the company payroll for up to a year even though they are not contributing to corporate profits.

As this collective response to social needs suggests, individual managers are increasingly following the dictates of their consciences in dealings with the public. To some extent, of course, the "rhetoric exceeds the progress," but as managers continue to stress high ideals over personal biases it is not unlikely that corporations will move to the forefront of social change.

Ethics and Age

Certainly, any businessperson who adheres to the standards outlined above will be highly ethical regardless of age. But given the widespread publicity accorded any major incident where a manager's expressed ethical beliefs do not coincide with actual behavior, it is not surprising that many people are somewhat cynical about the ethical practices of established business. Today's young people have openly rejected the kind of double standard such behavior represents. Many college graduates have hesitated to seek business employment because they fear they will be asked to violate their ethical standards.

As noted above, however, a new emphasis on business ethics and corporate responsiveness to public needs has emerged in recent years and corporation executives generally agree that this trend is "largely the result of young people. Each new generation of employees and managers demands more than the last."[5] Louis B. Lundborg puts it more bluntly—"It's the young people that keep pushing us upward. When we talked to college graduates ten years ago, we did all the questioning. Now they ask us just as many, sometimes more. They want to know our record of social performance, our standards for running a business."

This widely held opinion that the impetus for improved business ethics has stemmed primarily from the young is not borne out, however, by the results

[4] John Getze, "Businessmen Accept New Responsibility," *Los Angeles Times,* May 4, 1975, p. 1. The material in this section is drawn from this article.
[5] Ibid.

of two exhaustive studies.[6] The researchers questioned more than 1500 executives from a variety of firms and managerial levels and more than 1000 M.B.A. students. In contrast to the viewpoints expressed above, their conclusions indicated that older executives and those with longer business experience strive for higher ethical standards than do managers and students who are younger and less experienced.

Regardless of the source, there can be no question that the present trend toward sound business ethics—from manufacturing quality products to avoiding pollution and discrimination—bodes well for the future of American firms. Perhaps the most significant reflection of this trend is the growth of company codes of ethics, an increasingly common practice in firms of all types and sizes.

Ethical Codes

A valuable activity for any company is formulating a code of ethics for company employees at all levels. In the process of codifying company practices, it is likely that managers will learn a great deal about themselves both individually and collectively. There are many types of codes. They may be arbitrary, legalistic, or vague; they may be reasonable, clear, and concise; they may be specific or general; they may truly confront problems by company employees or they may simply make impressive wall plaques. But one thing is certain—any company that endures the experience of putting together its own code of ethics will have a better idea of where it stands than it had before.

Expressing company policies in the form of a code of ethics will affect everyone who comes in contact with the company. The simple act of asking the searching question, "Why are we in business?" will produce numerous internal benefits. To identify what the firm or group recognizes as desirable practices or acceptable standards is sure to be revealing. The fact that unscrupulous individuals might misuse codes of ethics should not discourage firms from adopting codes, any more than possible abuse of advertising, the profit motive, or aggressive competition discourages them from supporting these concepts.

There will be advantages to employees when a code of ethics goes on paper. For the new employee, a written code eliminates a great deal of uncertainty which is often associated with learning a job. Codes should help a firm attract higher-caliber employees, since they will give evidence of the firm's concern for ethical standards, strengthen the resolve of employees to act ethically, and also provide a source of resistance to ethical apathy.

Customers will benefit from a company's code of ethics. The customer will have a reason to feel assured that they will be treated in an ethical fashion. A company that makes it known that its practices are guided by a code of ethics can expect a rise in public trust. Codes can be valuable apart from their role in professionalization. Yet, a well-defined code of ethics is essential for a vocational specialization to become a full-fledged and legitimate profession.

[6] Based on R. C. Baumhart, "An Exploratory Study of Businessmen's View of the Ethics of Businessmen," Ph.D. Thesis, Harvard Business School, 1963, and Robert M. Fulmer, "Business Ethics: Present and Future," *Personnel Administration,* September 1971, pp. 48–56.

I will recognize that management is service which requires responsibilities to my subordinates, associates, supervisors, employer, community, nation, and world.

I will be guided in all my activities by truth, accuracy, fair dealings, and good taste.

I will earn and carefully guard my reputation for good moral character and citizenship.

I will recognize that, as a leader, my own pattern of work and life will exert more influence on my subordinates than what I say or write.

I will give the same consideration to the rights and interests of others that I ask for myself.

I will maintain a broad and balanced outlook and will look for value in the ideas and opinions of others.

I will regard my role as a manager as an obligation to help subordinates and associates achieve personal and professional fulfillment.

I will keep informed on the latest developments in the techniques, equipment, and processes associated with the practice of management and the industry in which I am employed.

I will search for, recommend, and initiate methods to increase productivity and efficiency because of a strong sense of loyalty to my employer and the profession of management.

I will respect the professional competence of my colleagues in the ICPM and will work with them to support and promote the goals and programs of the Institute.

I will support efforts to strengthen professional management through example, education, training, and a lifelong pursuit of excellence.

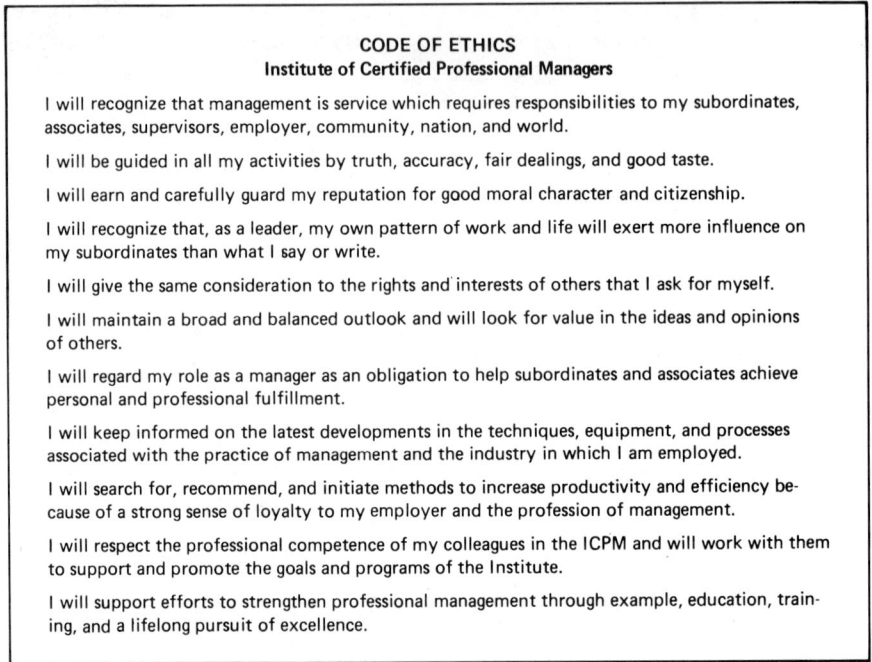

Figure 6-1. The Code of Ethics Adopted by the Institute of Certified Professional Managers.

Although each code should be made as specific as possible (the truly aggressive approach to ethics may demand a written code of ethics for the individual manager), there is always value in the comparison of individual codes. If several codes are intended for an organization, groups at each level should be familiar with the code of ethics that will guide the actions of those at the level above and below their own.

The sample code of ethics shown in Figure 6-1, which was adopted by the Institute of Certified Professional Managers, demonstrates the principles discussed above.

Summary

Ethics may be defined as a system of moral principles. Those principles become "the rules or standards governing the moral conduct of the members of the organizaton" when we are discussing the ethical concerns of professional managers.

Approaches to making ethical decisions usually fall into one of four broad categories: empirical, rational, intuitive, or revelative. However, more often a given attitude toward ethics combines two or more categories or overlaps one into another.

A truly ethical approach to management requires that the manager examine the company's responsibility to the community and personal responsibilities to the company. A manager must have an ethical self-image and an ethically responsible attitude toward an employer, workers, co-workers, associates at the same management level, the immediate supervisor, and the public whose needs the company serves.

Many questions concerning ethics and business are as yet unanswered. What exactly are a company's social obligations? Do people of different ages adhere to different ethical systems? Whatever these questions, codes of ethics seem to help companies pinpoint their own ethical concerns and begin finding meaningful answers. Codes help top management define its ethical values. They clarify the company's policies for employees, and they promote customer trust in the fairness and forthrightness of the organization. The code of ethics established by the Institute of Certified Professional Managers attempts to incorporate the basic values contained within several traditional and current ethical systems. However, regardless of the usefulness of such codes, the truly ethical manager will do more than is required by any code. He or she will examine and weigh values in light of the several duties and obligations that a manager must fulfill.

Key Terms

Code of Ethics. Written expression of ethical standards for an organization or group of individuals. Codes help individuals associated with a particular group know what they can expect concerning acceptable practice and behavior. Codes are also an essential part of any recognized profession.

Empirical Theory of Ethics. A branch of ethical thought which holds that the bases for ethical decisions can be identified, quantified, and measured. An empiricist is more interested in determining the way things are than the way they ought to be.

Ethics. A system of moral principles; also, the branch of philosophy that deals with values in human conduct. For the supervisor, ethics is the rules or standards governing the moral conduct of professional managers and supervisors.

Intuitive Theory of Ethics. Assumes that humans automatically possess an intuitive understanding of what is right or wrong. Often related to the concept of "natural moral law."

Professional Manager. An individual committed to the lifelong pursuit of excellence in management practice and ethical conduct.

Professional Responsibilities. Duties demanded of a professional individual in relation to other groups. For a manager or supervisor this includes responsibility to self, employer, subordinates, colleagues, higher management, and the public.

Rational Theory of Ethics. Assumes that the power of reasoning or logic can determine what is good and bad.

Revelation Theory. Based on the assumption that divinely inspired teachings provide answers to moral and ethical questions.

Social Responsibility. The debt owed by a manager or company to the society that allows the firm to exist. Generally, social responsibility requires honest delivery of goods or services according to the demands of the public. More recently, the concept of social responsibility has been expanded to include the demand that businesses avoid environmentally unsound or discriminatory practices.

Review Questions

1. Define ethics.

2. What are the four major theories in ethical philosophy? Write a short paragraph describing each theory.

3. Is there such a thing as an extreme position toward business ethics where a supervisor acts according to the letter of a code of ethics?

4. Describe the diverse responsibilities a supervisor should consider in making ethical decisions.

5. It is assumed that people have ethical responsibilities to others. Do people have ethical responsibilities to themselves? If so, what would your code of ethics say about your responsibilities to yourself?

6. Describe the benefits for a company of a formal, written code of ethics.

7. It is assumed that ethics are important in the business world, but it is extremely rare to observe employees talking about ethics in their work. How do we know a code of ethics is in operation if we cannot observe the code being used in the daily life of a company?

8. In what ways is ethics a business issue today? How would Ralph Nader or Jane Fonda describe the major ethical issues in business?

9. How does ethical behavior make someone a more effective supervisor?

Exercises

I. Ethical Problems and Attitudes

The following survey may reveal the patterns in your ethical system, not to discover faults or flaws but to let you better understand your standards and ethics. Because your instructor may wish to discuss how the class as a whole responded, fill out the survey without consulting your classmates.

A. Listed below are a number of statements that have been made by observers of the business scene. How do you feel about these statements? Please check the column that best corresponds to your feelings about each.

	Agree	Disagree
1. "Sound ethics is good business in the long run."	_____	_____
2. "Whatever is good business is good ethics."	_____	_____
3. "Clergy should not meddle in the social problems of business."	_____	_____
4. "American business executives tend to ignore the great ethical laws as they apply immediately to work. They are preoccupied chiefly with gain."	_____	_____
5. "For corporation executives to act in the interest of shareholders alone, and not also in the interest of employees and consumers is unethical."	_____	_____
6. "To get ahead in business, one must be willing to conform."	_____	_____

B. Imagine that you are the president of a company in a highly competitive industry. You learn that a competitor has made an important scientific discovery which will give it an advantage that will substantially reduce the profits of your company for about a year. If there were some hope of hiring one of the competitor's employees who knew the details of the discovery, would you try to hire that person?

C. A supervisor earning $15,000 a year has been padding the expense account by about $500 a year. What do you think? (Check as many responses as are applicable.)

1. Acceptable if other managers in the company do the same thing. _____

2. Acceptable if the supervisor's superior knows about it and says nothing. _____

3. Unacceptable regardless of the circumstances. _____

D. Many factors can influence a supervisor's decisions. From your experience, how would you rank each of the factors listed below according to its influence in encouraging an executive to make ethical decisions? (Indicate the *most* influential by placing a "1" beside it, the next most influential by a "2," and so on to "5" for the *least* influential).

	Rank
1. Formal company policy.	_____
2. Personal code of behavior.	_____
3. The behavior of an employee's peers in the company.	_____
4. Ethical climate of the industry.	_____
5. The behavior of immediate supervisors.	_____

E. In every industry there are many accepted business practices. Do you expect to find any practices which you regard as unethical? (Please check *one* only.)

No	_____
Yes, a few	_____
Yes, many	_____
I do not know	_____

If you answered "yes," describe the unethical practice you would most like to see eliminated.

Case 6 • David Butler

David Butler is a purchasing agent for Korn Snax, Inc., a "giant" in the nation's soft drink and snack foods industry. For twelve years he has been responsible for purchasing the commodities—corn, vegetable oil, salt, spices—necessary to produce all the products Korn Snax sells. Mr. Butler's annual "shopping list" amounted to more than $25 million, making him a significant buyer in the industry.

When another national company became interested in acquiring Korn Snax and began conducting its preliminary investigation of the company, its auditors discovered that Mr. Butler had financial interest in a company supplying Korn Snax with corn supplies and that he was receiving a consulting fee from a vegetable oil broker that supplied Korn Snax. Upon further investigation, it was revealed tht Mr. Butler was a very wealthy man as a result of these relationships. Eventually, this information came to the attention of top management at Korn Snax and Mr. Butler was dismissed. In addition, Korn Snax sued Mr. Butler for damages.

In the courtroom, Korn Snax had a difficult time demonstrating the actual harm it suffered as a result of Mr. Butler's handling of commodities purchases. He was widely acknowledged by commodities sellers as one of Korn Snax's key assets because he was unusually knowledgeable and a hard bargainer. In his own testimony, Mr. Butler stated that he saved Korn Snax $50 million over a five-year period because of his shrewd buying. It was also shown that since Mr. Butler's dismissal, Korn Snax was paying more for nearly all its raw materials than when he was in charge of buying. Finally, Mr. Butler believed that other company employees, including top management, had, with the knowledge of Korn Snax directors, invested in companies that provide Korn Snax with goods and services.

1. Has Mr. Butler engaged in unethical and illegal behavior?
2. If Mr. Butler is correct about top management's holdings in other companies, does this alter your position about the ethical or legal nature of his behavior?
3. If you had been Mr. Butler's immediate supervisor in the company and discovered the information about him yourself, what would you have done?

CHAPTER 7

The Supervisor's Legal Environment

If you laid all of our laws end to end, there would be no end.

Arthur Baer

Learning Objectives

- To analyze the relationships between the political and economic systems of the United States and their effect on the practice of supervision.
- To analyze the vital roles government plays in business.
- To describe specific areas where supervisors must comply with government regulations.
- To investigate the rationale for government regulation of business.

People in general, and business managers in particular, tend to view government as an unnecessary evil when it comes to regulating business practices. Perhaps firms could police themselves much more effectively than the government does, without the sacrifice of high production levels that seem to go along with bureaucratic red tape. Admittedly, government restrictions can act to curb the productivity of an individual business or even an entire industry. But businesses could not function freely without some regulation. The wise supervisor recognizes that legal restraints can actually guarantee flexibility rather than reduce it.

Ever since the founding of this country, America's economic system has been based on capitalism: competitive production of goods and services for sale in a free market. Capitalism depends on a complex set of interrelationships among five different types of individuals and organizations: entrepreneurs, managers, workers, consumers, and government.

The role of each of the five components of the business network can be described very simply. The entrepreneur invests capital in some enterprise in the hope that it will make a profit and accepts the possible loss of the investment. Managers enter the picture when the entrepreneur can no longer control the organization because of size, complexity, or other factors. They are responsible for guarding the entrepreneur's investment. Workers provide the labor essential for production of goods and services in return for wages and other rewards. Consumers ultimately decide which business organizations will survive by choosing to buy particular products or services. Government oversees the entire process, regulating business for the protection of competition, workers, profits, and consumers.

The positive role of government in this network of business relationships is often overlooked. Government frequently operates as a "silent partner," entering the scene only when new regulations are needed or old ones violated. But today's supervisors are well aware that government's function is a crucial one. In fact, their jobs and the survival of their companies may depend on their knowledge of government regulations and processes of control.

The democratic form of government has provided a congenial environment for the operation of private free enterprise activities within the economy. Private enterprise implies that competition will exist. Competition means that the strongest, best-equipped businesses and industries are the most likely to survive. Thus, without regulation, and left to its own devices, competition would ultimately eliminate itself by allowing monopolies to form around the production of essential goods and services. Because the government has passed legislation that attempts to control monopolistic tendencies of big business, we have managed to preserve the free enterprise system at the level of the small entrepreneur. Further, the needs and demands of employers and workers are often at odds; maximization of profit has sometimes meant exploitation of labor, and government regulation has served a valid purpose in this area also. As a third function, regulatory laws help insure that consumers can rely on the honesty and good faith of manufacturers for the quality and durability of their products.

Many of the government's policing activities are directly related to the manager's daily work activities. Labor relations, job safety, hiring and firing practices, and consumer protection all involve supervisory duties and are closely regulated by both state and federal governments. The following sections will explore some of these areas in greater detail so that supervisors may become better acquainted with their "silent partner."

The Government as Protector of Competition and Consumers

Some of the earliest forms of legislation involving business were protective laws. Tariffs, or taxes on foreign goods, were introduced in this country as early as 1789 to protect businesses from overseas competition. In the 1800s states began imposing regulations on transportation industries, particularly the railroads, to make sure that customers were treated fairly. Farmers had complained for years of the railroads' unjust and discriminatory treatment and high fares, and their concerns were translated into state laws. In 1887 the Interstate Commerce Commission was created at the federal level to oversee all transportation industries. This commission today controls various aspects of shipping, trucking, railroads, pipelines, and air carriers that operate commercially.

Government control of public utilities followed shortly. These regulations covered companies that sold electric, gas, water, communications, and local transit services. Utility regulation differed greatly from transportation regulation, which serves to encourage competition, in that monopolies were set up to provide these public services more efficiently. Even stricter government regulations were imposed on these monopolies to protect the public from unfair pricing and poor service.

Protection took another form as well. In 1890 Congress passed the Sherman Anti-Trust Act, which prohibited mergers and acquisitions that tended toward monopoly and thus encouraged free competition in most industries. Other abuses of business and industrial power were attacked through laws controlling "unfair competition," including unfair pricing, advertising, and packaging methods. As suggested above, it is widely held that such controls on big business have unfairly penalized small firms, sometimes forcing them out of business. The absence of controls, however, might encourage the economic stagnation of monopoly.

Enforcing Contracts

One of the foundations of the capitalist system is the existence of legally enforceable contracts that spell out the nature of relationships, services and goods to be provided, costs, and so forth. The government's role in enforcing contracts protects the business executive, the supervisor, the worker, and the consumer, since all parties to a sale or other agreement know exactly what is expected of them and what the consequences will be if they fail to meet their end of the bargain. If contracts could not be enforced, it would be impossible to carry on business.

Contract law varies considerably from state to state, a situation that has created problems for businesses and individuals, especially with the rapid growth of interstate commerce. In 1952, the American Bar Association drew up the Uniform Commercial Code, a complex piece of legislation laying out specifics on contract contents in great detail. This code has been a tremendous help in minimizing confusion over interstate contracts.

Enforcing Competition

Competition is at the heart of the American business system. Government has intervened in two basic ways to provide a secure legislative base for continued economic competition. First, it has passed laws designed to prevent monopolistic combinations of businesses. Second, it has developed laws and regulations designed to enforce a certain amount of fair and reasonable competition. The United States is the most diligent country in the world in enforcing competition, although the European Common Market and some other countries are now developing similar controls. Below are four kinds of laws designed to enforce competition.

1. Antitrust laws. At the end of the nineteenth century, several states were severely distressed at the growth of huge business and industrial combinations such as the Standard Oil Company and the large railroad combines that monopolized some industries. These states passed legislation that outlawed such combinations, but there was little the states could do to enforce these laws.

The Sherman Act of 1890 and the Clayton Act of 1914 laid the groundwork for national regulation of monopolies. Since then, these acts, in revised form, have served as effective means for preventing unwanted monopolies in American business. When these laws were first passed, many monopolistic organizations tried to get around them by placing their businesses in the hands of a "trustee," thus forming a presumably legal "trust" as their organizational basis, but the laws were quickly adapted to outlaw this arrangement also. Hence the name "antitrust laws." Similarly, federal agents involved in monopoly regulation are known as "trustbusters."

Antitrust laws prohibit actions by business that would tend to reduce competition. Price fixing, the use of power to throttle competition, combinations leading to unusual power, and similar corporate actions are consistently found to be illegal under the antitrust laws. Companies have been forced to sell acquisitions and in some cases have been subjected to stiff fines and other penalties for engaging in illegal trust activities. In the latter half of the 1970s, the news media have been full of stories about the Justice Department and other regulatory agencies bringing suits against large corporations seeking mergers and acquisitions at home and abroad. No major industry has been overlooked in the government's efforts to prevent the creation of monopolies and unfair competition through "legal loopholes."

2. Laws enforcing fair competition. The Federal Trade Commission was established in 1914 to supplement enforcement of the antitrust laws. The commission is responsible for helping to maintain free competition by regulating and controlling unfair types of competition. The laws are fairly specific about what types of behavior constitute unfair competition. But the commission has developed, over the years, its own interpretations of the law, which are generally supported in court. Thus the commission has gained tremendous power over business.

3. Price discrimination. The Robinson–Patman Act of 1936, a major piece of trade legislation, was aimed at controlling price discrimination. Under this law, sellers may not cut prices in order to drive a competitor out of business. Further, it is illegal for a seller to maintain different prices of the same product for different customers unless the price differentials can be justified by quantity bought. Price reductions available to one customer must be available to all. Price setting is thus a fairly complicated enterprise, and most large companies seek legal counsel before changing their prices.

4. Unfair and deceptive practices.   The Federal Trade Commission regulates business practices that are designed to deceive the consumer. These activities include misleading and false advertising, misbranding of products, trade name simulation, obtaining trade secrets by spying or bribery, cutting off a competitor's source of supply, and making false or derogatory statements about a competitor's product. For instance, automobile companies were prevented from advertising a 6 percent financing rate when the actual interest rate was 11 percent per year.

Protection of Workers: A Growing Concern

During the early days of industrialization, men, women, and children often worked long, hard hours seven days a week for wages that barely kept them alive. The early 1800s brought some state legislation designed to end such practices. Connecticut and Massachusetts passed laws in 1842 that limited the labor of children under twelve years of age to ten hours a day in manufacturing organizations. Pennsylvania prohibited child labor six years later. In 1847, female employees were limited to a ten-hour day. But the twentieth century has brought the most far-reaching labor legislation, thus making the supervisor's job that much more complicated and important.

Since the 1930s, every business has had the government peering over its shoulder in dealings with employees. An employer must observe worker-oriented laws when setting hours and wages, determining physical working conditions for employees, and hiring people without consideration of age, race, religion, or sex. The employer is required to provide various forms of insurance for employees, either through taxation by government or through private insurance policies, including unemployment, accidental injury, occupational disease, and old age or retirement benefits. If the workers are represented by a union, employers are even more constrained; nonetheless, they must recognize the employees' right to be represented by a labor union and must not interfere with its operations.

Although state governments are still important in regulating health and safety conditions and providing unemployment or accidental injury compensation, the federal government is increasingly assuming the responsibility for governing the relationships between employers and workers. Various federal agencies have large responsibilities in the areas of child labor, requirement of a forty-hour work week (with overtime paid at the rate of one and one-half times the hourly rate), minimum wage regulations for most workers, and the rights of employees to organize and bargain collectively with their employers.

Further, since 1970 the federal government has begun to assume major responsibility for occupational health and safety conditions in places of employment, an area of regulation that touches the supervisor directly and extensively. For this reason, the Occupational Safety and Health Act of 1970 is discussed in detail below.

OSHA: Problems and Promises for Supervisors

The Occupational Safety and Health Act of 1970, the culmination of growing concern over the working conditions in many firms, had a powerful impact on both workers and employers. During the nineteenth century and earlier, employers displayed little concern for the welfare of their workers. They did not need to; a laborer was easier to replace than a horse. Though laws did exist to protect workers, they were full of loopholes and rarely enforced. In the early twentieth century, however, a reform movement swept the country; more and more people demanded that workers have some means of legal recourse in case of job-related accidents, diseases, or other undue occupational strains.

When states began enacting workmen's compensation laws, businesses had an incentive for improving working conditions. The safer and more healthful their work premises were, the less likely it was that they would be charged very high rates for compensation insurance coverage, since fewer of their workers would become injured or ill on the job. In addition, employer attitudes have changed. Most companies now recognize that trained labor is a valuable commodity and that employers have a moral as well as a legal obligation to maintain safe and healthful working conditions. But most state laws did not allow sufficient protection; thus Congress passed the Occupational Safety and Health Act to ensure that uniform standards would be applied throughout the country. Effective in April 1971, the act enabled the federal government to both set and enforce national standards for safe, healthful work environments. OSHA affects only businesses engaging in interstate commerce, but these companies represent a sizable proportion of commercial and industrial enterprises in our country today.

OSHA's Purpose

The act itself states its purpose as follows:

> To assure safe and healthful working conditions for working men and women by authorizing enforcement of the standards developed under the Act; by assisting and encouraging the States in their efforts to assure safe and healthful working conditions; by providing research, information, education, and training in the field of occupational safety and health; and for other purposes.

The Occupational Safety and Health Administration, created by the act, is an agency of the Department of Labor. It has been assigned the task of setting standards and enforcing them. Frequently, previously existing standards will be adopted as federal norms, as with those devised by the National Fire Protection Association. The Secretary of Labor may institute new standards or alter existing ones. Also, research into safety and health in occupational settings is being conducted by a national institute in the Department of Health and Human Services. OSHA enforces its standards primarily through on-site inspections of any location where people work. The OSHA agents do not need to give advance notice of their visits, and they may talk privately with owners, supervisors, or workers. However, owners can demand a search warrant, which can stall an inspection several days. Inspectors have complete access to health and safety records, which the federal government requires employers to keep, and can issue citations for any violations they find. If inspectors find that workers' lives are in imminent danger in their work situations, they have the power to obtain a court injunction to shut down the dangerous operation. Penalties for violations are stiff, with fines ranging from as high as $1000 for a single nonwillful violation up to $10,000 for a willful violation and fines of up to $1000 a day for failure to correct violations. Jail sentences can also be imposed on those who falsify records or cause death through a willful violation.

During the first year of OSHA inspections, almost 30,000 workplaces were visited, and about three-fourths of those were found to contain violations of the law. Almost half of the businesses inspected were proposed for penalties by the inspectors. The OSHA laws are frequently very specific and highly technical, and many small firms complained that they could not understand the law and in any case could not afford to comply with every detail. Congress exempted very small companies from OSHA inspections, but there is some feeling that this move was a dangerous one for workers, since smaller companies tend to have higher employee accident rates. This situation has been partially corrected in some states through the passage of legislation to regulate smaller businesses that do not fall under OSHA jurisdiction.

Who Is Affected?

Virtually any firm that does business and has employees must comply with OSHA regulations. Industry, farming, offices, nonprofit and service organizations, restaurants, transit companies, and other kinds of commercial organizations are all covered under OSHA. The Department of Labor estimates that nearly 60 million workers are covered by the administration's regulatory policies, although there are some exceptions for self-employed persons, family businesses with no paid employees, and unpaid domestic workers. Organizations that provide comparable protection under different regulatory agencies are also exempt. Federal, state, and local government employees are excluded from OSHA, for instance, but are covered by other protective plans. In addition, workers who are covered by mine safety and atomic energy safety acts are not included in OSHA coverage.

Keeping Records

Employers who are regulated by the act must keep records of all accidental injuries and illnesses that require medical treatment or loss of time from the job, or result in death, unconsciousness, handicap, transfer to another job, or termination. Minor injuries that are treated with first-aid measures are not included in OSHA record-keeping requirements. Records must be up to date and available at the place where employees normally report to work. Employers must retain OSHA records for five years. Each injury or illness must be recorded on a log (OSHA Form No. 100F; see Figure 7-1) within two days of its occurrence. In addition, a summary record (OSHA Form No. 101) must be filled out within six days of the injury or illness.

At the end of every year, the log and supplementary records are used to

LOG OF FEDERAL OCCUPATIONAL INJURIES AND ILLNESSES

This is the separate log for: Civilian Personnel ☐ ; Military (Non-combat) Personnel ☐

Recordable Cases: You are required to record information about: every occupational *death*; every nonfatal occupational *illness*; and those nonfatal occupational *injuries* which involve one or more of the following: loss of workdays, loss of consciousness, restriction of work or motion, transfer to another job, or medical treatment (other than first aid).

Case or File No. (1)	Date of Injury or Onset of Illness mo./day/yr. (2)	Employee's Name (First name or initial, middle initial, last name) (3)	Occupation (Enter regular job title, not activity employee was performing when injured or at onset of illness.) (4)	Department (Enter department in which the employee is regularly employed.) (5)	Description of Injury or Illness			Extent of and Outcome of Cases				
					Nature of Injury or Illness and Part(s) of Body Affected (Typical entries for this column might be: Amputation of 1st joint right forefinger Strain of lower back Contact dermatitis on both hands Electrocution—body) (6)	Injury or Illness Code See codes at bottom of page (7)	Deaths (Enter date of death.) mo./day/yr. (8)	Lost Workday Cases				Nonfatal Cases Without Lost Workdays (Enter a check if no entry was made in columns 8 or 9 but the case is recordable, as defined above.) (10)	Terminations or Permanent Transfers (Enter a check if the entry in columns 9 or 10 represented a termination or permanent transfer.) (11)
								Enter a check if case involved lost workdays. (9)	Lost Workdays			
									Enter number of days away from work due to injury or illness. (9A)	Enter number of days of restricted work activity due to injury or illness. (9B)		

(Parent Agency and Federal Establishment Code)

(Sub-Agency & Federal Establishment Code)

(Address of Sub-Agency)

Injury Code

10 All occupational injuries

Illness Codes

21 Occupational skin diseases or disorders
22 Dust diseases of the lungs (pneumoconioses)
23 Respiratory conditions due to toxic agents
24 Poisoning (systemic effects of toxic materials)
25 Disorders due to physical agents (other than toxic materials)
26 Disorders due to repeated trauma
29 All other occupational illnesses

Figure 7-1. OSHA Form No. 100F for Maintaining Log of Occupational Injuries and Illnesses, January 1976.

complete an annual summary of all occupational illnesses and injuries that required more than first aid treatment (OSHA Form No. 102F; see Figure 7-2), which is sent to OSHA headquarters. These figures may also be used to determine the rate a company must pay for its workmen's compensation coverage.

Figure 7-2. OSHA Form No. 102F for Summary Report of Federal Occupational Injuries and Illnesses.

SUMMARY REPORT OF FEDERAL OCCUPATIONAL INURIES AND ILLNESSES

A. This is the separate summary report for:

B. Report Period Ending Date ☐☐-☐☐-☐☐
Month   Day   Year

A.1 Civilian Personnel – ☐

A.2 Military (Non-combat) Personnel – ☐

Injury and Illness Category	Code	Total Cases	Deaths	Lost Workday Cases				Nonfatal Cases without Lost Workdays*	Termina-tions or Perma-nent Trans-fers
				Total Lost Workday Cases	Cases Involving Days Away from Work	Days Away from Work	Days of Restricted Work Activity		
Category	Code	Number of entries in Col. 7 of the log (1)	Number of entries in Col. 8 of the log (2)	Number of checks in Col. 9 of the log (3)	Number of entires in Col. 9A of the log (4)	Sum of entires in Col. 9A of the log (5)	Sum of entries in Col. 9B of the log (6)	Number of checks in Col. 10 of the log (7)	Number of checks in Col. 11 of the log (8)
Occupational Injuries	10								
Occupational skin diseases or disorders	21								
Dust diseases of the lungs	22								
Respiratory conditions due to toxic agents	23								
Poisoning (systemic effects of toxic materials)	24							✓	
Disorders due to physical agents	25								
Disorders associated with repeated trauma	26								
All other occupational illnesses	29								
Total—Occupational Illnesses (Sum of codes 21 through code 29)	30								
Total—Occupational Injuries and Illnesses (Sum of code 10 and code 30)									
Total man-hours worked by all employees	40								(This reporting period)
Average number of employees	50								(This reporting period)
Average work week for all employees	51	☐ Check this box only when average work week for all employees is (a) less than 30 hours or (b) more than 50 hours per week.							

(Occupational Illnesses is the vertical label beside codes 21–30)

*Nonfatal Cases Without Lost Workdays—Cases resulting in: medical treatment beyond first aid, diagnosis of occupational illness, loss of consciousness, or transfer to another job (without lost workdays).

The Supervisor's Legal Environment • 113

Uncertainties in OSHA Administration

Because the Occupational Safety and Health Administration has been in operation only a few years, it has not yet developed smoothly operating procedures or a positive image for every aspect of occupational safety and health it is empowered to regulate. Sometimes the provisions of the act are interpreted in different ways, leading to confusion among administrators, business owners, and supervisors. Aside from regulating aspects of business life that directly and obviously affect the health and safety of workers, OSHA also includes numerous regulations which are less obvious in their implications. It is easy to see how confusion and misunderstanding can arise when businesses try to comply with government regulations that are either very general or much too specific.

In the future, OSHA will have an enormous impact on business and industry. Its importance has been compared to that of the first industrial compensation laws in the early twentieth century. In many cases the costs of compliance with OSHA standards will be high. Supervisors must take major responsibility for knowing the requirements and making sure that their shops or departments comply with the law.

OSHA and the Manager

Good managers are always actively concerned about the on-the-job safety and health of their workers. The existence of OSHA means that safety and health has become a formal and major responsibility of every supervisor. They will have increased duties because of the act, and they are in the best position to ensure that the workforce and workplace comply with OSHA regulations.

The first thing the supervisor must do is become acquainted with the regulations that apply to his or her type of work organization. Technical or legal advice may be required in some cases to determine whether or not certain regulations apply. Once familiar with the regulations, the manager must do whatever is necessary to bring the company into compliance. This will often require cooperation and assistance from other managers and owners, since in many cases special equipment, safety devices, and other items must be purchased and installed.

For the most part, however, it is up to supervisors and managers to see that OSHA regulations are observed, without resorting to help from owners. For instance, firms are required to keep aisles and walkways clean and free of debris, oil, grease, and other trash. A first-level manager can assure that this regulation is met. Another area of increased supervisory responsibility is the enforcement of employee compliance with safety regulations. Goggles, protective clothing, gloves, and other safety devices are often uncomfortable or inconvenient for the worker. The supervisor must ensure that all employees comply with safety regulations regardless of their personal inclinations, as an employee violation results in a citation for the employer. Safety measures can no longer be ignored to increase production for a rush order. Managers need to run tight ships if they hope to prevent OSHA citations against their employers.

Employees are guaranteed a number of rights under OSHA, and the supervisor must be careful not to violate those rights while attempting to enforce safety regulations. Employees have the right to file anonymous complaints with OSHA against their employers, requesting on-site inspections. An employee may accompany the OSHA officer on any inspection of the place of work, and employees have the right to meet and talk privately with the inspector before and after the inspection. The act specifically prohibits employers from punishing or discriminating against employees who exercise these rights.

Dangerous though poor working conditions may be, they are not the major cause of on-the-job accidents. It has been estimated that as many as 90 percent of all work-related injuries result either directly or indirectly from some personal act. Thus, while managers must take responsibility for seeing that working conditions under their control are safe and lawful, their major duty is to ensure that workers are performing their tasks safely and are taking all necessary precautions against accidental injury.

Protection of Minorities

Since the 1960s the federal government has become increasingly involved in business through legislation designed to protect the working rights of minority group members. Civil rights and employment opportunity legislation has not only created new avenues of employment for people of different races, religions, and nationalities, but it has also opened a whole new area of legal responsibility for the supervisor.

The 1964 Civil Rights Act

Although this congressional act covers much more than occupational discrimination alone, it has had numerous important implications for the working rights of various minority groups. The Civil Rights Act was designed as a national statement against discrimination in occupations, voting, use of public facilities, and public education. Title VII of the Act, called Equal Employment Opportunity, is devoted specifically to employment. Under the provisions of this title, companies employing twenty-five workers or more, labor unions, and employment agencies must not discriminate against any person regarding hiring, firing, training, promotions, salary increases, or working conditions because of race, religion, color, sex, or national origin.

In 1967, further legislation was passed to prevent occupational discrimination against job applicants or employees from forty-five to sixty-five years old. After the Age Discrimination Act took effect in 1968, it was illegal for employers to discriminate against any person in the areas of hiring, firing, and wages because of age.

The 1964 Civil Rights Act contained at least one major loophole, however. Federal contract companies were exempted from the provision against sex discrimination, although all other regulations concerning minority discrimination applied to them. A subsequent executive order plugged this loophole, and federal contract holders must now comply with the law.

The Equal Employment Opportunity Commission

This commission (EEOC) was created by Title VII of the 1964 Civil Rights Act to administer and regulate the Act's provisions regarding discrimination in employment. During its first year, EEOC received almost 9000 charges of job discrimination. The majority of these complaints, about 60 percent, concerned racial discrimination, while 37 percent were charges of sex discrimination.

Unfortunately for many workers who felt they had been discriminated against, the EEOC was not given any punitive power. Its activities were limited to persuasion, conciliation, and education. Thus, during its first year of operation, EEOC was successful only 50 percent of the time in getting employers to comply with the law. Some people felt that EEOC should have more power to enforce the law, and subsequent executive orders corrected this powerlessness.

The Manager's Role

Most managers have little direct control over their company's personnel policies, hiring practices, or wage decisions. Many do, however, provide some input into these practices and decisions and thus can play a critical role in preventing discrimination against minority members. Further, first-level supervisors may be responsible for designing programs to increase the number of minority employees, or to train, promote, or reassign them within their sphere of influence. It would be easy to shift the burden of minority relations onto the shoulders of top management and owners, but, as with most other areas of management the immediate supervisor must take responsibility for what happens in the work environment. In many cases, supervisors can be held legally responsible for violations of civil rights employment laws.

Training is a particularly important area under the supervisor's control. Before they can adequately fill a job, many minority members will require training in reading, writing, mathematics, and new attitudes toward work if they are to survive in a full-time work environment. For instance, it is important that all workers get to work on time, but many minority members have not been trained to believe that being on time is important.

Managers should be particularly aware of the chance that a training program may be overly sensitive to minority group problems and end by practicing reverse discrimination. For instance, individual counseling of minority employees often increases their frustration and insecurity at holding a new job. Special handling is easy for most people to detect, and training programs that concentrate on this approach may well be resented instead of appreciated.

Managing Minorities

Even though America's population consists of nothing but various minority groups, the attitudes and values of one such group, middle-class white males, have been dominant over the years, often excluding or suppressing the values and rights of other groups. The recent interest in and concern for the rights of all citizens have made it important for supervisors to understand the special problems associated with minority group membership. In particular, supervisors must learn how the differences among minority groups may affect a worker's attitude toward the job or supervisor. Two goals should be kept in mind: maintenance of high-quality production, and individual growth for the minority worker.

With some background knowledge and special supervisory tools, it should be possible to meet both of these goals in a satisfactory manner.

Below, certain minority groups are examined as they are defined by the Civil Rights Act of 1964, including the classifications of race, color, religion, nationality, age, and sex. Handicapped workers are also discussed because, though not specifically mentioned in the act, they have been discriminated against in past employment practices of many companies. Following the special problems associated with each group are some supervisory techniques for handling minority relations within each category.

Race and color. Technically, race is a matter of physical, not mental or cultural, difference. Thus we usually group races by color: Caucasoid (white), Mongoloid (yellow), and Negroid (black). Because blacks have assumed a key position in civil rights movements in this country, we shall focus on them here.

In our nation's history, blacks have experienced the most severe racial discrimination as the target for a seemingly endless variety of social and cultural prejudices. Against this background of centuries of discrimination, the supervisor is likely to meet several distinct problems when working with black employees. Among unskilled and skilled black workers, problems may range from lack of self-confidence, distrust, shyness, and uncertainty to aggressive militancy and cynicism. Lack of confidence usually results from lack of education and job experience, plus the lifetime habit of taking a back seat to nonminority workers. Overconfidence sometimes results from government pressures on businesses to hire certain numbers of minority group members. A highly militant employee may damage a department's morale, and the manager must be alert in recognizing and dealing with such attitudes. There is the additional problem of white resentment of government intervention in a company's hiring practices. Recently, companies have tended to hire a black over an equally or better-qualified white so that racial quotas may be met. Whites will resent this policy and may become opposed to management that engages in the practice.

Religion. Since the sharp animosity between Protestants and Catholics that often affected company hiring practices in the nineteenth century has faded in the twentieth, the most common form of hiring discrimination based on religion probably involves non-Christian faiths. In particular, our nation's businesses have a long and deplorable history of denying jobs to qualified Jewish applicants. Among Christian faiths, certain groups whose religion prescribes an unconventional life-style, such as the Amish, may experience discrimination if they try to find employment outside their own religious communities.

The usual source of religious discrimination is the simple blind prejudice which holds that employees of one or another religion will somehow prove dishonest or try to "take over" the business. Some employers, however, try to justify religious discrimination on the grounds that religion shapes our beliefs and attitudes, and workers whose beliefs and attitudes do not coincide exactly with the employer's may somehow interfere with company goals. Of course, it is irrational to assert that an individual's religion, in and of itself, might reduce the effectiveness of his or her job performance. Indeed, too much emphasis on religious homogeneity (or any other kind) in a given firm may preclude the kind of vital, stimulating atmosphere that emerges when different types of people work together.

The Supervisor's Legal Environment • **117**

Gossip is a primary way of spreading information about a person's religious beliefs. Managers must ignore all such gossip unless there is clear evidence that a worker's religious beliefs are negatively affecting job performance. More often, as noted above, religious discrimination is the result of narrow prejudices and lack of contact with members of a particular religion.

National origin. An individual's country of birth or ancestry may have an important influence on customs, language, accents, manners, and dress. In the past, when America was the destination of large numbers of foreign immigrants, discrimination because of nationality was a critical and often violent problem. Waves of immigrants entered the country, took over the lowest-paying and dirtiest jobs, then gradually moved up into more "respectable" positions, leaving the lowest jobs to the next wave of immigrants. Thus the Irish, Poles, Italians, and numerous other ethnic groups have encountered job discrimination because of their national origin; today refugees from Southeast Asia and Cuba are objects of ethnic discrimination in this country.

Age. In 1979 Congress outlawed some mandatory retirement policies and severely restricted others. By amending the Age Discrimination in Employment Act of 1967, Congress made it unlawful to retire forcibly most public or private workers under age seventy. Exceptions include air traffic controllers, fire fighters, some law enforcement personnel, executives who are entitled to an immediate and nonforfeitable retirement benefit of $27,000 a year or more, and employees of companies with fewer than twenty workers. Initially, few workers are likely to take advantage of the changes. But many, both young and old, may feel the impact. Employers who are eager to reduce their ranks will encourage voluntary retirement. Performance standards will be stiffened, making it easier to dismiss marginal employees. Neither the original act nor the amendments restrict employers' right to dismiss employees for valid reasons, such as poor performance or misconduct. Although studies have repeatedly shown that older workers do as well as their youthful counterparts in most jobs, some do decline in efficiency. This has often been tolerated because of a worker's compulsory retirement. In the future, performance evaluations may be much more critical.

As the birth rate declines, this country's age composition will include larger and larger numbers of older people. Thus discrimination in hiring because of age—already a problem today—will become an increasingly important issue. In terms of ability, people age at greatly different rates. It is therefore a serious mistake to judge a person's competence solely on the basis of age. Many employers have in the past refused to hire workers over a certain age, usually forty-five or so, claiming that older workers tend to be less competent, more inflexible, and more often absent because of illness. In addition, employers believe that older workers increase the cost of group health insurance and pension plans. Of all these beliefs, only the last—increased cost of pension plans—is true. The company must invest large amounts of money in older workers without having access to most of their productive years. At the same time, older workers are frequently better workers. They have the benefits of greater experience and wisdom and are more likely to treat their jobs with respect, aware that they cannot walk out the door and immediately find another position.

The handicapped. These workers are not covered by the 1964 Civil Rights Act, but since they do constitute a minority group in occupational areas, we shall discuss them briefly here and at greater length in Chapter 19. Business organizations are only now discovering that handicapped workers can be valuable assets. Beliefs about their low productivity, need for extra care, and poor morale effect on coworkers have all been shown to be false. Like the older worker, the handicapped person is more likely to value a job because of its difficulty to obtain.

Some restructuring and redesigning of jobs may be necessary to accommodate a handicapped worker. Often these adjustments can be made for any new worker regardless of his physical or mental condition. Some handicapped workers can successfully fill positions which present problems to other workers. For instance, a deaf worker has no problem in a work area with excessive noise. People who are confined to wheelchairs make excellent telephone workers. Managers should make sure that handicapped people are hired to fill positions that emphasize their abilities and best utilize their skills and talents.

Women.   Women represent the largest minority group in America. In fact, in sheer numbers they are an actual majority. But discrimination does not depend on numbers so much as on values, and in America, men have always given themselves priority.

Women's rights groups have recently made far-reaching gains in promoting the rights of women against discriminatory employment practices. One reason for this gain has been the increasing numbers of women entering the labor force in the last few decades. In spite of their growing numbers, however, women remain concentrated at the low end of the pay and prestige scales, while men are much more heavily represented in the high-paying, prestigious occupations. Because of this discrepancy, women's lobbyists have been successful in forcing federal officials to enforce the Civil Rights Act provisions for women.

State legislation regarding fair employment opportunities for women has also given women's rights a push. Many court cases have been decided in favor of plaintiffs charging discrimination because of sex (both male and female), and the Equal Employment Opportunity Commission has been swamped with sex discrimination cases since it began operation.

The new liberal laws concerning working women have given employers considerable cause for thought. The traditional notion that women are not physically suited to a wide variety of jobs has been sharply undermined by the discovery that with relatively minor adaptations in tools and facilities, women can handle nearly all jobs formerly reserved for males—including mining, operating heavy equipment, riding as jockeys, and so on. Of course, women who pioneer in such fields often encounter opposition from their male coworkers—which usually fades when it becomes evident that they are competent, dedicated workers, capable of holding down tough, strenuous jobs on the same terms as men, who deserve the same amount of pay, and the same promotion considerations that a man ordinarily receives.

Every manager must be open-minded when it comes to hiring women. Women must not be denied the right to hold a job for which they are qualified solely on the basis of their sex. This means that qualified women must be allowed to drive fork-lift trucks, act as administrators, sell men's clothing; it also means that qualified men must not be denied the opportunity to work as secretaries, nurses, or flight attendants. Job performance, once again, is the key to determining the existence of discriminatory practices. If a woman or man is holding a nontraditional job and performing it well, there is no reason why she or he should not continue in the position, earn raises in salary, and be considered for promotion.

Supervisory Techniques for Fighting Discrimination

Faced with the new pressures for hiring members of all the minority groups, supervisors should be aware of two areas in which the government can help them deal with their increased responsibilities: affirmative action guidelines and federal training programs.

Affirmative action programs. The Equal Employment Opportunity Commission (EEOC) and the Office of Federal Contract Compliance (OFCC) both require affirmative action programs from employers to enforce the federal laws against employment discrimination. An affirmative action program is one that (1) eliminates the systematic exclusion of certain minority group members from hiring, pay increases, and promotion, and (2) makes positive efforts to discover and hire qualified minority members for positions within the company.

Affirmative action programs mean increased responsibilities for managers. First, they may be required to conduct interviews for new employees in an extremely careful manner so as not to discriminate against minority members. Second, increasing attention must be given to minority relations. Third, control must be exercised over white or male backlash against minority members who are hired with less stringent qualifications to meet affirmative action quotas. Fourth, managers may be closely involved in setting up training programs for disadvantaged minorities. Finally, they may be required to keep records for submission with their company's affirmative action report to one of the federal agencies regulating employment discrimination. Figure 7-3, an EEOC Employer Information Report, shows the kinds of information the federal government requires about minority participation in business.

Excessive governmental zeal in enforcing antidiscrimination laws, while valid, can also create severe problems for managers and their employers. Hiring unqualified people is always a waste of time and money, and the company may lose the competitive race if it concentrates too many of its resources on hiring and training unqualified workers. A more important reason, perhaps, is expressed in the following statement by Kenneth B. Clark, a well-known black psychologist:

> I cannot express vehemently enough my abhorrence of sentimentalistic, seemingly compassionate programs of employment of Negroes which employ them on Jim Crow double standards or special standards for the Negro which are lower than those for whites. I think this is a perpetuation of racism, is interpreted by the Negro as condescension, and . . . will be exploited but will not contribute to any substantive, serious, nonracial integration of minorities into the productive economy of business.[1]

The short-run advantages of meeting federal quotas for minority employees can sometimes be offset by the long-term disadvantages of lowered morale and suffering production. The manager can lend a hand by refusing to practice discrimination, by reviewing carefully the qualifications of all job applicants, and by instituting and operating adequate training programs for disadvantaged

[1] Quoted in *General Electric Campus Monographs,* 1972–73.

SECTION D—EMPLOYMENT DATA

Employment at this establishment—Report all permanent, temporary, or part-time employees including apprentices and on-the-job trainees unless specifically excluded as set forth in the instructions. Enter the appropriate figures on all lines and in all columns. Blank spaces will be considered as zeros.

Job Categories	Overall Totals (sum of col B through K) A	Number of Employees									
		Male					Female				
		White (not of Hispanic origin) B	Black (not of Hispanic origin) C	Hispanic D	Asian or Pacific Islander E	American Indian or Alaskan Native F	White (not of Hispanic origin) G	Black (not of Hispanic origin) H	Hispanic I	Asian or Pacific Islander J	American Indian or Alaskan Native K
Officials and managers											
Professionals											
Technicians											
Sales workers											
Office and clerical											
Craft workers (skilled)											
Operatives (semi-skilled)											
Laborers (unskilled)											
Service workers											
Total											
Total employment reported in previous EEO-1 report											

(The trainees below should also be included in the figures for the appropriate occupational categories above)

Format on-the-job trainees	White collar		
	Production		

Figure 7-3. EEOC Employer Information Report, Section D, EEO-1 Employment Data.

employees. Given the right atmosphere and the right set of circumstances, people can learn a new trade, how to write a sentence, or how to read a trade manual; they can even learn new attitudes and values. In the process, a supervisor will have learned a great deal about relating to fellow human beings, regardless of their race, color, religion, nationality, age, sex, or physical or mental condition. This growth and learning is important to both management and labor, and can only benefit their organization.

Federal training programs. In addition to the affirmative action requirement that managers help train disadvantaged minorities, the government has established many programs of its own to provide valuable job skills for unemployed or underemployed workers. As this emphasis on training suggests, the government recognizes that minority group members will benefit from the equal opportunity laws only if they are fully qualified for the jobs they receive.

Federal funds have been allotted to such programs as Outreach, Apprenticeship, JOBS, the Job Corps, Operation Mainstream, JUMP, and WIN. Program participants include a wide range of trainees, among them blacks, the urban and rural poor, white Appalachians, Mexican-Americans, Puerto Ricans, welfare mothers, displaced professionals from the declining aircraft industry, and Vietnam veterans. Most of these programs involve classroom training, on-the-job experience, or a combination of both. Program graduates are placed in such jobs as nurse's and teacher's aides, auto mechanics, and hotel personnel. Many of the programs have been poorly coordinated and supervised, however, so that their impact on the unemployed is not nearly as great as it could have been. Nevertheless, a substantial number of workers have been trained and placed under these programs.

One program which had some major successes was JOBS—Job Opportunities in the Business Sector. This program allowed companies to be reimbursed for half the salaries of hard-core unemployed persons whom the companies agreed to hire and train. Texas Instruments hired 2000 black women with very weak educational backgrounds to assemble electrical parts and taught them mathematics and English. Almost 90 percent of the trainees qualified for regular jobs in the company after completing their training program. Participants in the JOBS program include other companies from many different types of industries, including General Motors and Ford Motor Company, Xerox, IBM, and General Electric.

Although these federal programs have helped some minority group members prepare for and obtain jobs, they alone are not enough to stimulate minority interest in job training and education or employer interest in hiring and training minority members. More needs to be done to help all people fulfill their potential and lead productive lives.

The Minority Supervisor

The bulk of this discussion has centered on the assumption that managers are members of the American "majority," that is, white and male. Increasingly, however, this assumption is less valid, as qualified minority members move into supervisory and managerial positions in many businesses and other groups. It is unfortunate but true that, in most cases, minority supervisors will have to do a *better* job than their white male counterparts. To survive as managers, they will have to prove their ability to do the job, to regulate employee disputes and complaints, to see that the work flows smoothly and is done well. Having achieved his position through government pressure on the company, the minority supervisor is now in a position to show both his employer and his workers that minority discrimination is a senseless waste of talent and ability. Competent minority members in supervisory positions will do more to overcome job discrimination than all the legislation that can pass through Congress. Needless to say, the strains and tensions may be enormous, even overwhelming. But the rewards can be just as great, both individually and for society.

Summary

The American economic system is based on a complex set of relationships among entrepreneurs, managers, workers, consumers, and government. In this chapter we have reviewed some of the roles of government in regulating the business world. The government becomes involved in business in two principal ways: (1) protecting businesses, competitors, and consumers through enforcing contracts and enforcing competition, and (2) protecting workers' health, safety, and civil rights.

A major step toward the second objective was the Occupational Safety and Health Act of 1970, which established the Occupational Safety and Health Administration to develop and enforce regulations concerning job safety and occupational hazards. Failure to comply with OSHA regulations can result in stiff penalties for owners and managers. Under the act, employees are guaranteed a number of rights, and managers must be aware of those rights as well as the specific features of safety regulation applying to their organization.

Since 1964 the federal government has been involved in preventing job discrimination because of race, color, religion, nationality, or sex. The passage of the 1964 Civil Rights Act placed strict limitations on employers with regard to such discrimination. In recent years, affirmative action programs have been instituted, both to prevent discrimination and to seek out qualified workers. Because the manager is usually involved in personnel decisions such as hiring and firing, wage increases, training programs, record-keeping, and day-to-day supervision of minority employees, an active role is required in minority relations.

The federal government is far from inactive in the affairs of business and industry. Its regulations are far-reaching and extend into almost every aspect of commercial enterprise. The manager is affected in many ways by this governmental influence. It is essential that he or she be aware of federal regulations and learn to comply with them.

Key Terms

Affirmative Action Programs. A systematic attempt to eliminate the exclusion of certain minority group members from hiring, pay increases, and promotions. Employers with affirmative action programs make positive efforts to discover and hire minority members for positions within an organization.

Antitrust Laws. Legislation, such as the Sherman Act of 1890 and the Clayton

Act of 1914, which provides for national regulation of certain monopolies and the preservation of competition in other areas.

Capitalism. An economic system based on the competitive production of goods and services for sale in a free market.

EEOC. The Equal Employment Opportunity Commission, created by the 1964 Civil Rights Act to administer and regulate requirements of the act regarding discrimination in employment.

OSHA. The Occupational Safety and Health Act of 1970, which attempts to set and enforce national standards for safe, healthy work environments.

Price Discrimination. A business practice, illegal under the Robinson-Patman Act, where different customers are charged different prices for the same product.

Unfair Business Practices. According to the Federal Trade Commission, unfair business practices are those designed to deceive the customer, such as false advertising, industrial espionage, or other acts of misrepresentation or dishonesty.

Review Questions

1. List and describe the major components of the American capitalistic system.

2. Write a paragraph in which you describe what would happen in America if all government controls on business were removed.

3. The earliest laws regulating business in America covered competition. Why? Does this mean that in the 1980s there is no need to worry about competition in business?

4. List and describe the four types of laws that cover competition in business.

5. What is the primary purpose of OSHA? Are you surprised that such an act was not passed until 1970?

6. What types of employers are affected by OSHA regulations?

7. What was the purpose of the 1964 Civil Rights Act?

8. Identify the major functions of EEOC. Is there any real force behind the legislation?

9. Does religious discrimination exist in the United States? Why would someone discriminate against someone else in employment because of religion?

10. Characterize the role of the minority supervisor today. Balance your argument equally between the opportunities and the problems facing the supervisor.

11. Why are businesses not always able to regulate themselves? Is there a connection between the desire to make a profit and the lack of self-regulation?

Exercise

The Safety Inspection

You are surprised and just a little bit nervous to be asked to accompany an OSHA compliance officer and the plant manager through the assembly area of your department. As you walk through the assembly area, you are quite pleased to notice the orderly and efficient arrangement of the assembly tables. In one of the material bins, you notice that several random pieces of tubing are protruding about eight inches beyond the rack. You recall that someone had tripped over such a piece of tubing a few weeks ago. Almost at the same time, you see that one of the engineers has removed a portion of the protective rail around a heavy-duty source of power. The grill had been removed to facilitate an experiment with a new process. Evidently, somebody has forgotten to cover it.

1. Should you point out the two possible violations or remain silent?

2. What do you think will happen to your company as a result of this negligence?

3. How could these problems have been avoided?

Case 7 • Skip Little

Skip Little is a supervisor for Edmond Generator Company, a manufacturer of high-powered electrical generators for the steel industry. He supervises a team of three men and two women. Recently, an OSHA inspector identified a piece of equipment in the work area as dangerous because the insulation was worn through exposing a high-voltage coupling. The inspector dictated that the equipment could not be used until it was repaired; the OSHA regulations gave the company five days to repair the equipment. After that time, a $1000 fine would be imposed for each day the equipment remained unrepaired. If the equipment was not repaired within fifteen days, the plant would be closed and subject to more fines.

After reading the OSHA report, Skip called his workers together. "Well, those OSHA folks really like to swing their weight around. The inspector over-reacted to the exposed coupling. It is dangerous, but we can keep the machinery running until the replacement parts arrive. If we shut down the equipment, we'll fall off our production schedule. Everybody just be careful and keep quiet—okay?"

One of the employees, Steve Bows, replied, "Skip, I have to agree with the inspector. The coupling is extremely dangerous, and someone could get killed. I think we ought to wait until the insulation gets here from New Jersey." Skip replied that no one would know the difference and that the crew should go about its business as usual.

Another employee, Sally Finney, complained. "Skip, I'm not going to work as long as the equipment is dangerous. Either I work in another part of the plant, or I don't work!" Skip replied that she was over-reacting, and that he, not OSHA, knew what was safe. He suggested that everyone go home early today.

The next morning, Steve Bows came into Skip's office fifteen minutes before starting time. "Skip, the five of us met after work yesterday and decided that we are not going to work until the coupling is repaired. You can't force us to work, and if you send us home we will file a grievance with the company and notify OSHA of your position."

Skip Little's telephone rang. It was the plant manager. "Skip, we are having a little trouble locating the right kind of insulation for that piece of equipment in your area. We have to file the compliance report tomorrow, so come over to the office and sign this form for me. Then we'll get the piece of equipment installed whenever we can, maybe within a couple of weeks."

1. What should Skip Little do?

2. What are the risks of complying with the plant manager's request?

3. How would you respond to the employees? to the OSHA inspector? to the plant manager?

CHAPTER 8

Effective Decision Making

They are decided only to be undecided, resolved to be irresolute, adamant for drift, all-powerful for impotence.

Sir Winston Churchill

Learning Objectives

• To become thoroughly familiar with each step in the process of making effective decisions.

• To differentiate between problem solving and decision making and to learn when each process is appropriate.

• To recognize the importance of personal decision making as a foundation for decision making on the job.

• To gain ability in applying decision-making rules to every area of the supervisory job.

Many people feel that the ability to make decisions forms the core of supervision because every aspect of managerial responsibility involves making decisions and choosing among alternatives. In the final analysis, supervisors are paid for one major job: making decisions. In fact, the job of supervising is essentially the job of making decisions.

In the next chapter we will discuss planning as a part of decision making. Planning is actually a preliminary part of the decision-making process. Almost every supervisory task or responsibility involves making decisions. Throughout any day, supervisors will be involved in many major and minor choices. Unfortunately, some give up their right and duty to make decisions. They either decide not to decide, or they make a policy of giving "definite maybes." These supervisors have judged themselves unworthy of the position and thus prove that they are unable to fulfill their supervisory obligations.

Preventive Problem Solving

It is easy to confuse problem solving with decision making. At first glance, these words may seem to represent two terms for the same set of activities. Problem solving, however, is the *process* that guides a supervisor toward a decision. This process is a logical step-by-step method that enables the supervisor to narrow down a body of information, identify the main problem, and choose among alternative plans. This problem-solving process will be described in detail later in the chapter.

However, the best time to solve a problem is before it occurs. It is amazing how rapidly little problems can grow to crisis proportions. We are all familiar with the pressures of problem solving and the way making decisions during a crisis can bring us to the end of our emotional tether. After hours of dealing with uncooperative employees, pacifying angry customers, or handling sticky production problems, even a strong supervisor may wonder at the philosophy expressed by one successful inventor (General Motors executive Charles Kettering): "Problems are the price of progress. Don't bring me anything but trouble. Good news weakens me." A full day of crisis situations and difficult decision making can make any supervisor long for the "weakening influence" of good news.

Supervisors who cannot avoid crisis situations may find the following set of questions helpful.

What Is the Right Thing to Do?

For supervisors to make decisions effectively, they must have a clear idea of what is right before they can tell when things are going wrong.

At twenty-three, William Randolph Hearst was assigned to oversee the San Francisco *Examiner,* one of many newspapers in his father's chain. The paper was losing money. Young Hearst went to San Francisco, studied the problems, and wrote the following letter to his father. You can see that this letter sets forth well-defined, specific objectives for action:

Dear Father:

I am anxious to begin work on the San Francisco *Examiner.* I have all my pipes laid and it only remains to turn on the gas. One year from the day I take hold, our circulation will have increased ten thousand.

We must be alarmingly enterprising, and we must be startlingly original. We must be honest and fearless. We must have greater variety than we have ever had. We must print more matter than we have printed. We must increase our force and enlarge our editorial building.

There are some things that I intend to do new and striking which will constitute a revolution in the sleepy journalism of the Pacific slope and will focus the eyes of all that section on the *Examiner.* I am not going to write you what these are, for the letter might get lost, or you might leak. In two years we will be paying, and in five years we will be the biggest paper on the Pacific slope. We won't be paying for two years because up to that time I propose turning back into the improvement of the paper every cent that comes in.

> Your affectionate son,
> W. R. Hearst

Hearst met his objectives in three years. He understood that clear, realistic, and measurable objectives are as important in crisis management as they are in original planning.

Like opportunities, crises can too long go unrecognized. It is easy to overlook little problems until they become unmanageable. To do the job properly, the supervisor should solve minor difficulties before they turn into major crises.

What Can Go Wrong?

Edsel Murphy is renowned for formulating Murphy's Law of Management, which simply states, "If anything can go wrong, it will."

Most people have seen this law in operation, yet few take the time to anticipate problems before they happen. A healthy dose of pessimism is essential in anticipating problems, as long as your optimism then helps provide the cure.

Murphy's law has been extended to cover a wide variety of potential problem situations:

1. The more innocuous a design change appears, the further its influence will extend.
2. Firmness of delivery dates is inversely proportional to the tightness of the schedule.
3. In any given miscalculation, the fault will never be placed if more than one person is involved.
4. Any error that can creep in, will, and it will be in the direction that will do the most damage to the calculation.
5. All constants are variables.
6. In any given computation, the figure that is most obviously correct will be the source of error.
7. Any wire cut to length will be too short.
8. If a project requires n components, there will be $n-1$ units in stock.
9. A dropped tool will land where it can do the most damage. (Also known as the law of selective gravitation.)
10. Interchangeable parts won't.
11. After an instrument has been fully assembled, extra components will be found on the bench.

How Can I Prevent the Problem from Happening?

Sometimes, merely identifying a problem will suggest its obvious solution. If an organization is prepared to deal with crises, they are not likely to erupt too often. Trouble is less likely to visit a prepared supervisor. An analysis of a potential problem can lead to simple steps which can prevent the problem from occurring. As an example, a supervisor who has carefully planned a Sunday afternoon move would face a crisis situation if movers arrived to find the plant securely locked with no key available. Problem prevention in this case is simple: pick up the passkey Friday afternoon!

In any situation, when a number of potential problems have been identified, it may be useful to group them into categories denoting the relative seriousness of each problem. Some problems must be avoided at all costs. Others are so irritating or undesirable that considerable effort must be made to prevent them. Other problems are minor and will not require much attention. The planning decision sheet in Figure 8-1 will show you how to identify and allow for potential problems that could arise in completing a project.

Figure 8-1. Planning Decision Sheet. [With permission from the Macmillan Publishing Company, Inc., from *The New Management,* 2nd ed., by Robert M. Fulmer. © 1978 by Robert M. Fulmer.]

What:	The movement of furniture and office equipment.			
Where:	From the fifth floor of building A to the fourth floor of new building B.			
When:	Sunday, starting 9 A.M. and finishing 4 P.M. for inspection.			
Extent:	Twenty desks and tables, forty file cabinets, twenty typewriters, and twenty chairs.			

Potential Problems and Possible Causes	Probability That Problem Will Occur (in %)	Plan A: Preventing the Problem	Probability That It Will Happen Anyway (in %)	Plan B: What to Do if It Occurs in Spite of Plan A
A. Move will take too long.				
1. Not packed and ready.	75	Instruct; set deadline; inspect 3:00 P.M. Friday.	5	Have two packing crewworkers on hand
2. Not enough movers show up.	20	Check; get written commitment from movers.	10	Know of backup commercial mover.
3. Freight elevator not manned.	50	Check; arrange for operator.	5	Have backup operator on call.
4. Hand trucks not available.	20	Check and arrange.	0	Know where to borrow.
5. Lunch counters nearby closed, no food.	70	Check hours; locate nearest one that will be open.	10	Know catering truck service to call.
6. Doors locked, no one has key.	50	Get passkey.	0	
B. Items will be mixed up, things all confused:				
7. Items not properly labeled.	80	Instruct, inspect mid-P.M. Friday.	10	Have assistant who can label stuff.
8. Movers do not know where to put items.	100	Lay out rooms with chalk; use signs and labels.	5	Have assistant who knows layout.
9. Someone else moving in, same time.	10	Check with building superintendent.	5	Rearrange schedule; set up aisles to keep separate.
C. Items will be damaged:				
10. Breakables not properly packed.	40	Instruct; provide packing materials; inspect.	10	Have two packing crewworkers on hand.
11. Doors, corners, elevators not padded.	100	Check for critical spots; arrange for padding.	10	Have extra pads on hand.
D. Items will be stolen, lost:				
12. Unauthorized people come in, take things.	50	Place uniformed guards at doors; have mover post bond.	5	Spotcheck against list.
13. Desks, files not locked.	40	Instruct; check locks.	10	Have person lock same

What Is My Alternative Plan?

Even the best planning and foresight sometimes is not enough. Problems have a way of appearing even when the supervisor has anticipated and prepared for them. After doing eveything possible to keep the problem from happening, the wise supervisor will ask, "What am I going to do when something goes wrong anyway?" It is always wise to have an alternative plan available in case the original plan does not work out or something else goes wrong.

Decision making and crisis management are time-consuming tasks, but the effort is well spent. If a supervisor tries to avoid decision making by saying, "I really don't have time to do all this," it may well be necessary to go through the process all over again when problems arise.

When Should the Alternative Plan Take Over?

Although patience is usually considered a virtue, a supervisor can land in hot water by displaying too much patience in a crisis. You must be able to tell when the original plan has failed, and when it is time to put an alternative plan into action. It is usually easier to schedule Plan B's kickoff before pressure builds from a crisis situation. Using this method, you will be able to recognize a developing crisis and can better determine when to shift gears.

It is a good idea to set up mileposts to serve as an early warning system. When those mileposts are reached, a crisis is building, and it is automatically time to initiate Plan B.

Problem Solving

Once a problem has been identified, the problem-solving process has begun. The problem's cause is isolated, alternative plans of action are considered, and a decision is made. At each stage, unnecessary information is eliminated until the situation is refined and narrowed down. Isolating the problem's main cause helps us identify solutions and choose intelligently among them.

Suppose that your car stalls on the expressway. You put in a frantic call to your local mechanic. Upon arrival, he or she begins narrowing down the problem and seeking possible sources. Your mechanic knows, for example, that pushing the car until it could be jump-started would treat the symptom but not cure the problem itself. The mechanic will check the battery, ignition wiring, starter, and other potential sources of trouble. A problem exists whenever there is a difference between what *should* be happening and what *actually* happens. As the mechanic narrows down the field, the real problem begins to emerge.

As with everything else, adding a human element complicates the problem-solving process. Too often, problem solvers jump to an immediate conclusion after hearing a little information or too little of the facts or circumstances. They will then defend their conclusion at all costs, in spite of new evidence to the contrary. What would you think if your mechanic insisted your car's starter was faulty, even after your starter turned over properly? You would probably find another mechanic. Though we recognize such stubbornness in others, most of us occasionally decide on a particular solution without investigating other problem sources.

In spite of all the preventive actions you may take, unexpected problems will arise now and then. The following list suggests a series of steps that will help you pinpoint the exact problem, its source, and its solution:[1]

1. State the problem. The more specifically and clearly the problem is stated, the easier it will be to discover the solution.

2. Define the present state of affairs. State specifically and in measurable terms the exact situation at present.

3. State the objective. Write down the exact difference between what is happening and what should be happening.

4. List the possible causes. Think of all the possible reasons that might explain the present problem, and maybe even a few that seem impossible.

5. Select the most likely cause. This selection process itself may suggest other causes and send you back to Step 4.

6. List alternative solutions. Write down all the possible actions that would seem to solve the problem you have isolated.

7. Evaluate alternatives. Weigh each possible action by effort, cost, and risk. Will the solution cost more than solving the problem is worth?

8. Make a decision. Choose the alternative that promises the most effective solution with the least risk or cost.

9. Draw up a plan of action. Plan exactly the events that must occur if the solution is to work. Pay attention to specific dates and details.

10. Evaluate the results. When the plan has been executed, accept the credit graciously if it succeeds. If it fails, regroup, start again at Step 6, and find the next most likely cause of the problem.

The Decision Tree

The use of a decision tree, or a series of if-then statements can help isolate potential problems, sources, and solutions. The decision-tree concept can best be understood by following this simple example.[2]

The annual company picnic is coming up soon. The plant manager has assigned you the all-important task of deciding what to do if it rains. The company picnic has two main objectives: (1) that everybody have a good time, and (2) that it be a financial success. Your first step is to gather your picnic committee together and consider alternatives. You might come out with a list something like this:

1. If we plan an *outdoor picnic* there are three potential financial outcomes:

   • If it rains, *then* we lose $350.

   • If we have short showers, *then* we will make $300.

   • If it is sunny all day, *then* we make $500.

2. If we plan an *outdoor picnic* but also provide a temporary shelter and a movie, *then* we must invest an additional $50 but we have the following possible results:

[1] Adapted from Robert M. Fulmer, *The New Management,* 2d ed. (New York: Macmillan, 1978), pp. 78–99. See also Charles Kepner and Benjamin Tregoe, *The Rational Manager* (New York: McGraw-Hill, 1965) for one of the classic treatments of decision making and problem solving.

[2] For a popular and comprehensive treatment of decision trees, see E. A. McCreary, "How to Grow a Decision Tree," *Think Magazine,* March–April 1967, pp. 13–18.

- If it rains all day, *then* we break even (people will leave early but our costs are covered).
- If we have showers, *then* our emergency plan goes into operation and we still make $450.
- If it is sunny, *then* we still make $450, although we have spent money on the safeguards for nothing.

3. If we schedule an indoor picnic, *then* we can predict the following outcomes:
- If it rains, *then* we lost $100 because of low attendance despite the same general and promotion expenses.
- If we have showers, *then* we still lose $100.
- If it is sunny, *then* we lose $150 because people who planned to come may find personal activities that will enable them to enjoy the out-of-doors.

You now begin to gather information about the probability of rain, showers, or sunshine on the day of the picnic. You learn that the U. S. Weather Bureau predicts the following probabilities: 70 percent chance of sunshine, 20 percent chance of showers, and 10 percent chance of rain all day. According to your final analysis, the best alternative is to plan an outdoor picnic and have a shelter available. Since the probability of rain is so low, you may consider eliminating the shelter entirely. The third alternative, an indoor picnic, is no alternative at all. Who likes an indoor picnic?

When making up a decision tree, it is important to identify *all* the possible factors. It is equally important, however, to keep the growth of the tree within manageable proportions. If you are considering too many factors, the possibilities for actions and their outcomes will multiply beyond control. The assigning of probability values presents another problem area. For example, even the weather bureau occasionally errs in its predictions. It is also important to remember that in making a relatively simple decision, decision trees are time-consuming and usually unnecessary. Even without the information about probability, the decision tree may be built to demonstrate graphically the options and possible outcomes. Figure 8-2 displays the relative values of the three alternative

Figure 8-2. A Decision Tree.

			Expected Value
Outdoor	.10	Rain all day (lose $350)	− 35
	.20	Showers (make $300)	60
	.70	Sunny (make $500)	350
			+375
Outdoor with Shelter	.10	Rain all day (lose $.00)	0
	.20	Showers (make $450)	90
	.70	Sunny (make $450)	315
			+405
Indoor	.10	Rain (lose $100)	− 10
	.20	Showers (lose $100)	− 20
	.70	Sunny (lose $150)	−105
			−135

Decision

decisions. Finally, the decision tree should not be used as an "answer machine." It is a tool for setting up logical reasoning processes—it is not an answer in itself.

Approaches to Decision Making

Due to complicating factors, supervisors are seldom able to choose the decision that is unquestionably "best." Consequently, they must often be content with a decision that is satisfactory but not optimal. The challenge of decision making for the supervisor can be approached from one of several perspectives.

"Optimizing" Versus "Satisficing"

At first, it would seem logical that each supervisor attempts to make "optimal" decisions. Although there is a natural desire to make the best decisions possible, "possible" and "best" are not always compatible. Supervisors seldom have totally accurate and complete information; they do not always think and act in a totally rational manner. Finally, cost and reward cannot always be precisely calculated, especially where feelings, emotions, and attitudes are involved. In analyzing the many attitudes imposed on decision making, Herbert A. Simon suggested the *principle of bounded rationality:*

> The capacity of the human mind in formulating and solving complex problems is very small compared to the size of the problem. It is very difficult to achieve objectively rational behavior in the real world or even a reasonable approximation to such objective rationality.[3]

Since obtaining optimal results was often too difficult for supervisors and managers, Simon coined the word "satisficing" to define the process of reaching an acceptable decision. Few people will keep looking for the sharpest needle in the haystack after finding one to sew with. Research has shown that managers actually behave in this manner when making decisions. For his work, which challenged the assumptions about how managers make decisions, Simon received the Nobel Prize for Economics in 1978.

Lessons from the Orient

Peter Drucker suggests that American managers might learn something from the Japanese approach to decision making.[4] In America we tend to emphasize the answer, while in Japan the emphasis is on the question and the process of decision making. The Japanese procedure is to be very deliberate and careful in the initial stages of gathering information and finding out what other people think about the situation. The Japanese manager may consult with others throughout the company over a long period of time in order to derive a true consensus about what to do. American managers often ask their subordinates

[3] Herbert A. Simon, *Administrative Behavior* (New York: Macmillan, 1947).
[4] Peter F. Drucker, *Management: Tasks, Responsibilities, Practices* (New York: Harper, 1974), pp. 467–70.

but assume the personal responsibility for making the decision. Japanese managers actually make the decision on the basis of majority opinion. American managers tend to make their decisions much more quickly than their Japanese counterparts. But once the decision is made, the latter are able to implement decisions much more quickly. There is almost no need to initiate a program to "sell" the decision.

Group Decision Making

The idea of involving many people in a decision makes sense—until you sit through a committee meeting. Committees have a tendency to discuss the same question over and over again. When the group finally surrenders to an aggressive member of a "railroading" chairperson, no one feels good about the decision-making process. Committee work is often characterized by a sloppy, unstructured, loosely led "bull" session that goes on until everybody grows tired and gives in to some sort of compromise.

Recently, business researchers have explored two more structured approaches to gaining input into the decision process. The first is called the Delphi method; the other is known as nominal group technique (NGT).[5]

The Delphi method uses questionnaires sent through the mail or a computer terminal. Instead of using one questionnaire, several are sent as part of a planned process. When a participant receives the second questionnaire, he or she also receives a summary of what other people have said. If a group is attempting to rank several objects, this second questionnaire will show the ranking which developed in the first round. You may then decide to adapt your own opinion to correspond more closely with the group's, or you may explain why you feel that your choice is better than the group's. The administrator of the Delphi method may circulate a revised questionnaire one more time to obtain final input from respondents. Once all the questionnaires are collected and computed, a "most correct" decision can be reached from the consensus input. The technique can be used to forecast developments or to determine group consensus about an idea. Though the coordinator of this exercise must spend a great deal of time tabulating responses, panel members do not get involved in the endless discussion of a committee. Their time is conserved and the decision is usually more precise than a committee summary because persuasive individuals cannot pressure a member to change his or her mind.

The nominal group technique is similar to "brainstorming" that became popular a few years ago. In the NGT procedure, a committee sits around a table and lists every possible solution or relevant factor about the problem. Next, the group members consolidate their ideas into one list. At this point, there is no discussion of suggested alternatives except to clarify meanings. Once a master list is developed, the group begins to discuss the ideas and place them in priority order.

Although there is no consensus about the best way to get at a group's collective wisdom, researchers do agree that committees are slower than most individuals, less accurate than the best individual, and more accurate than the majority. A five-person group would generally take 50 percent longer than the average

[5] André L. Debec, et al., *Group Techniques for Program Planning* (Glenview, Ill.: Scott, Foresman, 1975), pp. 17–39.

individual working alone. Over 75 percent of groups, however, produce better performance than the average individual. Yet, most groups are worse than the best individual in the group.[6]

Making Decisions About Personal Goals

Systematic goal setting and decision making can prove a valuable tool for achieving individual development as well as organizational success. When you set personal goals, you give yourself a sense of purpose and create an inner motivating force in yourself to achieve those goals. As soon as you know where you are going, you are in a better position to gauge your success in getting there. Successful people know where they want to be and how they plan to get there. One classic self-help book sets forth this plan for becoming rich:

> First, fix in your mind the exact amount of money you desire. It is not sufficient merely to say "I want plenty." Be definite as to amount. Second, determine exactly what you intend to give for what you desire. Third, establish a definite date when you intend to possess or achieve your goal. Fourth, create a definite plan for carrying out the desire and begin *at once,* whether you are ready or not, to put this plan into action. Fifth, write out a clear, concise statement of the amount of money you intend to acquire or the goal you intend to achieve. Name the time limit for its acquisition.[7]

Finally, the book suggests that you read your written statement aloud twice daily, once just before going to bed and once after getting up in the morning. While reading, make every effort to see and feel yourself as having already attained your goal.

Of course, you cannot make a dream come true if you do not have a dream. Although personal goal setting is a little like dreaming, you should be realistic enough to set goals you can actually achieve. Many of history's great inventors were dreamers. Thomas Edison tried *ten thousand times* before seeing his dream of the electric light become reality. The Wright brothers imagined a flying machine and set about making that dream come true. After fantasizing, Marconi created the system by which our televisions and radios operate today.

Of course, all the dreaming in the world will not carry your goals into reality. Personal goals, once they are clearly stated, require lots of hard work to achieve.

The following is an example of one supervisor's personal goals for the next five years:

- To be making an additional $5000 per year
- To complete my bachelor's degree
- To be head production supervisor
- To finish building the new wing on my house
- To play tennis well

What kinds of things must be done to make sure these goals are achieved?

---

[6] Ross A. Webber, *Management* (Homewood, Ill.: Irwin, 1975), p. 527.
[7] Napoleon Hill, *Think and Grow Rich* (Greenwich, Conn.: Fawcett, 1960), p. 36.

Some Rules for Making Decisions

Although the following rules are not cure-alls or substitutes for the difficult job of decision making, they do provide a logical framework for collecting and analyzing information and reaching sound conclusions.

1. Collect the facts. When you have collected the available, relevant facts, then make the decision. If all the information is not in yet, wait until you get it. Collecting information can become an escape hatch when people use it to avoid making decisions at all, but collecting the facts is a vital part of decision making and a valuable use of time.

2. Consult your feelings. Most supervisors develop an intuitive "second sense" about many decision-making situations. Your knowledge and past experiences are valuable guides. Do not ignore them. Freud once said:

> When making a decision of minor importance I have always found it advantageous to consider all the pros and cons. In vital matters, however, such as the choice of a mate or a profession, the decision should come from the unconscious, from somewhere within ourselves. In the important decisions of our inner life, we should be governed, I think, by the deep inner needs of our nature.[8]

3. Time your decisions wisely. It is important to know when *not* to make a decision. Research studies have shown that when we are low and feeling blue, our decisions tend to be aggressive and destructive. On the other hand, when we are feeling good, our behavior becomes more constructive and balanced. Understanding your own moods and behavior is crucial for timing decision making.

4. Do not assume too much. Although feelings and emotions are important, they are not the only areas to be considered in decision making. We should carefully weigh and interpret our emotions when they contradict all available information. Filling in the gaps with intuition and jumping to emotional conclusions can prove a dangerous game. We all have a tendency to assume too much from limited information. Give yourself the quiz on page 138; then give it to a friend for comparison. You are already suspicious because of the warning about assuming too much!

5. Communicate your plan. Communications skills play a critical role in decision making. You must be able to communicate your objectives to everyone involved. The person collecting information must tell you clearly what has been found. The people carrying out the solution must know exactly what the problem is and how they are to solve it. As you can see, decision making often involves more people than the decision maker alone. Communication failures can prevent even the most brilliant plan from succeeding.

6. Make a flexible decision. Any good decision includes the flexibility to allow for unforeseen occurrences and new information. Remember that once you have said "Yes," it is difficult to reverse that decision, but a "No" can more easily be changed to a "Yes" if a changing situation demands it.

Franklin D. Roosevelt was a great believer in flexible decisions. Frances Perkins, his Secretary of Labor, said of him, "He rarely got himself sewed tight to a program from which there was no turning back."

---

[8] Quoted in Robert L. Heilbroner, "How to Make an Intelligent Decision," *Think Magazine,* December 1960, p. 2.

"We have to do the best we know at the moment," he told one aide. "If it doesn't turn out all right, we can modify it as we go along."[9]

7. Follow through with your decision. There is a delicate balance between perfecting the plan and carrying it out. People who are afraid of action tend to spend most of their time perfecting never-used plans. If you never pass the preparatory stage, you cannot be an effective decision maker, no matter how much information you manage to collect. If you find yourself searching for more information when enough is available to make a good decision, you are probably avoiding the commitment necessary to put a decision into action.

8. Make decisions with courage. Andrew Jackson once said, "One person with courage makes a majority." Given information of equal amounts and quality with almost identical alternatives, the forceful, courageous decision maker in a group will carry more weight than a weak, indecisive member—even if they both make the same decision. When you finally face making a decision, you must ask yourself, "Will I have the courage to do what is best—even if everyone else does not agree?"

Every supervisor encounters situations which demand such responses every day. Courage is needed to oppose a majority even when you know you are right. Remember that although others have provided input, the responsibility for making a decision ultimately rests with you.

Bubbles La Vroom has been killed. Police have rounded up six suspects, all of whom are known criminals. All of them are known to have been near the scene of the murder at the approximate time it occurred. All had substantial motives for wanting Bubbles killed. However, Dirty Dan has been completely cleared of guilt.

1. Dirty Dan is known to have been near the scene of the killing of Bubbles La Vroom.	T	F	?
2. All six of the rounded-up gangsters were known to have been near the scene of the murder.	T	F	?
3. Only Dirty Dan has been cleared of guilt.	T	F	?
4. All six of the suspects were near the scene of Bubbles' murder at the approximate time it took place.			
5. The police do not know who killed Bubbles.	T	F	?
6. Bubbles' murderer did not confess of his own free will.	T	F	?
7. Dirty Dan did not kill Bubbles.	T	F	?
8. It is known that the six suspects were in the vicinity of the cold-blooded assassination.	T.	F	?
9. Bubbles La Vroom is dead.	T	F	?

(Answers at end of chapter exercises.)

Summary

Every aspect of a supervisor's responsibility involves choosing among alternatives and making decisions. Many people feel that decision making lies at the core of supervision. To function properly, the supervisor must develop an ability to make rational decisions.

In a crisis situation a supervisor should ask several questions that will help point to the correct solution: (1) What is the right thing to do? (2) What can

---

[9] Ibid.

go wrong? (3) How can I prevent the problem from happening? (4) What is my alternative plan? and (5) When should the alternative plan take over?

Solving problems should not be confused with decision making. Problem solving is the process that leads the supervisor toward a decision. The ten steps in the problem-solving process are (1) state the problem, (2) define the present state of affairs, (3) state the objective, (4) list the possible causes, (5) select the most likely cause, (6) list alternative solutions, (7) evaluate alternatives, (8) make a decision, (9) draw up a plan of action, and (10) evaluate the results.

A decision tree, or a series of if-then statements, can help in isolating potential problems, sources, and solutions. Four problems to guard against in using decision trees are (1) considering too many factors, (2) assigning probability values, (3) using trees for simple problems, and (4) using them as "answer machines."

Systematic goal setting and decision making can serve individuals as well as organizations. If you know where you are going, you can tell if you are getting there. Personal goal setting has much in common with dreaming, but once goals are chosen, hard work is required to achieve them.

Eight rules for making effective decisions are (1) collect the facts, (2) consult your feelings, (3) time your decisions wisely, (4) do not assume too much, (5) communicate your plan, (6) make a flexible decision, (7) follow through with your decision, and (8) make decisions with courage.

Any supervisor who can internalize the decision-making process by using intuition as well as facts should have little trouble dealing with minor problems or major crises. The key to successful decision making lies in understanding the process, then deciding to decide!

Key Terms

Crisis Management. Supervising by solving crucial, unexpected problems through planning ahead to avoid those problems.

Decision Making. The process of choosing among alternative courses of action.

Decision Tree. A series of if-then statements about possible solutions to a problem in which alternatives are gradually eliminated in reaching the best decision.

Delphi Method. A process of collecting group opinion through a series of questionnaires; initial responses are fed back to participants so that subsequent decisions can reflect input from all participants.

Japanese Approach to Decision Making. An approach that depends upon input from many individuals. The process is slow and careful. Decisions that do not have group support are usually rejected; consequently, the need to sell decisions is greatly reduced.

Nominal Group Technique (NGT). A group decision process whereby individual opinions or ideas are solicited and merged into a master list for the entire group. During this consolidation process, these ideas are evaluated and ranked.

Principle of Bounded Rationality. A theory of decision making which recognizes that people cannot gather all the information they need, cannot formulate problems adequately, can rarely estimate the actual value of rewards and costs, and can achieve objectively rational behavior only with the greatest difficulty.

Problem Solving. A logical, step-by-step process that leads one toward making a successful decision. The problem is identified, alternatives are formulated, and information is gathered before choices are made.

Satisficing. Choosing the first available alternative course of action that meets one's minimum standards for satisfaction.

Review Questions

1. Do you agree that decision making is "the core of supervision"? Why or why not?

2. Do you agree that preventive problem solving is a workable method of supervision? Defend your answer.

3. What should a supervisor do when a crisis occurs?

4. What is Murphy's Law of Management? How would you alter the law to fit a situation you are familiar with?

5. Can planning prevent the need for crisis management?

6. What is the difference between problem solving and decision making?

7. What are the basic steps to follow in problem solving?

8. List the advantages of using a decision tree to reach a decision. What are its disadvantages?

9. List and describe the steps you would take, beginning now, to become independently wealthy in one year.

10. Do personal feelings have a place in decision making?

11. When can a decision be changed? Can a supervisor ever change a decision and continue to be respected by his or her subordinates?

12. List and describe the rules for effective decision making. Can you add to the list from your own experience?

13. Describe a decision you recently made. How many rules for effective decision making did you use? Would your decision have been different or arrived at more easily had you been exposed to the rules earlier?

Exercises

I. Using a Decision Tree

Your instructor is going to be out of town during the next session and has asked you to take charge of the class. You have these alternatives: (1) prepare a lecture from the text, (2) lead a discussion, (3) show a film, (4) ask some other class members to help with a presentation, or (5) arrange for a guest speaker. Prepare a decision tree to help you choose the best solution. Add other alternatives you might consider. Be prepared to justify your eventual choice.

II. Learning Crisis Management Skills

You have supervised a medium-sized production plant for a couple of years. During that time, employees under your control have been guilty of a number of petty thefts and minor shoplifting. Employees are allowed to take home small amounts of company products for their personal use—primarily batch overruns and leftovers with no commercial value. However, the petty theft problem has mushroomed, and last night there was a major theft—an expensive table saw is missing. Write brief answers to each of the following questions:

1. What will you do about the increasing petty thefts?

2. What are you going to do about this major theft?

3. How could thefts have been avoided altogether?

4. How will you justify your decisions to your employees and to top management?

III. Making Dreams Work for You

Write a description of your biggest dream. What would you most like to accomplish if no practical obstacles stood in your way? Now write your answers to the following questions:

1. What decisions would you have to make to achieve your dream?

2. What would be the consequences of those decisions?

3. What are the major obstacles to fulfilling your dream? How might you get around those obstacles?

4. If unexpected problems arise and you cannot accomplish your dream, what new direction might you decide to follow?

IV. Answers for Bubbles LaVroom Quiz

1.	?	**6.**	?
2.	T	**7.**	?
3.	?	**8.**	?
4.	T	**9.**	T
5.	?		

Case 8 • Rona Crawford

Rona Crawford is a route supervisor for Peters Publishing Company, which publishes and distributes a variety of trade magazines. Recently, she hired Doug Brody, a thirty-one-year-old bachelor with considerable marketing experience, but who had quit his previous job because of disagreements with his supervisor. Rona feels that he is a very intelligent person with a pleasant personality and that he wants to do an excellent job for her.

Since most of Doug's job involves distributing magazines (taking orders, deliveries, picking up unused copies, and so on), he is provided with a company car—a new full-sized model. His first five weeks with the company have been labeled by Rona as "start up" time; Doug is new to the company and his work can only be "average." Her responsibility is to communicate suggestions to him, especially in the critical area of customer relations. In their conversations, Doug is not afraid to disagree with Rona. Although this bothers Rona, she has decided not to say anything in order to see how he will handle her flexibility.

On Monday morning, Doug came into Rona's office to inform her that someone had backed into his company car Friday night outside a restaurant while he was dining. Rona was astonished when she saw the car; the rear end was totally caved in and the bumper bent almost into an "L." She told Doug that she could not believe that this much damage could happen from someone backing into the car in a parking lot. She insisted Doug show her the scene of the accident, but Rona could find no broken glass, chipped paint, or other signs of the collision in the parking lot. She told Doug, "I'm sorry, but I don't believe your story. Go home and call me when you're ready to tell the truth." Doug left without a word.

1. Did Rona do the correct thing? If not, what should she have done?
2. What would you have done? Why?

Part 2

The next morning, Rona was looking at an $1800 estimate to repair Doug's car and wondering what to do. Although the company carried and paid for insurance on its cars, she and Doug had to complete an accident report before the claim could be sent to the insurance company.

The telephone rang and it was Doug. "Rona, I'm sorry but I lied to you yesterday. I jumped out of the car on a hill in my apartment parking lot without setting the brake. The car rolled down the hill into a stone wall."

Rona asked, "Why didn't you tell me the truth yesterday?"

"I was afraid you would think I was irresponsible and fire me," said Doug.

1. Now what should Rona do? Why?
2. Do you think Rona would be justified in firing Doug?

CHAPTER 9

Purposeful Planning

Christopher Columbus was not a model planner:
He did not know where he was going when he left,
He did not know where he was when he got there,
He did not know where he had been when he got back home.
And he went all the way on borrowed money.

Anonymous

Learning Objectives

- To construct a model of the planning process.
- To analyze how planning helps the supervisor effectively discharge responsibilities.
- To recognize that planning is a never-ending process that requires careful and constant attention.
- To list the most common reasons for the failure of plans as a warning against these pitfalls.
- To learn how to apply the techniques of the planning process to every phase of the supervisory job.

In most cases, people who fail to plan, plan to fail. Regardless of how competent and well-trained employees may be, daily work, changes, and improvements cannot be successful unless planning takes place. Often people will complain that they do not have enough time to plan a job thoroughly, but they always find time to do the job over when everything goes wrong. After all, it does not matter how fast you are going if you are on the wrong road.

Planning is a very important management function, since it determines the nature of the supervisor's other functions. Planning involves choosing an objective, plotting a course of action, and moving along the course to the desired goal. Frequently, planning takes valuable time, but planning ensures a much greater chance of success. Since planning must precede any of the other basic supervisory functions, it is easy to see that the person who considers planning unimportant is courting problems at every step along the chosen path to a goal.

There are two basic elements to planning: (1) assessing the future, or deciding what is likely to happen or what should happen, and (2) providing the means to make the future what you want it to be. Whether you are planning for tomorrow's agenda or for the next ten years, your plans will include these two parts.

The American Management Association suggests that the manager should divide the time for planning in the following percentages:

38 percent on problems that come up the same day.

40 percent on events or deadlines to occur in one week.

15 percent on events or deadlines to occur in one month.

5 percent on events or deadlines to occur in three to six months.

2 percent on events or deadlines to occur in a year or more.

Of course, these percentages are not absolute, and the nature of an individual's responsibility will certainly determine the way planning time should be divided. Probably the most useful message of the suggested list is its emphasis on looking to the future. In some cases, when supervisors speak of planning time, they really mean figuring out some solution for immediately pressing problems.

Planning Is a Process

Supervisors can better understand their role as planner if they view planning as a process of orderly steps. You must remember, however, that these planning steps may not be so orderly in reality. Complex change can occur very rapidly. Thus supervisors must have a feeling for the proper steps in planning so that they can sense when a step has been missed or needs to be repeated. In the following material we will become more familiar with these basic steps and how to apply them.

Choose Objectives

Objectives are the goals you wish to achieve or the desired results of your planning process. If your objectives are not clear-cut and carefully considered, then you are, in effect, planning to fail.

Charting your personal objectives for the next five years may be a useful exercise to aid in understanding this phase of planning. People who can tell you where they want to be, how much money they will be making, and what they want to be doing in five years are more likely to attain their objectives than individuals who drift through life without a plan.

It is often easy to become so absorbed in the method of achieving the goal that we forget the goal itself. This is a common complaint about government agencies and other bureaucracies—they forget about ultimate goals because the means to achieving those objectives become goals in themselves. When this happens, the emphasis has slipped into the wrong factor. For example, you may plan to set up a new evaluation procedure for your department, which will require additional paperwork from you and several of your employees. Is your goal to see that the paperwork is done, or is evaluation your objective? Paperwork is merely the *means* to achieve your ultimate objective— better evaluation. Can you imagine what directions you might take and how different your values would be if paperwork instead of evaluation were your goal?

Peter Drucker has listed eight critical areas where objectives must be set: (1) market standing, (2) innovation, (3) productivity, (4) physical and financial resources, (5) profitability, (6) workers' performance and development, (7) work performance and attitude, and (8) public responsibility.[1] Naturally, some of these responsibilities for objective-setting fall to top management rather than the supervisor. Nevertheless, supervisors often contribute to objective-setting sessions, and several of these categories apply directly to the supervisor's functions. Innovation, productivity, resource use, workers' performance and attitudes are all areas of prime concern to the supervisor. They require effective planning if goals are to be set and achieved.

At the supervisory level, objectives are usually targets for you or your department. Typically, these objectives are designed to help the organization move to its overall objective of profit or service. Most supervisory goals are short-range. Ideally, these goals will be specific and measurable rather than qualitative. Table 9-1 identifies typical performance goals for a supervisor.

Communicate Objectives

Although you may not want to share your personal objectives with everyone in your organization, the organization's major objectives should be known and understood by all. For example, one of the authors consults with a franchiser of real estate companies in the Southern states. The owners of the franchise organization have developed the following major objectives for their company:

1. To be the largest and most profitable real estate franchiser in the country.

2. To make our employees the highest paid personnel in the industry.

3. To make the real estate brokers we serve the most profitable in the industry.

4. To be a socially responsible corporate citizen.

Every week, the regional supervisors hold staff meetings and remind their employees of these company goals. Every month the goals are read out loud

[1] Peter F. Drucker, *The Practice of Management* (New York: Harper, 1964), p. 63.

Table 9-1. Sample Performance Goals for a Supervisor.

Area of Measurement	Past Year's Record	Goals for Next Year
Absences, lateness	7% absences, 8% lateness	5% absences, 3% lateness
Labor stability	Three quits (two long-time employees), one transfer	No resignation of employees with over three years service
Rejects and rework	Less than 2% rejects, rework average 8%	Rejects less than 1%, reduce rework to 5%
Percentage of job costs held within 5% of standard costs	89% average, 95% highest, 77% lowest in July	90% average, bring up low figure to 85% or better
Percentage of total jobs completed on schedule	84% average, 93% highest, 63% lowest in August	90% average, minimum acceptable 75%
Accidents	One lost-time accident, 37 calls to plant infirmary for minor problems	No lost time accidents, reduce number of infirmary visits to 25

and copies are distributed to all personnel at the monthly management meetings.

In addition, the supervisor's objectives for a department or work group must be clearly understood by workers. If department objectives blend with corporate goals in the minds of workers, the manager has completed an effective job of communication. The most effective communication of objectives occurs, however, when a supervisor can describe departmental and organizational objectives in terms of each worker's personal objectives.

Management by objectives is an approach to communicating goals that has gained popularity in recent years. It is an effective way of ensuring that all employees know and understand their company's objectives and the role each employee plays in reaching them. (See Figure 9-1, Management by Objectives Worksheet, for an example of how a company might inform workers of their specific roles.) There are three basic components of the management by objectives approach:

1. Employees should be evaluated according to what they accomplish, rather than how they spend their time. Most company presidents still believe that if they throw out the time clock, chaos will reign. Though in some cases this may be true, it is also true that management's real objective is not to have every worker spend eight hours a day behind a desk or on an assembly line. The goal is to get the work done. Loyalty, trustworthiness, and bravery are all worthy traits, but in a work situation it is more meaningful to ask, "Did you get the job done?" and "Did you do it well?"

2. Employees should know what the objectives are. Some workers do their jobs for thirty years, never really aware of their company's objectives or even of their own goals. In addition, many employees never know the standards on which the company evaluates their performance. If the rules of the game must be figured out while play is in progress, the rules are likely to change quite frequently. This situation also fosters shifting evaluation standards for employees. Every employee should know what is expected in clear-cut and simple terms. Employees should also know how performance will be judged

Specific Area of Responsibility _____

Item No.	1. Specific Responsibility (Describe briefly)	2. How Results Will Be Measured	3. Areas of Improvement	4. Priority Long Range | Short Range	

Figure 9-1. Typical Management by Objectives Worksheet.

and that a standardized evaluation process will be fairly applied. The supervisor should sit down with each employee individually to communicate clearly the expected levels of performance for the specific responsibilities for the job. This is where a comprehensive job description can be an invaluable tool for communication.

3. Employees should have a part in setting their own objectives. One of the easiest ways to make sure everyone understands the objectives is to let everyone share in setting them. Joint goal setting can be a highly effective means of listing objectives which are both reasonable and comprehensive. Research has shown that individual workers tend to set their own goals higher than their supervisors would have. Supervisors who set all departmental goals but neglect to tell workers about them are not only serving as poor communicators—they are missing out on the potential for higher quality and quantity of production from employees.

Identify Assumptions

Certain assumptions underlie all plans of action. These are often called *premises*. In most cases, the planner makes assumptions about what the future will be like, based on current trends, predictions, and projections. This is not the time for gazing into a crystal ball, but for gathering all the available information about what the future may hold. This may range from determining which employees will be unable to work tomorrow (necessitating hiring of temporary workers), to looking at next year's production goals and determining if more machinery or space is needed by mid year.

Though the processes are similar, there are some important differences between long-range and short-range planning. Long-range plans may include a series of short-range plans. On the other hand, some plans that seem short-range may have implications for the organization or a particular department for many years. Risks are lessened when short-range plans are used—the supervisor who plans for tomorrow has a better chance of being right than the one who plans ten years ahead. But all plans must be evaluated in terms of both short- and long-term implications.

When making short-range plans, you can often assume that the future will be very similar to the past. Employee attitudes, production rates, working conditions, and relationships with outside suppliers or distributors may not change much from day to day. This assumption becomes more dangerous, however, when plans extend for more than a year.

Another assumption that may underlie both long- and short-range plans is the supervisor's attitude toward workers. These attitudes and assumptions will be discussed more thoroughly in the chapter on leadership. For now, you should understand that if workers are assumed to be lazy, incompetent, and uncooperative, the plan will be very different from one which assumes they are able and willing workers.

Survey Resources

We have spoken of general objectives—perhaps to increase production, achieve higher worker morale, get a pay raise, or all of these. Now we must consider what resources are available to help meet these goals. Each work situation includes problems and promises that will affect fulfillment of objectives. Unless you know what these are, you are dreaming and not actually working toward goals.

You may face resource limitations in time, money, work space, number of employees, type of employees, higher management considerations, staff assistance, material resources (raw materials, equipment, and services), and company, union, or government regulations. When you identify these limitations, you should then consider each one carefully. Remember that often what is seen as a limitation can become an excuse for doing nothing. If you allow these limitations to become excuses, you are limiting yourself even more.

At times it becomes obvious that there are simply not enough resources available to achieve a certain goal. Even so, the first stages of planning have not been lost. You must begin again by readjusting and setting more realistic objectives, but at least you are now aware of what can and cannot be accomplished.

Only in science fiction have people visited the future and returned to tell about it. No one can accurately predict what will happen, how technology will be altered, what resources will disappear and what new ones will become available. Estimating resource availability for the years ahead is a slippery business at best.

Check on Policy

In weak organizations, policy may be the exact opposite of common sense. Employees may remark, "Nobody knows why—it's just our policy!" In fact, of course, most policies are established to avoid repeating a trial-and-error process which has already indicated one best way to do something. Generally, they reflect careful study or extensive experience.

In this sense, policies are shortcuts for thinking. They also serve as limiting boundaries within which the supervisor must set objectives, excluding any course of action that would be unacceptable or unmanageable under company policy. Sometimes, the existence of policy obstructs a direct means to the goal. In many cases, however, the most direct means is not the most beneficial for the company or its employees. It may be unethical, too expensive, or too difficult.

Sometimes policies do not originate within the organization. Federal, state, and local government contains numerous regulatory agencies that control many aspects of business life. For example, several agencies lay out detailed instructions for the care and handling of workers, and the supervisor must be aware of these regulations and the limitations they place on objective-setting and planning.

Usually, policies are created at higher levels in an organization. For the most part, the supervisor's challenge is to apply existing policy in making decisions and interpreting corporate policy for subordinates. Although the supervisor may create departmental policies, the greatest challenge will be to interpret, implement, and explain the meaning of existing policies. To be able to exercise the responsibilities effectively, supervisors must fully understand existing policy and know how to apply it fairly and appropriately.

As mentioned before, policies often are substituted for thinking. Although many policies are based on logical, intelligent decisions, some policies become obsolete as time passes and should be retracted or changed. If a supervisor discovers obsolete policies blocking plans to create a more efficient, productive work force, he or she should investigate every possible method of effecting a policy change.

Develop Alternative Plans

If there is only one possible course of action, planning is not necessary. The possibility for alternative decisions makes planning necessary and challenging. Planning is really a series of decisions. Experienced supervisors know that in decision making, careful consideration and development of alternatives can often solve a troublesome problem.

If your objective is to create more comfortable, sanitary working conditions, you will want to consider the various ways to achieve this goal. You might ask top management for money to equip an employee lounge or dining room. You could divide clean-up duties among several lower-level workers. You could sponsor a contest among employees to see which section could keep its work area cleanest. You may require workers to dress in company-supplied uniforms. You may post cleanliness messages in conspicuous locations around the plant. In short there are many possible activities, all of which may or may not lead to the desired objective. Considering these alternatives can help you decide which course requires the least effort for maximum results.

Developing and considering alternatives can cause regrets later when the method not chosen might have worked out better in the long run. In his famous poem "The Road Not Taken" Robert Frost suggests,[2]

[2] From *The Poetry of Robert Frost,* edited by Edward Connery Lathem. Copyright 1916, © 1969 by Holt, Rinehart and Winston, Inc. Copyright 1944 by Robert Frost. Reprinted by permission of Holt, Rinehart and Winston, Publishers. Reprinted also by permission of the Estate of Robert Frost and Jonathan Cape Ltd.

I shall be telling this with a sigh
Somewhere ages and ages hence:
Two roads diverged in a wood and I—
I took the one less traveled by,
And that has made all the difference.

In most cases, though, regrets will be considerably greater when other alternatives are not even considered. Failing to consider alternatives may lead you to overlook an important option. You will learn to eliminate quickly those alternatives which are too costly, too time-consuming, unethical, or against policy. But it is always better to consider too many alternatives than to settle on one course of action without looking at others.

Compare Alternative Plans

When you have identified all possible alternative methods of reaching a goal, you should begin to evaluate each alternative in terms of cost, availability, and expected results. Some of the alternatives will be subject to the limitations mentioned above; some will be less efficient than others; and some can be successfully followed through.

Let us go back to our example in the previous section. You have identified all the alternatives you can think of in achieving your objective of more comfortable, sanitary working conditions. Now you begin to evaluate each alternative in terms of its feasibility and productivity. A talk with top management reveals the company cannot spare money for improvements or uniforms. The union prevents the assignment of those extra clean-up duties without its specific permission. Most of the alternatives have been eliminated by resource or policy restraints, and you are left with a choice between sponsoring a contest and posting messages in the plant. Neither of these requires considerable amounts of money, and both may make workers more aware of their surroundings and more willing to care for them properly.

In some cases, when considering the relative merits of various alternatives, you may want to use a series of if-then statements to clarify your thinking and to make your decision more objective and logical. As you know from Chapter 8, if-then statements compose a "decision tree" and work like this: "If I sponsor a contest, then workers may not respond. If they don't respond, then I can post messages. If I post messages, then the employees may start taking better care of their surroundings. If they start taking better care of things, then I will achieve my goal and maybe a raise, too."

Elaborate consideration of alternatives can appear a waste of time—until you begin to waste time because you have chosen a method without considering other possibilities.

Finalize the Choice

Whenever you decide not to decide, you make the worst possible decision. When you allow decisions to be made for you, your planning process has proved a waste of time. Courageous leadership is a key function of professional management. It is also an asset for the supervisor who learns to decide between attractive alternatives.

When you have identified a method that meets all requirements, conforms to all limitations, and will achieve your goal efficiently and effectively, you will realize that the process of eliminating alternatives has made the decision for you. Unfortunately, this ideal situation occurs only rarely in reality. Decisions are not often so clear-cut and simple. Usually, a choice must be made among alternatives only slightly more attractive than those already eliminated. Of the alternatives remaining, one may be only slightly better than the others. Of course, if decision making were a simple task, a supervisor would earn no more than regular workers.

When faced with alternatives and the necessity of making a choice, a supervisor must not be inflexible; when the decision is made, a commitment is required. In one of his fables, Aesop tells the story of a donkey that starved to death because it was an equal distance between two bales of hay. The donkey wanted to make the very best choice, but it deliberated until it was too late to choose either alternative. A supervisor who will not decide between alternative strategies and take a strong stand on a specific choice may be demonstrating some characteristics of the donkey.

Develop New Procedures and Rules

Rules differ from policies in that *rules* are generally specific, while *policies* are designed to describe a company's attitudes in general terms. Procedures and rules establish step-by-step guides for action within a general policy framework. In effect, procedures are the subpolicies of an organization.

Established procedures can be viewed as a sequence of steps that must be taken in order to accomplish some stated objective. Once a method is chosen which the supervisor believes will allow goals to be achieved most effectively, the next decision is how that method is to be followed. What new requirements will be made of workers? How will their behavior be altered? What are the best administrative procedures to use? How much paperwork will be involved?

In many cases, supervisors already have a list of procedures to follow. They play a key role in seeing that company rules are enforced and that discipline is swift and fair. Creating and enforcing procedures and rules are a necessary part of his job.

Procedures are useful in a number of other instances. If one operation must be performed many times, a standard of performance may be helpful to ensure that every worker grasps the preferred procedure and meets the standard, thereby maintaining the quality of output. The same operation can then be performed consistently by numerous workers.

When new employees receive training, procedures can help them learn the organization's standards and expectations and avoid the time-consuming and frustrating trial-and-error method of learning a task. Instead, they can follow a procedure worked out by someone with considerably more knowledge and experience.

Part of any supervisor's continuing responsibility is to improve accepted procedures. The professional manager is always alert to opportunities for improvement and never assumes that the traditional way is the only way. New approaches that save a step or a movement represent a victory that will help keep each worker's "streamlining instinct" at a peak.

The supervisor may choose to examine the effectiveness of the procedure under consideration by illustrating it with a flow chart, a graphic representation of a process from beginning to end. Standard flow-chart formats are available for most common job analyses, but the supervisor may need to create a specialized way of representing activities unique to the operation.

The surest route to improved procedures is careful attention to the factors of time, distance, and order. When these elements are out of alignment, inefficiency results. Most production tasks involve three distinct stages that may be analyzed for possible corrective measures.[3] There is the *make-ready stage*, when the employee is setting up a machine, getting information, or pulling together the resources required for the job. Next comes the *doing stage*, when the worker is actually producing or providing an item or service. Finally, there is the *putting-away stage*, which involves cleaning up, following up, or making arrangements for whatever comes next. The creative manager may discover ways to save money at each stage by resorting to any of these four approaches. Many tasks can be *eliminated* altogether. Others can be *combined* or *simplified*. And, sometimes, money can be saved by changing an operation's *position* in the process—the point at which a particular step is carried out.

Rules differ from procedures because rules generally stand alone—they are not usually part of an orderly sequence that must be followed. In football, rules of behavior are established in advance; referees do not discuss what an appropriate penalty should be. When the rules are broken, punishment results. Everyone should know what the rules of an organization are and the consequences of breaking those rules.

A wise supervisor recognizes, however, that all the planning in the world will not meet an objective without the cooperation and understanding of the employees involved. Procedures and rules are one means of ensuring that everyone understands what is expected.

Preparing a Budget for Approval

Budgeting may or may not be a factor in supervisory planning. If the supervisor's objectives and methods for reaching them require extensive financing or reallocation of resources, it would be foolish to proceed with the plan without preparing a budget. Although budgets are usually constructed in terms of dollars and cents, any unit may be budgeted—square footage, work-hours, or number of bottle caps used per hour.

Table 9-2 is an example of a budget prepared for approval by Janet Jones, production supervisor for a chemical manufacturing plant. Janet has reviewed worker efficiency and plant production carefully and has decided that production can be increased 15 percent within a year with no additional employees. Her method includes replacing several minor pieces of obsolete equipment, reorganizing the work force into more efficient and interrelated departments, and beginning an employee incentive program. She has talked with sales representatives about equipment pricing, has secured information on the cost of various incentive schemes, and has consulted the company's construction department for a bid on the carpentry work needed to reorganize.

[3] Based on Lester Bittel, *What Every Supervisor Should Know*, 4th ed. (New York: McGraw-Hill, 1980), pp. 504–505.

Table 9-2. A Budget Prepared for a Chemical Manufacturing Plant.

Projected Expenses	Cost
Equipment	
Automatic silk-screen printer (1)	$ 8,700
Thermostatic controls for raw material storage tanks (10 @ $55)	550
Semiautomatic bottle capper (1)	5,150
Construction	
Large work tables for packing and labeling department (2 @ $75)	150
Remove partitions between raw materials and chemical mixing departments	125
Incentives	
Trophy (one-time purchase) for monthly award to most productive department	25
Piece-rate bonuses for employees exceeding established quota (average monthly figure = $50 × 12)	600
Create training manual for job enrichment (1)	250
Subscription for monthly incentive posters	60
Total projected cost	$15,610

After Janet presents her budget to management, its task is to decide if her projected 15 percent increase in production is worth the expenditure of almost $16,000. She has given them the information they need in clear, understandable, and usable form. If the current value of annual production is $200,000 or more, the firm will certainly give serious consideration to Janet's ideas. What other questions should management ask?

Budgets are no more than statements of expected costs. They are not hard and fast factual statements of what costs will actually be. Flexibility must be built into any budget to allow for unforeseen expenses, but flexibility should not be used to mask inefficiency and waste.

Develop Timetables

Although the cost of a project is a major factor in planning, time can be an equally important ingredient. In fact, as one maxim points out, "Time is money."

Experienced supervisors will recognize the value of setting deadlines. When subordinates receive a task, it is useful for them to know when they will be expected to have the task completed. An exact completion date gives the worker a clear idea of the time limitation and provides an opportunity to budget personal time so the assignment can be finished.

Although completion dates are important, mileposts should also be laid out to check the progress of the project as it moves from phase to phase. When a milepost deadline rolls around, the supervisor can gauge whether or not the project is proceeding on schedule and anticipate exactly where unforeseen problems may delay completion.

In our previous example, Janet Jones estimates that it will take three months to complete the improvements and establish the programs in her plan. Her timetable might look something like that in Table 9-3.

Table 9-3. Sample Timetable for the Jones Plan

Project Phases	Expected Completion Date
Begin to implement plan	Jan. 1
Begin collecting data for monthly trophy award	Jan. 15
Complete construction work	Feb. 15
Begin awarding trophy on monthly basis	Feb. 15
Begin incentive bonus plan	Mar. 1
Begin posting monthly posters	Mar. 1
Complete equipment installation	Mar. 15
Complete job enrichment training manual	Mar. 30
All phases should be completed by March 30	

When February 15 arrives, Janet will be able to determine immediately whether the construction portion of her plan has been completed and whether the plan is proceeding according to schedule. She will also have indicated to management that she is aware of time constraints in planning and budgeting and has established a realistic schedule to help her efficiently control each phase of her report.

Establish Standards for Evaluation

Once the completed plan is put into action, that plan becomes a model of the expected result. For this reason the careful supervisor will build controls into the plans and determine in advance how performances will be evaluated. In one sense, evaluation can be a simple matter. If the project is completed and produces the desired results, then it can be considered successful.

Supervisors who plan their decisions help guide the future of their companies. From the "firing line," they can best see what needs to be done in their departments and how it should be done. Supervisors, then, must value those hours spent at the drawing board. Though some planning stages may seem tedious and unnecessary, they can pay off when a successful plan achieves the initial objective. There is no better proof of a supervisor's capabilities and foresight.

Why Do Plans Fail?

Successful planning requires involvement of every manager from chief executive officer to first-line supervisors. In a study of more than 350 U.S. and European corporations to discover common failures in planning,[4] results showed that unsuccessful plans can usually be traced to any of these factors:

1. Managers at all levels are not involved in determining corporate goals. Because all managers and supervisors have some degree of control

[4] K. A. Ringbakk, "Why Planning Fails," *European Business,* July 1970.

over and responsibility for what happens in their organization, their opinions, information, and support should be considered in planning or a company risks a much greater chance of failure.

2. Planning is not systematic or the phases of the planning process are not well understood. As we mentioned earlier, if one planning step is omitted, the planning process is incomplete. Personnel at all levels tend to overlook important factors and forget crucial limitations when some steps are forgotten.

3. A planning department has sole responsibility for corporate planning. Though the planning department may be replete with textbook experts, supervisors and managers involved in the organization's daily activities see firsthand many of the restraints and opportunities within the corporate structure.

4. Management assumes that once a plan is committed to paper, everything will happen on schedule. A carefully written plan, if filed away, holds no value for a company. Follow-up checks are necessary for each phase of implementing the plan. The supervisor would do well to keep the total plan nearby and make periodic checks on how the work in each phase is progressing.

5. The plan attempts to do too much in too little time. You cannot hope to completely reorganize your work force, replace all your equipment, and begin an "instant" incentive program in a month's time. Yet many corporate plans attempt too much too quickly. Knowing your limitations should help avoid this pitfall in planning.

6. Forecasting and financial planning are confused with comprehensive planning. As you can see from the list of planning stages, forecasting and budgeting are only two aspects of a very complex process. Any corporation that relies solely on these two activities for developing plans can anticipate serious trouble.

7. Inadequate information is obtained. If you have planned to reorganize your employees—assigning and changing duties and shifting work locations, for instance—and have failed to ascertain union regulations or information to make your plan workable, you have not collected enough information to make your plan workable. Information from all available sources must be gathered and assembled before a final plan can be successfully developed.

8. Too much emphasis is placed on a single aspect of planning. Some corporations spend all their planning time setting objectives, never investigating alternative methods or discussing how to achieve their objectives. In such cases, true planning has not taken place, and it is easy to see why failure occurs.

Summary

In most cases, people who fail to plan have planned to fail. Planning determines the nature of a supervisor's other functions. It usually takes time to plan, but planning greatly increases your prospects of success.

There are two basic elements to planning: (1) assessing the future, and (2) providing the means to carry the plan out. Planning is a process of orderly steps. In reality, of course, change is rapid and complex, so a supervisor should develop an instinctive sense of when the proper steps have been followed. The basic steps in planning are these:

1. Choose objectives. Make certain your goals are clear-cut and easily understandable, and that means are clearly separated from ends.

2. Communicate objectives. Make sure everyone involved knows what the objectives are. Management by objectives is a popular technique for ensuring communication and accomplishment of goals.

3. Identify assumptions. The assumptions underlying planning decisions may include ideas of what the future will bring as well as the supervisor's assumptions about employees.

4. Identify assumptions. The assumptions underlying planning decisions may include ideas of what the future will bring as well as the supervisor's assumptions about employees.

5. Survey resources. Find out what resources are available and what limitations exist.

6. Check on policy. Policy will spell out some limitations imposed by the company, the union, or the government.

7. Develop alternate plans. It is better to consider too many alternatives than to settle on one course of action without looking at others.

8. Compare alternative plans. Once alternatives are identified, you can evaluate them in terms of cost, availability of various resources, and expected results.

9. Choose a method for achieving the objective. Considering alternatives and identifying limitations will help you narrow the field. You must then make a decision and stick to it while remaining fairly flexible on details.

10. Develop new procedures and rules. Where necessary and possible, revise and improve established courses of action that inform all employees of management's expectations.

11. Prepare a budget for approval. Collect information on the cost of implementing your plan, and present it to management for consideration.

12. Develop timetables. Time is money, and a timetable will help you avoid the inefficient use of time while implementing your plan. Milestones and completion dates give you a means of periodically reviewing progress.

13. Establish standards for evaluation. If your plan achieves its objective, it has been successful.

The following major causes of planning failure have been identified:

- The total management system is not involved in forming the corporate goals.
- The planning is not systematic.
- The planning department has sole responsibility for the corporate planning.
- The management assumes that a plan on paper will work itself out.
- The plan attempts to do too much within too little time.
- Forecasting and financial planning are substituted for comprehensive planning.
- Inadequate information is obtained.
- Too much emphasis is placed on a single aspect of planning.

Without effective planning, all the supervisor's other functions will be ill-defined. With this skill, however personal, departmental and corporate success is more likely.

Key Terms

Assumption. A statement or belief generally expected to be true without the proof that may underlie other statements, beliefs, or actions.

Budget. Usually, a schedule of estimated expenses and financial limitations in planning. Also a numerical expression of expectations.

Forecast. A prediction of what may happen. Forecasts in business, either long-range or short-range, involve certain assumptions about the economy, including the labor force and sources of supply. Planners use forecasting to plan the course of their organizations.

Management By Objectives. A system of managing in which the supervisor and subordinates together set goals and evaluate performance by the workers' ability to meet goals within specified time and financial restraints.

Milepost. An interim deadline within a plan or time schedule.

Objective. A goal, something to work toward.

Planning. The process of choosing an objective, plotting a course of action, and following the steps toward the desired goal.

Policy. Limitations set by the company, the union, or the government that the supervisor must consider in setting objectives and accomplishing them.

Procedure. A series of steps that must be performed in sequence to accomplish the stated objective.

Rule. An action guideline that is usually not part of a sequence and is more specific in imposing limitations than a policy statement.

Timetable. A plan for accomplishing the objective, which includes expected completion dates of various project phases.

Review Questions

1. Write a paragraph in which you describe to the supervisor the importance of planning.
2. In choosing objectives, what is meant by the distinction between means and ends? Describe ways in which you can guard against concentrating on the means and neglecting the end result desired.
3. How can a supervisor's failure to communicate objectives affect the planning process?
4. What role does forecasting the future have in planning?
5. What planning resources are available to supervisors? Why is it important to know the resources that are available, and in what quantities?
6. Describe the functions and limitations of policy in planning.
7. Are there strategic alternatives in every supervisory situation?
8. What are the roles of forecasting and evaluation in comparing alternative plans?
9. List the differences between policy and procedure.
10. List the differences between procedures and rules.
11. It is said that budgets and timetables are valuable in planning. Why?
12. What is the final step in the planning process? Why is it important?

13. It is said that most plans fail. Why?

14. Can a supervisor "supervise" and leave planning to others? Why or why not?

Exercises

I. Where Do You Want to Be in Five Years?

Write down your personal goals and objectives for the next five years. What kinds of things would you like to accomplish? Where do you want to be in terms of a career and your personal life? The following list of topics may be helpful as a guide, but you should cover only those which are important to you. Add any unlisted areas that interest you.

- Place of residence.
- Job—type of work; status of position.
- Annual income, savings, investments.
- Family.
- Education.
- Hobbies or talent.
- Social life.

II. Where Do You Want to Be in One Month?

A. Think about what you want to accomplish in the next month (based on some of the areas listed above if they apply). Make a list of these objectives and draw up a timetable for completing them. Be sure to set up mileposts along the way so you can check your progress from time to time.

B. During each week in the month, try to make some progress toward accomplishing the objectives on your list. At the end of the month, compare your actual achievements with those you hoped to achieve. Were you a good planner and manager of your own time? If you did not reach most of your goals, what went wrong? Why? How might these problems be overcome?

Case 9 • Mike Matson

Mike Matson is the administrative manager of the adult education program of a community college. His departmental budgets are due in the dean's office in one week and he has two staff supervisors on the assignment: Karen Burton is in charge of the word processing center, and Jim Chapman is in charge of student services and information. Each has been a supervisor for about three years at the college.

Mike calls them into his office to ascertain their progress on their budgets. Hearing that all is going well and that they will both submit them to his office before the deadline, Mike decides to ask them how well their representative departments faired for the past year, assuming that they have enough data to make some preliminary predictions.

Karen responds: "Overall, my department has done well. Our total output in the past eleven months is 13 percent above the previous year. Requests for work to be redone are down by 17 percent, absenteeism is down 7 percent, and turnover is down 10 percent. We should end the year 3 percent under budget. However, I am concerned about photocopying, which is up 20 percent, and carbon paper consumption, which is up 18 percent. I don't know what I can do about carbon paper use, but I have issued a directive that daily photocopying counts must be submitted to me by each employee. I am really discouraged because I've tried so hard to make everything work out right."

Jim brought no detailed figures with him to the meeting, but he was optimistic about his unit's performance. "Basically, everything in my department is going great. We haven't had as many problems this year as we've had over the past three years, and the problems that have developed have been handled efficiently. My people seem to be happy and I think they do a good job. We are operating well within budget. In fact, I think we will have a little left over at the end of the year."

1. Evaluate the approaches to planning taken by the two supervisors.
2. Can you suggest ways for each supervisor to improve the planning process?

CHAPTER 10

Let's Get Organized

Organize a great venture as you would cook a small fish. Don't overdo it.

Lao-Tse

Learning Objectives

- To identify the purposes and problems in organizing large numbers of people.
- To compare *organization* and *efficient organization.*
- To identify the complex relationships among the various factors in organized production, such as division of work, processes, structure, and span of control.
- To devise techniques of working effectively within the organization to achieve goals and objectives.
- To increase the individual's ability to cope with strains created by the growing size and scope of organizations.

Organization and Efficiency

Like an orchestra, a business organization is not composed solely of individual contributions, but of the relations formed between them. Carry this analogy a bit further. In each, the structure restricts the individual expression of each musician or worker. The orchestra members play many different instruments and fulfill different roles, but to produce a concert each member must be restricted in some way from "doing his or her own thing." The supervisor (conductor) knows the organizational plan (the musical score) and has the overview necessary to direct the group toward its final goal.

Because organization implies a group of people working together toward a common purpose, departmental organization is the *result* of a supervisor's efforts. The result may be good or bad, efficient or inefficient, but an organization does exist wherever people are trying to accomplish some common goal.

To organize is a function of supervision. When supervisors set up relationships between people, resources, and work, they organize. They are responsible for making sure that the goals are accomplished and that everyone understands what to do and why. If a supervisor organizes effectively, the goal will be achieved efficiently.

Efficient organization groups people and processes together in ways that prevent wasting time or resources. Note the difference between *organization* and *efficient organization* in the following message, which was handed down by top management of a not-so-thriving young company:

> "AEGIIIMNQSTTTUW." The boss's secretary had organized each letter in the memo alphabetically. Somehow, this orderly arrangement of letters failed to impress the supervisor or the workers. When the letters were more efficiently organized and the proper relationship established, the message read: "QUIT WASTING TIME."

Whenever all parts are present in *some* order, organization exists, but efficient organization exists only when parts are arranged in their *most productive* relationships. When supervisors organize people and resources efficiently, they and their people enjoy the satisfaction of high productivity and the accomplishment of their mutual objectives.

Foundations of Organization

Traditional discussions of organization focus on four areas: (1) division of work, (2) scalar and functional processes, (3) structure, and (4) span of control. We shall use these four topics to organize our discussion of organization and to simplify and categorize elements of classical organization theory.

Division of work is the earliest and most basic foundation of organization. All other areas of organization are based on this foundation. Scalar and functional processes consist of dividing tasks into specialized areas. Structure refers to the distribution and nature of authority-responsibility relationships. Finally, span of control problems are concerned with the number and complexity of specialized functions under a supervisor's control.

Division of Work

Eighteenth-century Scotch economist Adam Smith is credited with creating the phrase "division of labor" in his book *The Wealth of Nations* (1776). The process was in use, however, long before it was given a name. Even in prehistoric times, some members of a tribe hunted, some planted crops, others made pots or ornaments or weapons, and a few served as leaders. In medieval England, centuries before industrialization, the textile industry was divided into groups of workers specializing in spinning, weaving, dyeing, and printing.

Studies of the eighteenth and nineteenth centuries indicate that the division of work concept was used in manufacturing pins. Production was broken into several steps and spread out among several workers. For instance, a small pin manufacturer employed ten people, each completing one to three steps of the total process. Working in this way, the group manufactured 4800 pins every day. If each worker had produced a pin from start to finish individually, the group as a whole would have produced no more than 200 pins a day.

Advantages of specialization. Economists who studied early examples of manufacturing discovered three reasons why dividing the work increased production. First, workers' skills increase when they concentrate on a particular task. Second, no time is lost in shifting from one task to another. Third, a division of labor encourages the invention and use of specialized machines capable of greatly increasing production.

Supervisors who experimented during the 1800s placed great emphasis on the classical concept of division of labor. They considered increased productivity their chief goal. Consequently, they paid little attention to possible ill-effects on their workers, whose creative satisfaction and emotional well-being was often severely neglected.

Disadvantages of specialization. Recently, behavioral scientists have begun to criticize the classical division of labor. They argue that workers suffer from boredom, monotony, and dissatisfaction when limited to overly specialized task assignments. When division of labor is too specialized, it treats a person like a machine. If individuals repeat the same operation with monotonous regularity every day, they lose interest in the work and cannot relate the job to the final product. Because they cannot deviate from the prescribed way of completing a task, there is no opportunity for creativity to improve the product or increase production.

In the early 1950s, Charles R. Walker and Robert H. Guest studied the dehumanizing effects of division of labor on workers in an automobile assembly plant.[1] They found that many workers intensely disliked their jobs because they were mechanically paced, repetitive, and gave no sense of accomplishment. Naturally, morale among these workers was very low. The study also found that workers who performed more operations tended to be more satisfied with their jobs. Additional studies[2] confirmed these findings and led to the following insights and recommendations.

Making jobs bigger and better. Some organizations have developed special strategies to combat the social and psychological problems caused by division of labor. Among these strategies, job enlargement, job rotation, and participation in decision making have often proved effective.

Job enlargement structures the production process so that each worker per-

[1] C. R. Walker and R. H. Guest, *The Man on the Assembly Line* (Cambridge: Harvard U. P., 1952).
[2] Robert H. Guest, "The Man on the Assembly Line Revisited," Paper delivered at the Thirty-Sixth Annual Meeting, Academy of Management, Kansas City, August 12, 1976.

forms several steps. Workers must be more highly trained, but they suffer less from boredom. Many companies have found efficiency increases and morale rises when workers perform several different operations rather than a single, mechanical task.

Perhaps the most famous study of the effects of job enlargement occurred at IBM's Endicott plant.[3] Thomas J. Watson, Sr., then president of the company, found a young woman standing idle by her machine waiting for the setup person to make an adjustment. In talking with her, Watson found that she knew how to adjust the machine herself but was forbidden to do so by company rules. Watson then decided to let the operators make their own adjustments. The results in improved morale, productivity, and quality were startling. IBM then began to expand some job responsibilities at the Endicott plant, and worker interest and efficiency continued to increase. When the reorganization was complete, each machine operator was responsible for setting up the job, sharpening the tools, operating the equipment, and inspecting the work. This start-to-finish progression allowed each operator to see the importance of his or her own role in the total process.

The Endicott findings suggest that job enlargement can raise employee morale and interest, lower production costs, and improve product quality. In addition, the task of supervision was greatly simplified, since workers became responsible for many aspects of their jobs which had been closely supervised by others.

The concept of job enlargement can be applied to many areas which are more sophisticated than an assembly-line operation. Think for a moment how you might expand the following jobs to raise the interest and morale of the workers:

> David Nichols works part-time for a large discount department store. His job consists of moving cartons of merchandise, collected by the warehouse supervisor, to various departments, where department supervisors take charge and direct the shelving of the merchandise by other employees.
>
> Susan Dennis operates a camera at another department store, which records each customer's check, identification, and photograph. The customer service representative is then responsible for checking that customer's signature card and identification and approving the check after Susan has recorded it on camera.
>
> Allan Martin's job in a chain restaurant is to make sure customers' water glasses are kept filled.
>
> Janice Johnson works all day at a ten-key adding machine, adding up the previous day's checks and invoices for the bookkeeper at a large insurance company.
>
> George Watts works for the physical plant department of a large factory. His job is to empty trashcans in a major assembly building.

After this exercise in hypothetical job enlargement, it should be easier for you to apply this concept to your own supervisory problems.

Job rotation involves periodically moving a worker from one job assignment to another. Individuals who switch jobs have less opportunity to become bored and disinterested with what they are doing and are better able to grasp the total picture of the company's operation and their role in it. If supervisors choose to use this strategy rather than job enlargement, the supervisor can select the best time to rotate a worker, and jobs do not have to be redesigned.

There are, however, some disadvantages to job rotation. Even though workers may not be as bored, considerable retraining may be required to enable employ-

---

[3] See Ernest Dale, *Organization* (New York; A. M. A., 1967), p. 132.

ees to change tasks. Second, workers may come to feel that just as they develop skill at a particular job, the company moves them on to another one. Finally, and perhaps most seriously, informal work groups that arise whenever people work together are disrupted. These disruptions can diminish employee morale, which may offset any gains made by decreasing boredom.

The participation approach allows employees to participate in decisions affecting them and their jobs. In this strategy, authority is redistributed and "moved down," in a sense. Companies that employ this approach reason that people are more likely to accept decisions they helped to make. Some companies have set up employee committees to make decisions relating to job design, salary, promotion, retirement plans, and complaint and appeal procedures. Naturally, this approach assumes that supervisors are willing to relinquish some of their authority to gain increased employee satisfaction through participation.

Peter F. Drucker has outlined some guides for designing individual jobs:[4]

1. The job assigned to an individual or a group should constitute a distinct phase of the work process—a phase that enables the employee to see a specific result from some completed chore.

2. The speed and rhythm of the job should always depend only on the performance of the person or group that performs it; the worker should be allowed to perform it a little faster at times and a little slower at other times.

3. Each job should embody some challenge, some element of skill or judgment.

Scalar and Functional Processes

The term *scalar and functional processes* can be more easily understood by looking at supervisory processes within an organization in terms of a "ladder," or a chain of command. This organizational theory assumes that there is someone "at the top" who makes final decisions. Other positions on the ladder include various functions and responsibilities delegated by the boss. Although a supervisor may head a particular chain of command, chances are that he or she is responsible to a superior in the organizational structure.

Delegation is an important supervisory skill and one that is often abused. Though supervisors are responsible for many jobs, they cannot and should not attempt to do every job. Delegation seems a simple skill—you simply allow the worker to do the job. In reality, it is usually quite difficult. Supervisors who take their jobs seriously are often unwilling to trust those below them on the organizational ladder to do their jobs competently.

When supervisors designate an employee to do a particular task, they must be willing to "let go" and trust the worker to accomplish the job satisfactorily. Employees often complain, "My boss wants me to do the job but won't give me the authority I need to do it." Both sides of this statement must be understood if the supervisor is to delegate effectively. First, the boss should provide employees with adequate authority to complete their tasks. On the other hand, the supervisor is ultimately responsible for the acts of subordinates. Whatever happens, the supervisor will get praise or blame from the high ups in the company.

[4] Peter F. Drucker, *The Practice of Management* (New York: Harper, 1954), pp. 295–96.

Responsibilities should be pushed as far down the organizational ladder as possible. People at the lowest structural level who possess the necessary competence and information should be allowed to take responsibility for their jobs. Many workers apparently feel that they are not responsible for the quality of their work and, therefore, do not need to perform efficiently and effectively. Delegation of authority often eliminates this attitude and increases employee morale and job interests.

A supervisor delegates job duties (but not ultimate responsibility) and authority to get the job done. Job duties define the task. Responsibility is the obligation to account for what has been done. Authority gives the power to act officially within the scope of delegation. In delegating a job, the supervisor is telling the employee, "I trust you to get the job done. Your actions, and even your mistakes, will be acceptable to me. I am willing to take responsibility for your acts, and, in return, I expect you to do your job well."

Delegation can be satisfying or frustrating to all concerned. The result depends on whether all these implications are understood by both supervisor and worker. Clear-cut communication must be established between supervisor and employee at the beginning of any delegation process to avoid serious misunderstandings. Theodore Roosevelt summed up the essence of delegation when he said, "The best executives are the ones who have enough sense to pick good people to do what they want done, and self-restraint enough to keep from meddling with them while they do it."

One major management source identifies the following personal characteristics as those common to supervisors who delegate effectively:[5]

1. Receptiveness.   They are open to suggestions and are willing to give other people's ideas a chance. They allow employees to think creatively.

2. Willingness to let go.   They are not afraid to give decision-making power to subordinates. They trust workers to do their jobs in the best way they can without constant supervision.

3. Willingness to let others make mistakes.   They are patient with workers and think of them as human begins, not gods or machines. Although they expect some mistakes, they do not hover over workers like anxious hens.

4. Willingness to trust subordinates.   They know that if they cannot trust subordinates, they had better begin trading them to the competition.

5. Willingness to use broad controls.   They stay in touch, keep the communication lines open, and are available when subordinates need help but resist the temptation to take the job back to complete personally.

Unity of command is simple to define but often difficult to put into practice. In the ideal organization, employees should receive instructions and commands from only one immediate superior. In reality we know that employees often receive conflicting and confusing commands. When it is difficult for an employee to determine which order to obey, there is a temptation to choose the one delivered in the loudest manner. The result is that wise orders are often tossed aside for those which appear to carry more authority.

Chaos can result from this failure of communication at numerous levels of supervision. Since most departments are to some degree interdependent, it is essential that supervisors communicate effectively with each other. Cooperation among departments is as important as cooperation among fellow workers. Communication builds the bridges necessary for good relationships.

[5] Harold Koontz and Cyril O'Donnell, *Principles of Management,* 6th ed. (New York: McGraw-Hill, 1976), pp. 282–84.

Every time a task is delegated, the importance of communication grows. If good reporting and feedback channels are established, work can be accomplished across departmental lines as well as within departments. As long as everyone knows who is supposed to do what and how well they are doing, delegation will serve as a useful tool. Earlier an entire chapter was devoted to the communication process. For now, it is enough to remember that clear communication is the first step in effective organization and delegation.

Structure

Every organization, no matter how complex or simple, has a structure. Employees and their activities are grouped in particular ways. Structure is the framework of the organization—the method of determining individual responsibilities and tasks, processes of delegation, and the distribution of authority. There are probably as many organizational structures as there are organizations, for each type of business operation has its own special selection of people, resources, and goals.

Since most supervisors assume jobs in existing organizations, structure is something they must adapt to as part of their job situations. It is, however, important for you to be aware of some components of organizational structure. Understanding the structure of a company will help you understand why people relate to each other as they do and why the business operations proceed in an orderly or untidy manner. We shall discuss structure in relation to departmentalization, the organizational chart, levels of authority, and organizational size.

Departmentalization is one of the major components of any organizational structure. Essentially, it means *how the workers are divided up*. In ancient times, armies were departmentalized by simple nose count—"department heads" were captains of tens, of fifties, and of hundreds (centurions). In peacetime activities, however, there were more productive ways of grouping workers.

In modern businesses, there are five main ways to departmentalize employees—function, geographic area, product line, type of customer, and process or type of equipment. Workers are often grouped by *function*—sales, marketing, financial bookkeeping—and production employees are grouped to work together toward common goals. Grouping employees by *geographic area* is another common method, particularly when better service or coverage is desired. "The Southwestern sales district" combines function and geographic designators.

A more recent means of dividing workers is on the basis of *products* or *product lines*. Here, authority and responsibility can be delegated efficiently, and workers in each department focus on a particular product, service, or line. Personnel groupings in the children's department of a retail store or the paper products division of a consumer goods company illustrates this approach.

Departmentalization may be governed by the *type of customer* involved, as with a wholesale grocery sales force specializing in quick-service food stores. The Small Business Administration is a governmental approach to departmentalization by customer.

Finally, departments may be set up according to the *process* or *type of equipment* used, as in the bottle-filling department of a chemical manufacturer.

Most companies use some combination of these methods to group their employees effectively. Identify the departmentalization strategies used in this job description: Southwestern regional supervisor of the fifty-person marketing department of the college textbook division for a major publishing company.

The *organizational chart* shows the skeletal structure of an organization (Figure 10-1). It shows clearly and concisely the functions, positions, and chain of command existing in that organization. It spells out relationships that must be maintained if the company is to progress. Although most supervisors are not involved in the actual drawing up of organizational charts, they should keep in mind that the chart is a symbolic representation outlining company functions and the way they operate.

Most organizational charts show two basic authority relationships in an organization—line and staff. The manager with line authority takes orders from those above and passes them on to workers below. The person with staff authority reports to someone with line authority and is not actually involved in the chain of command. The line supervisor tells others what to do; the supervisor with staff authority must sell his or her ideas.

Levels of authority lead us again to the chain of command. The levels of authority establish power relationships among workers in a company. Authority levels can determine workers' social status and choice of associates, provide them with varying amounts of authority, and affect the way they see their roles in the organization. An individual may occupy one of several positions

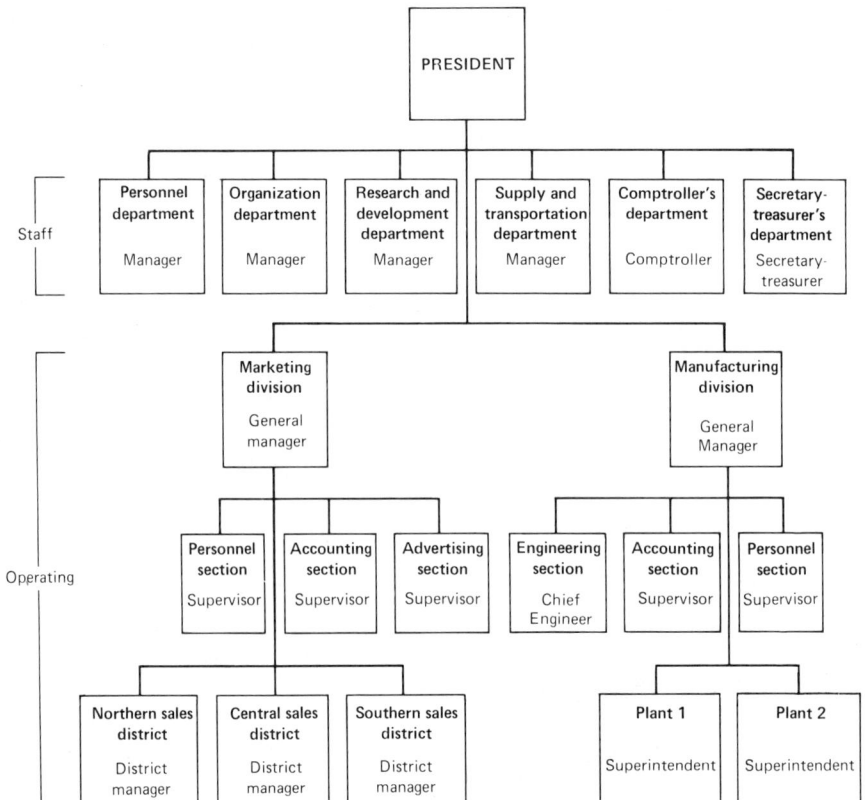

Figure 10-1. Sample Organizational Charts.

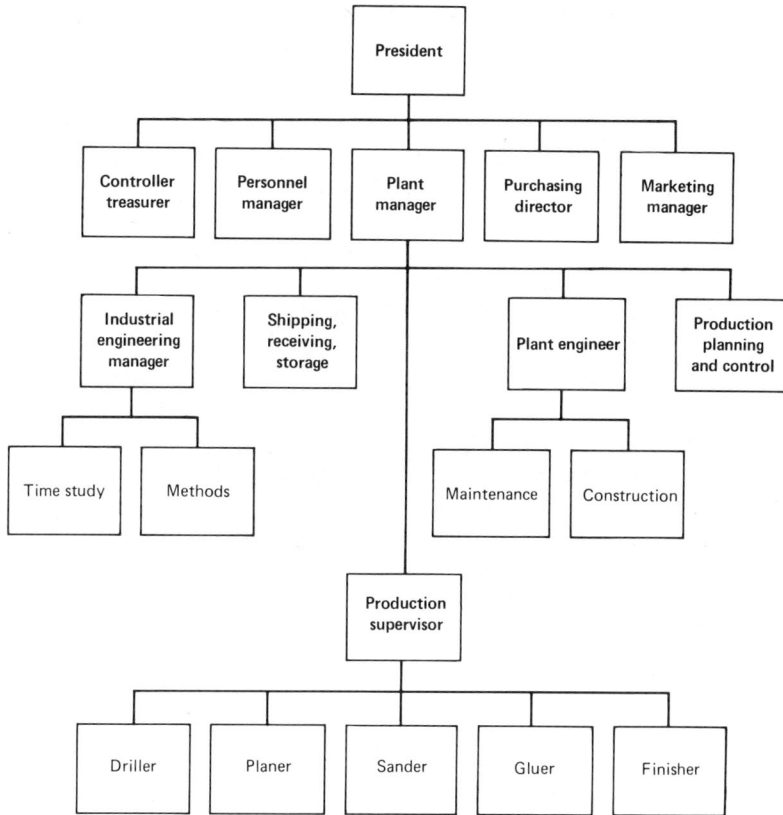

Figure 10-1. *(cont.)*

on the organizational ladder: a trustee, a member of the board of directors, an executive manager, a departmental manager, a "middle manager," or a first-level manager.

The position of first-level managers has often been neglected in the corporate structure. Often, higher-level managers become so involved with paperwork decisions that they forget the problems and needs of supervisors who bear the ultimate responsibility for job accomplishment and who must deal effectively with people and their problems every day. This supervisor usually occupies the lowest organizational level authorized to delegate responsibility. It is especially important to realize the necessity of these "firing-line" managers who communicate the final instructions to begin each task, then maintain production schedules until the job is done.

A famous study involving over 100,000 employees of Sears, Roebuck and Company during a twelve-year period demonstrated the following:

1. As organizations become more complex, relationships worsen between management and employees.

2. Overspecialization results in low employee morale and poor production. Groups completing tasks from start to finish show the highest morale.

3. When work is divided into very small units, close supervision is required to maintain production quality. Rules become rigid and exert a negative effect on employee morale.

4. Supervisors who use pressure to control employees are quite common in organizations that are very complex.[6]

When the structure of an organization becomes too rigid and inflexible, it actually hinders the efficient operation of the company. In order for organizational levels of authority to operate smoothly and effectively, employees must know where they stand, and no one should fear authority or feel hemmed in too tightly.

Organizational size is the final aspect of structure that must be considered. The size of a company can have considerable effect on its employees. Usually, larger companies experience lower employee satisfaction rates and higher absenteeism.

The size of a company's *local* work force is the important variable in measuring the effects of an organizational size. A department store that is part of a 10,000-employee chain, but employs only 50 people, will have "size effects" more like a small company than a larger one. In smaller operations, an employee is more likely to know most of the people he or she works with, and relationships are more easily established. Also, since departmentalization cannot occur on a widespread level in such a small store, employees often see the results of their efforts and better understand their importance in the total operation.

Span of Management

Span of management refers to the number of workers actually reporting to one supervisor. Classical theory imposed strict limits on the span because every supervisor possessed only so much knowledge, energy, and time. In fact, the Bible reveals an example of limitations on the span of management, as told in Exodus 18:

> Moses sat to judge the people, and the people stood about Moses from morning till evening. When Moses' father-in-law saw all that he was doing for the people, he said, ". . . What you are doing is not good. You and the people with you will wear yourselves out; for the thing is too heavy for you; you are not able to perform it alone. . . ."
>
> So Moses gave heed to the voice of his father-in-law and did all that he had said. Moses chose able men out of all Israel, and made them heads over the people, rulers of thousands, of hundreds, of fifties, and of tens. And then judged the people at all times; hard cases they brought to Moses, but any small matter they decided themselves.

More supervisors at lower levels. Modern limits on the span of management are based on two major lines of reasoning. First, many people feel it is much easier to supervise the work of many plant workers or cashiers than to supervise a few employees at a higher level. More people can be successfully supervised at lower levels because their tasks are often more repetitive and less creative (though this need not be true). Higher-level jobs tend to be more complex and require more steps to complete; one person can effectively supervise only a few employees with higher-level jobs.

Second, the number of possible relationships among people increases geo-

---

[6] James C. Worthy, "Organizational Structure and Employee Morale," *American Sociological Review,* April 1950, pp. 169–79.

metrically as more people join the group. This will be easy to see from a simple example. If a group contains Supervisor A, Subordinate B, and Subordinate C, the diagram (Figure 10-2) shows the possible relationships that may exist among these three people.

If a third subordinate joins the group, eighteen possible interactions can result. A fourth subordinate raises the potential number to forty-four. Five subordinates and a supervisor can engage in 100 different interactions, and a supervisor with eight subordinates must deal with 1080 potential relationships! Of course, all possible relationships will not occur every day, but the warning is clear—do not take on more people than you can effectively supervise.

How to know how many. The National Industrial Conference Board provides these guidelines for determining the number of employees any one individual can effectively supervise under given conditions:

1. The competence of the superior and subordinates.
2. The degree of contact or interaction between the people being supervised.
3. The extent to which the supervisor must perform nonmanagerial duties, and the demands on personal time from other people and units.
4. The similarity of the activities being supervised.
5. The incidence of new problems in the supervisor's unit.
6. The degree of standardized procedure within the organization.
7. The degree of physical distance between activities.

Stretching the span. One advantage of broadening the supervisory span is that it results in less red tape and fewer communication difficulties—the organizational structure is compacted so that operations require a shorter chain of command. A broader span also encourages more extensive delegation and more general, rather than close, supervision. These factors in turn can help raise employee morale.

Organizations: tall or short? In a "tall" organization with many levels of authority, an employee tends to become "boss-oriented." The superior interacts with the employee daily and supervises the work closely. The employee reacts by learning the superior's personality quirks, likes, and dislikes in order to

Figure 10-2. Interaction Expansion.

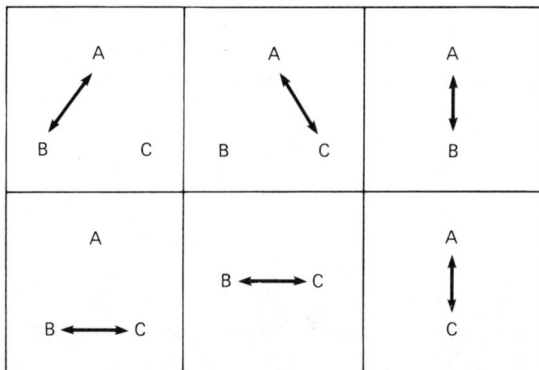

get along better. Naturally, organizational structures that foster playing "personality games" will find they do not contribute to accomplishing the task and can even divert time and energy from the actual organizational goal.

A "flat," or "short," organizational structure, with widely distributed authority and fewer strict controls, is a good environment for people who like to do things on their own. This structure encourages initiative and ideas, and employees learn to take responsibility for their own work. Some controls, of course, must be maintained. A successful flat organization depends primarily on its supervisors to keep their eyes open, make good decisions, take responsibility, and cooperate to achieve organizational objectives.

Although organizational experts may want to limit supervisory responsibility to six employees or develop formulas computing the proper span of supervision, it is the supervisor's skill and the unique situation that will ultimately determine the number of employees he or she can manage effectively.

Summary

Because our world is organization-conscious, there is a constant danger of organizational patterns getting out of control. To some extent, every employee should be part of a continuing committee for re-evaluation and refinement of the company's organization—the way people and activities relate to each other in accomplishing company goals. The wise supervisor, however, understands the difference between *organization* and *efficient organization*.

There are four major foundations of organization. (1) *Division of work* is the most basic of the four. It has been criticized for stifling individualism and dehumanizing workers for the sake of increasing production. To correct this, some organizations have developed special strategies, such as job enlargement, job rotation, and participation in decision making. (2) *Scalar and functional processes* refers to the ladderlike pattern of authority and responsibility within an organization. This approach relies on the processes of chain of command, delegation, and unity of command. (3) *Structure*, or the way employees and their activities are grouped, makes possible the management of complicated enterprises. Four important components of organizational structure are departmentalization, organizational charts, levels of authority, and organizational size. (4) *Span* of management refers to the number of persons a supervisor oversees directly. Many studies have tried to determine scientifically the optimum number capable of being supervised effectively. In the final analysis, of course, the supervisor's skills and the situation must determine the proper number of subordinates.

In itself, organization is neither good nor bad. It is a tool that enables us to accomplish goals more efficiently or may become an overbearing slavedriver. If we are aware of organization's potentials and pitfalls, our choice can be an intelligent one.

Key Terms

Delegation. Designating a subordinate to handle a particular task and granting the authority and the freedom to accomplish that objective.

Departmentalization. The divisions of workers that exist in an organization.

Division of Work. The specialization of individual tasks to achieve greater group output.

Hierarchy. The ranking of individuals or positions in an organization according to prestige, responsibility, authority, or other factors.

Job Enlargement. A structuring of the production process that allows each worker to perform more steps.

Job Rotation. The periodic reassignment of a worker from one job to another. The individual has less chance to become bored with the work and may form a better "total picture" of the organization and his or her function within it.

Levels of Authority. The chain of command or series of power relationships among workers and management in an organization.

Organizational Chart. The skeleton of the organizational structure, showing functions, positions, chains of command, and relationships that must be maintained if the organization is to function effectively.

Organizational Structure. The framework of the organization; the method of determining individual responsibilities and tasks, processes of delegation, and the distribution of authority.

Participation Approach. A method of job enrichment in which workers are allowed to participate in decision making that concerns them or their jobs.

Scalar and Functional Processes. Aspects of an organization that determine chains of command, delegation procedures, and processes by which the organization can be maintained.

Span of Control. The number of individuals a supervisor oversees. The proper span of control for any supervisor depends on personal abilities, the competence and diversity of workers, the physical constraints of the job situation, the frequency of problems, the total demands made on the supervisor's time, and the extent of standardized procedures within the organization.

Unity of Command. The degree to which employees receive unified statements and instructions from all levels of management and supervision. Conflicting and confusing commands destroy the unity of command necessary for efficient operation.

Review Questions

1. List and describe the positive and negative features of organization.

2. What is meant by the term *efficient organization?* Describe an example in detail.

3. List and describe the four foundations of organization.

4. What is meant by division of labor? List and describe its advantages and disadvantages.

5. Is it possible for a job to be too specialized? What might some of its disadvantages be to the worker?

6. How is it possible to delegate such personal characteristics as "authority" and "responsibility"? How would you go about delegating each of these?

7. In the organization structure of a corporation, what are some ways departments may be assigned?

8. It is said that as the number of employees under a supervisor increases, the challenges of being a supervisor also increase. Explain.

Exercises

I. Understanding the Organization Chart

Draw a chart showing the chain of command or organizational hierarchy in your current job, or a job you have had in the past. Include your own group of subordinates, yourself, and management immediately above you. What does your chart tell you about who has responsibility and/or authority to see that certain tasks are done? Is there a formal or informal organizational structure among your group of workers? What changes or improvements would you like to make in your work hierarchy? Why?

II. Analyzing Organizational Structure

A. In groups of four to eight, think of a product that can be made of paper without adhesives to hold it together. Any product will do, as long as the group agrees on it. Develop a production plan for your item and construct as many as you can in thirty minutes. When the time is up, the group with the most creative product and the group producing the most items each win.

B. After the exercise, discuss the following questions within your group:

1. Was there a group leader? Who was it? How did the leader perform the leadership role? How was this person chosen?

2. Were there task specialists in the group—people who had ideas for products, production techniques, or organizational structure? Who were the task specialists and how were their roles divided?

3. What organizational structure did you develop to handle production? Did you use the division of labor principle? If so, how?

4. How could your group have been more effective in meeting its goal of maximum productivity?

C. After each group has discussed its performance and organization, one member of each group should report the results of the discussion to the class. After these reports, the class as a whole should discuss these questions:

1. Did all groups operate in the same manner, or were different organizational structures devised?

2. Which organization proved the most effective in terms of production? Why?

3. Which was most effective in terms of creativity? Why?

Case 10 • Harry Higgins Revisited

Harry Higgins has been a supervisor in the order processing department of the K. D. Nickel Company for about four months. His boss Rex Harris has called Harry into his office to suggest ways of improving delegation. Harry is concerned by this "lecture" because he has tried very hard to be a good supervisor.

Harry muses, "It isn't fair. When I was given this job, I spent several days considering reorganization. I developed a detailed job description for each of my ten employees and carefully explained my ideas to them. I've stayed at work late many evenings to check output and to see if there were any snags in my system. When I've discovered mistakes, I've diplomatically pointed them out to the workers and always showed them how to avoid problems in the future.

"The only turnover in the unit was two workers upset that they didn't get my position. I've replaced them with new people I've personally trained. When I check over the work sheets each night I find few mistakes, so what could be the problem? I really think Mr. Harris doesn't appreciate how hard I've worked."

1. Discuss Harry's concept of organization.
2. Has Harry failed to recognize any basic principles of delegation?

PART

THREE

Managing People, Information, and Events

CHAPTER 11

The Supervisor's Personnel Function

It often happens that when a fellow gets a job, he stops looking for work.

Standard Democrat

Learning Objectives

- To recognize that personnel functions for the supervisor involve more than routine administrative work and that human relations skills are essential to effective personnel supervision.
- To list the steps in the personnel or staffing function.
- To incorporate planning and evaluation in all phases of personnel administration.
- To learn to apply personnel techniques for more efficient supervision.

Human assets often represent an organization's most valuable resource. Without competent and willing workers, even the best-equipped company is destined for failure. Any supervisor who has worked in a situation with a high rate of personnel turnover recognizes the value of dependable human resources. Each employee represents a sizable investment in recruiting, training, and supervision. The cost of finding and training replacements mounts rapidly, and a supervisor soon realizes these duties can command the bulk of his or her time.

Every company encompasses a system of jobs that must be filled if the organization is to function efficiently and profitably. Supervisors will often have direct hiring control for a number of these jobs. Depending on how he or she chooses and manages people, muscle or flab can be added to the organizational skeleton.

In some companies, the supervisor's role in personnel selection is limited. New workers are often sent down by the hiring office or personnel department. The supervisor may only recommend that less-than-competent workers be terminated. Even in these cases there is an important part to play in evaluating workers and in training new workers.

Regardless of how broad or narrow the supervisor's personnel functions may be, they represent critical factors in the success of any organization.

The Staffing Process

Staffing is the area most likely to be ignored or poorly performed by supervisors. The problem seems to lie with the fact that it is "people work," not paperwork. A supervisor must combine many skills—creativity, communication, leadership—in choosing workers, evaluating their performance, and making or contributing to decisions regarding compensation, promotion and termination.

Because people are involved, it is difficult to perform the staffing process within a foolproof set of rules or handy checklist. There are, however, several easy-to-use steps in building a good team. Briefly, these steps include (1) determining needs, (2) recruiting, (3) orientation and training, (4) evaluating performance, (5) compensation, (6) promotion, and (7) termination. In any supervisory position, it is important to be aware of your role in each of these seven areas and to perform well in each area in which you have authority or influence. Effective training is a *process,* not a single event.

Determining Needs

It is easy to overlook this logical first step or to assume that someone else has determined your staff needs. You have seen, though, that it becomes easier to reach a goal when you know what it is.

Earlier we mentioned the organizational skeleton. In any company, certain jobs must be filled. On the other hand, some jobs serve no real purpose but are grounded in tradition or have been created to retain employees laid off in other areas. Whenever a job vacancy occurs in the department, a supervisor should ask a few questions instead of immediately filling the position: Is this function absolutely necessary to this department? What would happen if the position were not filled? Could the tasks be divided among other workers without negative effects?

Once the supervisor decides a particular position is essential, the next step is to outline or review the job's duties and skill requirements. Finding the right employees is easier if you know exactly what the position demands. Qualifications for the job should be written in clear, down-to-earth terms, stressing necessary skills and expected performance levels rather than strict educational or experience requirements. The actual duties to be performed in the position should also be listed. This job description procedure helps supervisors avoid misunderstandings in hiring new workers because applicants and new employees know exactly what is expected of them. This process is discussed more thoroughly in the next chapter.

Another factor in determining needs is to decide *how many* new workers are needed and *when* they will be needed. Supervisors realize that seasonal shifts can change the tempo of production. At certain times of the year, more workers are needed to keep the organization running smoothly under pressures of increased demand. At other times, fewer workers will suffice because demand is not as great. The supervisor who reviews previous sales or production records can form an accurate projection of seasonal variations in production. A toy manufacturer, for instance, will have a production "boom" when toys must be stockpiled for the Christmas season. A retail store, on the other hand, may not need extra workers before mid-November. A janitorial service company may employ extra workers just prior to schools' opening in the fall, while a lawn-care firm will experience greater demand for its products in spring and summer. A continuing awareness of your company's seasonal production cycles will help you avoid two problems: (1) being caught short-handed with rush orders to fill, and (2) having too many workers with not enough to do.

Selection and Recruitment

Should a supervisor consider selection before beginning to recruit? The answer is yes. Much of the selection process is over once the job's requirements and duties have been spelled out in writing. If this procedure is not followed, however, it is easy to fall into several traps once the recruiting process has begun.

Selection pitfalls. Unless there is a procedure for selecting new employees, the supervisor may be directing a fast-thinning team. Careful attention to such factors as age, years of service, "promotability," seniority, and pay scales is essential. A strong department or division is built up over years of perceptive hiring, and if all employees are too similar in experience, age, promotability, pay scales, and job development, a supervisor has not ensured the long-term health of the department.

The supervisor may also fall into the trap of assuming that the right employee will come along when one is needed. The supervisor who does not recruit in advance to fill future needs can land in serious trouble by being short-handed during production peaks. Often this recognition will require detailed negotiation with the personnel department or higher management.

Another common pitfall is the assumption that the supervisor's personal judgment is enough to determine whether an applicant is qualified or not. If selection procedures are set up and qualifications are defined within flexible limits, the danger of relying on one's personal judgment is greatly reduced. The supervisor should take a dim view of anyone who comments that a particular applicant is right for the job because "He has that gleam in his eye," or "She reminds me of myself when I was a kid."

A system for selection. Establishing a method of selection and sticking to it can help the supervisor avoid problems. Lack of planning and reliance on personal feelings have caused the downfall of many businesses and many more individual supervisors!

The first step in recruiting is the screening of applicants. The supervisor who needs a position filled may wish to do the screening. In other cases someone else—perhaps the personnel department or an assistant—will do this job. Screening involves matching the qualifications of potential employees with the job's requirements. The person doing the screening must understand the goals of the company as well as the policies and procedures of the department. When applicants clearly do not meet the job's requirement, the recruiter should terminate the interview quickly and tactfully. On the other hand, the screening process allows people who do not quite meet the requirements to display unusual potential.

A good recruiter will attempt to create an environment in which the applicant will be put at ease and encouraged to talk frankly, aggressively, and positively. A specific set of questions should be prepared and asked of each applicant, and an opportunity for questions from the candidate should be solicited by the interviewer. Direct eye contact and few interruptions are additional facilities of a good interview.

Once it has been determined that an applicant meets the requirements and is interested in the position, the supervisor or personnel officer should encourage commitment. At this point, wages, benefits, and advancement opportunities are discussed. The supervisor is on dangerous ground at this point, for the challenge is to sell the company without overselling it. It is easy for a new employee to become disillusioned in a job that has been "oversold" during the hiring process.

The final selection should be made by all those who have interviewed the applicants or will be dealing directly with the new employee. If the personnel department has handled things up to this point, the supervisor should certainly play a role in the final selection. After all, the supervisor will be working daily with the new employees helping them fit in effectively with other workers and checking to see that they are able to perform duties competently. This final conference is not the time to be nice or to overlook storm warnings. If an applicant is not quite right for the job, it is better to find out before a job offer is made.

Some companies use rating charts or forms to determine whether a particular applicant is qualified for a job. Others use psychological tests, interviews, trials, performance tests, and a variety of other methods. Whatever the method or combination of methods used, *any* method of selection and recruiting is better than none. For a sample selection procedure chart, see Figure 11-1.

Orientation and Training

Once a new employee has been hired, he or she must be introduced to the organization, co-workers, and the new job. Without some knowledge of company policies and procedures, the new worker cannot be expected to feel

To warrant employment,
an applicant must meet the standards at
each step of the selection procedure
and must qualify for the job in all
five respects

JOB QUALIFICATIONS

The qualifications to look for at each
step are keyed as follows:

≡ See if the applicant appears to have
the qualifications.

▓ Look for evidence that the applicant
has the qualifications.

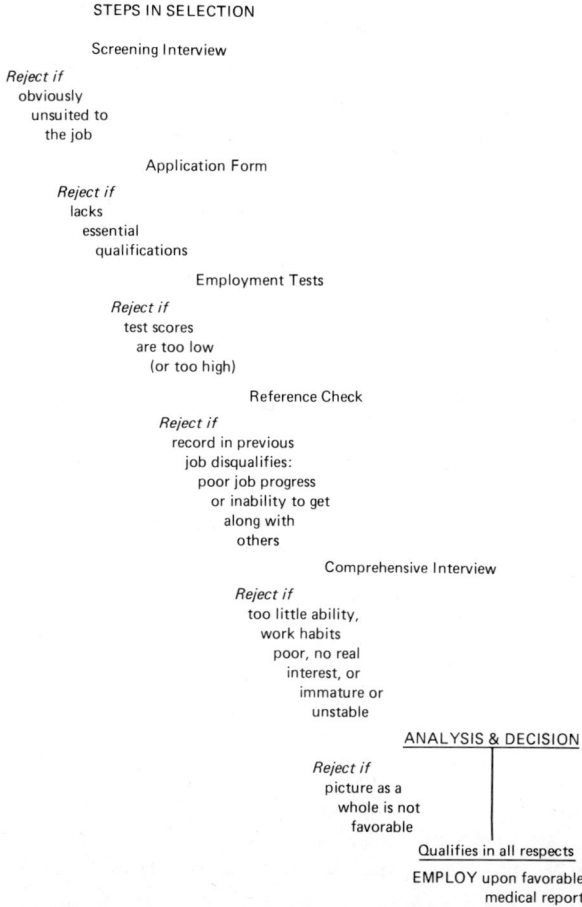

Capability for the job

Acceptability to others

Perseverance—Industry

Interest in this job

Maturity—Stability

STEPS IN SELECTION

Screening Interview

Reject if
obviously
unsuited to
the job

Application Form

Reject if
lacks
essential
qualifications

Employment Tests

Reject if
test scores
are too low
(or too high)

Reference Check

Reject if
record in previous
job disqualifies:
poor job progress
or inability to get
along with
others

Comprehensive Interview

Reject if
too little ability,
work habits
poor, no real
interest, or
immature or
unstable

ANALYSIS & DECISION

Reject if
picture as a
whole is not
favorable

Qualifies in all respects

EMPLOY upon favorable
medical report

Figure 11-1. Summary of a Selection Procedure. (With permission from AMA Research Study No. 47, "The Employment Interview," by Milton A. Mandell. © 1961 by the American Management Association, Inc.)

comfortable with the situation. For this reason, a period of orientation should follow the hiring of a new employee.

If the supervisor is alert to the possibilities, some of the information required for orientation can be discussed during the interview. Salary structure, benefits, holidays, and vacations can be discussed in broad terms. In addition, the supervisor will want to pay close attention to the ease with which the applicant grasps the broader goals and policies of the company. Naturally, in some cases a knowledge of company philosophy is not essential to the job at hand.

On the other hand, a prospective employee who picks up this kind of information readily is giving clues about competence, alertness, and promotability.

In some companies, the personnel department turns orientation into a major production. They may arrange to present a film, a set of slides, a formal lecture, or a panel discussion in introducing the new worker to the company. In other organizations, orientation is more informal and may consist of a discussion between supervisor and worker. In any event, subjects like these are usually covered:

1. Company history, products, and major operations.
2. Company policies and regulations.
3. Relation of supervisors and personnel department.
4. Rules and regulations regarding:
   (a) Wages and wage payment.
   (b) Hours of work and overtime.
   (c) Safety: accident prevention and contingency procedures.
   (d) Holidays and vacations.
   (e) Methods of reporting tardiness and absences.
   (f) Discipline and grievances.
   (g) Uniforms and clothing.
   (h) Parking.
   (i) Badges and parcels.
5. Economic and recreational services such as:
   (a) Insurance plans.
   (b) Pensions.
   (c) Athletic and social activities.
6. Opportunities:
   (a) Promotion and transfer.
   (b) Job stabilization.
   (c) Suggestion systems.

Naturally, new employees are not expected to remember every detail discussed during orientation. The real purpose is to introduce them to the company, to give them an overview. After the official orientation is over, the real orientation begins. As the new employees start the job and circulate among other employees, they are able to fill in the official overview of the company with specifics from the day-to-day situation. It has been said that more valuable orientation takes place on coffee breaks than in all the personnel presentations that will ever be made. Where else can a new employee learn such valuable information as who will take phone messages and who will not, whom to see for specific kinds of problems, and what the company president is *really* doing when the office door is closed!

The training of new employees is a more complex subject. At this point, it is enough to remember that training is education, and that in matters of education, time and experience remain the best teachers.

Evaluating Performance

Many students object to getting grades in school because they feel there is no accurate way to determine how much an individual has learned. This same attitude is often voiced when it comes time to evaluate performance on the job. How can someone who is not involved with the job on a day-to-day basis effectively evaluate the performance of another person?

Of course, there are many difficulties in evaluating performance, but, so far, no better system has been found for determining raises. Some method of performance evaluation must be used so that productive workers are rewarded and nonproductive workers are discovered and encouraged to perform. Evaluation serves other purposes as well. It helps the supervisor to allocate resources wisely. It provides a means of giving feedback to workers on their progress. Finally, evaluation helps the supervisor maintain fair relationships with workers. If used properly, evaluation keeps communication lines open. The next chapter will explore this challenge in more detail.

Fair Pay

The basic purpose of compensation is to attract and retain good employees. This is done by providing fair pay for fair work, rewarding good performance, and providing incentives for higher achievement. Our entire economic system is based on the notion that people should be rewarded according to their talents or skills, what they produce, or the risks they take. Although many things are more important than money, we still tend to base many of our business decisions on financial considerations. Money is a unique incentive—it can satisfy our basic needs for food, clothing, and shelter, our psychological needs for status and prestige, and our higher needs for esteem and recognition.

Table 11-1 lists the roles of various levels of management in the compensation function. Many workers in industry are paid according to incentive plans—the more they produce, the more money they make. Under this plan, productivity almost always increases, and labor costs per manufactured unit decrease. Workers not familiar with wage incentive plans usually possess the ability to increase their production, and wage incentives have proved successful in releasing that potential. In fact, some industries have increased production over 300 percent and reduced labor costs over 20 percent after beginning a wage incentive program.[1] In cases like these, money obviously talks!

The supervisor may believe the department could be more productive with a wage incentive program. Naturally, such a program must be discussed with top management, carefully planned, and then implemented. Workers who are already producing at their peak levels should not be penalized, but those who can improve their performance should be rewarded for extra achievements.

So much for the workers. Now what about the supervisor? In Chapter 17 we shall discuss the impact of money on supervisors and workers. There is an obvious distinction in the type of work they do. Assembly-line workers are compensated for doing their jobs. Supervisors, on the other hand, are usually paid according to *how* they do their jobs. Supervision requires a large number of subtle skills and abilities, and money alone may not prove to be a supervisor's best motivator.

There is a complicated and important relationship between incentive systems and the behavior of an organization's employees. Although supervisors may

---

[1] Keith Davis, *Human Relations at Work,* 5th ed. (New York: McGraw-Hill, 1977), pp. 480–81.

Table 11-1. Levels of Management and Compensation. (With permission from Richard Henderson, "The Changing Role of the Wage and Salary Administrator," *Personnel*, November–December 1976, pp. 56–63.)

Activity	Top Management	Senior Management	Middle Management	First-Line Management–Operative Employees
Base compensation 　Job evaluation 　Pay surveys	Consultant	Coordinator Implementer	Implementer	Implementer
Employee benefits 　Employee security 　Time not worked 　Employee services	Coordinator Catalyst Consultant	Coordinator Consultant Catalyst	Coordinator Consultant Catalyst	Coordinator Consultant Catalyst
Incentive programs 　Individual pay for 　　performance 　Cost reduction 　Profit sharing 　Base-pay premiums 　Dangerous-job 　　premiums	Consultant Coordinator	Coordinator	Coordinator Implementer Catalyst Consultant	Coordinator Implementer Catalyst Consultant

Top management: Chief executive officer, president, and senior vice-president.
Senior management: Regional, divisional, and functional managers and senior professionals.
Middle management: Department and unit managers, superintendents, professionals, and senior paraprofessionals.
First-line management-operative employees: Foremen, supervisors, paraprofessionals, skilled craftsmen, technicians, and semiskilled and unskilled laborers.

not have control over company policy, they will surely play a major role in determining the compensation for individuals under their supervision. The supervisor's work may be critical in determining who will get a pay raise and who will not, or whether the company or department will adopt an incentive system. There is a delicate balance between corporate profits and worker satisfaction. The supervisor who is aware of this balance can help the company achieve the best of both worlds—increased profits *and* motivated workers.

Indirect Compensation: The Fringe on Top

Recently, fringe benefits for employees have risen twice as fast as wages. The U.S. Chamber of Commerce estimates that fringe benefits add as much as one-third to the value of a worker's wages.

Management offers fringe benefits to make the compensation package more attractive to employees. In this manner, they hope to be able to attract and maintain capable, committed, productive employees. Unfortunately, many employees take fringe benefits for granted. Supervisors can perform a valuable service by pointing out to employees the value of these benefits. There are four major categories of fringe benefits:

1. Extra pay for work. These benefits include the premiums paid for work beyond forty hours a week, holidays, weekends, or night shifts. Some companies include cost of living bonuses in this category.

2. Pay for not working. Many employees receive wages even though they do not work; examples include lunch periods, rest periods, military duty, vacations, and severance pay. Sometimes, workers are compensated for time to clean up and get ready to leave the factory, when they are serving on juries, and when they vote.

3. Payments for sickness and security. Today, employers are expected to assume a portion of the responsibility for insurance programs to protect workers. This can include life, accident, hospitalization, surgical, and major medical insurance; payments to Social Security, state disability insurance plans, unemployment insurance, and workmen's compensation; and stock purchase plans and other pension programs.

4. Special employee services. The range of services offered to employees is too broad to be concisely summarized. Some of the employee benefits appear to have little connection with work. They include company-subsidized cafeterias, tuition refunds for educational programs, medical services, day-care facilities, scholarships for workers or their families, company-sponsored athletic teams, recreation facilities, legal aid, and employee picnics or parties.

Promotion

A familiar form of compensation is a promotion to a higher position. Though promotion usually means increased pay, there are other appealing aspects that have nothing to do with money. Promotion involves new status and prestige and represents a form of direct praise. Promotions tell the workers, "You have been doing such a good job that you are now ready to meet new challenges."

Of course, people can be promoted out of their area of competence. Just because a person has performed well at one job does not necessarily mean that a more difficult job can be handled equally well. A good teacher may not make an effective administrator, and the fastest production worker in the line may perform miserably as "chief" of a work group.

Promotion from within is the most common type a supervisor will encounter. In a growing company, workers with the most experience or seniority may be made heads of departments. Promotions from within the department give a supervisor a chance to delegate some authority and to spread out responsibility among competent employees. In other cases, performance evaluations will play a meaningful role in deciding who should be promoted.

Seniority and merit of performance are the two general factors in consideration for promotion. Unions typically argue that seniority should be the sole factor for promotion, assuming acceptable job performance. Others argue that seniority should carry no weight whatsoever, but performance is all that counts. Many managers and entrepreneurs of small, growing companies hold this perspective. Obviously, neither is totally right or wrong and both have some merit. The successful supervisor will clearly communicate to employees his or her criteria for promotion.

Termination

The last major area in the supervisor's personnel function is the business of getting people *out* of the organization. There are three main types of termination, each having its own special circumstances and methods of handling: retirement, resignation, and dismissal.

When an employee retires, he or she has fulfilled all obligations to the company and has earned the right to stop working. Retirement income theoretically comes from money earned during the productive years and set aside for the leisure years. However, retirement often causes problems for both company and worker. Some people remain productive and useful long after they have reached the official retirement age. Others should be able to retire much earlier, as their usefulness to the company declines due to illness or other disabilities. Retirement policies have often proved shortsighted and heartless. As with compensation activities, different levels of management develop different retirement policies. The primary role of the supervisor is to make certain that employees understand the policies and programs in existence. A supervisor should recognize deficiencies and needs in this area and communicate potential solutions for these oversights to upper management.

In the supervisor's world, another word for resignation is quitting. Mobility has infected people at all levels, and workers often seek greener grass in another valley. A high turnover rate is some cause for concern because it can mean that conditions are not good in the department. It can also mean that the nature of the job is such that workers become quickly dissatisfied. Of course, some workers who resign because of dissatisfaction may be equally dissatisfied anywhere. In this case, their leaving probably means the department is better off without them. The supervisor should not be alarmed by an occasional resignation among the workers. But if the turnover rate becomes too high, the causes of worker dissatisfaction should be actively investigated.

The last and most unhappy type of termination is dismissal. In slow seasons, workers may have to be laid off temporarily. If the worker, rather than the company, is not making it, the supervisor must fire the employee. Dismissal, like evaluation, is not the appropriate occasion for venting anger or frustration. It is a last resort, and the supervisor should use it wisely to show the employee what has gone wrong and why he or she must leave. Sometimes dismissal can be a positive occasion—a worker who does not perform well in one situation may be released to find a more suitable outlet for his or her abilities. These people have been described as being "fired with ambition."

Summary

No matter what the supervisor's specific personnel functions, they must be handled with intelligence and understanding. A work team is only as strong as its members, so a supervisor should make every effort to see that the team is built with solid personnel practices.

The seven steps in the staffing process for supervisors are (1) determining needs, (2) selection and recruiting, (3) orientation and training, (4) evaluating performance, (5) compensation, (6) promotion, and (7) termination. Depending upon company policies, a supervisor will have varying responsibilities in these areas.

Key Terms

Incentive Plan. A method of compensation by which workers are paid according to how much they produce.

Orientation. The introduction a new worker receives to the job, co-workers, and the organization; an overview of policies, procedures, benefits, and opportunities.

Promotion. A step up the organizational ladder, usually resulting in more status, prestige, money, benefits, authority, and responsibility.

Screening. Matching the qualifications of potential employees with the requirements of an available job.

Termination. Leaving employment through retirement, resignation, or dismissal.

Review Questions

1. To a supervisor, what does this phrase mean: "using to the maximum the available human resources?"

2. What role does determining staffing needs play in the personnel process? How can personnel needs be determined and clearly stated?

3. It has been said that establishing selection criteria before beginning recruitment is placing the cart before the horse. Do you agree? Why or why not?

4. What are the proper steps in recruiting? What are some questions *you* would ask as a recruiter?

5. What is the supervisor's role in compensation? Without control over wages, is a supervisor unable to motivate or satisfy workers?

6. How can employment be terminated?

7. It is frequently argued that the personnel department should handle every aspect of hiring. Do you agree? Must a supervisor get involved in personnel selection?

8. List and describe the four major categories of fringe benefits. Would you agree with some that there are "psychological fringe benefits" to certain jobs, such as teaching, working for the government, and counseling?

Exercises

I. Applying Personnel Skills

Imagine that you are the supervisor of a discount department store. A new department is being added—lawn and garden supplies—and a whole new group of employees begins work at the store on Monday. Personnel for the department includes a lawn and garden specialist who will serve as department head and "resident expert," two sales clerks, two cashiers, and a stockperson. You have asked the new group to meet with you Saturday afternoon for orientation.

Now you must develop an orientation program that will rapidly and effectively acquaint this new group of employees with store policies and procedures, training practices, advancement opportunities, and other aspects of their new jobs. Develop an orientation session that will adequately introduce these new members of the team to your store, keeping the following questions in mind:

1. What topics will you cover?
2. What methods will you use to inform the new employees?
3. Will you include some job training in the orientation session?
4. Will you use a formal or an informal approach, or a combination of both?
5. What do you hope to accomplish with your Saturday afternoon orientation?
6. How will you allow for feedback to make sure that the new employees are getting the kind of information they need?

II. Retirement Day

After reading the story below, discuss the questions that follow.

Arnold Miller dressed slowly that Friday morning. His wife had made coffee and scrambled eggs, but he could hardly force his breakfast down. After finally giving up trying to read the newspaper, he began to pace around the kitchen.

"It will be nice having you home more often," his wife said. "We can catch up on all the things we've put off for so long."

Arnold did not reply. He was lost in thought. What would he do with so much time? How could he take up new hobbies or interests at his age? He was very good at what he did—the best in the city, in fact. For thirty years he had learned everything he could about his company and his job, and had moved up from assembly-line worker to quality control supervisor. In the years he had supervised quality control, a bad batch had never been shipped to a customer. He was well aware that his company's reputation depended to a large extent on his consistent performance in quality control. Would the new man be able to handle the job? Did it make any difference?

When his wife finally became exasperated with him and pushed him out of the house, Arnold left reluctantly for work. His thoughts followed him as he maneuvered on the expressway, pulled into the parking lot, and entered the office for the last time. It seemed that everyone greeted him with too-hearty smiles, and he walked quickly back to the plant.

The day wore on very slowly, as Arnold finished cleaning out his desk and giving last-minute instructions to his replacement. Several minor problems arose during the day which he dealt with quickly and fairly. Finally, everything appeared to be in order; at 4 P.M., Arnold straightened up his shoulders and walked into the cafeteria. Management and employees assembled quickly, and the ceremony began.

Fred Bumble directed the show, as he had for sixty-five years. At eighty-five, he was a physical wreck and showed definite signs of memory loss and growing incompetence. But as president, he was still going strong. Mr. Bumble did a passable job of getting through his speech, congratulating Arnold for his fine years of faithful service, and admonishing him to enjoy his declining years in comfort and relaxation. Arnold took it like a stoic. He accepted the engraved plaque and the bonus check with a smile and a firm handshake, said a few words, and left the company forever.

On the way home, Arnold remembered that Mr. Bumble had been only a few years younger than Arnold was now when they first met, thirty years ago. It was not fair. . . . Arnold was sixty-five and still young, while Mr. Bumble should have retired long ago. But policy was policy, and he would just have to fill his time in other ways. He only hoped he could find something as meaningful as his job had been to him for so long.

1. What are some of the problems of retirement illustrated by the story?
2. What do you think of a company president who does not follow his or her own policies?
3. What alternatives does Arnold have for filling his days?

4. Is it right for every worker to be retired at a fixed age?
5. Do competent people always become less competent as they grow older?
6. What kinds of problems does retirement present for people whose work has been meaningful to them during their lives?
7. What do you think would be a fair retirement policy?

Case 11 • Angela Byars

Angela Byars is personnel supervisor for Southland Department Stores. Southland currently has two openings in its supervisory training program, and Angela has just completed a visit to local colleges where she and an assistant interviewed numerous graduating seniors for the program. She has narrowed the field to three candidates from the colleges and one candidate currently employed at Southland.

The first is Stephen Glenn, a business major who attends one of the largest state universities. He has average grades (2.8 on a scale of 4.0) but is very involved in campus activities. He is head of the intramural program for his fraternity, a student senator, and a varsity cheerleader. Angela noted on her interview form, "He was very personable and seemed quite articulate and self-confident."

The next candidate is Batsell Barrett, an engineering student from a small private college with an excellent academic reputation. He has a high grade-point average (3.4) and is a member of numerous honorary societies, but has been involved in few social activities at his school. He decided to postpone graduate school even though he was accepted by fifteen schools. Angela noted, "He was very intelligent but rather shy and introverted."

The third college candidate is Candice Kane, a classics major at an exclusive women's college. Candice has excellent grades (3.8), is active in student government, and is editor of the campus literary magazine. Angela recalled, "She was very ambitious, socially sensitive, and rather aggressive."

The fourth candidate, from the ranks of Southland, is John Charles Walton. John has worked for Southland three years while completing a marketing program part-time at a local community college. Even though working full-time, he made excellent grades. During her interview with him, Angela was impressed by his determination, energy, and knowledge of retailing.

1. Who should get the job? Why?
2. What other kinds of information would be useful in making a determination from this group of candidates?

CHAPTER 12

Evaluating Work and Job Performance

There is a difference between wanting to *get* a good salary and wanting to *earn* a good salary.

Bits & Pieces

Learning Objectives

- To identify and understand the characteristics of a fair compensation system.
- To identify and understand the elements of the job evaluation process.
- To understand and compare the different ways of writing job descriptions.
- To develop an understanding of the formation and use of performance standards and evaluation techniques.

Job Evaluation

The supervisor is responsible for helping higher management decide upon methods of ranking jobs and helping employees understand why some jobs pay more than others, how the rankings are established, and the reasoning behind the rankings. Knowing the characteristics of various jobs will help the supervisor devise a fair compensation system and match jobs to workers who are most likely to succeed in these positions. There are numerous job characteristics, but we shall consider nine basic factors that are most frequently considered in connection with ranking or classification on a pay scale.[1]

1. Degree of physical exertion required. Most workers prefer jobs with small amounts of physical exertion.

2. Pleasantness or unpleasantness of the work environment. Pleasant surroundings are usually described as being free from dirt, excessive noise, danger, darkness, and odors. They can include carpeting, office furnishings, and an employee cafeteria.

3. Job location. This factor includes considerations of indoor versus outdoor preference, stable (factory) versus shifting (construction jobs) work location, and single work space versus no work space (sales representatives).

4. Time required to do the work. Many jobs require constant, relatively untiring time inputs, while others require long, intensive hours of work followed by long leisure periods. Some jobs are full-time, some part-time, and some require short bursts of intensive effort.

5. Amount of specialization required. Different jobs demand various degrees of specialized knowledge, but some jobs are so highly specialized that almost no knowledge or mental skill is required to perform them. Both considerations must be included and evaluated for each job.

6. Education required. Minimum amounts of certain types of education are required for certain jobs. Some supervisors can use this as a "cop-out," however, by not considering the amount of education *actually needed* to perform the job, but by using education as a selection or "weeding out" device.

7. Experience needed. Certain skilled jobs can be learned only through apprenticeship training, but many jobs can be quickly learned by an inexperienced worker. Most supervisors want to hire only "experienced" people. If they re-evaluate their hiring and compensation policies, supervisors will discover that in many instances "inexperienced" employees are eager and quick to learn. If experience is really needed for a particular job, this factor must be considered in evaluation.

8. Human interaction. Jobs that require a great deal of personal contact and interaction (such as a salesperson) require a different set of skills than those requiring contact with a machine and a supervisor (such as an assembly-line worker).

9. Psychological factors. If there is a lot of freedom, innovation, risk taking, and responsibility, and the worker has to perform work according to a personal standard, the compensation rating should be higher than for a job requiring minimal levels of effort in these areas.

These general job characteristics will differ among organizations and jobs, and few supervisors will have comprehensive knowledge about all the positions under his or her jurisdiction. It is necessary, however, to collect as much information as possible for effective job evaluation.

[1] Edwin B. Flippo, *Principles of Personnel Management* (New York: McGraw-Hill, 1976), p. 294.

```
┌─────────────────────────────────────────────────────────────────────────┐
│                                                                           │
│   Job Title _____   │
│                                                                           │
│   Indicate:  H for high ability needed        L for low ability needed    │
│              A for average ability needed      O when not needed for this job │
│                                                                           │
│     1. Work rapidly for long periods      25. Memory for written directions │
│     2. Strength of hands                  26. Arithmetic computation       │
│     3. Strength of arms                   27. Intelligence                 │
│     4. Strength of back                   28. Adaptability                 │
│     5. Strength of legs                   29. Ability to make decisions    │
│     6. Dexterity of fingers               30. Ability to plan              │
│     7. Dexterity of hands and arms        31. Initiative                   │
│     8. Dexterity of foot and leg          32. Understanding mechanical devices │
│     9. Eye-hand coordination              33. Attention to many items      │
│    10. Foot-hand-eye coordination         34. Oral expression              │
│    11. Coordination of both hands         35. Skill in written expression  │
│    12. Estimate size of objects           36. Tact in dealing with people  │
│    13  Estimate quantity of objects       37. Memory of names and persons  │
│    14. Perceive form of objects           38. Personal appearance          │
│    15. Estimate speed of moving objects   39. Concentration amidst distractions │
│    16. Keenness of vision                 40. Emotional stability          │
│    17. Keenness of hearing                41. Work under hazardous conditions │
│    18. Sense of smell                     42. Estimate quality of objects  │
│    19. Sense of taste                     43. Unpleasant physical conditions │
│    20. Touch discrimination               44. Color discrimination         │
│    21. Muscular discrimination            45. Ability to meet and deal with people │
│    22. Memory for details (things)        46. Height                       │
│    23. Memory for abstract ideas          47. Weight                       │
│    24. Memory for oral directions                                          │
│                                                                           │
└─────────────────────────────────────────────────────────────────────────┘
```

Figure 12-1. Worker Characteristics Required. [With permission from Donald A. Laird and Eleanor Laird, *Psychology: Human Relations and Motivation,* 4th ed. (New York: McGraw-Hill, 1967), p. 375.]

Methods of Information Collection

The three most common methods of gathering job evaluation information are (1) questionnaires completed jointly by workers and supervisors, (2) interviews conducted with supervisors and employees, and (3) observing actual job performance.[2]

Questionnaires are not very reliable techniques. Direct observation is the most reliable method *if* the limited observation does not give a distorted picture of a complex job. For best results, proper job evaluation requires the collection of two types of information: (1) data about the job surroundings, and (2) characteristics of the tasks as they relate to employee characteristics. The nine factors mentioned earlier should serve as a guideline for data collection for most situations. Figure 12-1 presents a more complete list of job characteristics for rating individual jobs.

Any supervisor can adapt this type of job analysis to the needs of his or her organization. Job titles can be misleading, since specific characteristics will differ from job to job. Figure 12-2 illustrates another way to compare jobs on key variables by a simple and understandable method.

[2] George Strauss and Leonard Sayles, *Personnel: The Human Problem of Management,* 4th ed. (Englewood Cliffs, N.J.: Prentice-Hall, 1960), pp. 595–96.

Task	Stock Clerk		Carpenter's Assistant	
Dimension	High	Low	High	Low
Degree of physical exertion				
Degree of physical unpleasantness				
Outside work (high) Inside work (low)				
One place work				
Hours				
Degree of specialization				
Degree of freedom				
Degree of risktaking				
Degree of responsibility				

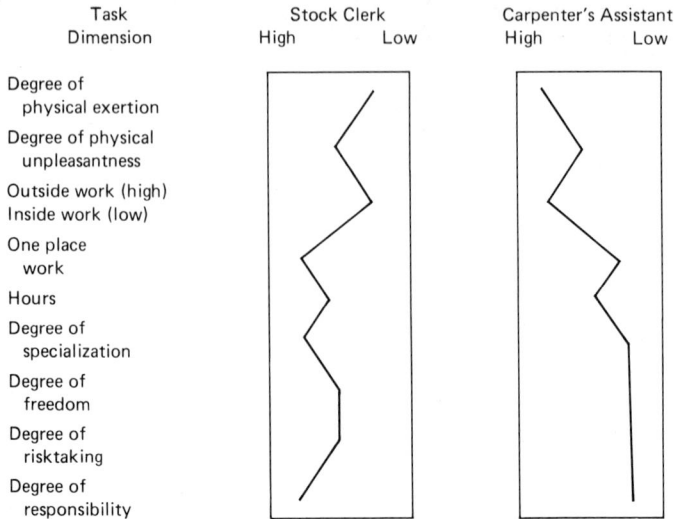

Figure 12-2. Task Dimension Differences for Stock Clerks and Carpenter's Assistants. [With permission from William F. Glueck, *Personnel: A Diagnostic Approach,* rev. ed. (Dallas, Tex.: Business Publications, Inc., 1978), p. 49.]

Methods of Job Evaluation

There are three basic methods of categorizing jobs in relation to a pay scale: (1) ranking, (2) classification, and (3) factor-point totals.

Ranking. This uncomplicated (and least reliable) method of evaluating jobs is accomplished by supervisors considering the importance and complexity of each job in their organization and placing it somewhere in a rank order from high to low. This allows for a great deal of subjectivity on behalf of the supervisor but may be acceptable for very small or simple organizations. Most organizations, however, require a more accurate rating method.

Classification. This technique groups occupations into work categories that are ranked according to responsibility and complexity. Groups of similar occupations are classified by salary ranges known as "grades." These pay grades may range 30 to 50 percent from lowest to highest and allow for merit and across-the-board increases. The competitive element can serve as a motivational opportunity for supervisors and employees. Figure 12-3 illustrates salary structures based on pay grades and occupational classification into groups.

Factor-point totals. This is probably the most objective and professional method of evaluating and ranking jobs. All jobs in the organization are rated and ranked on the same point scale after receiving a point total for each factor on which evaluation is based. Since each factor is evaluated separately, a job that might receive a low point rating on one factor, but medium or high rating on other factors, would not necessarily reduce its pay because of the possible negative stereotyping it may have because of one low rating. At least three precautions must be taken when using the factor-point total method

Consider promotional policies versus salary increases in the same job (what is the employee flexibility in jobs for the company?), for example, company policy: to move employees fast into other higher-rated jobs and promotional increases (if many separate jobs exist) versus merit increases (up to a point) for the same job over a considerable time span, or if there are only a very few separate jobs, then fewer grades are necessary (1 versus 2).

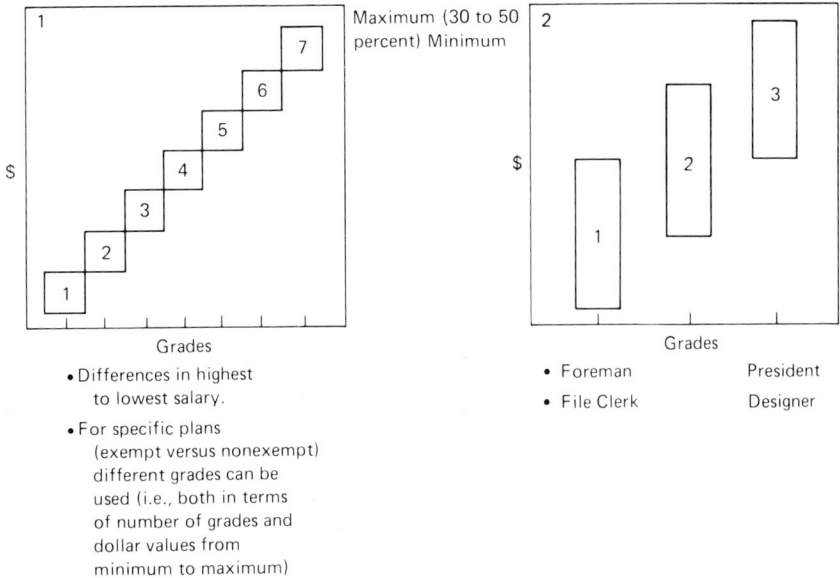

Figure 12-3. The Salary Structure. (With permission of the Pepsi-Cola Management Institute.)

of job evaluation: (1) selected factors must be applicable to all the jobs that are evaluated; (2) the factors must not be overlapping; and (3) the factors must be clear, easy to understand, and have concise reference points (such as 1 for poor and 10 for excellent) to easily determine distinctions between grades. Figure 12-4 provides an example of factor-point rating for job evaluation.

Regardless of the rating method selected by a supervisor, objectivity and fairness are essential ingredients for employee acceptance of the method. Pay scales must be satisfactory to workers and must closely reflect the workers' perception of their position in the organization. Workers expect supervisors to rank employees, and employees rank themselves against other employees. A supervisor should remember that wages determined by these rating systems help determine the workers' life-style and self-image.

Fairness in Compensation

Wages and salaries must be reasonably related to job requirements and work performance for workers to believe that their compensation is fair and equitable. If jobs are not fairly assessed and performance is not wisely evaluated, two unpleasant consequences can result: (1) worker discontent that can lead to high turnover and absenteeism, or (2) paying very high salaries for worker performance, thus making the company owners or stockholders unhappy.

The perception of fair compensation has two distinct sides: supervisory and

	Lowest (File Clerk)	Mid (Office Manager)	Highest (President)
Knowledge			
Education	15	45	60
Experience	10	30	65
Skill			
Creativity	0	25	50
Judgment	0	25	50
Foresight	0	15	50
Scope and impact			
Effect on sales	0	10	25
Effect on decisions	0	15	25
Company commitments	0	18	25
Relationships			
Internal	10	20	30
External	0	20	45
Direction over others			
Direct	0	9	50
Functional	0	7	25
	35	238	500

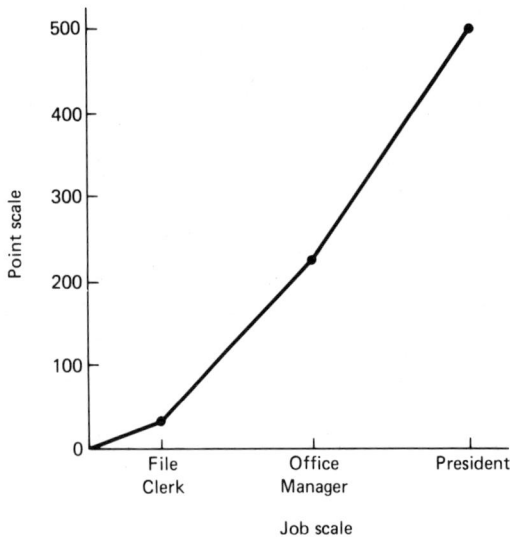

Figure 12-4. Example of Factor-Point Rating for a Low, Middle, and High Job. (With permission of the Pepsi-Cola Management Institute.)

employee. Fair compensation to the supervisor may mean paying as little as possible for the required work to be done. Fair compensation to the employee may mean getting a day's pay for a day's work, "plus a little extra for showing up." Both sides may be attempting to get as much as possible for the least amount of money or effort. This subjectivity underscores the need for organizations to establish standards for employee compensation.

Necessity of Standards

Job ranking and performance evaluation standards possess two categories of factors affecting compensation decisions: (1) the knowledge or ability required to perform the job satisfactorily, and (2) working conditions surrounding employees and their jobs.[3] Usually, jobs requiring more skill or higher levels of training will demand more pay than those requiring less skill or training. Jobs that are performed in dangerous, extremely noisy, or dirty surroundings often require more pay to keep workers than those jobs with pleasant physical and social surroundings. Most employees and supervisors agree on these general characteristics of a fair *system* of compensation, but the tangle comes in agreeing on fairness for individual pay.

Factors for Fair Pay

A fair compensation system should be characterized by several factors.

1. Logical. Pay scales must coincide with generally agreed-upon and understood criteria that are established by management. For example, an average regional salary or wage for a particular job would be logical for a forty-hour week of work; it would be illogical if a company expected sixty hours of work if other companies were paying comparable wages for forty hours.

2. Consistent. Favoritism based on personality attributes cannot be tolerated. Workers who meet the performance standards should receive equal compensation, regardless of their personality. Paying relatives, sweethearts, or friends more than other employees with the same jobs creates tremendous problems for the supervisor and the company.

3. Equitable. Supervisors must ensure that workers understand why some jobs receive higher pay than others and what are the specific criteria for merit (or good performance) increases. Good communication is the key to success so that employees can understand the quantity, quality, difficulty, and supply and demand concepts of jobs as they relate to compensation.

4. Competitive. Employees must have an incentive to perform in an outstanding fashion, over and above the call of duty. If an organization gives only cost-of-living or seniority increases it will seriously damage the motivation and morale of its above-average employees. Psychological or monetary rewards must be large enough and directly related to increased results in order to motivate employees to be exceptional.

A fair and well-understood compensation system is a powerful motivational tool for supervisors and a team-building device that is beneficial for everyone in the organization.

The Value of Job Descriptions

The accuracy and success of job evaluations depend greatly on accurate job descriptions. These descriptions contain information collected through questionnaires, interviews, or direct observation. A good job description should be a concise one- to two-page statement of the principal job responsibilities and duties. It should be developed by the supervisor and upper-level management. This can help to clarify the role expectations of that job. Role expectations

---

[3] Wendell L. French, *The Personnel Management Process,* 3rd ed. (Boston: Houghton-Mifflin, 1974), p. 210.

```
POSITION: PROJECT SUPERVISOR

 1. Assemble materials price quotes for new jobs.
 2. Assemble subcontractor price quotes for new jobs.
 3. Coordinate with the president on plans take-off.
 4. Help assemble the total bid and submit to the president for final review.
 5. Job start:  Coordinate with the secretary preparation of Field Coordinator folder and job
    book.
 6. Job start:  Coordinate contact of all subcontractors.
 7. Job start:  Coordinate preparation of purchase orders.
 8. Job start:  Order all job facilities.
    (a)  Telephone.
    (b)  Electricity.
    (c)  Permits.
    (d)  Temporary toilets.
    (e)  Storage trailer.
    (f)  Temporary utilities.
 9. Daily communication with Field Coordinators on:
    (a)  Job materials supply.
    (b)  Job construction details and addendums.
    (c)  Coordination of carpentry substitutes.
    (d)  Coordination of all substitutes and substitute performance problems.
    (e)  Scheduling of equipment.
    (f)  Daily job progress.
10. Handle all warranty work:  phone calls, inspection, and follow-up.
11. Periodically visit sites, at least three times during construction.
12. Continually review plans, specifications, and detail drawings.
13. Meet weekly with the president and staff to review progress and conditions on all jobs.
14. Manage and control warehouse materials and equipment.
```

Figure 12-5. A Job Description.

have been defined as "the attitudes and beliefs that people who interact with the job incumbent and his or her activities have about what the incumbent should and should not do."[4] An accurate job description will help keep role expectations realistic and mutually understandable. Figure 12-5 shows a job description developed for a construction company.

Usefulness of Job Descriptions

Job descriptions should not be haphazard summaries or comprehensive, detailed descriptions of job duties. They should, however, provide any person with a composite picture of the job and its principal tasks. This information can, of course, be very useful to supervisors and employees alike.

1. They can stimulate supervisory discussion regarding the necessity of each position.

2. They can establish required qualifications for workers holding the jobs.

3. They can aid planners and recruiters in their efforts to fulfill the organization's personnel needs.

4. They can more quickly orient new workers to the nature and scope of the job. They are not, however, a substitute for thorough orientation and training.

[4] David W. Belcher, *Wage and Salary Administration* (Englewood Cliffs, N.J.: Prentice-Hall, 1959), pp. 268–69.

5. They can serve as a basis for the establishment of quantitative and qualitative performance standards.

6. They can serve as a partial basis for job evaluation. David Belcher has stated that "job evaluation is the process of determining the relative worth of jobs within an organization, and job descriptions, if written with this objective in mind, can provide the basic information for making these evaluative decisions."[5] Job descriptions are not, however, a magic wand that will solve a supervisor's evaluation responsibilities. They can create problems if handled improperly and have several pitfalls for which supervisors should be alert.

Abuses and Misuses of Job Descriptions

Job descriptions can be very helpful when they are carefully written and properly used. Inadequate descriptions can also contribute to serious problems.[6]

1. Disagreement in understanding. Inaccurate job descriptions are dangerous and often result in disagreement between supervisors and workers who assume that a description accurately describes and reflects the job. When this occurs, supervisors should re-examine their facts and obtain more data on the job itself.

2. Obsolescence. Antiquated job descriptions should be revised and updated quickly. If not, decisions and evaluations may be based on invalid data.

3. Static rather than dynamic. Ignoring dynamic qualities of jobs results in describing the job under its former holder and not the present one. All employees bring unique work habits and ways of doing things into a job that alter the job structure.

4. Sloppy writing. Job descriptions have no value if they cannot be understood or are too general. This is a major problem with many organizations' job descriptions.

5. Overdependence. Inequitable compensation systems and poor managerial decisions can result from overreliance on job descriptions. They must be used wisely as a tool in conjunction with other information and sound judgment.[7]

Job Descriptions for Supervisors

This chapter has emphasized assisting supervisors to write job descriptions, evaluate jobs, and establish performance criteria. But what about the supervisor's job? How is it described and evaluated? Peter F. Drucker has identified four functions of the supervisor's job.[8]

1. The job itself. The supervisor is hired for the job itself. The job is relatively permanent and will be needed for an indefinite period of time.

2. Temporary assignments. Special jobs occur every day in a supervisor's activities that may or may not be written in the job description. These challenges must be met regularly and successfully.

---

[5] Ibid., p. 227.
[6] Strauss and Sayles, *Personnel*, p. 592.
[7] Robert M. Fulmer, *Practical Human Relations* (Homewood, Ill.: Irwin, 1977), p. 340.
[8] Peter F. Drucker, *Management: Tasks, Responsibilities, Duties* (New York: Harper, 1973), pp. 414–15.

3. Multitype human relationships. Supervisors are in continual communication with superiors, subordinates, and staff. They must deal openly and honestly with all of these individuals regardless of position.

4. Information. Supervisors are initiators, receivers, and transmitters of information. They report progress and problems to superiors, communicate decisions to subordinates, and receive information from various sources for processing and transmission to other persons.

Supervisors should keep these four factors in mind as they write and follow their own job description. They should continually update and define their positions and evaluate their own performance if they are to be successful supervisors.

Performance Standards

Criteria by which an employee's job performance is evaluated are called *performance standards.* They may be quantitative, qualitative, or both. Supervisors use performance standards for evaluating employee progress. Performance standards are developed on the basis of job descriptions and organizational goals.

Job descriptions specify what tasks must be accomplished, and performance standards indicate how well, how much, or how often they must be performed. Sales people may be evaluated by how many products they sell, a secretary by how fast or how many letters he or she can type, a commissioned artist by how well the task is performed, and a supervisor may be evaluated on the basis of all these criteria—and more.

Determining Performance Standards

The determination of performance standards within an organization depends greatly on executive decisions about overall standards of performance including company profit, employee wages and salaries, job satisfaction for workers, fairness in performance evaluation, and even the future of the company. Top management first has to outline the organization's goals clearly and translate these goals to the requirements needed at the supervisory levels of the company. There must be an understanding of the relationship between upper- and lower-level activities in order to translate a 10 percent return on investment goal for the organization into 1500 units of output per week for the average assembly line worker or file clerk.

The supervisor's responsibility will be to obtain job descriptions for his or her employees and determine which employees are responsible for the various aspects of the organization's total set of activities. The supervisor may be assisted by a team of personnel specialists, an operating manager, or a consulting group. Each job should be discussed in terms of what can and should be accomplished by the job holder.

Based on the organizational goals and job descriptions, supervisors should set minimum levels of performance where goals can be realistically met. Standards should be translated into specific task expectations for each job and explicit criteria should be established for judging minimum performance. Workers must not be left in the dark about their own job expectations and the kind of performance they should exhibit. Figure 12-6 provides a partial list

Compliance with Performance Standards Is Adequate when:

I. Medical treatment for occupational injuries or disease, first aid treatment for certain non-occupational conditions, and other care as necessary for the industrial health program is provided.
   A. There is no increase in Workmen's Compensation claims due to inadequate medical care within the Division.
   B. The medical reviews of employee Workmen's Compensation Claims are completed within seven days.
   C. The number of dispensaries is adequate to handle the treatment of the plant population considering the geographic location of the area the dispensary will serve, the number of employees that can adequately be handled per shift by a nurse (50 calls), and the hazards of the area.
II. We have recommended and developed industrial health policies.
   A. Incidence of occupational disease as noted by Workmen's Compensation claims and our frequency rates if 1 per 100 employees per month or less.
   B. Evidence that health programs are being adequately engaged in as indicated by current procedures and current physicians' program manuals.
   C. There are no reported employee terminations due to environmental factors that the Medical Section has failed to correct by preventive medical plans.
   D. The Corporate Director of Health and Safety approves and supports our program.

Figure 12-6. Performance Standards for the Medical Director in an Industrial Relations Department. [With permission from Wendell L. French, *The Personnel Management Process,* 3rd ed. (Boston: Houghton-Mifflin, 1974), p. 221.]

of performance standards for the supervisor of the medical department of a large corporation. Note that some standards are quantitative and some are qualitative.

Pitfalls in Determining Standards of Performance

The consideration of employees and the presence of a union are two potential problems in developing and using consistent performance standards.

When performance standards are designed solely by supervisors and dictated down to employees, they are likely to be resented and resisted by workers. Many researchers have discovered that people not only like to have input in setting standards for themselves, but will often set standards higher than management would have set them. With joint standard setting, the standards are usually more fair, fulfilled more frequently, and result in greater job satisfaction among employees.

Performance standards may be built into the labor contract of a unionized organization. Changes in the standards may necessitate contract renegotiation, which can be more trouble than the potential benefit. Historically, unions have resisted management attempts to increase performance standards and have argued for unchanging uniform standards. When a union cooperates in establishing fair and realistic performance standards, however, they can be developed with greater practical value.

Performance Evaluation

Performance evaluation is the practice of *using* performance standards that have, hopefully, been rationally and realistically developed. Unfortunately, job

Table 12-1. Purposes for Merit-Rating Programs in Companies with Both Blue-Collar and White-Collar Employees. (With permission from the National Industrial Conference Board, "Personnel Practices in Factory and Office: Manufacturing," Studies in Personnel Policy, No. 194, 1964, p. 17.)

Purposes	Number of Companies	Percent
Wage or salary determination, or both	114	69
Promotion	112	73
Training and development	102	61
To help supervisors know their employees	101	61
To let workers know their progress	102	61
Transfer	98	59
Follow-up interviews	57	34
Discharge	77	46
Layoff	44	27
Personnel research	48	29
Total companies with merit-rating programs	166	100

descriptions and performance standards are often unused or misused and lead to much frustration for workers and supervisors.

Merit Rating

Most organizations use some form of a merit-rating system for appraising employee performance and determining compensation increases. A report by the National Industrial Conference Board indicated that white-collar jobs are more likely to be merit rated than blue-collar jobs. Sixty-three percent of manufacturing companies surveyed used merit-rating systems for white-collar jobs and 43 percent did so for blue-collar jobs. Most blue-collar workers are paid standard hourly rates rather than a range of possible wages according to employee performance. The additional uses of merit-rating programs in companies having such programs for both blue- and white-collar workers are listed in Table 12-1.

A typical frequency for evaluating rank-and-file employees is twice a year. Evaluation more often than this can cause the supervisor to get caught up in daily occurrences. Conversely, waiting too long can erase incidents that should influence the appraisal.

Who Rates?

Three groups of employees in an organization can contribute to the merit ratings of others: superiors, subordinates, and peers. Combinations of these groups are often used in rating employee performance, but most rating systems have superiors rate subordinates. Supervisors must evaluate the performance of their subordinates, but they should be aware of at least two other systems that might be helpful.[9]

[9] Eugene C. Mayfield, "Peer Nominations—A Neglected Selection Tool," *Personnel,* July–August 1971, pp. 37–43.

Peer ratings. Ratings by peers of equal position in the organization have been used for promotion and transfer decisions, and to improve supervisors' performance. It is used mostly in the military, and, wherever used, is most effective when the job calls for frequent interaction between peers.

Group ratings. A supervisor and his or her superior may rate those employees under the supervisor's control or a select group of subordinates, peers, and superiors may be chosen to evaluate a group of employees. More information can be made available to several persons than to one, and subjectivity can be minimized with this approach. Most supervisors, however, individually evaluate the performance of subordinates. How can they insure objectivity in evaluation and how can they effectively and constructively communicate the results of merit ratings to employees?

A System for Performance Evaluation

An effective performance evaluation system is a critical element of any effective compensation system. Therefore, it must be fair, logical, consistent, equitable, and competitive. To achieve these standards, an evaluation system must be based on performance standards established during the job evaluation process. If supervisor and subordinate know and understand the minimum performance standards for a particular job, then evaluating employee performance is easier.

Figure 12-7 is a sample merit-rating form that is based on the same principle as the factor-point rating system for jobs. After a set of important job performance characteristics is established, the employee's supervisor ranks him or her on the basis of perceived performance in each category. This particular form arranges categories in reverse and inconsistent order to prevent a supervisor from haphazardly running down the column checking for "poor," "good," "excellent," and so on. An astute supervisor will realize that any particular set of characteristics may or may not accurately describe a job. As mentioned earlier, the purpose of job evaluation is to provide standards of performance that are consistent with the organization's overall goals and the nature of the individual job. Supervisors should not blindly accept a set of pre-established merit-rating characteristics but should develop a realistic checklist that accurately reflects the duties and responsibilities of the job.

The Appraisal Interview

Supervisors should communicate the results of performance evaluations to individual employees. If handled properly, the procedure can be a motivating experience for the worker. If handled poorly, they can create anxiety, hostility, and misunderstanding. Some suggestions for making the appraisal interview a constructive activity are presented in the following paragraphs.[10]

1. Performance. Clearly communicate to the employee that you will discuss his or her actual performance in the interview.

2. Specific goals. Refer to specific goals in terms of what is expected and what was done. Do not generalize in performance evaluation.

[10] Robert J. Hayden, "Performance Appraisal: A Better Way," *Personnel Journal,* 1973, p. 613.

Dept.	Clock No.

1. Disregard your personal feelings. Judge the employee on the qualities listed below
2. Study the definitions of each factor, and the various phases of each before rating
3. Call to mind instances that are typical of employee's work and actions
4. Using your own careful judgment—check the phrase in each factor that is typical
5. If employee performs no supervision—do not rate additional factor for supervisory ability
6. Explain on reverse side any unusual characteristic not covered in regular factors

#	Factor	Range					Rating
1	Quality — Performance in meeting quality standards	Careless **4**	Just gets by **8**	Does a good job **12**	Rejects and errors rare **16**	Exceptionally high quality **20**	
2	Job Knowledge — Understanding in all phases of the work	Expert in own job and several others **25**	Expert but limited to own job **20**	Knows job fairly well **15**	Improvement necessary—just gets by **10**	Inadequate knowledge **8**	
3	Quantity — Output of satisfactory work	Turns out required amount but seldom more **8**	Frequently turns out more than required amount **12**	Slow—output is seldom required amount **4**	Exceptionally fast, output high **20**	Usually does more than expected **16**	
4	Dependability — Works conscientiously according to instructions	Dependable, no checking necessary **20**	Very little checking **16**	Follows instructions **12**	Frequent checking **8**	Continuous checking and follow-up **4**	
5	Initiative — Thinks constructively and originates action	Good decisions and actions but requires some supervision **9**	Minimum of supervision **12**	Thinks and acts constructively, no supervision required **15**	Requires constant supervision **3**	Fair decisions—routine worker **6**	
6	Adaptability — Ability to learn and meet changed conditions	Prefers old methods; does not remember instructions **3**	Learns slowly, reluctant to change **6**	Normal ability, routine worker **9**	Short period for mental adjustment, willing to change **12**	Learns rapidly—adjusts and grasps changes quickly **15**	
7	Attitude — Willingness to cooperate and carry out demands	Good team worker **10**	Cooperative **8**	Limited cooperation **6**	Passive resistance **4**	Poor cooperation; argumentative **2**	
8	Attendance — Amount of excessive absenteeism	2 to 3 days normal or 2 days own accord **6**	1 to 2 days normal or 1 day own accord **8**	No days lost **10**	3 to 4 days normal or 3 days own accord **4**	More than 4 days absence **2**	
9	Safety and Housekeeping — Compliance with safety and housekeeping rules	Safe and orderly worker; equipment well cared for **10**	Workplace clean and safe **8**	Occasional warning about safety and orderliness **6**	Warned repeatedly about safety and cleanliness **4**	Area dirty, safety rules ignored **2**	
10	Potentiality — Personal ability to lead and teach others	Has no more growth **2**	Future growth doubtful **4**	Slow development ahead **6**	Bright future growth **8**	Exceptional possibilities **10**	
11	Personality — Ability to get along with associates	Disagreeable **2**	Difficult to get along with **4**	Average or reasonable **6**	Well liked and respected **8**	Winning personality **10**	
12	Supervisory Ability — Additional rating for supervisors only	Poor organization and planning **7**	Inadequate supervision **14**	Nothing outstanding **21**	Good planning and effective organization **28**	Outstanding leadership **35**	

Date rated _____ Signed _____ Total _____

Use space on reverse side for remarks. Explain any rating that is abnormally low or exceptionally high.

Note that to minimize halo effect, rating scales for some factors are reversed, such as for job knowledge, dependability, attitude, safety, and housekeeping. Other scales are mixed in order, such as for quantity, initiative, and attendance.

Figure 12-7. Typical Employee Performance Rating Sheet. [With permission from Robert M. Fulmer, *Practical Human Relations* (Homewood, Ill.: Richard D. Irwin, Inc., 1977), p. 343.]

3. Credit. Identify and compliment the employee on tasks he or she has performed well. Give credit where credit is due.

4. Room for improvement. Point out responsibilities and duties where performance has been substandard. Communicate to the employee why improvement is necessary, suggest ways for improvement, and obtain the employee's suggestions for improvement.

5. Doing the specific job. Judge the employee's job performance, not the employee. Accept responsibility and blame if you have been partially at fault for the employee's performance, and work together on a solution. Do

Table 12-2. Appraisal Counseling: Three Types of Interview. [With permission from Norman R. Maier, *The Appraisal Interview: Three Basic Approaches* (La Jolla, Calif.: University Associates, 1976).]

Method	Tell and Sell	Tell and Listen	Problem Solving
Role of interviewer	Judge	Judge	Helper
Objective	To communicate evaluation To persuade employee to improve	To communicate evaluation To release defensive feelings	To stimulate growth and development in employee
Assumptions	Employee desires to correct weaknesses if he knows them Any person can improve if he so chooses A superior is qualified to evaluate a subordinate	People will change if defensive feelings are removed	Growth can occur without correcting faults Discussing job problems leads to improved performance
Reactions	Defensive behavior suppressed Attempts to convey hostility	Defensive behavior expressed Employee feels accepted	Problem-solving behavior
Skills	Salesmanship Patience	Listening and reflecting feelings Summarizing	Listening and reflecting feelings Reflecting ideas Using exploratory questions Summarizing
Attitude	People profit from criticism and appreciate help	One can respect the feelings of others if one understands them	Discussion develops new ideas and mutual interests
Motivation	Use of positive or negative incentives or both (Extrinsic in that motivation is added to the job itself)	Resistance to change reduced Positive incentive (Extrinsic and some intrinsic motivation)	Increased freedom Increased responsibility (Intrinsic motivation in that interest is inherent in the task)
Gains	Success most probable when employee respects interviewer	Develops favorable attitude to superior, which increases probability of success	Almost assured of improvement in some respect
Risks	Loss of loyalty Inhibition of independent judgment Face-saving problems created	Need for change may not be developed	Employee may lack ideas Change may be other than what superior had in mind
Values	Perpetuates existing practices and values	Permits interviewer to change his views in the light of employee's responses Some upward communication	Both learn, since experience and views are pooled Change is facilitated

207

not compare the employee with anyone else, but stick to what he or she has or has not accomplished on the job.

6. Goals. Let the employee know the specific goals that are expected over the next time period. This will better prepare the employee for the next appraisal interview and can contribute to motivated performance.

7. Sharing the job. Offer your assistance in improving the employee's performance. Ask what you can do to make tasks easier to achieve and to insure that goals are met. This will instill confidence and enthusiasm in the employee about his or her work.

Table 12-2 summarizes three types of appraisal interviews, the techniques used, the rationale behind each method, and the advantages and disadvantages of each. The manner in which a supervisor conducts appraisal interviews depends largely on his or her personality and attitudes toward employees, the job, and the organization.

Summary

Employees' life-styles are determined to a great extent by the amount of income they earn. Supervisors, therefore, are responsible for letting employees know what is expected from them by establishing job standards and evaluating performance fairly, logically, consistently, equitably, and competitively. Establishing an acceptable method of job evaluation is the first step to a fair compensation system in an organization. Three basic methods of job evaluation are (1) ranking, (2) classification, and (3) factor-point totals.

There are nine basic job characteristics that are most frequently considered in the evaluation of jobs: (1) degree of physical exertion required, (2) pleasantness or unpleasantness of the work environment, (3) job location, (4) time required to do the work, (5) amount of specialization required, (6) education required, (7) experience needed, (8) human interaction, and (9) psychological factors such as freedom and responsibility. Questionnaires, interviews, and direct observation are three ways to gather information used for job evaluation.

Job descriptions provide a composite picture of each job and form the basis for accurate job evaluation. They should outline the principal duties and responsibilities of a job in a one- to two-page, concise statement. Job descriptions can stimulate management discussion, aid in personnel planning, recruiting, training, orientation, and setting performance standards. Job descriptions can be misused, however, so supervisors must be wise and cautious in using them. The supervisor's job must also be regularly evaluated and ranked. It is characterized by at least four basic components: (1) the job itself, (2) temporary assignments, (3) human relationships, and (4) information flow.

Job descriptions and evaluations and organization goals form the basis for performance standards. Performance standards may be quantitative, qualitative, or both, and are the criteria by which an employee's performance is judged. Supervisors must insure that they are (1) communicated clearly and effectively to employees, and (2) consider union contractual agreements.

Most organizations employ some form of merit-rating system to aid in determining pay raises, promotions, transfers, to effectively communicate organization goals to the employees, and to receive their feedback. Most merit ratings are made by an employee's immediate superior, but peer and group ratings may enhance the fairness and objectivity of the process. Performance evaluation must also be fair, consistent, logical, equitable, and allow for competition among employees. Standard characteristics are not acceptable for judging performance on a particular job. A supervisor should consider characteristics that accurately reflect the nature of the job being evaluated. The appraisal interview is the best method for communicating performance evaluations to the worker. If handled properly, it can be a constructive, motivating opportunity for immediate and future performance.

Key Terms

Classification. A job evaluation technique that groups occupations into categories or grades with pay ranges that allow for merit and across-the-board increases.

Factor-Point Totals. Considered by many to be the most objective job evaluation method by rating and ranking all jobs in the organization on the same point scale after point totals have been established for each job factor.

Fair Compensation. From the employee's point of view, a subjective amount that represents a day's pay for a day's work.

Fair Compensation System. A system that relates pay to the work done in a logical, consistent, equitable, and competitive manner.

Job Description. A concise written statement of the principal responsibilities and duties of a job.

Job Evaluation. The process of classifying and ranking jobs for pay levels, based upon various factors (physical exertion, specialization, etc.) that determine the relative worth of each job in the organization.

Merit Rating. A form of performance evaluation where employee performance is appraised and appropriate compensation determined.

Performance Standards. Minimal levels of performance for use by workers in setting realistic goals.

Ranking. A method of job evaluation determining the importance and complexity of each job in the organization and placing it in rank order from low to high.

Role Expectation. Attitudes and beliefs people have about each other's jobs.

Review Questions

1. What role does the supervisor play in employee compensation?
2. List and describe the main factors in a fair compensation system.
3. List as many factors as you can that should be considered when classifying a job on a pay scale.
4. How does the supervisor collect information for a job evaluation?
5. What are the main methods for evaluating jobs? What are the advantages and disadvantages of each?
6. What is a job description? How is it used in an organization?
7. It is said that an appraisal interview should be a constructive event for the supervisor and worker. Describe how this is possible.
8. List and describe jobs that can be evaluated by quantity alone, quality alone, and a combination of the two criteria.

Exercises

I. Constructing a Job Description

Based upon what you have learned in the chapter, develop a detailed job description for yourself if you are a supervisor. If you are not a supervisor, choose someone you know very well and prepare a job description for him or her. Be sure to include measurable factors of performance in the description. (If you are married, you might try developing a job description for the supervisory role of husband or wife.)

II. Constructing a Job Evaluation System

You have just been made supervisor of a company that manufactures wooden children's toys. There has been a history of dissatisfaction with the company's compensation system, and you want to create a new job evaluation ranking that everyone will agree is fair. How would you rank the following jobs in your department?

Your secretary.	Planer.
Inventory schedule clerk.	Joiner.
Shipping and receiving foreman.	Gluer.
Equipment maintenance foreman.	Driller.
Facility custodian.	Finisher.
Cutter.	Packer.

What criteria did you use to rank these jobs? What assumptions did you make about each job? Did you find job titles misleading? Now compare your rankings with other class members. Which jobs were the most difficult to rank? Why.

Case 12 • Barry Heavener

Barry Heavener was just promoted to supervisor of the electronics maintenance and repair division of a large airline company. The employees in his shop are union members, some with twenty years of tenure with the company.

About three years ago, company management devised the following performance rating form to be completed by the supervisor for each employee.

In concept, Barry thought the rating system was a good idea. However, Barry learned that after the form was introduced, employees began refusing to sign it unless they were rated "excellent" in all three categories. When supervisors began turning them

---

Name of Employee _____

Job Title _____

	Poor	Good	Excellent
Job Knowledge	____	____	____
Job Quantity	____	____	____
Job Quality	____	____	____

_____   _____
Supervisor's Signature   Employee's Signature

I have seen this completed rating form
and it has been discussed with me by my
supervisor. I accept the ratings.

---

in without signatures, numerous grievances were filed with management at each rating period. In order to avoid the time and frustration of the grievance procedures, supervisors began giving each employee the highest ratings every review period. This completely eliminated grievance cases related to the rating form.

1. If you were Barry, what would you do?

2. What consequences do you imagine resulted from the submissiveness of the supervisors?

3. What needs changing in this company—the rating form or the supervisors? How would you improve the rating form? How would you improve the quality of the supervisory staff?

CHAPTER 13

Control: Staying on Top of Things

The trouble with most of us is that we would rather be ruined by praise than saved by criticism.

Norman Vincent Peale

Learning Objectives

- To list the basic steps in the process of control and to learn the importance of control in all phases of supervision.
- To be able to identify the characteristics of a good control system.
- To recognize the different types of control and their functions.
- To apply concepts of control to supervisory tasks and personal activities.

Experienced supervisors say, "Plan your work—work your plan." It is simple advice, but contained within those last three words is a perfect summary for this chapter. All books written about control lay down useful principles to help eager supervisors "work their plans."

This control process is so common to daily life it is often difficult to recognize the steps involved. Automatically, our bodies keep control of our body temperature. When it is cold, the body closes skin pores to save valuable heat. When it is hot, the body perspires, using a simple evaporation process to regain its normal temperature. But unless we run a fever or get the chills, thermostatic controls rarely come to mind.

Control techniques are essentially the same in every operation. Whether in terms of body temperature, cash flow, office procedures, morale, or product quality, control is needed to keep all components operating efficiently.

We should never need to discuss control if all the plans we set in motion proceeded without a hitch. Of course, this would take a lot of the spice from life, and though we can hope everything goes according to plan, the truth is that people thrive on challenge. Good supervision requires that we learn to appreciate pitting our wits against our problems, preferably before they occur.

The Basics of Control

The control process, regardless of its goal, can be boiled down to three steps: (1) establishing standards, (2) measuring performance against these standards, and (3) correcting deviations from standards and plans. To put these terms in down-home terminology, control is (1) sayin' how things oughta be, (2) seein' how things is, and (3) straightenin' out what's crooked.

Exact, specific standards must be established before any meaningful evaluation can be made. Almost all commodities—money, time, quotas—are measured in value against standardized scales because vague goals and values confuse and nullify evaluation.

Types of Standards

A standard is an expression of expected quantity or quality of performance. For example, a sales person's standard may be four calls a day, and at least four presentations a week. An assembly-line worker's standard may be to turn out 100 units of product a day.

Standards may be set in several ways. One is to base the standard on past experience. The result of such analysis is a statistical or historical standard. But no present-day standards for precision can result from repeating past performances. Competition with the past may be sufficient if best efforts have been exerted in the past, but remember that matching a poor effort probably presents no challenge to employees.

Gut-level appraisal by the person in charge is probably the most common method of setting standards. In some ways, this technique has never been surpassed. Information drawn from past experience can help set performance standards in profitability, market position, employee attitudes, and even public responsibility. But the best idea of what constitutes satisfactory performance comes from the supervisor's own mind. The relation between a supervisor's subjectivity-objectivity ratio and success is narrow. A supervisor must carefully balance the use of information with personal intuition.

One way to help ensure accurate appraisals is to develop standards based on observation of workers in action. Such engineered standards, reflecting careful analysis of specific situations, may usually be considered fairly objective. Workers, however, usually learn that it is wiser to take it easy whenever the people with the stopwatch come around. They know that the lower they "engineer" those engineered standards, the better they will look on day-to-day production reports.

Standards for Control

Although measurement of above-average performance is necessary to give standards a real purpose, in most cases we do it, measure it, and then fix it. The most important aspect in evaluation is stating the goal in measurable terms at the outset so that research, evaluation, and objectives can be effectively compared.

Cybernetics is the processing and interpreting of all this information. If supervisors are to set up and properly use valid control measures, they must work within these systems of control. To determine the value of information intended to measure and describe a certain performance, ask yourself the following five questions:

1. Is the information timely? Little benefit can be gained in receiving one month's data at the end of the following month. A good supervisor must oversee, rather than record, and may make decisions for two, three, or four weeks on the basis of a few days' information.

2. Are appropriate units of measure used? Statistics can be slippery communicators, so gains, losses, and status quos must be explained in clear, accurate terms relevant to the actual subject matter the numbers represent. Measurements determining quality, as opposed to quantity, may require different evaluation standards.

3. Is the information reliable? Because of the increased use of computers, more information can be tabulated, analyzed, and transferred more accurately and rapidly than ever. For standards to be meaningful, however, the data source must be dependable. The best processing in the world will not improve the quality of data that is basically faulty.

4. Is the information valid? Validity refers to the extent to which the stated information actually and accurately expresses what is being described. Suppose that there were only two cars in a race and the Ford finished first, and the Chevrolet second. How would you interpret the following press report from a Chevrolet public relations employee: "While our Chevrolet did come in second, the Ford finished next to last." The figures are accurate and the information source reliable, but the conclusion is misleading.

5. Is the information being channeled to the proper person? An effective control system will communicate right information at the right time to the right person. Information must flow to the proper person with the responsibility and authority to make decisions that will positively affect the operation. The astute supervisor will insure that valuable information does not fall on the desks or ears of indifference or incompetence.

Measuring the Performance

Measuring the performance is the indispensable second step in the control process. It is at this point that discrepancies between the ideal and the actual first show up. Without evaluation a standard is useless, but without corrective action results will not improve. For example, suppose the standard for the paint department of a boat manufacturer is twenty completed boats per week. Daily output may vary by one or two boats, but each Friday the supervisor could either check a production report or physically count the finished inventory. If the weekly output is fewer than twenty, the supervisor should investigate the reasons for not making the standard, and provide whatever resources and assistance are needed to make up the loss during the following week. If weekly output is twenty or more, the supervisor should praise the employees using human relations and communications skills discussed elsewhere.

Correcting mistakes is the supervisor's strongest defense against future control problems. The sooner a correction can be made in a procedural problem, the faster a desired goal can be reached. Once the problem is pinpointed, the supervisor can choose from several solutions. The final decision may entail redrawing plans, changing goals, reorganizing functions, reassigning duties, adding staff, and retraining or even firing workers.

A supervisor must decide which individual style of control suits his or her personality best. Few incidents are more confusing or comical than an easygoing supervisor who decides it is time to get tough.

Characteristics of a Good Control System

Although broad generalizations may be made about the desirable characteristics of a control system, it is only natural that each individual system requires a special design. However, these ten characteristics should always be considered when forming control systems.[1]

1. Controls must reflect the nature of the activity. Control practices of a professional football team will differ drastically from those used by the Girl Scouts. Methods for control should be created to suit specific situations. Poor blocking and tackling in a game may mandate more weight lifting, running, and dummy-hitting to improve for the next game. A camping group that gets lost and runs out of food may mandate more map reading and survival practice before the next expedition.

2. Controls should report errors promptly. It is more advantageous to know things are about to go wrong than to learn they are out of control. The controlling supervisor should give as much attention to ominous trends as to actual failures.

3. Controls should be forward-looking. Although some mistakes are inevitable, a controlling supervisor understands the system well enough to predict a good portion of problems that lie ahead.

4. Controls should point out exceptions at critical points. Because supervisors cannot possibly watch over every phase under their authority, they must be careful to handle only those situations that are out of the ordinary. Since they cannot treat all problems simultaneously, they must wisely budget both time and effort to solve the more important discrepancies first.

[1] Harold Koontz and Cyril O'Donnell, *Management,* 7th ed. (New York: McGraw-Hill, 1980), pp. 734–39.

5. Controls should be objective. Business transactions are commonly thought to be conducted coolly and objectively. But most critical business decisions are based on personal, subjective feelings. The supervisor must strive to keep control activities free from influences of personality.

6. Controls should be flexible. Although objectivity is essential, it must not be carried to such extremes that the system lacks flexibility. Alternative plans for situations that may arise must be built into the control system. Only then is a supervisor prepared to use another route to correction if the first choice proves inadequate.

7. Controls should reflect the organizational pattern. Numerical information must specifically designate the exact locations of problem areas. General information about a malfunction somewhere can lead only to accusations and buck-passing between departments.

8. Controls should be economical. A supervisor should guard against establishing an overly complicated system. Sophisticated systems reflect well on a supervisor's intelligence, but danger lies in the temptation to make the system a goal in itself. Controls should always be considered a means to an end.

9. Controls should be understandable. The system must be easy for the workers to comprehend. Impressive, complex charts are displayed by some supervisors though they do their actual work through another, simpler system. In such a case, the displayed control system does not represent actual activities of the operation.

10. Controls should indicate corrective action. A functioning control system must do more than simply flash a red light. Decisions about emergencies must be made before a problem actually occurs. Control systems should show where failures are occurring, who is responsible for them, and exactly which remedies would be most helpful.

Control Categories

Control processes fall into five general categories: *inventory control* is concerned with the steps involved in storing ice cubes or twenty-foot igloos; *production control* monitors and adjusts quantities of things from peanuts to grease paint; and *quality control* tests and adjusts qualities like crunchiness and pizazz. A fourth area, *financial control,* ensures that expenses or delays dictated by any of the other control procedures will not send the company into bankruptcy.

Production Control

Production control consists of six functions:

1. *Routing* determines the operations to be performed, their sequence, and the flow of materials through a series of operations.

2. *Loading* assigns work to a machine or department in advance.

3. *Scheduling* of production determines the time when each operation is to take place.

4. *Estimating* involves determining in advance the probable cost of producing a job so that the sales department can make a profitable bid.

5. *Dispatching* is the process of actually ordering work to be done.

6. *Expediting* is a follow-up activity that checks to be sure plans are actually being executed.

Inventory Control

Inventory control deals with (1) raw materials, (2) work in progress, and (3) finished goods. Inventory controllers must answer the following questions:

1. What is the optimum amount of inventory to carry?

2. What is the economic lot size for an order?

3. What is the record system for showing the status of inventory on hand?

Quality Control

Maintaining excellence in a firm's product is the primary concern of quality control. Specific tests may be conducted to ensure that the product is the correct size (it is often tested to within one one-thousandth of an inch) or strong enough to do its job.

Though each stage of a missile assembly is tested several times, it is impossible for a frisbee manufacturer personally to check out each item in the line. Instead, random samples are selected for examination so that quality can be checked via these individual items. By applying methods of determining probabilities, estimates will be made of total production quality. For this reason, quality control specialists want to be sure the sample they select is typical of the whole product line.

Financial Control: Balancing the Budget

Almost everything is influenced by financial control. Whether money is the object or a major factor of business activity, methods of controlling finances rank high in the system. The unattentive supervisor who neglects the financial aspects of the job is in for a shock upon reaching that toll gate at the road's end. Profit margin, investment returns, and budgets can get out of hand faster than any other aspect of an operation.

Because many people see budget limitations as obstructions to the successful completion of their projects, the word *budget* possesses a powerful negative ring. But financial planning should be the slave of business, not its master. Exact financial plans and firm budget parameters can help supervisors know exactly where they are headed.

No matter how big or how small the operation, an organization's budget is really a summary statement of several figures from other budgets. Five of the most common budgets are (1) revenue and expense budgets; (2) time, space, material, and product budgets; (3) capital expenditure budgets; (4) cash budgets; and (5) balance-sheet budgets. The master budget gathers together all other budgets of the departments involved.

As discussed in the chapter on planning, some pitfalls in the budgeting process must be avoided lest the tail wag the dog. Budgeting is a tool that helps a company accomplish its goals. Whenever meeting the budget becomes more important than the company's goals, things are out of order. Overbudgeting, for instance, can burden workers with such meaningless detail that they are accounting for paper towels when they should be concentrating on goals. A too-rigid budget—often the result of sloppy planning or data gathering—can cripple a supervisor and create serious financial dilemmas.

Variable Budget.   One method of budgeting now gaining popularity is the variable budget. Here, a certain minimum amount is set aside for operational costs. Budget amounts may then be changed on a percentage basis. Fixed costs are set and remain the same, but costs that tend to vary with the ups and downs of company income are arranged on an increasing scale. The variable budget is often favored in rapidly changing business climates because it can provide money for materials, labor, and advertising in proportion to sales.

Break-Even Analysis.   The break-even chart is similar to the variable budget. In fact, the two are so much alike they are often confused. These budgeting methods, however, have quite different purposes. Though the variable budget chart sets percentages to keep amounts flexible, the break-even chart sets specific amounts of time, money, products, or other commodities. The beginning point for the break-even analysis is the amount at which all expenses have been paid and the profits start rolling in. Break-even analysis charts a business beyond the point where income increases proportionately with each sale. A publisher might say, "As soon as we sell ten thousand copies of this book, we will have paid all the cost of development and production. After that, everything else is *gravy.*" If, however, a writer must receive royalties on the book, a break-even chart could demonstrate the growth of both royalties and company profits as income increases.

The break-even analysis chart can be used as a control device through its emphasis on the coverage of production costs. Such a chart clearly shows the effect of increased sales after costs and expenses have been met. A budget-analysis chart seems to say, "See—it's simple—more productivity, more profit!"

Ratio Analysis.   When computing rates of growth, ratio analysis is often helpful. This method can show a company's actual growth, and sometimes even make the facts more impressive by using relationships between years and between businesses, rather than using absolute figures as do the variable and break-even analyses. Which company would you prefer—one with sales up 7 percent from last year, or one with item sales up 100 percent? Such comparisons must always be carefully examined, so do not answer too quickly—one might be selling 7 percent more aircraft and the other 100 percent more chewing gum.

Return on Investment.   Imagine that Bill and Bob are two real estate agents who work for the same agency. They both work forty hours per week for a year. Bill makes twenty sales and Bob makes one sale. Which of the two men received a better return on investment of time? The surprising answer illustrates the return-on-investment concept. Bob received a higher return on his investment of time because his one sale was a $4 million shopping center and land development deal that netted him a $240,000 commission. Bill, who sold twenty residences during the year, made $36,000 in commissions.

In nearly every job, time, money, and effort must be invested in order to make a profit. The return-on-investment chart is useful in discovering possible alternative ways to make that profit while controlling the amount put into production time and expenses. Workers on lower levels understand the comparative values of the system better when they can measure profits against the cost of making each dollar. Supervisors who use the return-on-investment method are always comparing profits with the bills that will have to be paid eventually. They realize that anybody can achieve a high gross income simply by selling below cost, but that net income *after* costs is what determines the success of a company.

Figure 13-1 shows how the various factors affecting return on investment relate to one another. Essentially, ROI is determined by dividing total investment into earnings to determine a percentage rate of return (200,000 ÷ 500, 000 = .40). Incidentally, a 40 percent return on investment is fantastic. You

Figure 13-1. Return-on-Investment Concept. [With permission from Robert M. Fulmer, *The New Management* (New York: Macmillan Publishing Co., Inc., 1974. © by Robert M. Fulmer.)]

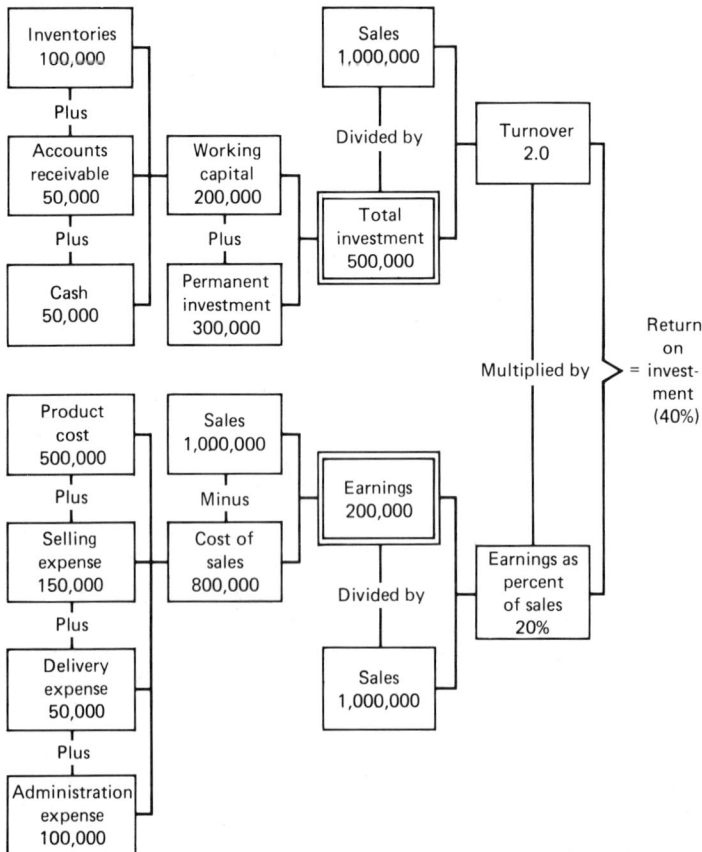

might want to buy stock in this imaginary firm! What other conclusions can you draw about the firm from the chart?

A return-on-investment approach allows the company controller to see things as they really are and to correct the slanted perspective conveyed by the sales manager's charts: all profit, no overhead. Trouble spots can be easily identified. Is too much inventory building up? Is the cost of selling the product getting out of hand? The supervisor can pinpoint the problem and apply corrective action. Without these checks and balances, sales may skyrocket to an all-time high while the business sinks into bankruptcy. Remember that basing a control system on profit alone can undermine personal budgets as well as a company's budget. Return-on-investment thinking can save a college student as well as a company president from the dangers of an uncontrolled budget.

Tools for Control: Old and New

As the tasks involved in starting any new project began to multiply because of increasingly sophisticated technology, supervisors sought better methods of coordination and control. When millions of dollars can be lost by a single day's delay, things have to start on time. This is especially true with new procedures not previously tested for smooth operation.

The Gantt Approach

Around the turn of the century, a management consultant named Henry L. Gantt realized that a good production plan is made of interlocking projects so totally dependent on each other that they must work in harmony or the entire effort will fail. To facilitate such plans, Gantt came up with a bar graph approach showing the relation of time between the "events" or actual happenings in a production process. The creators of later, more complicated tools used Gantt's chart as a basis for their own work. Figure 13-2 shows a Gantt chart designed for a research paper.

Figure 13-2. Gantt Chart for Research Papers. [With permission from Robert G. Murdick, *Business Research* (Scranton, Penna.: International Textbook Company, 1969), p. 118.]

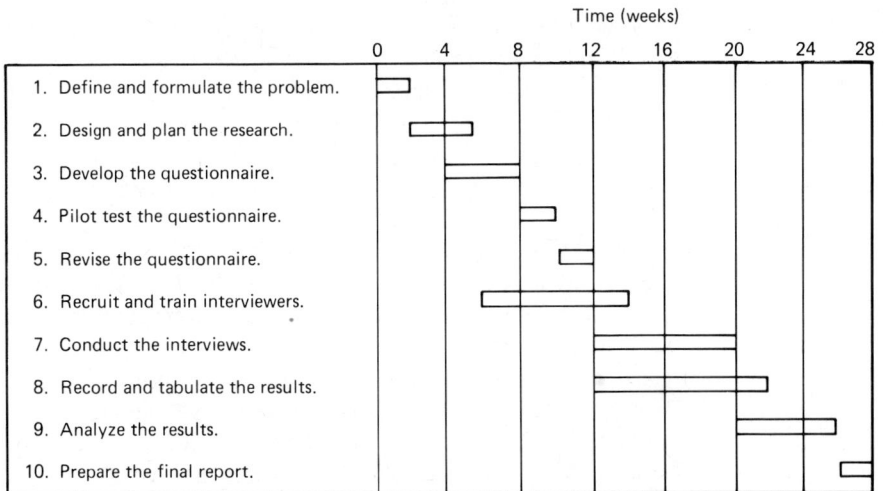

Network Analysis

The planning approach that stresses an awareness of every step in the production path is known as *network analysis,* a technique that makes full use of computers to attain maximum efficiency in planning and control.

Communication can also be improved by this method of supervising projects, because a visual representation of the entire project helps workers understand more clearly the importance, interdependence, and necessity of their jobs.

Network analysis systems simplify project planning because supervisors are forced to concentrate on only four main ingredients in establishing the *critical path* for production—the shortest route to a project goal:

1. A clearly recognizable end point or *objective.*

2. A list of separate, clearly defined, interrelated *events.*

3. The *time* required to complete each activity.

4. A *starting point.*

PERT and CPM. The two most common network analysis approaches are PERT (program evaluation review technique) and CPM (critical path method). These two planning tools were developed within weeks of each other during 1959. While the Navy was developing PERT to help with production of the Polaris Fleet Ballistic Missile, E. I. du Pont de Nemours & Company was developing CPM to reduce the time required for equipment repair. PERT is credited with saving two years on the missile project, and du Pont claims that CPM reduced equipment maintenance hours from 125 to 93. Figure 13-3 provides an example of a simple PERT chart for a research project that might apply to a wide range of areas, from a college term paper to an industrial marketing study.

The PERT user obtains three time estimates for the completion of an activity: the most optimistic time (if everything goes right), the most likely time (if an average number of things go wrong), and the most pessimistic time (if everything goes wrong). The three estimates are used to calculate the expected completion time of an activity using a statistically based formula. Thus a single time estimate is associated with each activity. From these estimates the expected completion time of the project is calculated.

Although PERT's great strength lies in saving time, budget controls were later added to the approach by including a cost comparison factor that would evaluate the allocation of limited resources and make more accurate information available for time-cost trade-off decisions. For example, it may be worth paying a group of employees triple-time to work over a holiday weekend in order to complete a project ahead of schedule and receive a large bonus.

The PERT system is used primarily for first-time projects needing complicated research and development; CPM is used with projects of a repetitive nature. The main advantage of the latter approach is its accurate computations of time and cost factors. CPM takes numercial information from previous projects and calculates how much time and money was spent in each step of these earlier operations. CPM works well in complex projects involving construction and maintenance in which time limits are definite and cost is a significant factor. If three CPM activities are happening at the same time, each requiring different amounts of time, the critical path follows the method expected to

Complete interviewing

10
8
6 ⑥

Complete preliminary
survey of literature

5
2
1

⑤ Complete preparation
of interview questionnaire

Complete design
and path of the
researcher

Tabulation and
analysis of results

3
2
1

①
3
2
1

2
1
.5

③

2.0
1.6
1.2

10
6
4

④

3
⑦

6
4
1

End
15

5
3

Start
0

6
4
2

.5
.2

②

⑩ In-depth study and
evaluation of literature
completed

5
2
1

⑭

2

3

Complete
formation of
the research
problem

8
5
3

⑪ Replies received

5
2
1

Draft of report
completed

Formulation of
definitions

Complete preparation
and testing of mail
questionnaires

⑧

1.8
1.4

2
1

⑬

1.2

.5

5
3
1

Replies received

⑨

⑫ Follow-up
mailing

Questionnaires
mailed out

Unit of time: weeks

Activity: ——→

Event: ◯

Critical path: 0-2-3-4-8-9-11-12-13-7-14-15

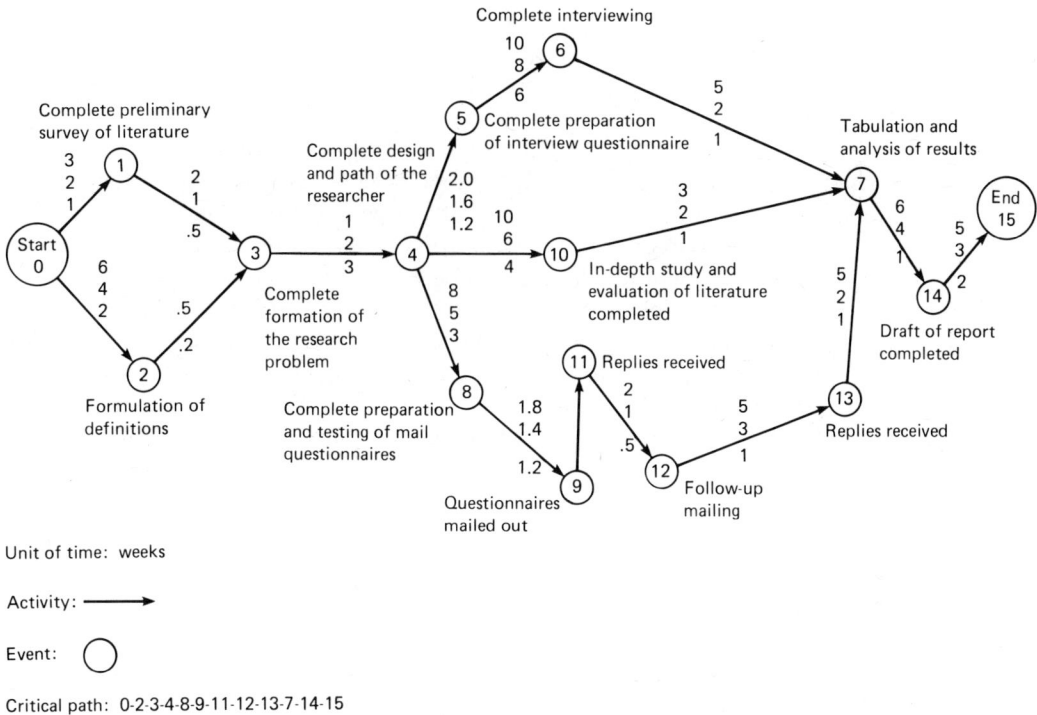

Figure 13-3. PERT Chart for a Research Project.

take the longest. Shortening the most time-consuming steps can shorten the overall project length.

GERT. The latest development in control programs is the graphic evaluation and review technique (GERT). Unlike its predecessors, GERT includes statistical concepts in the network model. GERT gives a statistical read-out of optional paths to pursue that the other processes do not. Conditional branching is allowed at selected points to represent uncertainty associated with the actual outcome. This ability has enabled managers to develop more realistic models of projects that involve high levels of uncertainty and has overcome one of the major criticisms of PERT and CPM.

Like PERT and CPM, GERT is a practical approach only in the design and development of a mass production system. Once an assembly line is set up and working, it would be expensive and useless to monitor the repetitious production process by network analysis. When better systems of planning and control are developed, it may well be PERT, CPM, and GERT charts that help us develop them.

Direct Control

Control systems are a must. But some think that the major responsibility for control should rest not on some lifeless chart or timetable but on a living, breathing, supervisor. In other words, the supervisor should use only those controls he or she thinks are needed, remaining personally responsible for successful project completions.

Direct supervisory control is founded on the idea that personal responsibility for problems will forestall any difficulties as long as the administrator lays down a definite set of rules. The direct control philosophy is based on four valid assumptions: (1) trained supervisors make fewer mistakes, (2) supervisory activities can be reduced to measurable terms, (3) principles of supervision can serve as a standard for comparison, and (4) the manner in which a supervisor follows management techniques can be reliably measured.

Control of control by controlling the controllers has several good points. First, it is simpler and more direct—each supervisor can expect a call on the carpet when things go wrong. Second, it is surer because regular checks should discourage supervisors from putting off and covering up. Third, it is fairer. Supervisors can rely on standards of performance by which their superiors will judge them.

Key Result Areas

One method of evaluating different controlled operations is through a system called key-area evaluation. This system was instituted by General Electric in the 1960s in order to compare organizational units. Each area was measured according to the way it was accomplishing stated goals in eight key areas: profitability, market position, productivity, product leadership, personnel development, employee attitudes, public responsibility, and the balance between short- and long-range goals. Though few supervisors will have enough control to monitor factors like social responsibility or market position, this concept shows the importance of controlling more than one factor in a single situation.

General Electric developed the key-area system to counteract one troublesome tendency: using profits alone to judge various departments' success. A department supervisor could work only to gain immediate, short-lived profits, get promoted, and escape the whole mess before long-term problems eventually appeared. In this way, one supervisor's quick-and-dirty profit approach could bring a department crashing down around the unsuspecting, innocent successor. However, GE realized that each key area is closely tied to a company's success and ultimate profit capability.

Management Audits

Periodic examination of financial records and accounts is done by an impartial outside auditor in most sizable organizations. Perhaps in the future, a consultant supervisor from outside a company will audit nonfinancial factors of the business' progress. Maybe then the idea of a supervisional audit will gain the professional acceptance of the financial audit.

Self-appraisal systems to discover and correct errors of management have been developed over the past forty years and are relatively common today. The questions involved can range from complicated scientific inquiries to magazine questionnaires covering topics such as deskside manner or coffee break finesse. A worthwhile self-appraisal should cover company policies, organizational structures, personnel practices, physical facilities, managerial methodology, control behavior, and human relations philosophy.

A self-examination will be valuable only if performed regularly and impartially. Of course, from the supervisor's point of view, these are the two characteristics hardest to control. There is rarely the extra time to conduct an involved self-analysis, and it is difficult to muster the objectivity to do justice to such an analysis. Few supervisors like to use precious time finding personal shortcomings.

Three Types of Control

Almost every type of control falls into one of three major categories. These have been given various names, but the simplest way to remember them is by their time relationship to the event being controlled. They are the (1) *before,* (2) *during,* and (3) *after* controls.

Preliminary controls (before the event) aim at preventing mistakes by taking care of every possible malfunction in advance. Preliminary controllers try to smooth out the wrinkles in everything that might go wrong, including humans, finances, and materials.

Concurrent controls (during the event) try to look over the operation while it is going on. The concurrent controller tries to keep qualities and quantities at standard levels by monitoring through instructions and supervisory activities. Usually, the concurrent controller asks one other person to help watch over the operations because controlling by overview is normally too large a job for one person to handle.

Feedback control (after the event) is used to improve the next attempt. Feedback methods used in business include analysis of budget, standard costs, financial statements, quality control, and pilot programs. This type of control derives its name from the fact that past results usually guide future approaches.

Summary

Control techniques are not noticed at all when they are functioning at their best. Ideally, controls in business processes will be more like the thermostat than the slave-driver.

The control process, wherever it is found and whatever its objective, can be reduced to three steps: (1) establishing standards of "saying how things ought to be," (2) measuring performance against standards of "seeing how things really are," and (3) correcting deviations or "straightening out what's crooked."

Judgment standards may be derived from a study of past performance, a subjective appraisal of the process to be measured, or an objective analysis of the parts of that process. Effective measurement standards will yield positive answers to the following questions.

- Is the information timely?
- Are appropriate units of measure used?

- Is the information reliable?
- Is the information valid?
- Is the information being channeled to the proper authority?

There are ten requirements of an adequate control system.

1. Controls must reflect the nature of the activity.
2. Controls should report deviations promptly.
3. Controls should be forward-looking.
4. Controls should point up exceptions at critical points.
5. Controls should be objective.
6. Controls should be flexible.
7. Controls should reflect the organizational pattern.
8. Controls should be economical.
9. Controls should be understandable.
10. Controls should indicate corrective action.

Financial measurements form the basic control in profit-dependent endeavors. Financial control may be assisted by budget refinements, variable budgeting, the break-even analysis, or return-on-investment charting. Nonbudget control tools recently developed include PERT, CPM, and GERT, and systems for supervisory control through evaluation of key-result areas; supervisory self-audit; and evaluation by outside consultants.

Three types of control generally recognized in terms of an event's time frame are preliminary, concurrent, and feedback. They can also be called *before, during,* and *after* controls.

Key Terms

Break-Even Analysis. A control device that compares the effect of increased sales to costs, profits, or expenses.

CPM. Critical path method, a network analysis that identifies the "critical path" (shortest route to a specified goal) for major projects done before but often repeated.

Concurrent Controls. Controls in effect during an operation.

Control. Regulation of, direction of, or influence over a procedure or course of action.

Cybernetics. The processing of information.

Data. Information, usually in numerical form.

Dispatching. The process of actually ordering work to be done.

Engineered Standards. A standard of evaluation based on an objective analysis of a specific situation.

Estimating. Determining in advance the probable cost of carrying out a job or project.

Expediting. A follow-up activity which ensures that plans are actually being executed.

Feedback Controls. Controls applied after the completion of a project, which help to improve performance on the next attempt.

Financial Control. The restrictions placed on operations by the availability of money.

Gantt Chart. A bar graph showing the relation of time between the events that represent steps in production.

GERT. Graphic evaluation and review technique—similar to PERT, but includes statistical probability event concepts to develop more realistic models of projects with great uncertainty.

Inventory Control. Controls that monitor and adjust quantities of raw materials, equipment, and products.

Key Area Evaluation. A method of comparing different organizational units with each other by using preselected functions for evaluation purposes.

Loading. Assigning work in advance to a machine or department.

Management Audit. A review and evaluation of management practices and effectiveness through self-audit or outside audit.

Network Analysis. A planning and control approach that identifies every step in the production process.

PERT. Program evaluation review technique—a time-saving control device that calculates ideal, most likely, and most pessimistic times for completion of a project.

Preliminary Controls. Controls in operation before a procedure or project begins.

Production Control. The processes of routing, loading, scheduling, estimating, dispatching, and expediting in production.

Quality Control. Controls that seek to maintain a standard level of quality in a product or process.

Ratio Analysis. A method of showing a company's actual growth by using relationships between years or companies, rather than absolute figures or amounts.

Return on Investment. Profit viewed as a percentage increase over the original investment.

Routing. Determining the operations to be performed, their sequence, and the path or flow of materials through a series of operations.

Scheduling. Determining the time at which each operation is to take place.

Standard. Unit of measurement established by authority to serve as a model or criterion.

Review Questions

1. How is control related to the expression "working your plan?"
2. Describe the three basic steps of the control process.
3. What are standards? List the types and give examples of each.
4. Why are standards important to a control system?
5. List and describe the ten characteristics of a good control system.
6. Describe the three categories of control, and show how they differ in function.
7. It is said that budgeting and financial control are crucial to a company. What is this form of control, and what is a supervisor's role in it?
8. Describe the return-on-investment concept.

9. Network analysis is important in clarifying four main features of the planning process. What are those features?

10. How would a supervisor use a PERT chart in controlling an assembly line?

11. It is said that direct supervisory control is the best way to handle many problems of control. What does this mean?

12. What would happen if profits were the only basis for evaluating and controlling the performance of a department or a business? What technique was developed to prevent this from happening?

13. How could a management aduit help a supervisor perform more effectively?

14. Can the concepts of control be applied to your personal life as well as to your job? How?

Exercises

I. Applying the Control Process: Writing a Research Report

You have just learned that a research project is due in three weeks. During that time you must do the necessary research, organize your ideas, write the paper, and type it. Develop a control system that will aid you in completing the project with a minimum of trouble. You may want to include the three basic steps of the control process and establish controls in terms of time. When you have finished your control plan, ask yourself these questions:

1. Is this control system too complicated for the job I am trying to do?
2. Can I easily follow the steps I have outlined for myself?
3. Have I included mileposts that will help me check my progress?
4. Have I allowed for possible snags by keeping alternative procedures in mind at various points along the line?
5. How will this control system help me complete the paper in time and with good results?

II. Comparing Control and Leadership

Write a paragraph in which you discuss the relationship between control concepts and leadership styles. What relationships exist? What types of controls would most likely be used by a democratic leader? An authoritarian leader? Do control methods have anything at all to do with styles of leadership?

Case 13 • Roger Travis

Roger Travis is one of six job-site superintendents for the Pinkerton Construction Company. His job is to supervise all aspects of the construction of single-family homes by the firm. Single-family homes account for about 40 percent of the company's annual construction business.

Roger enjoys his work, but recently has been growing dissatisfied with the company because he thinks it is trying to grow too fast. As a result, he feels it has not carefully hired new employees, especially supervisors, and that this accounts for the fact that the company lost money last year for the first time in its seven-year history. This meant that Roger did not receive a bonus he had counted on to buy a new automobile for his family. He feels that he has been penalized for the failures of others—management and supervisors—because all his jobs came in under budget. To make matters worse, he has just received his performance review from Mr. Pinkerton, and it is not entirely favorable.

"He probably hasn't been on one of my sites more than five times during the entire year," Roger complains, "yet he said that it was his impression that I was too lenient with my workers and that I sometimes left the job during the middle of the afternnon for a couple of hours!

"Even if I don't yell at my workers, they get the job done on time and under budget. And of course I leave the job site sometimes, usually to pick up supplies in order to save the project time and the company delivery charges! Why didn't Mr. Pinkerton mention that my last house came in $3000 under budget—a company record? Instead, he mentions that I'm 50 percent over my allocation of nails. I think he's spending too much time traveling these days and simply doesn't know what's going on anymore. He's only concerned about the big shopping center contracts and not the company's traditional bread-and-butter."

1. Evaluate the control system at the Pinkerton Construction Company.
2. Is their compensation system related to the control problem? Explain.

CHAPTER 14

Managing Information

The computer is a moron. The people who operate the computer don't have to be.

Peter Drucker

Learning Objectives

- To recognize the importance of accurate, adequate information, and the dangers of "information overload."
- To learn about several information systems that can be useful in supervisory work.
- To learn efficient means of gathering and analyzing necessary information.
- To become acquainted with the computer and to list its functions in processing information, as well as its limitations.
- To use the concepts of information systems as tools in supervision.

In all places and at all times, people are creating information and passing it on. Today, the amount of available information is so great it can be difficult to use it effectively. One study discovered the average office worker was spend-

231

ing nearly five and a half hours of each eight-hour day handling information. Almost three and a half hours were spent writing, and just a little less than that amount was used up in reading.[1]

But the information flood spreads far beyond the business world. Every day we are confronted with hundreds of commercials and other advertising messages. Trivia, new words, and valuable information pour out of every imaginable source until they threaten to overwhelm us.

As information grows and information needs change faster and faster, it is increasingly important for people—especially supervisors in business—to stay up to date.

Supervision Depends on Information

Every day the supervisor makes decisions that affect the growth and success of a department and perhaps an entire organization. The biggest obstacle in making those decisions is often a lack of reliable information.

Information has nourished every type of leader—presidents, generals, popes, and supervisors. To collect needed information, such leaders have relied on scholars, seers, and professional committees. A supervisor must depend on workers below and commands from above for information in making decisions.

Information Indigestion

Supervisors, of course, rely on other sources of information as well. However, with data processing machines reading and writing at the rate of four full-length novels a second, and our nation's amount of data growing at a rate faster than the gross national product, supervisors often wonder if it is possible to receive too much information. Even though most Americans, with their huge appetites for facts, might insist they can never get enough, they must learn to know which information is of value. Sometimes a business person is faced with information that is not wanted or needed.

So, our real concern should focus on how well we digest and use the raw data we receive. Too many undigested facts can turn an active person to an inactive one, paralyzed with indecision. Just as industrial raw materials must be refined and combined, information must also be processed, packaged, and marketed before it becomes useful.

Sources of Information

Organizing and assembling data is a constant challenge for anyone in management. Familiarity with valuable information sources is a must. At the same time, supervisors should be able to choose sources that will help solve each specific problem. Then they must sort through the information they collect and weed out whatever material is unreliable or unimportant.

---

[1] Quoted in Dennis Murphy, *Better Business Communications* (New York: McGraw-Hill, 1975).

One helpful source of information is the company's records. The flow of accounting data is information basic to every business. This *primary information* includes statistics on sales, inventory, equipment, and wages that could explain the problems of a business and suggest possible solutions.

The best source of marketing information is the consumer. Through surveys and interviews, you can get some idea of how buyers feel about a product or a marketing program.

For the manufacturer, *intermediate sources* such as wholesalers and retailers provide useful information on trends and new developments.

The largest source of business information in the world is the U.S. government. Regular listings published by the Government Printing Office give supervisors a good idea of the publications available. Other valuable sources of data are Small Business Administration publications and the *Statistical Abstract of the United States.*

Professional and trade organizations also provide businesses with considerable information. Specialized business areas such as marketing, supervision, and statistics have found professional groups that publish periodicals and research studies.

Trade associations provide information to their member firms through studies and magazines. Small businesses that cannot afford their own research programs often benefit from these.

Business executives and business students are better informed if they read one or more general business publications. The most popular of these include *Fortune, Forbes, Business Week, Dun's Review,* and the *Harvard Business Review.* Day-to-day information on domestic and international business and economic conditions may be found in daily newspapers, particularly the *Wall Street Journal. Supervisor, Supervisory Management,* and *Management Review* are excellent publications you may wish to read regularly. They contain many "how to" articles for supervisors in the public and private sectors.

Finding Secondary Information

Although it is easier and less time-consuming to have someone else search out secondary information, the supervisor should be aware of where and how to find it. As you will inevitably do library work, you may discover that a little extra knowledge can be of considerable help to you.

The library index used depends on the type of information needed. The *Reader's Guide to Periodical Literature* is a general reference classifying by subject matter articles that appear in hundreds of general-interest magazines. The *Public Affairs Information Service* lists books and articles covering the areas of economics and public affairs. Still another useful guide is the *Business Periodicals Index,* listing articles from numerous business publications.

Recently, the leasing manager for a real estate development firm needed a demographic site analysis conducted for eight proposed shopping centers, including population totals and growth trends, per capita income, daily traffic counts, and competitive information. The manager offered a fee of $850 for each site analysis, surprising because all the information needed by the leasing manager was contained in the local library and regional council office. Had he been aware of where to find the information, either he or a staff assistant could have saved their company $6800 for just two to three days' work!

The Supervisor's Information Systems

The onslaught of data can make or break a supervisor. To save sanity and the organization, each supervisor must find an orderly, reasonable way to deal with data. Many firms have *management information systems* for this purpose. A *system* is simply a collection of things that work together toward some common purpose. A bicycle is a system made of hardware, chrome, and rubber. More complicated systems compensate or change when new information is put into the system. A thermostat is one such *closed-loop* system. It takes regular readings of a room's temperature to decide whether to switch to heat or air conditioning. In much the same way, a management information system takes a regular reading of data, then sends a summarized message to the person in charge.

Supervisors may use several types of systems in dealing with information overload. We now discuss three types.

1. Environmental information. An environmental system considers the community in which the business exists or is planning to settle. By collecting information on population, prices, and trends, such a system aids in planning for the future.

2. Competitive information. This system tries to explain the past performances, activities, and plans of competing businesses. Alert managers monitor how well the competition is doing. By getting information on the successes and failures of other firms, supervisors can see their firm's record and decide what changes may be needed to improve future performance.

Good information on products, markets, and prices of competing businesses can help a supervisor choose what to do with materials and products. When the price of a product in a competing firm drops, a supervisor may attempt some reductions in the price of goods. Future plans of competitors also forewarn a manager about increased or new competition.

3. Internal information. This information is basic to making business decisions. In addition to the time a supervisor spends weighing the major strengths and weaknesses within a department, time must also be spent to present financial information in precise, exact terms and report on such matters as customer complaints, labor turnover, and—most important—sales and earnings growth or decline.

Although computers are steadily usurping the data-gathering functions for all three of these information areas, there are older and reliable "systems" still used by supervisors to collect valuable information: telephone calls, questionnaires, schedules, reports, and talking directly with employees, customers, suppliers, competitors, and colleagues. These noncomputerized information systems should be continually utilized by the supervisor in conjunction with the information input from computerized data sources.

Information and the Computer

Most of us take the wonders of science and invention pretty much for granted. When the parents of today's students were young, they were fascinated by the rapid pace of progress and perhaps imagined that the distant future would resemble the adventures of Buck Rogers and Flash Gordon as depicted in the Sunday papers. While reading of those who zoomed through space in their rocket ships and talked by television with people on other planets, few dreamed that in a few short years we would be watching astronauts walk on the moon on our own television sets, or that grade school students would carry calculators in their pockets to help them with mathematics.

The first electronic computer was, in fact, created in the days when Flash Gordon roamed the comic strips. It was far too large, however, to be carried around. Its hundreds of tubes gave off so much heat that it required an elaborate air-conditioning system. By 1960, a much smaller computer, using nonheat-producing transistors, cut the original model's time for performing operations. In time, even the transistorized computer was replaced by computers automated by pinhead-sized components. In the 1960s, the integrated circuit replaced the transistor. This new part was an entire system of transistors and components placed on a small silicone "chip," which made computers faster and more energy-efficient. In the 1970s, large-scale integration and the development of microprocessors enabled several separate circuits and functions to be assembled on a single silicone "sliver" that can replace 20,000 transistors, retail for about $15, and possess more information capacity than IBM's first computer, which cost over $1 million and was large enough to fill a room!

Computers are even smaller now, but they remember more than they used to. One computer can hold enough information to fill 300,000 books and can retrieve that information within microseconds (a microsecond is one-millionth of a second).

Each day's problems seem to uncover a new computer skill. We can now reserve an airplane seat, a motel room, or a baseball game ticket by dialing a telephone number, listening to a report of what is available, choosing from the selection, and reading the operator a credit card number.

Because of its speed in performing difficult calculations, the computer has drastically modernized today's business operations. It can function as a kind of chief clerk by making out payrolls, checking inventory, and billing customers. The computer is even capable of making an executive decision by choosing the best of several alternative problem solutions.

Although computer use had not filtered down to the supervisory level as heavily as in other areas of organization, we believe that the time is near when supervisors will regularly use the computer for problem-solving and decision-making activities. Therefore, it is important that you begin now to understand the basics of computers and become familiar with the language and concepts that will inevitably be a routine part of your life.

Computer Concepts

Most computers use numbers in their operations and calculations and are called *digital* computers. They operate on a *binary* code, which resembles a set of yes-no answers that describe every letter or number by opening or closing electrical circuits. Using this binary code, the computer can perform five basic operations: (1) input, (2) memory, (3) arithmetic, (4) control, and (5) output.

Input is the process of receiving information or instructions by the use of computer punch cards, lights, magnetic tape, or other devices. *Memory* is one of the most unique features of the computer because it can store millions of pieces of information and recall or "retrieve" them instantly. Memory units originally consisted of networks of magnetic "cares," or tiny wires that accepted electrical charges in a yes-no binary code manner. IBM developed semiconductor memory in 1961, which consists of memory "modules" containing two silicone chips which each contain 128 memory circuits within an area of a fraction of a square inch. This speeded up memory retrieval and reduced storage size dramatically.

Arithmetic is the process of adding, subtracting, multiplying, dividing, and comparing answers in any combination or sequence. The *control* function is comprised of instructions stored in the computer's memory that can be retrieved in order to tell the computer what to do next. *Output* is the form of information that becomes usable by other machines or people. Output may be printed by high-speed (2000 lines per minute) printers, put on small cathode-ray video screens, or activate electrical currents that trigger switches on other types of machines.

Hardware and Software

Shortly after computers were developed, the term *hardware* was applied to describe the physical machinery of computers. *Software* became the term referring to the ideas, programs, systems, and methods required to operate the hardware.

Categories of Hardware

A computer's hardware is divided into two sections. The system's heart is the central processing unit, or CPU. All the devices that support this unit make up the second section of a computer's hardware.

The CPU is like a busy, efficient supervisor, giving orders, requesting services, and combining results. The supporting devices are like a supervisor's workers. Each section is essential to the whole system—the CPU cannot function without its supporting devices, and the supporting devices are worthless without a CPU.

New varieties of hardware are being developed on a regular basis. Optical scanners can read printed matter and translate it for computer understanding. Data transmission equipment makes computer service available via telephone lines. High-performance data storage and retrieval units are capable of automatic storage and recall of important data.

Computer hardware costs remain relatively high but are likely to drop because of improved manufacturing technology. Companies can purchase "time sharing" on computers owned by other companies. The basic hardware cost must be supplemented by proper environmental controls (temperature, humidity, as well as power), and skilled personnel to program, operate, and repair the machinery. In the last twenty years, the speed of data processing has increased from 375 to 5 seconds for an average series of calculations and the cost of this operation has dropped from about $15 to about 20 cents.

Computer Software

Software in computer parlance refers to the written programs needed to run the system's hardware. It is software that organizes and orders a computer into action. But software does not handle all of a computer's instructions. Human direction is still the ultimate authority. Each time a computer must "learn" to do something new, software experts have to make an adjustment within its system. Software is more expensive than hardware, but the value of the new ideas produced can easily justify the cost involved.

Software preparation includes systems and program flowcharting, programming, keypunching the program and data, and documenting.[2] *System flowcharting* depicts the interaction of people, equipment, and information required to accomplish a specific data processing task. *Program flowcharting* explains the sequential operation that the computer must perform to process the data effectively. The program flowchart is the basis upon which the actual computer program is written. *Programming* is the actual coding or writing of the computer program based on the program flowchart.

Different computer languages are used to program the computer. BASIC, COBOL, and FORTRAN are common computer languages used today. BASIC is a simple language and is frequently used by the home computer hobbyist. FORTRAN stands for "formula translator," and is used in scientific work. COBOL stands for "computer business orientation language" and is most widely used in business applications.

Once you have found the proper language for a particular computer, there are several ways to communicate. Punched cards remain the most familiar means of communication. Holes punched in each card are translated into numbers or letters as it scans the card. Punched paper tape also provides a communication bridge between programmer and computer.

Magnetic tape has become the most popular way to record data in a computing system. Electronic charges set on the tape are then read as significant messages by the computer. Magnetic discs and drums can collect information even more rapidly than tape.

In the 1970s, IBM introduced the data entry "diskette" system, which reduced dependence on punched cards. With the new system, information can be transferred directly to a small recordlike disk, sometimes called the "floppy disk." It replaces 3000 punch cards! Data placed on the disk can be transmitted directly to the CPU.

Technological advances continually emerge in the computer field and are likely to have significant impact on the supervisory levels of organizations. Bulky paper printouts of data are being replaced by cathode-ray video display that allow instant input and feedback (output) of information for decision making. Even "talking computers" produce verbal responses from a prerecorded vocabulary.

Documentation is the last stage of software preparation and provides a permanent record and reference for all completed work. See Figure 14-1 for a graphic summary of the essential elements of a computer.

---

[2] Hugh J. Watson and Archie B. Carroll, *Computers for Business* (Dallas: Business Publications, Inc., 1976), pp. 8–17.

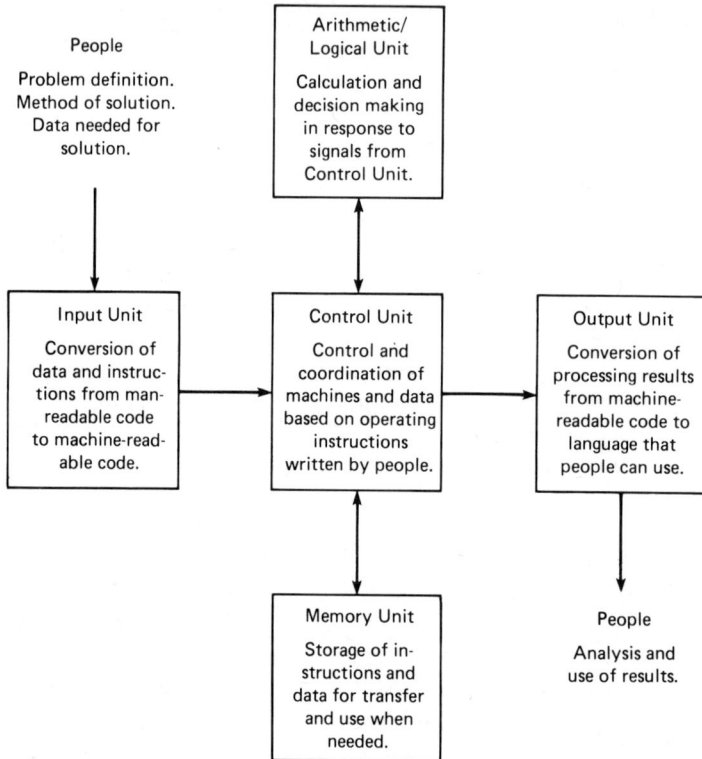

Figure 14-1. Essential Elements of a Computer. (Courtesy of the International Business Machines Corporation.)

Computers at Work in Organizations

The purposes of computers are limited only by the imaginations of those who use them. In fact, computers are rather like superhumans, ready at all times to carry out whatever task is assigned to them.

Routine Procedures

As suggested earlier, a computer can serve as a business' extremely efficient and able chief clerk. It is so speedy in working out arithmetic problems that it can take total charge of making out payrolls, keeping track of inventories, or billing customers. Still, the computer must have strict supervision because it will make the same mistake over and over unless it is given correct instructions.

A computerized payroll is a quick, accurate, economical way to keep track of the many deductions that must be figured for each employee when making out paychecks. The computer also stores and updates employees' personnel files, including promotions and job transfers. A computer can even record the times a worker clocks in to work.

Information Storage

One of the greatest problems of business used to be the time-consuming process of assembling sales or shipment records. Reports were usually made at the end of each month and came out about two weeks late. With computers, reports can be put out so fast they can even include the previous workday's results. Specialized languages have been developed to report documents more rapidly to management for control purposes. For example, RPG or "report program generator," is a special language developed for small business computers that need simple computation and processing for preparation of more detailed reports.

Solutions to Problems

Supervisors will find no other aid in problem solving as valuable as the computer. When there are several ways to solve a certain problem, the computer can scan all the solutions and analyze each. Computers can weigh the relative costs of different types of materials and different sources of supply and then suggest to a supervisor the cheapest possible way of getting a specific job done.

Although the computer can operate completely on its own once it has been given a basic formula and the necessary data, the supervisor's word is still essential in making any final decision about a problem. From the many possible solutions available, the computer may choose three of the best. At this point, the supervisor must exercise judgment. One solution may be less expensive than the others, but a supervisor may anticipate its detrimental effect on employee morale. The supervisor can see the intangible human aspects of a problem, while the computer cannot. So, for major decisions, the judgment of a wise, experienced supervisor is usually considered superior to the computer's strictly factual output.

Accounting and Billing

The computer can figure the most complicated bill with ease. It can also subtract payments and allowances, address the bill's envelope, and send reminders to customers when their payments lag. In this way, too, the computer is a great help in simplifying a supervisor's work load.

The computer can also maintain inventory records and monitor warehouse stock. In some retail stores, the cash register tape feeds into a computer that records the sale's amount and the collected tax, then checks inventory and sends orders for needed replacements. The computer can also help the supervisor by analyzing shopper trends and measuring the relative effectiveness of various forms of advertising.

The Limitations of Computers

Although the computer's abilities are certainly far reaching, it cannot do everything perfectly. Supervisors still find it necessary to watch over computer operations, just as they do with employees. Although workers may go on strike, computers may break down. And though no computer has a drinking problem, occasionally a programmer does.

Another drawback in using the computer is, of course, cost. There is always a newer, more efficient model coming out that just happens to be more expensive. Even though the machine will not ask for higher wages, the staff working with it will.

Because supervisors often are not sure what to expect from a computer, they are often disappointed after one has been installed for their use. The computer is not a magic genie that makes all the old problems disappear. Supervisory people must be willing to take time to understand what the computer can and cannot do for them. They must educate themselves in computer use or they will feel dubious and resentful about the value of this machine.

On the other hand, computer experts themselves must be open-minded about the supervisor's problems in using the computer. These two groups, if they are sympathetic to each other's problems, will avoid forming negative attitudes about the "new-fangled contraption."

Getting the Most from the Computer

As mentioned, the computer will play a more significant role with supervisors in the future, but already in many organizations supervisors are either users of computer information or are primary input sources for company reporting and control activities. Whatever your role, four suggestions can help you get the most out of the computer.

First, do not ask for more information than you really need from the computer. Most supervisors and executives suffer from "information overload," rather than too little input. Information that is convenient or interesting may not be essential to control and decision making, and may only waste your time.

Second, be willing to compromise when information duplication or overlaps occur. If you request a listing of inventory items by part number and colleague in another department wants the same information by order number, suggest a simple list with both numbers to save expense and time.

Third, communicate with the computer operator, especially about any excess information or inadequacies in output. Computers are famous for sending duplicate and triplicate copies of reports that are wasteful and expensive! Also, a minor programming error can delete entire sections of important information, so you must keep your data processing department informed.

Finally, be certain to make your own data collection accurate, succinct, and relevant. Set a good example for efficiency and relay information immediately for timely utilization.[3]

Summary

Handling a surplus of information will probably continue to be one of the unsolved problems in every business. People in business should think about

[3] Adapted from Lester R. Bittel, *What Every Supervisor Should Know,* 4th ed. (New York: McGraw-Hill, 1980), p. 558.

their information problems, define their information needs, and find an efficient information technique.

Making an information system that satisfies these goals is no easy task. Environmental, competitive, and internal information needs to be carefully examined, simply presented, and thoroughly organized before it can give a business energy and direction.

Meaningful data are always necessary to a business, and the computer presents the best method for working with it. Computers have drastically modernized nearly all of a business' operations. Many jobs that once required dozens of clerks are now completed in moments by this electronic brain. This machine can store information and instructions, make rapid calculations, and print out the answers faster than any person can read.

The person who tells the computer what to do is the computer programmer. This employee studies the problem to be solved, sets it up logically, and translates it into computer language. He or she will then translate the computer's answer into language that humans can understand.

The practical uses of computers in business are endless. They can figure payrolls, keep track of inventories, and bill customers. They can store huge amounts of information and make it instantly available. By analyzing solutions, they can even help supervisors with their most difficult decisions.

Because of their high cost, computers must be kept busy. A small company may share part of a computer's time with other companies. Above all, it is important to understand both the advantages and limitations of computers. They are useful machines that do a great deal of work, but they cannot solve all of business' problems, and they can never replace the human element supplied by a skilled, experienced supervisor.

Key Terms

Competitive Information. Data dealing with the past performance, present activities, and plans of competing businesses.

Computer. High-speed, efficient, data-processing machine.

Computer Programmer. Person who tells the computer what to do.

Environmental Information. Data concerning the community in which a business exists or is planning to settle.

Hardware. The computer's machinery—its central processing unit and supporting devices.

Intermediate Sources. Wholesalers, retailers, trade associations, and the U.S. government can provide secondary general information about businesses.

Internal Information. Data concerning the major strengths and weaknesses within an organization.

Primary Information. Any company records that can help explain the problems of a business and suggest possible solutions.

Software. The parts of a computer that organize and order it into action.

Supervision Information Systems. Methods used by supervisors in dealing with their information overloads.

Review Questions

1. What is meant by the term *information indigestion?* Make a list of the ways you have experienced this phenomenon.

2. List and describe the sources of information available to a supervisor to aid in evaluating his or her operations.

3. What is a company's most basic information system?

4. What is the best source of primary information? Of secondary information?

5. How can the computer be useful to a supervisor in everyday operations?

6. List and describe the differences between computer "hardware" and "software."

7. Many developments in computer software have been made in recent years. What developments would you like to see made in software in the next decade? Would these developments have any impact on your personal life? On your role as supervisor?

8. List and describe the ways in which a small business would benefit from a computer.

9. List and describe the pitfalls that may result from a small business becoming overly reliant on a computer.

10. How can a supervisor get the most out of a company's computer?

Exercise

Collecting Information

You supervise a large printing department for a paper manufacturer. Management has decided that your department should be restructured in terms of equipment, job duties, location, and general organization. The boss has asked you to research the alternative possibilities for making these changes and then offer suggestions for the most convenient, effective procedure. Write a few paragraphs answering the following questions:

1. How will you collect the information you need?

2. What primary and secondary sources will you use?

3. Can you use resource people as information sources? What kinds of resource specialists might be appropriate?

4. Once the information is collected, how will you analyze it?

5. Might a computer be useful to you in working out the final suggestions from the information you collect?

6. What information will you give the computer?

7. If you have no computer availabe, how will you organize your information to formulate your suggestions?

Case 14 • Todd McKay

Todd McKay has been a supervisor at Gyroscope Gifts, Inc., for nearly four years. Gyroscope is a leading national mail order firm with burgeoning sales over the last two years. Todd's department staff processes orders for one of five regions in the country and consists of a representative cross section of company employees—four order receivers, eight order processors, and eight order shippers. Up to now, all operations by his staff have been handled manually with the support of a large central core of secretarial and accounting personnel. Todd's major responsibility as a supervisor has been to maintain accurate and up-to-date order fulfillment within his regional unit.

This is an on-going task because of the manual system. Todd's department has always received excellent marks for its work.

Lately, order processing has been falling behind for the company as a whole, although Todd's unit has processed its orders on schedule. Concerned that this problem may jeopardize the company's public image as a swift fulfillment company, Gyroscope's owner, Mrs. Mary McEvoy, has decided that her company needs a computer. She has addressed a detailed memo to all supervisors explaining her research into computers and her opinion that a computer may be the panacea to her company's problems. She has called a meeting of all supervisors and top management in two weeks. She has asked each supervisor for recommendations on the type of computer that should be secured, the functions it should perform, and the immediate needs in order processing it could fulfill once "on line."

1. In your opinion, will the computer help Gyroscope?

2. What effect will the computer have on employees? On supervisors? On top management?

3. What should Todd tell top management in his report? What potential problems might he alert them to in the transfer from the manual system to the computer?

CHAPTER 15

Working with Groups

People who are busy rowing seldom rock the boat.

Anonymous

Learning Objectives

- To explore the nature and complexity of an individual's membership in different groups.
- To identify the principles of group formation and group dynamics.
- To recognize the process by which groups grow and mature.
- To identify the various roles individual members play within groups.
- To apply concepts of social control in groups related to the job.

How many groups do you belong to? Some people would say "none." You may be able to think of only a few, but you are probably overlooking many informal groups that play a crucial part in your development as an individual, your relationships with other people, and your role in society.

Formal organizations such as the church, Lions Club, Boy Scouts, Campfire

Girls, and school activities usually come to mind whenever we are asked about group membership. But from the day we are born, we join and leave many different, more informal groups. Some of these overlap while others remain quite separate. Most of us are members of several family groups—the family we grew up in, a family by marriage, and various extended families of grandparents, cousins, aunts and uncles, and in-laws. Our friendships may make us part of one or more informal groups. In addition, thousands of club members group together to enjoy common interests like hobbies, consumer or political activities, volunteer work, and recreational activities. Your class forms a group, and there may be many smaller groups within the class itself. As a supervisor, you may be part of the management group, a member of a departmental crew, a newcomer to a work-related friendship group, and captain of the company bowling team.

We enjoy associating with other people, and we depend on others to fulfill many of our personal needs. Why is it important to understand how groups function in the work environment? Could we not perform our tasks more efficiently if every employee worked exactly as he or she was supposed to, and never wasted time with interpersonal relations?

The fact is, the combined efforts of a group can greatly surpass in results the efforts of isolated individuals. Many critics of group activity have focused on the apparent inability of committees to get anything done. From this observation, some critics label all groups as useless and insist we would be better off if we did not make things harder for ourselves by forming groups to accomplish tasks. These critics have missed the point of group activity and fail to see that in many cases, two heads *are* better than one.

Two Plus Two = Five?

Synergy is a word popularly used to mean that, in problem solving or creative thinking, one plus one often equals three or more. You probably have heard that common table salt is a synergistic combination of two highly poisonous substances, sodium and chlorine. When these two dangerous elements are combined, a useful and beneficial product results. Groups blend the good characteristics of many individuals, so it is important for a supervisor to understand the unique possibilities a group presents and be able to use them effectively in the work situation.

The principle of synergy was discovered at the grass-roots level many years ago. In 1885, the World Series of Mule Team Competition was held in Chicago. The winning team of mules was able to pull 9000 pounds, while the second-place team pulled somewhat less. Someone decided to try hitching both the first and second teams to a load. Together the teams pulled a 30,000-pound load, more than three times what they had pulled separately. This example of synergy was duplicated in Death Valley when a young foreman named Stiles noticed that a team of twelve mules was hauling loads twice the size that eight mules could have. He began to think and experiment. Can you guess what size was found to be most efficient? A twenty-mule team wound up pulling ten tons—about half the capacity of a modern railroad freight car.

This was the origin of "Twenty Mule Team Borax"—once a household word and an international trademark. It was also synergy in action.[1]

You would have a hard time getting your staff to pull ten-ton loads, but consider the possibilities when you begin to take advantage of the combinations of skills and abilities represented in any group of workers. In the remainder of this chapter, we shall discuss some of the group processes that occur naturally and aid or prevent effective problem solving and goal attainment. Working with groups can be as frustrating as it is rewarding. The only way to endure the difficulties is to remember that those who can draw on the strengths, talents, and knowledge of other people emerge the ultimate winners.

Group Dynamics—Fad or Fact?

It is only in the last fifty years or so that small groups have become the subject of rather intense study. Naturally, some conclusions drawn from early small group studies became the basis for today's popular ideas on the benefits and problems of working with groups. For some people, group dynamics represented a panacea curing marital problems, production lags, and the common cold. Others discovered that small groups revealed the natural processes that occur whenever individuals relate to each other in work settings or other situations.

Recently, several popular writers have pointed out the increasing use of groups in corporate creative and decision-making areas. They conclude that a strong emphasis on groups means an inevitable decline in the importance of the individual. Other writers have stressed the inherent problem-solving capabilities of groups—the synergistic reactions that occur when people exchange ideas—and have suggested that groups should be used in solving a wide variety of problems and creating original and useful ideas.

Management approaches, in particular, have tended to focus on group behavior rather than individual efforts. For this reason, it will be useful to review some studies that have supplied managers with many of their ideas about the value of group behavior.

In the 1920s, a group of researchers at the Harvard Business School found that production workers tend to form small, informal work groups that influence worker morale and productivity.[2] In the 1930s, another study showed that the attitudes of an informal group's leader played a significant role in the morale and productivity of the work group as a whole. More recent studies have uncovered other aspects of group formation and dynamics, including information about how groups are formed, how leaders are selected and what roles they play, and the kinds of specialized roles that develop among individual group members.

Managers tend to adopt completely the findings of these studies and often attempt to apply them to their own organizations. Their enthusiasm sometimes

[1] From a speech by J. W. Travis, then vice-president and general manager of the Southern Bell Telephone & Telegraph Company, before the J. Epps Brown Chapter of the Telephone Pioneers of America, June 7, 1968, Charleston, S.C.
[2] See Elton Mayo, *The Human Problems of Industrial Civilization* (Boston: Harvard Business School, 1946).

results in applying the right techniques to the wrong group. What works for a group of high-powered managers, already motivated, educated, and interested, may not work on the production line or in the distribution department. To use group dynamics effectively, the supervisor should first study the employees to discover what patterns of organization they prefer and who their informal leaders are. This makes it easier to raise production and morale by applying the correct group processes and techniques.

How Do Groups Form?

Several factors contribute to the process of group formation. Some groups form for more than one reason and fulfill more than one function, while others form to attain a specific goal or to fulfill a particular need.

Proximity is the first and most obvious cause of group formation. People who live in the same neighborhood may form a social group, just as people working at the same company or in the same department might gather in a work group. Physical closeness, however, cannot totally explain why people form groups, because physical proximity often follows from members' common interests or goals. Consider, for example, the result if a company lumped all its employees in the same large room. Would the secretary, supervisor, bookkeeper, and vice-president tend to form a work group if they found themselves in the same corner of the room? Or would people who serve similar functions congregate, changing their physical location in the room to save time and increase convenience? Although physical location is a factor in group formation, it often reflects some other, more basic factor.

Economic factors have always influenced group formation, and they are becoming increasingly important. Labor unions did not form because all their members lived in the same neighborhood or liked the same movies. Some work groups form because the members believe they can gain more economic benefits by joining together. People joined together for economic considerations are united by a common goal, but are likely to share little else in common.

An economic crisis at the national level can mean disaster to individuals, but people can sometimes avoid personal financial setbacks if they form groups for a specific, money-saving purpose. Car pools save money on gas and help solve pollution and transportation problems. Neighborhood parents frequently form children's play groups. Other examples of economic interest groups are coops that purchase commodities in large quantities for sale to their members at a discount.

Although work groups are not always formed for economic reasons, an economic goal can inspire a group. For instance, when management promises a bonus for the work group exceeding its monthly quota by the largest amount, togetherness and cooperation are likely to rule. In this case, individual gain depends upon the group's performance, and individual members are likely to put group goals first in achieving this common end.

Human needs were discussed earlier as motivators of individuals. These needs also play a crucial part in the formation of groups. Needs for security, esteem, and self-actualization are very difficult to meet outside a group. Informal group structures can often satisfy many of these needs.

Security needs operate on two levels in group formation. Some groups form to fulfill security needs at the personal level. People need the reassurance and support of other people in order to function as individuals. Other groups form to fulfill security needs at the economic level. The labor union movement began during a period when there were far more workers than jobs. With ten people waiting in line for each job, workers were somewhat reluctant to make demands of the boss. When workers joined together to bargain for job and economic security, they discovered a new power. Would it be surprising to see the formation of management and supervision groups to obtain security from excessive union demands? Consider what forms such a group might take and how it might seek to meet its own security needs.

Social needs are almost always present in any discussion of why groups form. In fact, all groups are social in nature. We need other people in order to fulfill our own needs. Groups often form because the members enjoy each other—the company softball team or bowling league are good examples. It is no accident that solitary confinement is considered the harshest punishment that a criminal in any penal system can receive.

The importance of groups in fulfilling social needs has been demonstrated by a study of American POWs during the Korean conflict. An unusually low escape rate among American prisoners coincided with many reported instances of collaboration with the North Koreans. This study revealed that prisoner treatment may have played a significant role in this situation.

> The North Koreans were careful not to allow social groups to form or continue. Officers were separated from enlisted men. Groups were broken up and prisoners were regularly transferred between barracks. The fact that informal groups could not be formed on a continuing basis could explain the low escape rate. The men were unable to develop the organization necessary to hatch an escape plan. Also, prisoners were unable to develop the necessary trust in each other that was so essential for an escape. Without mutual trust, the escape possibility was eliminated and the overall morale among POWs was very low.[3]

Most businesses have few problems with "escape attempts," but worker dissatisfaction can quickly become a major difficulty. Informal work-social groups should not only be permitted, but encouraged wherever possible. Many studies have shown that workers isolated from one another on their jobs are more dissatisfied than those who can socialize while working.

Esteem needs are also met by joining groups. We all like to think of ourselves as successful. Some employees will be attracted to groups they perceive as having high social standing. Others will join groups in which their personal status is very high. If the members of your group look up to you as competent and successful, that group fulfills your need for esteem from your peers. Even though esteem needs are difficult to identify, they are nonetheless important in recognizing the reasons for group formation.

Self-actualization needs are often the foundation of professional groups and associations that allow workers in the same type of job to communicate with each other. Exchanging shop talk is an important function of many groups and helps to fulfill individual needs for self-actualization. No clear dividing lines run between those groups formed to meet esteem needs and those that fulfill self-actualization needs. Many professional organizations professing to

---

[3] Edgar Schein, "The Chinese Indoctrination Program for Prisoners of War," *Psychiatry,* May 1956, pp. 149–72.

satisfy self-actualization needs operate instead to provide security, economic bargaining power, or self-esteem.

Knowing why a group has formed is useful in dealing with it, especially in a work situation. Now that we understand some reasons for group formation, we shall consider the stages groups pass through as they evolve and increase their ability to fulfill the needs of their members.

How Do Groups Grow?

Groups mature, just as individuals do, and pass through recognizable stages of growth and development. As the group matures, members learn to trust and understand one another and are better able to tackle decision-making and problem-solving situations. Of course, some groups never really get started. They continue to use a wasteful approach to every task instead of combining their abilities and applying the principle of synergy. When groups do not mature, their members miss out on two important benefits. First, each member wastes time and money by inefficient use of personal resources. Second, each has missed the self-actualizing experience of working successfully with a group of other individuals. Precision teamwork—not individual skills—is what made basketball a popular spectator sport.

In fact, it may be useful to illustrate the steps of group growth by following the development of a company softball team. One researcher has developed a four-step process describing the development of groups.[4] We shall apply these four steps to the formation and perfection of our company softball team.

Step One: Mutual Acceptance

The Acme Manufacturing Company has initiated a program to improve worker morale through a series of competitive games with workers from other companies in the area. Since many of the workers enjoy playing softball, management decides a softball team should be formed. Plant supervisor Lefty Smith is informed that he will be the new team's coach. Lefty recruits his players through persuasion and threats, and finally gets together enough workers to form a respectable ball club. From the first day of practice, the Acme Aces must begin to accept each other. Naturally, each person is apprehensive about his or her own abilities, the coach, the fans, the other players, and the job implications of team membership. These feelings of insecurity, if they persist, can spell doom to such a group. If shared and dealt with, these factors can bring the group closer together. For the moment, let us assume that, as time passes, the Aces learn to trust each other and communicate openly among themselves.

Step Two: Decision Making

As the Aces discover each player's skills and the individual points of view about the game, they will begin to work out strategies for making their jobs

---

[4] Bernard M. Bass and Edward C. Rytherband, *Organizational Psychology,* 2nd ed. (Boston: Allyn, 1978).

easier on the ballfield. As they work together in practice sessions and in actual competition, they will learn each other's quirks and strong points. In many cases, the whole team will join in formulating some new strategy or system that will help them all perform more efficiently. They will make or accept decisions about positions, batting order, and uniforms.

Step Three: Motivation

As a group matures, its members' motivation will change from the individual perspectives to a group viewpoint. In Coach Smith's first encounter with his Aces, he saw a group of nervous, hopeful individuals, each ready to use the group to meet its own goals. Unfortunately, many group members (and employees) never let their motivation mature beyond their initial, individual perspective. Luckily, the Acme Aces recognized that it was more meaningful to be a member of a consistently winning team than the star of a losing one. The Aces learned to channel their individual efforts into solidarity and teamwork. They cooperated with each other, encouraged each member to shine in his or her special area of skill, and achieved a rewarding result while satisfying individual needs.

Step Four: Control

In the early days of the team, Coach Smith may have had to get tough with his Aces to keep them in line. He told them what to do, when to do it, and what would happen to them if they did not do it. At this point the Aces were externally controlled, rather than applying discipline among themselves. As the individual members began to form a tightly knit group, the group itself assumed control functions. They agreed on rules and regulations designed to keep them performing successfully and yet protect the rights of individual members. The group now controls itself, and the individual members control themselves for the benefit of the group.

Mature groups tend to be self-regulating, self-motivating, and self-directing. They take care of their own needs and solve problems arising within the group. At this point, Coach Smith can begin spending more time on supervisory duties, basking in the glow of creating, coaching, and belonging to a championship softball team.

How Are Group Members Ranked?

After the Bolshevik revolution, its leaders decided that everyone should enjoy equal status. The army abandoned all its traditional rank, insignia, and uniform distinctions. No one could tell a general from a private because everyone wore the same uniform and the same insignia. Within a short time, this decision made a mockery of the army. Orders were mistrusted and then ignored, while individuals abused the rights of others. To repair the chaos, the army quickly returned to a ranking system everyone understood and order was soon restored.

Who Is the Leader?

Groups will always choose one or more leaders, but the appointed leader, for example, may not be the employee who really has the most influence over other workers. In other words, the group's actual leader may not occupy the official leadership position.

Recognizing the actual group leader is critical to implement change successfully. No amount of legislation or official regulation can change attitudes or behavior if the group's leader is opposed to any alterations. Though the supervisor always has more authority than any employees, the support of the informal leader is necessary to get anything done.

Formal leaders, like supervisors, usually have the authority to discipline or fire members of their work groups. Informal leaders, however, gain status through consensus of the group members. They work to help the group meet its needs through cooperation and mediation. The informal group leader knows the values and needs of the group, and uses whatever means are available to see that those values are upheld and the needs met. As a communicator, the informal leader is able to organize the needs and values of the group and translate them to nonmembers.

The formal leader and the informal leaders of a group can usually be distinguished by their relative dominance. The formal leader is *task-oriented,* eager to get a job done in the quickest, most effective manner, even if authority must be used negatively. The informal or natural leader, on the other hand, is *group-oriented* and works to enhance group welfare by obtaining consensus and compromise in accomplishing the task at hand. The authority figure uses negative motivation in many cases and relies heavily upon discipline and punishment. The natural leader is working *for* the group, and members may look to this individual for support in negotiations with the formal leader or higher management.

Status Seekers in a Group

As a group begins to gain maturity, a status system will develop within it. Members may try to move up the status ladder in various ways. Most groups do contain status hierarchies clearly perceived by the members. For example, in grocery stores, stockers have more status than sackers, but checkers enjoy more status than either. To gain in esteem and prestige within a work group, an employee may seek to "graduate" from stocker to checker, thus gaining status within the group.

Status is often based on the prestige of particular jobs held by individual members. If supervisors are to cope effectively with human relations problems on the job, they must recognize the status system that exists within the work group and understand why group members relate to each other in particular ways. The effective supervisor will show respect for each individual's status and encourage leadership from those with more prestigious positions. Most employees, whether they admit it or not, desire more recognition and status at work. It is the supervisor's job to fulfill much of that need if maximum performance is to be realized from the work group.

Who Are the Followers?

Does anyone like to be considered a follower instead of a leader? There is much talk about the value of good followers—people who can follow directions and accomplish their tasks with a minimum of friction. It seems, however, that often rewards go to the leaders and rarely to their loyal workers. Like movie stars and winning politicians, leaders often publicly thank the hard workers who made the accomplishments possible—then accept the rewards themselves.

We all claim that our society's economic success and our personal achievement depend upon followers and back-up crews. If this is true, we should start rewarding those who labor behind the scenes. Efficient, faithful workers are necessary to any group process, and the wise supervisor will recognize and cultivate these supportive employees. Rewards do not have to be financial to be effective (Chapter 17 discusses several means of motivating workers when the supervisor has no control over company purse strings), but they should always be prompt and meaningful.

Conducting Meetings

Supervisors are often asked to attend or conduct meetings. These meetings may be designed to disseminate information, share ideas, and make decisions, or they may be training sessions. Each supervisor should become familiar with the techniques of leading group meetings so that they are effective and fulfill their purposes.

Meetings are not popular with most individuals. Because meetings can be used to avoid accountability, many feel that by hiding behind group action, no one is really responsible for the ultimate decisions. Others feel that too frequent meetings are an indication that leadership is lacking. Though meetings can be a waste of time and expensive, and retard individual expression and responsibility, they can be helpful by involving workers in the activities and decisions of an organization. If meetings are not called too often, individuals may feel complimented that they have been included in a group approach to a problem. Further, effective meetings can create a synergistic reaction or a better decision than could be achieved with individuals working alone on the problem.

As a supervisor, you are responsible for leading productive meetings. There are several suggestions that should be helpful in meeting this challenge.

1. Develop and distribute an agenda in advance of the meeting so that the group knows what to expect. The agenda can help keep the meeting on track, especially when irrelevant issues are brought up.

2. Encourage others to offer their opinions before you offer yours. This prevents you from railroading ideas through the group.

3. If you reserve the right to make the final decision on an issue, let the group know this from the beginning of the meeting.

4. Encourage the participation of each person at the meeting, but silence long-winded discussions as they develop.

5. Try to involve the nonaggressive, quiet members at the meeting. Prepare specific questions and ask these individuals directly.

6. Make certain that you or someone else takes notes or minutes of the meeting so that you and others in attendance can have a record of what decisions were made or what activities were planned.

7. Do not fail to follow up on decisions reached at the meeting. Failure to do so will make workers feel that they wasted their time attending the meeting.

Social Control in Groups

Nobody likes to be thought of as a manipulator, but we all know how to get what we want. Getting a group to do what we want it to do is a more complicated affair. Most groups use processes of control to keep their members in line. A discussion of three of these control mechanisms follows.

Group Pressure

Group pressure is a powerful people motivator. Many of our decisons are based consciously or unconsciously on a desire to conform to our groups' standards of behavior. In a work setting, group pressure can cause headaches for the supervisor. Let us follow an example to see how groups can effectively oppose a supervisory decision.

Ellen Green supervises a group of ten workers in the shipping and receiving department of a large department store. Management has learned that the workers' lunch period does not coincide with the lunch period of truckers making deliveries. Since the store employees break for lunch from 12:00 to 1:00 P.M. and the truckers from 1:00 to 2:00 P.M., the shipping and receiving department is effectively closed for two hours each day instead of one. Ellen's group is told to begin having lunch from 1:00 to 2:00 P.M. to allow more efficient operation of the department.

When Ellen breaks the word to her workers, she is greeted by dead silence. Then the grumbling begins, "We've *always* had lunch at noon." "Why don't the truckers change *their* lunch period?" "We won't be able to last another hour without lunch!" And on, and on, and on. Ellen lets the employees know that the decision is final; starting today, they will break for lunch at 1:00. Havoc reigns the rest of the morning. Most of the workers cannot seem to concentrate on their jobs; instead, Ellen finds them talking in tight little groups that fall silent as soon as she walks by.

As noon approaches, every worker except one becomes more and more fidgety. Crates are thrown around and some merchandise is broken, but none of the workers seems to care. At noon, work virtually ceases. The lone worker, who has been doing his job all along, is unloading a huge shipment all by himself. None of the other workers makes a move to help. Unfortunately, Ellen has been called to a management meeting and does not see what has happened in her department.

About 12:30, nine unhappy workers get together, break out their lunch sacks, and start eating. The tenth is still unloading crates. The group seems a little hostile to him, and indulges in harsh talk about "rate breakers" and "the supervisor's boy." When Ellen gets back at 1:30, she sees all the workers breaking for lunch and assumes that they have accepted the decision. When they all return to work at 2:00, she still does not know she has a problem.

Throughout the week, the one employee who has accepted the new lunch hour is excluded more and more from the work group. The other workers begin to shun him, and he becomes more and more unhappy with the situation. Ellen, too, begins to sense tension in the air. Finally, she calls a meeting with the workers to determine the problem. Nine are uncommunicative; the tenth tries to tell Ellen that all the workers are unhappy with the new lunch hour. As he speaks, the others talk among themselves and pay no attention to him. Can you guess what has happened? The tenth worker has grown so unhappy at being left out of the group that he has finally joined them in opposing the new rule. Presented with a unified group of dissatisfied employees, Ellen negotiates with management to compromise the lunch schedule. Finally, workers and management both accept a compromise arrangement whereby the workers have lunch from 12:30 to 1:30 P.M. Is everybody happy now? Nine workers and Ellen are happy, but that tenth worker has some hard work ahead of him to be reinstated by the group, since he insisted on opposing them at first.

The power of social approval and disapproval should never be underestimated. Above all, people need to feel accepted by their own group, and winning group approval encourages members to follow the rules.

Group Enforcement

This method of group control is actually an extension of group pressure. It can, however, become quite hostile and damaging to the group member who is being disciplined. In the example above, the work group decided that one of their members had stepped out of line. They set about enforcing their decision by not speaking to this member, by not helping him when he needed help, and by showing hostility toward him when he tried to negotiate with the supervisor. A group using the enforcement method may even sabotage the worker's performance to ensure conformity to group standards.

Group pressure may exist only in the mind of the individual member. Group enforcement, on the other hand, is quite visible. Being excommunicated from one's group is an unmistakable situation and a harsh punishment. Most group members cannot stand up to group enforcement and will adjust their personal convictions to suit the needs and norms of their group.

In a series of experiments, Solomon Asch illustrated the effects of group pressure by examining social forces as a constraint on individual beliefs and attitudes.[5] He used a group of students and informed them that they would be asked to compare the lengths of lines drawn on cards. Two sets of cards were shown to the students, and they were asked to perform the simple task of matching the card.

[5] Soloman E. Asch, "Opinions and Social Pressure," *Scientific American,* November 1955, pp. 31–5.

Prior to beginning the comparisons with the cards, Asch had "rigged" the assignment by asking all but one student to choose cards that did not match. The results of observing and recording reactions to this assignment demonstrated the profound influence group pressure has on individual judgment. In more than one-third of the cases, the uninformed student denied his or her own accurate perceptions of line length and conformed to the pressure of the group's "correct" decision.

Personal Values

Some people like to think their personal value system was created in a vacuum, with little influence from anyone else. In reality, groups often initiate value systems that are then personalized by individual members. In cases where a member's personal value system differs from that of the group, it will be difficult to withstand the pressures of group enforcement. When the group manages to homogenize the conflicting personal values in its members, the individuals will often assume that the values of the group are morally right.

Being able to recognize the processes of group control is important for any supervisor who wishes to understand a work group. Groups do control their own members, and a supervisor can sometimes use the mechanisms of group control advantageously. The total acceptance of new rules, regulations, and work procedures depends to a large extent not only on acceptance by the group's leadership, but also on the group's ability to enforce behavior patterns among its members.

Summary

Even though critics often claim that groups cause individuals to lose their identities, the combined efforts of a group can greatly exceed the abilities of individual members. The word *synergy* is used to describe this phenomenon: the whole equals more than the sum of its parts.

Research in the last fifty years has uncovered many group processes that were formerly not well understood. Though management tends to accept these research findings without question, the supervisor must study each work group to find out which methods will work best.

Some factors leading to group formation are physical location, economic motivations, and human needs such as security, social satisfactions, esteem, and self-actualization.

Groups pass through recognizable stages of growth and maturity. These stages can be described as mutual acceptance, decision making, motivation, and control.

Every group includes various roles for its members. Some of these roles are formal and informal leaders, specialized area leaders, status seekers, and followers.

The three most important forms of group control are group pressure, group enforcement, and group values.

Key Terms

Formal Leader. The group leader in a position of formal authority who often possesses the power to discipline other group members.

Group Dynamics. The patterns and processes of interaction, growth, status, and social control that take place in groups of people.

Informal Leader. A group's "natural" leader, who rises to power through consensus of group members and works to help the group achieve its goals through cooperation and mediation.

Social Control. The methods by which groups control the behavior of individual members.

Specialized Leader. A task specialist: one who becomes a temporary or partial leader because of some special skill or ability required by the group.

Synergy. The combined or cooperative efforts of two or more individuals that achieve results greater than those that could be obtained by the separate actions of the individuals.

Review Questions

1. Give an example from your personal experiences of a synergistic relationship. How common are such relationships in your life?

2. How can a supervisor misuse the information from group dynamics studies?

3. List and describe the factors involved in the formation of groups. Why is each of these factors important?

4. It is said that a recreational group like a softball team and a work group have much in common. How is this possible? What do they have in common?

5. What is meant by a mature group? List and describe its characteristics.

6. Distinguish between formal and informal group leaders.

7. One kind of specialized leader is the "risk taker"; often this person has the highest credibility in the group because he or she takes the biggest risks. How does such a leader emerge in a group?

8. Describe the ways in which groups maintain social control of their members.

9. Why is social approval such an effective means of controlling individual behavior?

Exercise

Group Analysis

List all the groups you belong to—social, job-oriented, academic, and so on. When your list is complete, answer the following questions:

1. Can your groups be categorized according to their major function (professional, social, civic, religious, recreational, etc.)?

2. Do any of your groups have more than one function? If so, what are these functions?

3. What role do you play in each of your groups (leader, follower, task specialist)?

Case 15 • Ira South

Ira South was recently hired by Marin Redwood Industries, Inc., to work on a crew assembling hot tubs. The company president had decided to enlarge the size of crews from three to four persons based on a recommendation from a management consulting firm engaged to look at all aspects of the company's operation. With changes in the assembly procedure and the addition of a fourth worker, Marin Redwood hoped to increase its output.

The crew that Ira was joining consisted of Bill Strigley, Alma Smith, and Larry Nix. They had worked together for about one year, and their individual and group performance records were excellent. Bill was the youngest member of the group, just recently celebrating his twenty-second birthday. He worked extremely hard and was willing to work additional hours at any activity Marin Redwood would assign him because he was buying an expensive sports car. Alma was thirty years of age, and since she was the sole woman on the crew, she enjoyed the attention she received. Her husband was a long-distance truck driver who made an excellent salary. Alma decided to work at Marin Redwood in order not to be alone while her husband was on the road and to be engaged in physical activity. Larry was in his forties and the senior member of the work group, having been with Marin Redwood since its beginnings fifteen years ago as a quality hardwood supplier. He enjoyed fishing and looked forward to retirement so he could spend more time in British Columbia, where he owned a small cabin.

Since the group began working together, Bill had been the informal leader when the group needed one. He thought of himself as the most physically capable worker and someone the others respected enough to turn to in time of need. However, since Ira South's arrival, things have not been the same. None of the group has been able to achieve its individual production goals, and morale has dropped.

Bill muses, "Things just aren't like they used to be. Every time I look up, Ira is pushing another tub unit at me to finish. We don't talk together like we used to, and no one seems to enjoy work. Alma is thinking of quitting and Larry wants to be transferred."

1. Analyze the group dynamics at work in this situation.
2. If you were in a position to intervene in this situation, what would you do?

PART

FOUR

The Supervisor's Environment

CHAPTER 16
Lessons in Leadership

The job of a leader is to make it easy for people to do the right things and difficult to do the wrong things.

Anonymous

Learning Objectives

- To identify the leadership demands of supervisory work.
- To list various approaches to studying leadership.
- To learn how external factors determine effective leadership styles.
- To learn how to apply leadership concepts and skills on the job.

Leaders have existed for as long as people have worked together in groups. Why do some choose to be leaders and some followers? What is the unique quality that makes some people "natural" leaders? Can anyone be a leader? These problems have been the subject of much study in recent years. Since a supervisor's job is basically to lead, it will be useful to review the concepts and theories concerning the talents of leadership and study the qualities that make an effective leader.

Leadership involves both the ability to convince others to strive for a goal, and the skill to help them reach it. Although much has been written about the qualities of leadership, it is easy to see that one leader may differ greatly from another. Any two leaders may have different personality characteristics, use different styles, and emerge from totally different situations. Despite the fact that individual leaders are not the same, each may be equally qualified as a leader.

A supervisory or management position alone cannot guarantee that an individual will make a good leader. The title may provide a start, but many leaders do not function well in an organizational setting. Leadership is an important part of supervision but only a part. To be a strong supervisor, a person must be a good leader, but if someone is a good leader and a poor supervisor, workers will faithfully follow to the wrong goal. Unless leadership is combined with supervisory skills, workers will lack the direction and motivation they need to accomplish their aims.

Leadership or Popularity?

Many people believe, mistakenly, that leadership and popularity are one and the same. Leaders are often chosen on the basis of their popularity, yet no one considers that they may not be able to understand the goals and guide their groups. The best-looking, friendliest person on the graveyard shift may win the fellowship award, but he or she may make a very poor supervisor. On the other side of the coin, leaders too often play popularity games with their employees, seeking to win affection but failing to properly direct the group. Whether the group is selecting a leader or the leader is directing the group, popularity represents a short-sighted basis for decision making about leadership.

The confusion between leadership and popularity makes it very difficult to evaluate the performance of an American president while that person is in office. Though opinion polls tell us weekly how the president rates in popularity, they are little help in evaluating actual performance in office. Such evaluations are best made with historical perspective. With the passage of time, the effects of a president's work can be more clearly seen and the performance evaluated more fairly.

Lack of popularity, of course, does not necessarily mean a person is a poor leader. Some supervisors indulge in rudeness and unpleasant behavior but remain efficient, courageous leaders.

Perhaps the best way to tell a good leader from a bad one is to look at the followers and the quality of their work. How many followers does the leader have? What kind of people are they? Are they strongly committed or just along for the ride? Are they reaching their goals? The final question is the crucial one. If the group goals are wisely chosen and are being achieved, then the group has an effective leader.

Leadership or Enthusiasm?

Leadership is also often confused with aggressive behavior and enthusiasm. Though the aggressive and enthusiastic person may indeed be a leader, there are times when these qualities are undesirable and even dangerous. Sometimes the leader serves best by staying in the background, keeping pressures off the group, letting others develop their ideas, and calming group members when they panic. A good leader functions from three basic positions: at the front of the group, pointing toward the goal; in the middle, encouraging the majority of members; and behind the group, picking up stragglers.

Most leaders in organizations have a certain amount of authority that comes with their titles. The influence of some leaders, however, will extend beyond this authority in ways that may be either beneficial or detrimental to the organization. A good leader, who exercises power wisely, will increase that power by gaining the natural respect and recognition of group members. By contrast, the supervisor who takes the position that "I may not be right, but I'm the boss" will command obedience without demonstrating real leadership.

Approaches to Leadership

Since people first recognized leaders, they have attempted to understand and classify the characteristics that make a good leader. Over the years, leadership has been defined and described in a variety of ways. We shall look briefly at three methods of classifying the fundamental characteristics of leadership: the trait approaches, the behavioral approaches, and the situational approaches.

Trait Approaches

These approaches to leadership center around characteristics or traits shared by individual leaders. It was long believed that, while leaders were somehow different from the rest of us, they had many things in common with each other.

Physical traits were probably the earliest characteristics to be singled out in studies of leadership. In early groups, the strongest member was likely to lead. If members of the group disagreed, someone exercised leadership with a club. Of course, even the strongest person had to sleep—and could then easily be killed by jealous or spiteful group members.

Eventually, people realized that an effective leader had to be chosen on the basis of qualities other than physical strength alone. In the Middle Ages, the cleverest and most ambitious warriors became the feudal rulers and passed their thrones on to their offspring—who were presumably as clever and ambitious as they. And the line of succession remained in one family until a more powerful warrior came along to overthrow it.

Today, at least in countries which accept the philosophy that all people are created equal, nobody will follow a leader simply because he or she is taller, faster, stronger, blonder, or descended from King Alfred. Whether in government, business, church, university, or any other sphere of modern life, leaders are chosen because their experience and policies suggest that they will fulfill their responsibilities better than anyone else.

Mental traits, then, may be seen as the common key to today's successful leaders. We want our leaders to read fast and talk well, and we are often impressed when they surround themselves with "brain trusts." Politicians, in particular, benefit from associating with intellectual constituents—so long as the voters remember they are just down-to-earth folks!

Leaders *do* tend to be more intelligent than their average follower. The difference is small, but probably rests on broader talents. After all, the leader's job utilizes an ability to see broad problems and complex relationships and to synthesize knowledge, the group's talents, and available resources to solve problems efficiently. The leader must also possess good communication skills in order to get ideas across, motivate workers, and understand what others are saying.

One pioneer study[1] showed that leadership ability is associated with the leader's language skills and ability to make accurate judgments. Another study[2] concluded that, within a certain range, a person's intelligence is a good indicator of leadership ability. Above and below this range, however, leadership cannot be successfully predicted. Common sense tells us that intelligent people do not always make good leaders, and that although leaders must be smart, an individual can be too smart to be accepted as a leader by a group.

Personality traits are probably the most accurate indicators we have of who will make a good leader. This is true because "personality" is such a broad term it includes almost every aspect of an individual's physical, mental, and social makeup. It cannot be denied that a leader's personality is a key to success. We run into problems, though, when we try to say that one personality type is more suitable for leadership. Two individuals with completely different personality types can be successful leaders, given a specific group or particular situation.

Leaders usually display a wide variety of interests and participate in many kinds of activities. They are able to accept defeat and success gracefully because they are emotionally mature. They do not often become frustrated. They rarely display hostility toward others or indulge in temper flare-ups. They are sure of themselves and have a reasonable amount of self-respect.

Leaders are usually interested in "accomplishment." When they complete one project, they immediately begin another. Frequently, leaders have several projects going at the same time. They are always seeking to satisfy their own needs and the needs of their groups. They work hard because work satisfies them, not because of the external rewards they will receive. A leader will often be surprised when someone says, "You're working too hard." "How can it be work?" they respond. "I enjoy it too much!" Leaders are eager to accept responsibility and are faithful in carrying out their duties.

Successful leaders understand that the job gets done with or through their workers. They develop skill in human relations and in effectively managing groups of people. They display a healthy respect for their workers that helps ensure cooperation. They are more likely to approach problems in terms of the people involved than in terms of the problem's technical aspects.

These *trait approaches* illustrate characteristics that often identify leaders. Yet we are never sure whether an individual's traits have made for successful leadership or whether success as a leader has made the traits more noticeable.

[1] Ralph Stogdill, "Personal Factors Associated with Leadership," *Journal of Applied Psychology,* January 1948, pp. 37–71.
[2] E. E. Ghiselli, "Managerial Talent," *American Psychologist,* October 1963, pp. 631–41.

Behavior Approaches

This approach to defining leadership focuses on the way leaders act. Some theorists believe leaders have a particular way of doing things that distinguishes them from their peers. In this section, we shall review several methods of classifying behavior that seems to indicate leadership ability.

Benevolent autocracy is a convenient way to describe the all-powerful boss who listens patiently to employees' ideas and then does what he or she wanted to do in the first place. The benevolent autocrat's motto is, "I want to be democratic about this matter as long as it's done my way." Sometimes whole companies are operated in this manner, but even the smallest department within a company can have an autocratic leader. Though the term sounds suspiciously like a dictatorship, benevolent autocrats will argue that we should not try to apply democratic principles where they will not work.

Some observers believe that the "real world" of business and competition is no place for democratic systems of supervision. Too many independent thinkers, they say, will spoil a decision. If you have ever tried to accomplish anything through a committee, you can understand the benefits of having a benevolent autocrat in charge. He or she can take a failing project, tell each person what to do, and move the project decisively toward accomplishing its goal. The benevolent autocrat is a manager or supervisor with enough power and prestige to get workers to obey without question. In return, the leader is interested in the problems of subordinates and makes it easy for them to communicate. By using this balance of power but remaining in charge, the benevolent autocrat can discover problems as soon as they occur and take prompt action to correct them.

The *absence of democratic corporate leadership* and the rise of the benevolent autocracy is explained by the following factors:

1. The climate within organizations is unfavorable to individualism on the lower levels. The "captains of industry" have worked hard to attain their positions in the managerial hierarchy. They are typically hard-driving leaders who like controlling the destiny of the firms they created or helped to create. These individuals are not likely to favor delegation of decision-making power.

2. Because most organizations must make difficult decisions rapidly, it is more pragmatic to maintain control with a centralized authority. Freedom of action, therefore, is limited by the firm's need to make rapid decisions, and democratic leadership is not feasible because it encourages freedom of action and is more time-consuming.

3. Democratic leadership concepts are relatively new and unproved. Most successful firms (those that have made profits) have followed traditional leadership principles. These are generally compatible with autocratic and not democratic leadership. Once a firm has begun to develop autocratic leaders, these leaders tend to perpetuate themselves.

Of course, many supervisors adopt the benevolent autocrat approach to leadership without ever knowing its name. They are guided in their choice both by their own personalities and the type of people they lead. Benevolent autocrats assume that they understand and their employees do not. Such leaders are often willing and eager to listen to employees' ideas and help them deal with their problems, but when the company is in trouble, they may be more autocratic than benevolent.

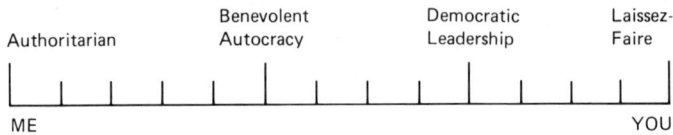

Figure 16-1. Leadership Attitudes Continuum.

As with most theories, neither the benevolent autocratic nor the democratic leadership approach can be considered best for all situations. Each method works for different leaders in varying situations. The leader's personality characteristics, skills and abilities, and situation all combine to dictate the proper behavioral approach to leadership.

Another approach, closely related to the benevolent autocracy, suggests that leadership attitudes toward employees can accurately be placed along a *continuum,* as in Figure 16–1. At one extreme is the total authoritarian, the hard-nosed supervisor who rules employees with an iron fist. This leader is the sole source of authority and the final decision maker. At the other extreme is the laissez-faire leader who allows workers to do their jobs any way they please. This leader places trust in others by emphasizing their freedom. The extremes in this continuum can also be interpreted as showing opposite centers of concern. The authoritarian leader is completely self- or job-centered, while the laissez-faire leader is almost totally employee-centered.

The differences between these two styles are based on the leader's assumptions about human nature, authority, and the source of supervisory power. The authoritarian leader believes that workers are naturally lazy, unreliable, and incompetent (sometimes called Theory X). Workers are often told in no uncertain terms what to do, how to do it, and when it is to be done. If there were enough time, this manager would prefer to do all the work personally.

The democratic leader, on the other hand, feels that people are basically self-directed, and that they can accomplish wonders if allowed to participate in decision making which relates to their jobs (sometimes known as Theory Y.) This type of leader will set objectives for the group and serve as a resource person, but will allow workers to accomplish their goals in whatever way suits them best.

At the extreme end of the scale is the laissez-faire leader. This represents the least-structured approach to leadership. Under this system, employees are free to do whatever they wish—including setting their own objectives, policies, and procedures.

The *managerial grid* is another behavioral approach to leadership patterns (Figure 16–2). Its originators, Robert Blake and Jane F. Mouton, developed descriptions of the various supervisory personalities that might be represented by various points within the grid.[3] With this matrix, a supervisor's leadership style can be pinpointed by weighing the concern shown for people against the desire for high productivity.

Five specific styles of leadership are illustrated on the grid. A specific supervisor's leadership style might fit any one of the eighty-one squares, according to concern for production and concern for people. The following attitudes describe the personalities represented by these five grid points:

[3] Robert Blake and Jane F. Mouton, *The Management Grid* (Houston: Gulf Publishing Co., 1964).

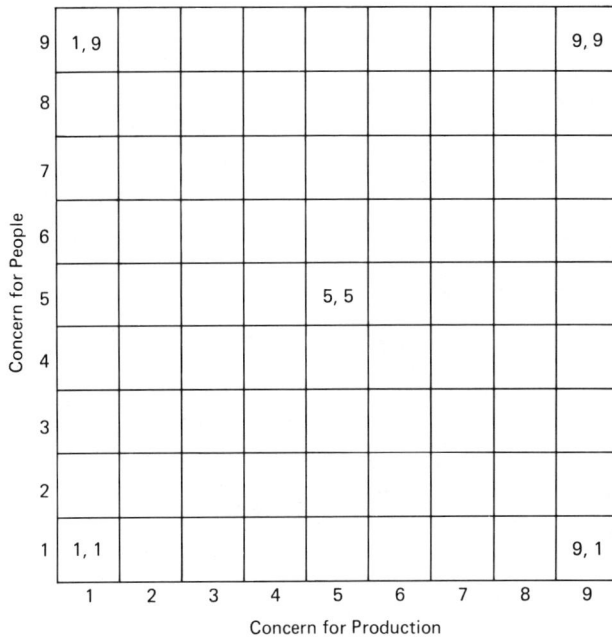

Figure 16-2. The Managerial Grid.

- 1,1 Impoverished: "Don't make waves; do only what is necessary to keep the boss happy."
- 9,1 Taskmaster: "The job's the thing. Accomplish the objective even if all the troops are lost in the battle."
- 1,9 Country Club: "If my people are happy, production will take care of itself."
- 5,5 Middle of the Road: "People and production are both important. It depends on the situation which factor needs the most emphasis."
- 9,9 Team Spirit: "Yes sir! This is the finest group any manager could want to work with. They really work as a team to accomplish team goals!"

Every company president's dream is to see all managerial positions filled by people who fit into the 9,9 grid square. Though this dream is only a fantasy, all supervisors should try to shape their attitudes toward that ideal.

Situational Approaches

A final approach to leadership concentrates on the supervisor's particular job situation. Theorists researched and developed this approach when they recognized that trait or behavior types did not adequately explain leadership qualities or styles. Situational theorists suggest that a leader is concerned with two "objective" factors in a job: to accomplish specific tasks and to establish meaningful interpersonal relationships with employees. A leader may determine how favorable his or her leadership position is, or what style should be used for maximum

Situation	1	2	3	4	5	6	7	8
Leader-member relations	Good	Good	Good	Good	Moderately poor	Moderately poor	Moderately poor	Moderately poor
Task structure	Structured	Structured	Unstructured	Unstructured	Structured	Structured	Unstructured	Unstructured
Leader position power	Strong	Weak	Strong	Weak	Strong	Weak	Strong	Weak
	Favorable for leader						Unfavorable for leader	
Most productive leadership style	Task	Task	Task	Relation	Relation	No data	Task or relation	Task

Figure 16-3. Relationship of Leadership Style to the Situation. [With permission from L. W. Rue and Lloyd L. Byars, *Management: Theory and Application,* rev. ed. (Homewood, Ill.: Richard D. Irwin, 1980), p. 356.]

effectiveness, by considering three factors: (1) leader-member relations, (2) task structure, and (3) the leader's position of power.[4]

A leader's situation is more favorable when there is strong support and loyalty from employees because the leader relates well to the group and gains support (good leader-member relations). Specific goals and methods of evaluating tasks assist group members in knowing what and how to do things and contribute to a more favorable situation for the leader (high task structure). Leaders with more ability and power to reward and punish subordinates—financially or psychologically—are in a more favorable situation (strong position of power).

Fred Fiedler is the leading researcher of the situational approach. Figure 16–3 illustrates his eight-part classification of leadership situations and the most effective leadership style for each situational module. The diagram suggests that in highly favorable or unfavorable situations, a task leadership style is most productive. A relationship-oriented style seems most appropriate where conditions are "moderately" favorable or unfavorable—depending on one's perspective.

This research suggests that it is easier to alter the work situation than it is to change one's motivation toward task accomplishment or establishing enviable interpersonal relationships. If the situations are too difficult to change, a leader should move to another group where his or her goals are more compatible with the new situation.

In effect, this approach to leadership takes into account both the leader's personality and the behavioral characteristics of the group. The success of a leader depends on the unique combination of special traits and abilities with a particular situation. As an old American proverb puts it, "Leadership is what happens when preparation meets opportunity."

Determinants of Effective Leadership

Considering the leader and his or her personal characteristics does not give us the full picture of leadership. There are several outside influences that often affect an individual's ability to lead effectively.

The size of the organization in which the leader must operate plays a definite role. Almost without exception, large organizations are slow organizations.

---

[4] See Fred W. Fiedler, *A Theory of Leadership Effectiveness* (New York: McGraw-Hill, 1967).

An elephant carries more weight than a monkey, but an elephant cannot leap from one treetop to another. A large organization can accomplish objectives a small organization could never consider, but its size and bulk often hinder individual leadership attempts. Organizational bigness is not in itself a bad thing, but it tends to discourage independent thinking.

To encourage individual leadership in large companies, supervisors must seek creative ways to overcome the sluggish communication system and slow decision-making processes that characterize big firms by developing his or her highly effective and efficient "organization within the organization." Rigid, formal policies and procedures seem to accompany increased size in a corporation, but the outstanding supervisor should not accept this situation without a strategic fight. Often, the advantages of bigness can be maintained while individual contributions are fostered and encouraged. For example, most big and small companies' computer capacity is underutilized. That is, their hardware is capable of doing much more than it is programmed to do. The software applications have not kept up with the hardware development. Innovative leaders will encourage their personnel to suggest ways in which the computer might assist performance of their job duties or streamline communication and decision-making systems for their department.

The amount of interaction taking place within an organization also encourages or inhibits the growth of leadership talents. Operations requiring more interaction among employees improve leadership skills. For instance, a production plant has relatively little need for total interaction among all employees. As long as each person does the job and supervisors are alert to conditions in the plant, interaction between employees can remain at a minimum. Consider now the case of a company specializing in advertising or market research. In such an organization, the total operation's success depends on communication between employees. Ideas must freely circulate from one person to another, and all workers must have access to the information and resources they need to do their jobs well. Sometimes even companies relying heavily on modern technology depend on input from experts all over the organization. As the need for interaction increases, cross-checking and collective thinking will also become more important. Leaders thrive in organizational structures that permit information and ideas to flow freely.

The personalities of the leader and group members make up the third factor influencing leadership functions. Sometimes leaders cannot use the type of leadership best suited to their own personalities. The personalities of followers or the nature of a situation may force an autocratic supervisor, for instance, to allow union representatives to participate in negotiation sessions. An example of a leader forced to deviate from personal preference is Douglas M. McGregor, one of the first supporters of the human relations approach to supervision. After a distinguished career as a university professor, McGregor became president of Antioch College. In reflecting upon this experience he wrote:

> I believed, for example, that a leader could operate successfuly as a kind of advisor to his organization. I thought I could avoid being a "boss." Unconsciously, I suspect, I hoped to duck the unpleasant necessity of making difficult decisions, of taking the responsibility for one course of action among many uncertain alternatives, of making mistakes and taking the consequences. I thought that maybe I could operate so that everyone would like me—that good "human relations" would eliminate all discord and disagreement.
>
> I couldn't have been more wrong. It took a couple of years, but I finally began

to realize that a leader cannot avoid the exercise of authority any more than he can avoid responsibility for what happens to his organization.[5]

The style of leadership chosen by the supervisor must conform to the organizational structure and to the personality and expectations of subordinates. Employees who do not expect to participate in decision making and who are dependent on others for motivation are best led by the benevolent autocrat. But those who expect to participate and who are self-motivated will react best to the type of leadership that allows them a voice in what happens.

If everyone in the company has the same goals, it is easier for effective leadership to develop and flourish. When corporate goals and employee goals differ, the authoritarian or autocratic method of leadership must be employed to ensure that company goals are met. When everyone's goals are the same, however, a less formal structure and more lenient type of leadership works best.

The level on which decision making is encouraged constitutes another factor affecting leadership skills. If the people who must carry out the decisions also make them, decision making can lead to more effective leadership. In other words, if the supervisors in the shipping and receiving department are the ones to make shipping and receiving decisions, chances are effective leadership will result. If the decisions come from someone higher up who has not seen a packing crate in twenty years, shipping and receiving employees may take their time following instructions or contributing to problem solutions.

Finally, *the organization's health* has a great deal to do with the amount and strength of organizational leadership. A failing company can rarely afford the luxury of democratic decision making. When a corporation is in poor health, authoritarian leadership offers a better chance of saving it.

A company in poor health might consistently show a loss. In this case, the president should make or closely oversee decisions. This leader cannot afford to delegate too much authority and responsibility to lower-level managers and supervisors. Though the president may have long-range plans for improving the health of the organization, short-range goals will include cutting costs at all levels. One of the fastest ways to cut costs is to reduce the payroll, and the president will have to make layoff decisions as promptly and wisely as possible.

The Unexplainable Ingredient

Individuality is the ingredient that makes the vital difference between a good supervisor and a poor one. Even identical twins, with the same training and benefits, should not be surprised to find their careers heading in different directions. One might apply leadership abilities to heading a big manufacturing firm; the other might make an outstanding college professor.

Why does this happen? What is the ingredient that makes some people leaders and some followers? For now, about the best we can do is to call it the "soul of the supervisor"—a mixture of personality, training, philosophy of life, and approach to other human beings. Unfortunately, this component is not something we can measure, buy, sell, or trade. If an individual has it,

[5] "On Leadership," *Antioch Notes,* May 1954, pp. 2–3.

he or she can be developed and nurtured into an effective leader. Without it, all the leadership training courses ever invented cannot make a leader. Of course, even if an individual has this component, it will require a combination of talents, skills, personalities, and situations to reveal those leadership qualities.

Behavioral science researchers from the University of Michigan conducted a number of studies to determine what leadership characteristics were associated with high productivity and job satisfaction. If you would like to improve your leadership abilities, you might consider the following suggestions:[6]

1. Try to develop a general approach to supervising workers rather than a close, detailed approach.

2. Spend as much time on your supervisory activities as you do worrying about production work.

3. Emphasize the planning of regular activities and special tasks; anticipate rather than react.

4. Attempt to engage employees in the decision-making process.

5. Show sincere interest in the needs and problems of employees and individuals as well as concern about high production.

Summary

In this chapter, we have studied several attempts to define and classify the mystical component of leadership. Could they all be saying the same thing in different words? Is any one theory "right" and the others "wrong"? If leadership were something that could be readily defined and separated into parts, it would be easy enough to create leaders in the laboratory.

People have followed leaders since prehistoric times, long before the experts began classifying and categorizing their leadership styles. If you wish to serve as a successful leader, you must seek to identify and develop the factors in your own personality that indicate you could lead well. Be aware of the situations surrounding you when called to lead. And understand that, in the end, the indefinable mixture of your abilities, your followers, and your situation will determine the proper type of leadership for you.

Remember that leadership is the ability to convince others to seek some goal and the skills to help them get there. Leadership is often confused with popularity, aggressiveness, enthusiasm, or success, but none of these is a definite indicator of leadership.

Three theories have been advanced in an effort to explain the leader. The trait approach suggests that leadership can be attributed to specific physical, mental, or personality traits possessed by leaders. The behavioral concepts propose that the leader's success lies in the way he or she acts and reacts. The situational approach claims that the appropriate leadership style must be determined partly by the conditions existing in each situation. Various approaches to leadership behavior have been expressed in terms of the benevolent autocrat, the democratic leader, the laissez-faire attitude, the continuum of approaches, the managerial grid theory, and group dynamics.

[6] C. Dorwin Cartwright and Alvin Zander, eds., *Group Dynamic Research and Theory* (New York: Harper, 1961), pp. 554–70.

Several external determinants of leadership effectiveness were discussed. Among them are the size of the organization, the amount of interaction, the personalities of the members, the existence of common goals, the level at which decisions are made, and the health of the organization.

Though all of these approaches have much in common, there remains an elusive indefinable ingredient that might be termed *soul*. This rare attribute may constitute the crucial factor in determining leadership ability and success.

Key Terms

Authoritarian Leader. One who is the sole source of authority and the final decision maker; a leader who supervises with an iron fist.

Behavioral Approaches. An approach to leadership centering on the supervisor's behavior toward employees.

Benevolent Autocracy. A manager or supervisor with so much power and authority that subordinates obey without question. This leader is interested and concerned about employees and will listen to what they have to say, but will make final decisions alone.

Democratic Leader. One who encourages worker participation in decision making and is willing to take into consideration the opinions of subordinates when decisions must be made or problems solved.

Laissez-Faire Leader. One who trusts workers to the extent of allowing them to do their jobs any way they please. This leader takes a very unstructured approach to leadership.

Leadership. The ability to convince other people to attempt a goal and the skills necessary to help them reach it.

Managerial Grid. A method developed by Robert Blake and Jane Mouton to identify types of leaders based on their concern for production and people.

Situational Approaches. Approaches to leadership that emphasize the supervisor's particular job situation. Situational approaches combine the individual leader's characteristics, the group's personality, and the situation.

Theory X. The philosophy of a leader who does not trust subordinates to do anything well, exhibits an authoritarian approach to leadership, and would much rather do all the work personally.

Theory Y. The philosophy of a democratic leader who feels that people are basically self-directed and creative, and who encourages participation in decision making.

Trait Approaches. Approaches to leadership that focus on physical, psychological, or biological characteristics of the leader. Physical strength, leadership by inheritance, intelligence, and personality traits have been used in these approaches to identify leaders.

Review Questions

1. It is said that unless someone is "born" a leader, he or she can never be a "natural" leader. Do you agree?

2. Distinguish between "popularity" and "leadership." What other characteristics are often confused with leadership?

3. What are the common personality traits of good leaders? Why are they important?

4. Which type of leader makes the best supervisor: a benevolent autocrat or a democratic leader? Why?

5. Describe in detail the characteristics of Theory X and Theory Y styles of leadership. Which are you?

6. How can the managerial grid be useful to a supervisor?

7. How do situational approaches to leadership relate to the other two approaches?

8. It is said that the type of employees a supervisor has to work with has an influence on the type of leader that supervisor can become. How is this possible?

9. Can training and education help develop a leader? How?

Exercises

I. Leadership Seminar

You have been given the task of developing a one-day seminar in leadership training. You have freedom to plan the program, and you have a small operating budget. The participants will be a group of 25 to 30 production and distribution supervisors. Develop the program for this one-day seminar. The following steps may be useful:

1. Decide what objectives the program should attempt to meet.

2. Outline the topics, skills, and information you wish to cover.

3. Decide how you will encourage participation.

4. Develop a simple evaluation plan to determine the seminar's success.

II. Leadership Traits

A. Perform this simple experiment to see what characteristics other people consider most important for leadership. Show the following list to ten people outside your class and ask them to rank the traits from 1 to 10, with 1 the most important leadership skill and 10 the least important:

Achievement orientation, aggressiveness, authority, creativity, decisiveness, emotional maturity, enthusiasm, intelligence, physical build, popularity, respect for people, respect for self.

B. Tally your results by grouping characteristics at the top, middle, and bottom of the list according to the ten reactions you surveyed.

C. Compare this grouped list with the three-part lists of other class members and answer the following questions:

1. Overall, which characteristics were considered most important and least important for leaders?

2. How would *you* have rated these characteristics?

3. How does your personal ranking compare with those of your sample and the findings of your classmates as a whole?

4. Can you find logical reasons why the people you consulted responded as they did?

Case 16 • Ron Danner

Ron Danner is a packer in the stamping department of Southwest Metals, Inc. He began his employment with Southwest about two years ago because he needed a job and at the time had no idea about the direction of his career. But after maturing and learning more about the world of work, Ron decided to enroll in business courses at the community college in order to improve himself and his potential for promotion. He is currently enrolled in a "principles of supervision" course that meets twice a week in the evenings. His class is studying a unit on leadership. Rather than help Rob to understand his experiences at Southwest, what he has learned about leadership has only made him more confused. In short, his experiences do not fit the textbook descriptions! To make matters more of a puzzle for Ron, he has been given a course assignment to describe a supervisor he has worked with and that individual's style of leadership.

Ron thinks to himself, "Nothing we have talked about in class fits my boss. Frank Ceccato likes to say he is 'firm but fair'. In some ways, he is an autocratic manager, keeping close tabs on everything that goes on in our operation, and he really chews you out if you report to work late or fool around. At the same time, he can be really considerate when you've got problems at home or at school and need to leave work a little early.

"Sometimes he'll work us like slaves, and then, when we get a big order completed, he'll take us down to Archie's tavern and buy us a round or two. I think the guy has a split personality! I mean, he can be hard-nosed and gruff sometimes, but in other situations, he can be pleasant and considerate.

"Another thing that is really confusing to me is that he will always ask our opinion about a problem, but after you've offered your suggestions, he'll say something like, 'Well, I appreciate your input, but I think we'll do it this way.' I mean, why does he ask if he's not going to take our suggestions?"

1. Do you agree that Ron's boss does not fit the "textbook" descriptions of a leader?
2. How would you explain Frank's "erratic" behavior?

CHAPTER 17
Motivation at Work

We know nothing of motivation. All we can do is write books about it.

Peter F. Drucker

Learning Objectives

- To study the problems and possibilities of motivation presented in everyday life and on the job.
- To explore the complex relationship of personality, behavior, and motivation.
- To recognize different approaches to motivation.
- To contrast the potentials and limitations of various motivators, and to begin applying techniques of motivation on the job.

Motivation comes from the Latin word *to move,* which implies behavior that will cause someone to move toward the achievement of a goal. When a person has a need (i.e., hunger), it will create a motive or drive within the individual (i.e., search for food), that, hopefully, will result in accomplishing a specific goal (i.e., eating) that satisfies the initial need. Needs and motives come in many forms both on and off the job, which confirms the concept that motivation lies behind everything we do. The intriguing part of dealing with motivation in people is that a supervisor can observe only exhibited behavior in employees, not the hidden needs or motives that impel or drive the manifest behavior.

Some people assume that motivation is something applicable only in a job situation. But even as infants, we recognize motivation as more. As soon as we learn that crying brings our parents running, we have started getting people to do what we want them to do.

As children grow, they gain skill in motivating people. They begin to evaluate each situation in terms of what they want and what other people can do about it, and soon learn new techniques for fulfilling their desires. Much of this learning takes place subconsciously, but it is continuous and basic to everyone's actions in later life. Sometimes children will use methods that are inefficient or socially unacceptable. When they try to get someone's attention by throwing something, they may get a response they did *not* want. Whether the response is good or bad, they learn to adjust behavior to the demands of other people. During this process, the child is developing and molding the characteristics of an adult personality.

Personality, Behavior, and Motivation

Personality is made up of behavior patterns, attitudes, interests, and values. Our behavior varies as we learn to use different methods of motivation. Sooner or later, most of us choose particular ways to motivate others, and our personalities are built upon these choices.

A supervisor's personality depends, to a large degree, on ideas about people. Certain attitudes about "what makes people go" will determine behavior in most situations. Unfortunately, many people fail to develop beyond a simple, childlike conception of the things motivating other people. The reasons why people act as they do rest on a complex and intertwining series of relationships.

We have already discussed some of the basic ideas about human behavior. In this chapter we shall consider some of the more widely used approaches to human motivation. At one level, these approaches remain theories about the nature of people. At another level, they serve as useful concepts for anyone who must deal with people.

What Makes You an Individual?

Your personality is made up of your everyday behavior, attitudes about people and things, and expectations about life. As these components change, your personality, too, adapts to influences from a number of factors. Your personality may be influenced by your physical size and strength, your sex, or the way you wear your hair. Another important influence in shaping personality is membership in certain groups. All of us belong to groups, both formal and informal. Each group holds a different set of expectations, and in each you play different roles by showing different facets of your personality. Consider, for example, the different roles you might play as parent, child, supervisor, employee, student, and basketball coach. When we say there is a time and a place for everything, we are admitting that we must present different parts of our personalities to meet varying situations. Remember, personality must be viewed as a dynamic process.

The components of personality are not isolated from each other. Instead, they form a network of interdependent relationships, all of which help to shape and alter a person's personality. For this reason, no single influence can "make or break" any individual.

Behavioral Building Blocks

Are actions governed totally by chance? Or is there something that leads us toward certain actions and makes us avoid others? Action forms the foundation for personality. In the same way, many people believe that motivation, in all its various forms, is the basis of behavior. When you consider that motivation also fosters manipulation, the possibilities may become frightening. However, only the insecure part of us balks at the idea of manipulating people to get what we want. When our aggressive side takes charge—when we want to effect a change for our benefit—we automatically become motivators: "*Why* did he say that?" "How can I get her to change her mind?" "What can I say or do to win their support?"

Literature on human motivation could easily fill a large library. Throughout the ages, people have been compelled to write about the sources of human behavior. Authors have outlined schemes for understanding behavior and thereby controlling it. Needless to say, there is no simple answer to the complex problem of what motivates humans to act as they do.

The supervisor need not be concerned with abstract theories of human motivation. More specific approaches will be useful to help relate to workers. One of the supervisor's primary tasks involves motivating workers to become achievers. Unfortunately, this problem is not at all easy to solve, and differing approaches may be required in varying situations.

In the next section, we shall look at some popular approaches to motivating behavior. Though these approaches are generalized, the supervisor will easily recall examples from day-to-day experiences. You should remember that an approach successful in a particular situation may fail under different circumstances. Always be ready and able to adapt your behavior according to the personalities and demands involved in each situation. As Mark Twain once remarked, "A round man cannot be expected to fit in a square hole right away. He must have time to modify his shape."

Approaches to Behavior Motivation

The Classical Approach

What happens when the hard-working, energetic young woman discovers she earns no more at her job than the lazy fellow who gets away with everything he can while doing as little as possible? It is possible that our energetic worker might become discouraged and dissatisfied, and would soon stop trying to do her best.

The classical approach to motivation is founded upon this simple example.[1] The basic idea is to make it possible for workers to earn more by producing more. The introduction of this approach set the stage for stopwatches and the piecework pay system in many organizations. Jobs can now be scientifically evaluated, and performance levels clearly defined and rewarded.

This approach usually establishes production quotas for particular jobs. If workers produce their quota, they are rewarded accordingly. If they exceed the quota, rewards are proportionately increased. This system differs from straight piecework pay scales because above-average productivity is rewarded at a higher rate. Thus workers can greatly increase earnings by increasing production.

Money is clearly considered the best motivator in the classical approach. The approach assumes that workers will act in whatever manner brings them the greatest financial reward. Many people agree with this approach, but its validity has never been clearly determined. Though every person may have a price, the price of some people may be measured in something other than money.

In some situations, opportunities for increased earnings bring definite improvements in production. This may be especially true in jobs where other motivators are not available or not often used. There is danger, however, in believing that *only* money motivates people. Individuals at all working levels have risen above the dollar and seek other rewards and pursue other satisfactions.

The classical approach to motivation attempted to establish money as the simple solution to production problems. As we stated earlier, there is no simple solution. Money is certainly a motivator, and usually a good one, but the classical approach failed to take into account other factors that affect an individual worker's motivation.

The Human Needs Approach

The classical approach was too simple a solution to answer every motivation problem. Few of us ever reach the point where we feel we have enough money. On the other hand, we probably all agree there is more to life than earning a dollar. The human needs approach takes into account other factors affecting motivation on the job.[2]

As discussed in Chapter 2, once our physical needs for air, water, food, shelter, and clothing are satisfied, we seek security as well as physical safety. Social needs for companionship and acceptance are the next to be fulfilled.

When we have been accepted by a group, we then seek to gain their respect and our own by developing our talents in a manner useful to and appreciated by the group. The highest level of our needs—self-actualization—can never be completely fulfilled because no one ever develops abilities to their fullest capacity.

[1] Frederick W. Taylor [*Scientific Management* (New York: Harper, 1919)] is generally viewed as the founder of this approach.

[2] Abraham H. Maslow ("The Theory of Human Motivation," *Psychology Review,* July 1943, pp. 370–96) is generally associated with this approach.

There are gradations of needs among workers and, indeed, all people around you. As a wise supervisor, you may study your people to find out their needs. You can then employ different techniques of motivation according to the need level of your individual workers.

We have spoken so far as if the supervisor's workers were the only people to have differing levels of needs. The supervisor also has human needs to fulfill. Several years ago, a group of male managers and supervisors of AT&T were studied over a period of five years.[3] Interviews with the young men during this time showed their need levels developed as their tenure with the company increased. The following list of findings may be helpful to you in analyzing your own need structure:

1. For all supervisors, the need for achievement and esteem increases over the years they are with a company.

2. Supervisors who have met high standards of performance will be rewarded with promotions and pay increases or with success.

3. Successful supervisors achieve a great deal and are given increased managerial responsibility. Therefore, by their fifth year their achievement and esteem satisfaction rank significantly higher than those of their less successful colleagues.

4. Possibly as a result of greater achievement and esteem satisfaction, successful managers become more involved in their jobs. By the fifth year, work is significantly more essential to their overall need satisfaction than it is for the less successful group.

5. With increased job involvement, supervisors are more likely to be successful in future assignments. Thus they ride an upward spiral of success.

The Human Relations Approach

Some people feel the top three levels of the human needs approach exert the greatest influence in human motivation. Social, esteem, and self-actualization needs make up the human relations approach. This approach assumes that, in our society, the physical and safety needs are overwhelmingly met for the vast majority of people. The approach concentrates instead on the fulfillment of higher-level needs.

The human relations approach emphasizes the motivator rather than the person to be motivated.[4] Supervisors are encouraged, for example, to use many techniques and methods to motivate their workers. These techniques include incentive plans, awards, and special recognition ceremonies, as well as stimulating the worker's curiosity or desire to be creative. The difference in the human relations approach is its emphasis upon the supervisor rather than the employee. Techniques such as those mentioned above serve as the supervisor's *tools,* but are not considered motivators in themselves.

Advocates of the human relations approach feel a highly productive department is characterized by good *human relations*—the workers get along well with each other and with the supervisor, they like their work, and they are happy with the organizational establishment. In brief, people involved in pleas-

---

[3] See Robert N. Ford, *Motivation Through the Work Itself* (New York: AMACOM, 1969).
[4] See Rensis Likert, *New Patterns of Management* (New York: McGraw-Hill, 1961).

ant, productive relationships with other people are likely to be motivated toward goal fulfillment. Therefore, the supervisor who follows the human relations approach encourages workers' participation in decision making, and allows them to use their creative and leadership abilities to work toward company goals.

The supervisor who uses this approach thinks more of workers than the classical supervisor. Classical supervision techniques assume that a worker cannot handle anything but a simple, uncomplicated task assignment. Human relations techniques attempt to make the worker a part of the team. If an individual feels like a significant member of the group, this will provide the highest form of motivation.

As might be expected, there is considerable merit but a high degree of impracticality in this approach when carried to its ultimate extreme. A manager who must direct a department of 300 production workers must limit the amount of participatory decision making. It is difficult to feel like a member of the team when the team has 10,000 members!

The Two-Factor Approach: Maintenance and Motivation

A study of over 200 engineers and accountants led to the development of a two-factor explanation of motivation and behavior among employees.[5] According to Frederick Herzberg, the first factor involved in any job situation is composed of *maintenance* characteristics—the necessities of adequate compensation, working conditions, job safety and security, and fringe benefits. These characteristics must be present before the worker can begin to be motivated. Ten maintenance factors were identified:

1. Company Policy and Administration.
2. Technical Supervision.
3. Interpersonal Relations with Supervisor.
4. Interpersonal Relations with Peers.
5. Interpersonal Relations with Subordinates.
6. Salary.
7. Job Security.
8. Personal Life.
9. Work Conditions.
10. Status.

The second factor consisted of *motivational* characteristics. Once maintenance needs were satisfied, the following six factors became critical in developing worker motivation and dedication:

1. Achievement.
2. Recognition.
3. Advancement.

[5] Frederick Herzberg, *Work and the Nature of Man* (New York: World, 1966), and Frederick Herzberg et al., *The Motivation to Work,* 2nd ed. (New York: Wiley, 1959).

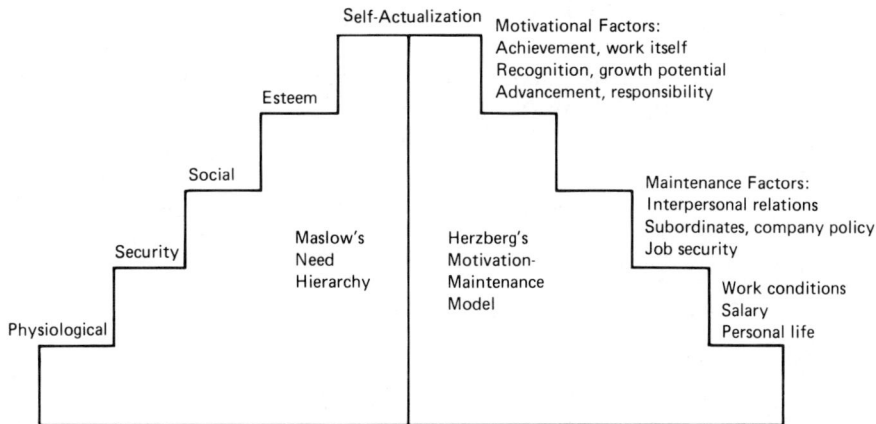

Figure 17-1. Comparison of Maslow and Herzberg Models.

4. The Work Itself.

5. The Possibility of Growth.

6. Responsibility.

How do these factors fit into the stair-step arrangement of needs in the human needs approach?

It should be obvious that what really motivates a worker involves *the job itself,* not peripheral matters. The real message of the two-factor approach is this: if you want to motivate your worker, do not give the work area a new coat of paint each year—give the worker a bigger share in the job itself.

The maintenance needs in the two-factor approach can be related to the lower levels in the human needs approach. Similarly, the motivational factors are quite similar to the upper three need categories. Figure 17–1 shows the similarities between these two approaches.

R. J. House and L. A. Wigdor analyzed the results of a number of studies involving the two-factor approach and produced a list of "satisfiers" and "dissatisfiers" present in most job situations.[6] Compare the responses in Table 17–1 and try to identify those elements which are most likely to cause worker dissatisfaction.

The supervisor has a responsibility to both workers and the company. As much as possible, he or she must see that workers are satisfied with their jobs. Especially productive workers should receive the recognition they deserve. At the same time, all workers should be motivated to increase productivity and ensure that company goals will be met. Table 17-1 illustrates which factors should be emphasized to increase morale and give each worker a bigger share in the job itself.

Any supervisor who is responsible for motivating workers may find it helpful to remember the following three summary questions, suggested by M. Scott Myers,[7] former personnel research director of Texas Instruments.

[6] "Herzberg's Dual-Factor Theory of Job Satisfaction and Motivation," *Personnel Psychology,* Winter 1967, pp. 369–89.

[7] M. Scott Myers, "Who Are the Motivated Workers?," *Harvard Business Review,* January-February 1964, p. 73.

Table 17-1. Re-analysis of Satisfier-Dissatisfier Data. (With permission from R. J. House and S. A. Wigdor, "Herzberg's Dual-Factor Theory of Job Satisfaction and Motivation," *Personnel Psychology,* Winter 1967.

	Reported as	
Factor	**Satisfier**	**Dissatisfier**
Achievement	440	122
Recognition	309	110
Work itself	175	75
Responsibility	168	35
Advancement	126	48
Policy and administration	55	337
Supervision	22	182
Working conditions	20	108
Relations with superior	15	59
Relations with peers	9	57

Total number of respondents for each factor: 1220.

What Motivates Employees to Work Effectively? A challenging job that allows a feeling of achievement, responsibility, growth, advancement, enjoyment of the work itself, and earned recognition.

What Dissatisfies Workers? Mostly factors peripheral to the job—poorly conceived work rules, poor lighting, regimented coffee breaks, inconsistency in awarding job titles, overemphasis (or underemphasis) on seniority rights, inadequate raises or fringe benefits, and the like.

When Do Workers Become Dissatisfied? When opportunities for meaningful achievement are eliminated, they are sensitized to their environment and begin to find fault. If you are totally involved in trying to solve a particular problem, or using your creative abilities to their fullest, are you likely to notice whether or not your office floor has a carpet? Opportunities for meaningful achievement can override many physical disadvantages in the work situation.

Vince Lombardi, the late coach of the Green Bay Packers, once observed:

> Running a football team is no different from running any other kind of organization— a business, an army, a political party. The problems are the same. The objective is to win.
>
> Winning is not a sometime thing. You don't win once in awhile. You don't do things right once in awhile. You do them right all the time.
>
> Winning is a habit. Unfortunately, so is losing. There is no room for second place. There is only one place in my game and that is first place.
>
> Every time a football player goes out to play, he's got to play from the ground up. From the soles of his feet right up to his head. Every inch of him has to play. Some guys play with their heads. That's okay—you've got to be smart to be number one in any business—but more important, you've got to play with your heart. With every fiber in your body. If you are lucky enough to find a guy with a lot of head and a lot of heart, he's never going to come off the field second.[8]

[8] Jerry Kramer, "Motivate *Your* Employees—The Vince Lombardi Way," *Supervisory Management,* March 1973, p. 4.

The challenge of the successful supervisor is to develop and motivate employees to work with their heads and their hearts.

The Preference-Expectation Approach

This approach is more an explanation of behavior and motivation than a concrete plan for motivating behavior.[9] The ideas are useful, however, in helping us see the relationship between a worker's goals and the means available for achieving those goals.

Numerous possible outcomes can result from a single activity. In each case, the worker will harbor a *preference* for a particular outcome. For instance, if a worker speeds up production and makes more pieces, several things could result: a raise, a bonus, a trophy, a certificate, or a promotion. On the other hand, this could make co-workers jealous and the worker might be avoided by the work group. Perhaps nothing would happen, or something might happen that was not anticipated. The only certainty is that the worker will have definite ideas about the preferred outcome.

Despite likes and dislikes, unless the worker has an *expectation* that desired outcomes are at least possible, preference will not affect performance. No matter how much preference there is for a bonus, increased production is unlikely if no bonuses have ever been awarded in the company. Limited expectation that outcomes can occur will always modify enthusiasm.

A person may believe that a particular outcome is very important, but unless personal actions can help bring about the desired outcome, there will be no reason to act. The more one believes that actions *can* bring about the desired results, the more motivation there will be. Consider the motivation of a person who is self-employed and one who feels trapped in a meaningless job within a gigantic organization. Who works harder, and why?

The preference-expectation approach allows for a great deal of individual difference in motivation. This approach helps us understand some of the complex relationships between motivation and behavior. To apply preference-expectation effectively, however, motivators would require a deeper knowledge of each worker's expectations than the supervisor can be expected to obtain.

"X" and "Y" Supervisors

Everyone has certain ideas about what does and does not motivate people. These ideas relate to the perceptions we hold about people in general and to our total outlook on life. Perhaps your approach to supervision agrees perfectly with one of the approaches we have already discussed. Or, you may have a totally different idea of human nature and motivation. In any case, we use our ideas about people whenever we seek to change their behavior.

[9] See Victor H. Vroon, *Work and Motivation* (New York: Wiley, 1964).

Beliefs about the nature of workers and appropriate means of motivating them can be neatly divided into two opposing categories: Theory X and Theory Y.[10]

As discussed in Chapter 16, a Theory X supervisor is one who runs a tight ship, maintains close control over workers, believes in centralized authority, and likes to make all the decisions. This type of supervisor operates on the basis of certain assumptions, which can be stated as follows:

1. The average person dislikes work and will avoid it whenever possible.
2. Most people have to be forced or threatened by punishment before they will make the effort necessary to accomplish organizational goals.
3. The average individual is basically passive and therefore prefers to be directed, rather than assume any risk or responsibility. Above all else, he or she prefers security.

Theory Y supervisors hold a different set of assumptions. They usually maintain a looser organizational environment, rely less on coercion and punishment, delegate authority more readily, and allow participation in decision making. Theory Y supervisors assume:

1. Work is as natural as play or rest and, therefore, is not avoided.
2. Self-motivation and inherent satisfaction in work will motivate workers more effectively than coercion.
3. Employee commitment is a crucial factor in motivation, and it is won by rewarding individual effort.
4. Given the proper environment, the average individual learns to accept and even seek responsibility.
5. Many workers have the ability to be creative and innovative in the solution of organizational problems.
6. In modern business and organizations, human intellectual potential is often ignored and wasted.

Which approach leads to the best results? It may be easy to believe that Theory Y always produces the best results, since it is more humanistic and less harsh, but many businesses have achieved tremendous success under authoritarian leadership.

Workers, like supervisors, are not all alike in their drives and needs. Some workers prefer to be told what to do in no uncertain terms. Others balk at strict control and prefer to have more responsibility and self-determination in their jobs. A particular work situation may demand a humanistic approach, while another may call for authoritarian treatment. Even within the same work situation, a supervisor may deal with various workers responding to different types of leadership. Each situation, assessed on its own merits, must suggest the appropriate supervisory style.

In this section, we have reviewed several major approaches to supervising and motivating employees. Figure 17-2 brings these different approaches together so that we may compare them more easily. Is any one approach right all the time? Or should the supervisor be prepared to use different approaches and combinations, depending on the situation?

[10] See Douglas McGregor, *The Human Side of Enterprise* (New York: McGraw-Hill, 1960).

APPROACH	BASIC CONCEPTS
1. Classical	People will be highly motivated if their reward is tied directly to performance.
2. Need	When basic psychological needs are satisfied, higher-order needs become dominant and must be included in motivational plans.
3. Human Relations	Managers are the key factor in motivation. They must make the workers feel that they are members of the team and individually important.
4. Two-Factor	Maintenance factors (working conditions) can make employees unhappy but will not motivate them. Motivational factors are higher-level needs, such as recognition, the work itself, and the possibility of growth.
5. Preference-Expectation	Motivation depends on the extent to which workers expect to receive those things that are important to them as a reward for excellent behavior.
6. X and Y	Supervisors who see employees as disliking work, passive, and seeking security while avoiding effort maintain close control over their employees (Theory X).
	Supervisors who see workers as self-motivated and capable of finding inherent satisfaction by offering creative suggestions and joining in decision making maintain looser controls and supervise more through delegation than coercion (Theory Y).

Figure 17-2. Major Approaches to Motivation. [Adapted from Robert M. Fulmer, *The New Management,* 2nd ed. (New York: Macmillan, 1978), p. 297.]

Money and Motivation

There is no doubt that money is something magic in our society. From all sides, we are encouraged to collect as much of it as we can. But when we look behind the uproar, we find it is not money itself we are striving for, but the things money can bring us. What we really seek is security, independence, social status, and a sense of accomplishment. Motivators, in fact, might be wise to forget about financial incentives and offer more direct means of obtaining security, independence, status, and accomplishment.

In the days before easy credit, it was difficult to accumulate *things* without having *money.* Today, of course, we are not limited in purchasing power by our bank balance. Whereas owning an expensive new car used to prove one's wealth and independence, today it usually means a long-term obligation to the finance company. On the other hand, very few of us could individually afford a lengthy hospital stay, but even the lowest-paid employee enjoys virtually the same medical insurance benefits as the company president. Taxes have severely cut the dollar's take-home value, and as a result, salary is not the incentive it used to be.

Supervisors who work with hourly-wage employees rather than salaried staff may find that money as a motivator ranks quite low. One writer estimates that only 10 percent of the production workers in this country would respond to a financial incentive plan by increasing their production to increase their earnings.[11] Other researchers suggest that three conditions must be present for money to be an effective motivator: (1) The amount of salary increase must be perceived as substantial enough to justify additional work effort; (2) the salary increase must be perceived as directly related to increased performance; and (3) the salary increase must be perceived as equitable by other group members, even those not benefiting themselves.[12] Additionally, the employee must perceive that he or she is physically and psychologically capable of performing the additional work required to earn the additional salary.

Other writers have de-emphasized the importance of money as a motivator among wage earners. They focus instead on the work group as a motivational force. Production workers are not always highly skilled and their backgrounds have generally not included much success. Many factors, such as lack of ability, lack of stamina or psychological drive, a poor home environment, or an inability to get proper training, conspire to make production workers a real challenge for the supervisor. Forces in life have led them to have low expectations of success, and they are not likely to be easily moved.

Most production workers are meeting their basic physical and safety needs, but they have little opportunity or hope of ever meeting higher-level needs. In most cases, their opportunities for esteem and recognition lie only within their work group rather than in the job itself. For them, being an accepted group member certainly provides more feelings of self-fulfillment than tightening bottle caps on a production line.

This tendency of workers to seek satisfaction from work groups can cause problems for the supervisor seeking to motivate employees to new levels of production. Efforts to motivate individuals may not work at all, since rate busters are invariably snubbed by the work group. If a worker is not prepared to conform to the standards of the group, he or she must be prepared for unpopularity. It is unlikely that a worker will show such independence, since social approval and disapproval are among the most powerful motivators we know.

Any supervisor confronted by a tight group of workers that consistently refuses to increase production should study the group's social patterns. Most groups have chosen leaders who are influential in shaping members' opinions and behavior. If the supervisor can succeed in "winning over" the group leader to work toward increasing production, then that leader may encourage the group to follow.

Morale and Productivity

Everybody knows when good morale is in effect, but what is it? Definitions of morale include the absence of conflict, the presence of a feeling of happiness or satisfaction, good personal adjustment, good work attitudes, and a degree

[11] William F. Whyte, *Money and Motivation* (New York: Harper, 1955).
[12] Daniel Katz and Robert Kahn, *The Social Psychology of Organization* (New York: Wiley, 1965), pp. 352–53.

of personal involvement in one's job. Regardless of how we define morale, its presence or absence is noticeable and extremely important. In some organizations, workers definitely feel "What's good for the company is good for us." In other enterprises, the "Who cares" attitude prevails and is reflected in low production rates and profits.

Morale tends to remain high if conducive conditions are maintained. When everything is going well, workers and supervisors alike ride an upward spiral of success. Every positive happening leads to others, and the health of the company is beyond question. But when morale is low, the spiral plummets and is difficult to arrest. The company may be in grave danger. When motivational techniques succeed, one result is good worker morale.

One comprehensive definition says, "Morale is the extent to which an individual's needs are satisfied and the extent to which the individual perceives that satisfaction as stemming from the total job situation."[13] This definition emphasizes the "total job situation" and includes four relatively independent areas that may either contribute to or detract from job satisfaction. These constitute (1) intrinsic satisfaction with the work itself; (2) satisfaction with the company, its goals, policies, and procedures; (3) satisfaction with the relationship established between worker and supervisor; and (4) satisfaction regarding rewards and advancement opportunities.

In recent years, a number of companies have established job enrichment programs. As with other approaches, job enrichment solutions are never problem-free. This approach may not be feasible with all jobs, it may be poorly managed, and some people seem happier with trivia than with increased responsibility. Overall, though, job enrichment seems to offer possibilities of increased morale and improved production.

Some highly successful job enrichment programs have been introduced in the last few years by AT&T.[14]

In the Treasury Department of American Telephone and Telegraph Company, educated and intelligent women handled correspondence with stockholders. They worked in a highly structured environment under close supervision in order to assure a suitable quality of correspondence. Under these conditions, the quality of work was low and the turnover was high.

Using a control group and a test group, the jobs of the test group were enriched as follows: (1) the women were permitted to sign their own names to the letters they prepared; (2) they were held responsible for the quality of their work; (3) they were encouraged to become experts in the kinds of problems that appealed to them; and (4) subject matter experts were provided for consultation regarding problems.

The control group remained unchanged after six months, but the test group improved by all measurements used. These measurements included turnover, productivity, absences, promotions from the group, and costs. The quality measurement index climbed from the thirties to the nineties!

American Telephone and Telegraph Company also has achieved excellent results in other job-enrichment efforts. In the directory compilation function, name omissions dropped from 2 to 1 percent. In frame wiring, errors declined from 13 to 0.5 percent, and the number of frames wired increased from 700 to over 1200.

Obviously, the quality of an employee's work is affected by his or her attitude toward the job. Workers caught in jobs they consider to be meaningless are

---

[13] Robert M. Guion, "The Industrial Psychologist," *Personnel Psychology,* Spring 1966.
[14] Robert Ford, *Motivation Through the Work Itself* (New York: AMACOM, 1969).

not likely to pay close attention to producing high-quality results. It is only natural to wish that all workers could be equally motivated and enjoy a high morale in their jobs. But the supervisor considering job enrichment or other morale-raising programs must consider practicalities as well.

A few years ago an automobile manufacturer initiated a new approach. Factory workers would no longer mass-produce cars but would work individually and in small groups as automobile craftsmen. The workers reported increased job satisfaction, but the production cost of each car increased over 50 percent. This is, of course, an extreme example. But the lesson should be clear. Though mass production need not be the tedious, trivial work it usually is today, the cost factor does impose restraints on the kind of motivational methods a supervisor can employ.

Summary

An individual's personality is composed of patterns of behavior, attitudes, and beliefs about self and others, and expectations. The attitudes we hold about what motivates people to act will influence methods as well as results. Personality is not a particular characteristic, but a set of interrelated factors that is dynamic, or continually changing. We show different facets of our personalities with different people and in different situations.

Since motivation is one of the key concepts in the supervisor's daily experience, it is only natural that many approaches to motivation have been outlined and generalized. In this chapter, we considered several popular approaches to employee motivation. The classical approach emphasizes the value of money and allows workers to earn more by producing more. The human needs approach sets up a hierarchy of satisfactions people seek, and suggests that we do not seek to fulfill high-level needs until all our lower-level needs are met. The human relations approach concentrates on the fulfillment of higher-level needs. This approach contends that most people have already met their lower-level needs such as physical, safety, and security requirements, and thus are seeking to fill social, esteem, and self-realization needs. The preference-expectation approach shows us that workers anticipate and prefer certain results to come of their actions, but they will not be motivated to act if they have no expectation of attaining the desired outcome. The two-factor approach is closely related to the human needs approach. It establishes two types of characteristics for any work situation: maintenance factors and motivational factors. Maintenance factors must be present to avoid worker dissatisfaction, though motivational factors are the means of increasing worker satisfaction.

Every supervisor chooses a method or combination of methods, depending on what is most appropriate in a given situation. Theory X and Theory Y characterize the basic assumptions of the iron-willed autocrat and the democratic leader. Probably the best approach might be considered a flexible combination of the two approaches to allow for differences in people and conditions.

Although many people assume money is an effective motivator, studies have shown in many cases it is not. Only a very low percentage of wage-earning production workers typically respond positively to financial incentive plans. Group membership and group approval seem to be more important than money as a motivator among production workers. In most cases, worker morale is a much better motivator than money. If the worker can be given a bigger share in the job itself, higher morale may solve the supervisor's motivation problems. Some supervisors believe people cannot be motivated by an external source. They believe the supervisor's job is to create an environment that will allow any inherent motivation to be released.

Key Terms

Achievement Motivation. A drive causing an individual to strive for the attainment of goals and objectives.

Esteem Needs. The needs for respect from family, peers, and other significant people in an individual's life.

Personality. The regular patterns and qualities of behavior that make every person both human and unique.

Physical Needs. The human needs for food, air, water, and shelter.

Safety and Security Needs. The need to be relatively free from danger.

Self-Realization Needs. The human needs for self-fulfillment, the realization of an individual's potential talents and abilities.

Social Needs. The needs for contact with other people, for acceptability by other people, and for recognized membership in a group.

Theory X. A concept of life or style of supervision that emphasizes a hard-nosed, distrustful view of people and a "do-it-yourself-if-you-want-it-done-right" attitude toward work.

Theory Y. A concept of life or style of supervision that considers each worker a valuable addition to the team effort and encourages participatory decision making, democratic leadership, and reliance on subordinates' abilities.

Review Questions

1. Why does a supervisor need to understand the behavior of other people?
2. In the classical theory of motivation, what is the primary motivator? What are the advantages and disadvantages of this motivator?
3. Describe the human needs approach to motivation.
4. Distinguish between the human needs and human relations approaches.
5. The preference-expectation approach to motivation places a great deal of emphasis on the individual's inner drive and ambition. Why does it make this emphasis? Are people more motivated by circumstances or inner drive?
6. List and describe the characteristics of Theory X and Theory Y. How might the two be combined?
7. List and describe factors that reduce the importance of money as a motivator.
8. For a supervisor, what is meant by "good morale?"
9. How can a worker's attitude toward a job affect the quality of his or her work?
10. Which approach to motivation seems the most reasonable to you? Why?

11. What motivates you? For instance, if you chew gum, what motivates you? If you recently bought an expensive pair of Italian shoes, what motivates you? How many people do you know who are motivated by the very same things? What relation does this have to your role as supervisor?

Exercises

I. A Motivated Employee

Identify an employee you consider to be motivated. Write a short paragraph in which you characterize this individual. Now, identify an employee you consider to be unmotivated, and prepare a similar characterization. Compare the two descriptions with the theories of motivation covered in the chapter. Is *all* behavior motivated? As a supervisor, will any motivated behavior be acceptable?

II. Motivation by Employee Rank

Interview three or four employees from the lowest rank or first line of your organization. Ask them to list and describe ten things that motivate them. Repeat the interviews with three first-line supervisors or middle managers, and the owner or a corporate officer of the organization. What are the similarities and differences in their responses? Can you explain the replies from each?

III. Maslow and Herzberg

The following are factors in a working environment. Where do each of these fit into Maslow's hierarchy and Herzberg's two-factor theory?

Pension Plan.	Bonus Plan.
Vacation Schedule.	Employee Holiday Parties.
Employee Cafeteria.	Educational Scholarships.
Work Environment Music.	Company Physician.
Wages or Salary.	Promotion-From-Within Policy.
Protective Equipment.	

Case 17 • Chris Poole

Chris Poole is a supervisor for Atlantic Construction Company, a small but rapidly expanding firm specializing in the construction of franchise restaurants in the southern states. Chris is in his fifties, lives near Tampa, and has been in construction most of his life. He came to work for Atlantic after his original employer went bankrupt. He has done an outstanding job on every restaurant project for Atlantic except one when he was supervising two jobs simultaneously in different parts of North Carolina.

Recently, the company engaged a management consultant to help formulate long-range corporate goals, establish a middle-management project team, and develop a new compensation system for all employees, including a retirement program and a profit-sharing bonus plan for each construction job. At the meeting where the new plan was explained to employees, Chris was one of the most enthusiastic and outspoken proponents of the bonus plan and the retirement program.

Shortly thereafter, Chris was assigned to two simultaneous jobs in South Carolina. About one month into the projects, Ben Frampton, the principal owner of Atlantic, began experiencing problems with Chris. The projects were behind schedule, and when questioned, Chris would blame the subcontractors for the delays. But Ben also noticed unusual behavior that suggested Chris might be responsible for some of the problems. He misled the franchise owners about the completion dates for certain phases of the buildings, and on two occasions told Ben that particular phases were completed, when in fact they were not. In addition, Chris was leaving work at lunch time on Fridays and driving back to Florida for a weekend of hunting and fishing.

Ben did not know what to do about Chris. He hated to fire him because he had been an outstanding employee, and he would be difficult to replace, especially in the middle of two construction jobs. But Ben was in an embarrassing position with the restaurant chain because of Chris's deception, and he feared this might jeopardize the future of his company.

Within a week, Ben's problems with Chris were solved for him. Late on a Friday afternoon, Chris arrived unannounced in Ben's office in Florida and informed him he was resigning from Atlantic. He was very pleasant and relaxed in explaining that he did not like the traveling and being away from home for ten to twelve weeks at a time. Although the pay was good, he had an opportunity to work in Alaska on the oil pipeline for three years where he would be able to make enough money to retire. He had worked on the pipeline for fourteen months a few years ago and did not like the isolation from his family. But he and his wife were willing to tolerate the separation again because of the payoff of early retirement.

1. What do you think motivates Chris Poole?
2. If you were Ben, would you make an effort to keep Chris from quitting? Do you believe you could be effective in keeping Chris with Atlantic?

CHAPTER 18
Understanding Unions

A union is a group of people who singly can do little, but together can decide that a little or a lot will be done.

Richard Brackan (adapted)

Learning Objectives

- To trace the historical development and significance of labor unions in the American economy.
- To compare different types of unions and their functions.
- To gain familiarity with common expectations and terminology in union contracts.
- To learn how to cope with collective bargaining in negotiations.
- To identify the supervisor's position in labor relations and to learn to deal effectively and fairly with both labor and management.

Dealing with unions is a fact of life for many managers and supervisors. We have seen that part of the supervisor's job is to help provide an atmosphere where workers can effectively and efficiently accomplish company goals. Unions, however, have goals of their own. Basically, unions seek to protect and promote the interests of their members, even if they must do so at the expense of the employer.

For this reason, business and union leaders frequently clash over different interests and goals. Railroad and construction unions have often opposed practices that would increase efficiency in these operations. Other unions, such as the coal miners' organization, endorse increased efficiency, but perceive the companies' resulting profit margins as a source of higher wages for the workers. Sometimes union pressures have forced autocratic business leaders into improving working conditions and wages and fulfilling other obligations to their workers. In other cases, unions have effectively prevented competent managers and supervisors from doing their jobs while union members reaped new benefits.

Every field of business and industry must deal with employer-employee relations. In recent years, virtually no field has remained immune from the challenges introduced by organized labor. Managers, supervisors, and labor union members, however, must learn to coexist in our competitive economy if business is to survive.

A Conflict of Rights

The philosophical foundations of our present-day unions were laid during this country's revolutionary days. Alexander Hamilton and Thomas Jefferson sparked a running battle of rights that has raged for two centuries. Hamilton argued that "rights of property" were the highest rights a new nation should guard. Jefferson, on the other hand, held that "rights of persons" were the most precious. Modern management may share Hamilton's attitude, while labor sides with Jefferson, but supervisors are caught in the middle. They must uphold management's property rights and workers' personal rights. The balance is a difficult one.

Today, American industry seems to support Jefferson's ideals while it profits from Hamilton's philosophy. This balance may appear a simple one, but the relationship between modern management and labor is much more complex than these founding fathers could have foreseen.

Though management has certain rights, it also owes obligations to its workers. Labor's rights must be respected, but employees are required, in return, to fulfill obligations to their employers through loyalty and productivity. This relationship is solidly based on economic values, but, because people are involved, a balance is often difficult to maintain.

Increased productivity and lower costs can mean higher standards of living for both management and workers. Yet, each must adopt these goals and strive for them cooperatively. Each side can meet its goals more quickly and easily if each uses every tool in *human* relations, as well as labor relations.

Background of the Labor Movement

Everything seems to have been simpler in the founding days of our nation. During the colonial era, most people lived and worked on farms. Any manufacturing took place in small shops or "cottages" near the owner's home. Typically, boys pledged themselves to masters as *apprentices* eager to learn a trade. Though the boy usually received no income except room and board at the home of his master, he could seek employment in the business world as a *journeyman* in five or six years.

When the industrial revolution introduced machinery to do much of the physical work, factories were filled with large work groups serving a single master. Supervision became a very different challenge when numerous superintendents, plant managers, and supervisors separated the master from the apprentices.

During this period, labor was generally viewed as a commodity that could be bought and sold. Laborers had few rights, but as employees they had few real responsibilities. Most workers could not vote, and, as late as 1835, workers could send their children to public schools only if they swore that they were paupers. The work week was six days long and encompassed seventy-five hours in winter and eighty-two hours in summer. Children as young as seven worked in factories from dawn until night during the early 1800s.

The First American Union

Conditions like these bred worker dissatisfaction. In 1792, the Cordwainers (shoemakers) of Philadelphia formed the first craft union for collective bargaining. A few years later, they were charged with "criminal conspiracy" for attempting to raise wages. This "conspiracy doctrine" was used frequently to prevent unions from exerting any real pressure on their employers. By the 1850s, most states were allowing unions to organize, but not to campaign aggressively for workers' rights. Strikes, pickets, and boycotts were generally viewed as illegal.

Employers applied pressure effectively through many avenues. Union members were sometimes fired, organizers were blacklisted and unable to find jobs, and many employers simply ignored union representatives. Some firms also instituted a *yellow-dog contract* that required new employees to pledge they would never join a union while working for that organization.

Unions Make Small Gains

The labor movement during this early era was marked by violence and fear. In 1886, Chicago's Haymarket riot brought death to several striking workers and policemen. More than a hundred people died in a clash between federal troops and strikers in 1877. Despite these incidents, however, unions were making some progress. In 1849, federal employees won a ten-hour day. In 1868, a federal law provided for an eight-hour day in federal jobs. Several states passed laws restricting the use of child labor, and the first permanent federation of unions—the American Federation of Labor (AFL)—was founded in 1886, while Samuel Gompers reigned as leading labor spokesman of the day. Gompers once defined the union movement's entire objective in one word. When asked what workers really wanted, Gompers replied, "More!"

Although it was the nation's largest and most powerful union group by the early thirties, the AFL suffered from squabbling within its ranks, and in 1935, some skilled craftsmen dropped out to form their own organization—the Congress of Industrial Organizations (CIO).

The First Labor Laws

By 1914, the Clayton Act had exempted unions from the Sherman Anti-Trust Act. The Act made picketing legal, but it did not stop employers from bringing civil suits for damages. Because of the depression of the 1930s, the federal government looked more favorably on union activity. In 1932, the Norris-LaGuardia Act severely restricted employer use of injunctions to halt union activities and outlawed yellow-dog contracts.

One year later, union membership mushroomed when the National Industrial Recovery Act gave employees the legal right to organize and engage in collective bargaining.

The National Labor Relations Act

Declared unconstitutional on May 27, 1935, the NIRA was replaced only a month later by the National Labor Relations Act. Also known as the Wagner Act, this legislation added considerable muscle to the union's clout. The NLRA gave employees these rights:

1. To organize, form, or join labor unions.
2. To bargain collectively and select their own representatives.
3. To engage in concerted activities to bring about their goals.

In addition, this act policed employer behavior toward unionized employees. Section 8 of the NLRA says employees cannot:

1. Coerce or otherwise interfere with employees in the exercise of their rights to unionize, including threatening to close or move the plant and spying on union meetings.
2. Dominate or interfere with the formation of a union, or contribute financial support to it.
3. Discriminate against an employee because he or she has filed charges or given testimony under this act.
4. Refuse to bargain collectively and in good faith.

This act also established the National Labor Relations Board (NLRB) to enforce the rights of workers and the responsibilities of employers. This board recognizes bargaining units, conducts representative elections to see if employees actually want a union, and prosecutes cases of unfair labor practices.

Labor-Management Relations Act of 1947

This legislation, also known as the Taft-Hartley Act, attempted to amend the Wagner Act and to create a specific set of union responsibilities. The Taft-Hartley Act retained most of the Wagner Act's basic provisions, but forbade several unfair labor practices by unions. These included specific prohibitions against unions:

1. To restrain or coerce employees by mass picketing or violence, for example, or attempt to prevent nonunion employees from entering a plant.
2. To cause an employer to encourage or discourage an employee about joining a union.
3. To refuse to bargain in good faith.
4. To require an employer or self-employed person to join a union.
5. To force an employer to bargain with one union when another is already serving as the certified representative.
6. To engage in secondary boycotts (attempting to force an employer to stop doing business with, or handling the products of, another employer)
7. Engage in jurisdictional strikes by forcing an employer to assign certain work to one union's employees rather than to another.
8. To charge excessive initiation fees.
9. To engage in featherbedding practices (requiring wages for services not performed).

These restrictions also eliminated the *closed shop*. Under a closed shop, all eligible workers were required to be union members, and all new hires had to be members or become members at the time of hiring. A *union shop,* requiring all eligible workers to join the union within a specified period, such as thirty days, remains a legally recognized concept. This act also linked supervisors and foremen to management rather than to employee ranks. Under the Taft-Hartley Act, the President can call for a "cooling-off period" of up to eighty days whenever a labor dispute threatens to create a national emergency.

Labor-Management Reporting and Disclosure Act of 1949

This legislation is generally called the Landrum-Griffin Act. Enacted to control the corrupt practices in some unions during the 1950s, this act polices internal union affairs and revises certain provisions of the Taft-Hartley Act. The major points of the act follow.

1. The bill of rights. Union members must be given the right to nominate candidates for union office; to participate and vote in union meetings, elections, and referendums; to testify and bring suit when unions infringe on members' rights; and to receive notice and a fair hearing before any union disciplinary action can be taken for other than nonpayment of dues.

2. Reporting. Unions, union officers, employers, and consultants must file various reports with the Secretary of Labor revealing any administrative practices or financial matters that could show conflicts of interest between union goals and management policies.

3. Trusteeships. Certain rules govern the establishment of trusteeships by national or international unions over their local unions. The rules protect local members' rights.

4. Union elections. This section specifies time periods within which elections must be held and spells out democratic procedures governing how the elections are to be conducted.

5. Fiduciary duties. Trust relations in connection with union funds are detailed and regulated. Willful misappropriation, embezzlement, abuse, or illegal use of union funds is a federal crime.

6. Amendments to the Taft-Hartley Act. Restrictions against organizational picketing were strengthened; strikers have the right to vote in new presentation elections held within one year after the strike began.

The States and Labor Legislation

Several states have supplemented federal labor legislation with laws of their own. Some states prohibit strikes by public employees, eliminate the closed shop (where no worker is hired unless he or she is or becomes a union member), and prohibit compulsory unionization. The Taft-Hartley Act of 1947 granted state legislatures the right to outlaw closed shops, union shops, maintenance of union membership, and preferential hiring.

Supported by this legislation, many states (particularly in the South and Southwest) enacted so-called *right-to-work* laws. These laws guarantee that no workers can be forced to join a union in order to obtain or keep their job. The following states have passed right-to-work laws:

Texas	Arkansas	Utah
Nevada	Mississippi	Nebraska
Georgia	Iowa	Virginia
North Carolina	Arizona	Kansas
South Carolina	North Dakota	Indiana
Tennessee	South Dakota	Louisiana
Alabama	Florida	

How Unions Are Organized

Locals

The local union is probably the most important organizational level to individual members, since local officers handle the day-to-day problems of workers. The "nationals" and "federations" are administrative and service organizations to local unions and are very important, but no union member really belongs to these large organizational bodies except through membership in the local union. Local union officers are elected by the members and frequently work without pay from the union. They serve in the following functions: negotiating labor agreements and grievances; disciplining union members who violate contract rules; and promoting social, educational, political, and community activities of the union to improve its public image and support.[1]

Although it is difficult to determine the exact number of union members in the country today, estimates place the figure at around 20 million workers out of about 90 million total workers. It is easy to see that even workers on

---

[1] Arthur A. Sloane and Fred Witney, *Labor Relations,* 3rd ed. (Englewood Cliffs, N. J.: Prentice-Hall, 1977), p. 171.

a local level exert considerable pressure when backed by a nationwide parent organization.

Nationals

The national unions are comprised of elected delegates from the local unions and the officers elected by delegates and the staff personnel they choose to hire. The nationals exercise considerable power over local unions through the following functions: (1) locals must obtain permission from the national to strike or lose many benefits; (2) all local collective bargaining contracts must be reviewed by national officers; (3) the national constitution sets guidelines and standards for local operations and governance; (4) nationals aid locals in grievance procedures and arbitration; (5) nationals provide certain benefits to striking employees; and (6) nationals aid locals in membership drives, political lobbying, and arranging educational programs.[2]

There are approximately 190 national labor unions in America. The Teamsters, United Auto Workers, and United Steelworkers each have well over 1,000,000 members. At the other end of the scale, the International Association of Siderographers (engravers on steel) has fewer than thirty members. The following list provides membership enrollments among the nation's largest unions, according to recent figures:

Teamsters	1,859,000
United Auto Workers	1,486,000
Steelworkers	1,200,000
International Brotherhood of Electrical Workers	922,000
Machinists	865,000
Carpenters	820,000
Retail clerks	605,000
Laborers	580,000
Meatcutters	494,000
Hotel	461,000
State, County, Municipal	444,000

Most local unions are affiliated with a national union, but some are strictly local and seek no affiliation. These unions feel they can do an adequate job of defending their members' rights without joining one of the larger organizations.

Federations

Federations represent the highest level of union organization. They may exist at the city, state, regional, or national level. Federations are composed of unions that pooled their resources to increase their bargaining power or provide better services for their members.

The federation's main functions are political activity and mediation. A federation may represent the labor movement as a whole in dealing with public

---

[2] Ibid., pp. 157–71.

officials and helping to settle arguments among affiliated unions. They may also take stands on broad public issues, serving as the "conscience" of the labor movement and leaving collective bargaining to local and national unions.

During the improved labor climate of the 1950s, the AFL and the CIO were reunited and joined their names as well as their membership lists. Since the American Federation of Labor-Congress of Industrial Organizations is cumbersome for conversation, this group is usually referred to as the AFL-CIO. It is the nation's largest federation.

Craft and Industrial Unions

The members of craft unions have skills that take several years to acquire. Plumbers, electricians, and carpenters are among the occupations now organized in unions. Craft unions serve a valuable function for their members in acting as a placement agency. Many members operate as independent contractors working for several different employers during a single year. The craft union's role as a "placement agency" gives it considerable power in the labor market—employers must hire workers through the union, and the union can control the supply of skilled employees. Craft unions also tend to establish rigid requirements for entrance into their occupations. Members often serve long apprenticeships before they become fully qualified members or "journeymen."

Industrial unions, on the other hand, have little control over employer hiring. The retail clerks, automobile workers, and institutional service workers are examples of industrial union members. Industrial unions gain most of their power through controlling the internal labor market of a particular business. They may help set promotion policies, raises, and job ranks within a company. In addition, they try to establish seniority regulations, grievance procedures, and wage rate policies. On the whole, though, industrial unions enjoy far less control over the labor market than do the craft unions.

Management Views About Labor Unions

Since the beginning of the labor movement, management has consistently criticized union power and programs. Business leaders often complain that unions interfere with efficient business operation. Their most significant criticisms are described below. As a supervisor you should study and contemplate these views so that you will have a more comprehensive understanding of unions on your organization, your employees, and you. Your own philosophy about unions will affect your behavior and strategy in working with workers and their organizations.

Monopoly Power

Strikes can cripple a business or industry because an employer is prevented from hiring replacements by union picketing. Businesses argue they cannot form monopolies with other companies, but they are badgered by monopolistic labor forces.

As management points out, the general public suffers whenever a strike shuts down a critical industry. The Taft-Hartley Act and other legislation provide mechanisms for holding off strikes in important national industries, but their powers are limited. In extreme cases, such as a railroad strike, Congress has sometimes passed special legislation forcing an end to a serious strike.

Make-Work Rules

Some unions require employers to hire workers who are not really needed. For many years, American railroads kept steam-boiler crews on diesel locomotives. Their union still requires their presence on passenger trains. Movie studios have been required to hire full-time electricians whose only job is to plug in a light. For years, painters' unions limited the width of the paint brush a union member could wield, and the separation of duties in the building industry protects and limits each worker's duties through a complex system of job descriptions. Recently, newspaper shutdowns have resulted from disputes over staffing now that new technological advances, such as computer composition, have reached the newspaper industry.

These practices seem to predominate among craft unions. These organizations argue that craft skills must be respected, and workers protected from heavy work loads. In addition, these unions feel their workers should not suffer when commerce introduces technological improvements.

Interference with Management Rights

When unions tamper with hiring, layoff, and promotion policies, management complains loudly. Many managers feel the union's seniority system interferes with their right to hire the most efficient, productive employees they can find and to use their own discretion in layoffs and promotions. Union contracts forbid incentive pay for individual production and may specify that, after a trial period, a worker cannot be fired unless the union agrees. Transfers between jobs and overtime policies—traditionally considered management's prerogatives—have fallen largely under union jurisdiction.

Assumption That All Productivity Increases Are Due to Labor

Dividing total company output by the number of labor hours spent in production results in a figure for output per labor hour. Unions often see this figure as an argument for increasing wages. The picture they present, however, is greatly oversimplified. It is easy to see how output could be increased by new tools, equipment, methods, and other factors not directly related to the efficiency of individual workers.

Labor's Complaints About Management

Naturally, there is another side to the story. Unions feel management has been remiss in meeting employee needs. Some of labor's most common complaints about management are discussed below.

Impersonality

Workers often get the impression that management cares little for them or for their feelings. They are transferred arbitrarily, laid off impersonally, recalled at the company's discretion, and generally treated like replaceable components. Though human relations practices have greatly improved this condition in many companies, the impersonality of the large corporation may encourage the worker to seek closer relations with colleagues via the union.

The Profit-Making Function

From the worker's point of view, the company's main function is to provide a job. Failing to recognize that profits are essential to protect that job, workers often see company leaders as overly occupied with making money and too little concerned with meeting human needs.

Achievements of Unions

Unions sometimes feel that management fails to give them credit for their sizeable contributions to the quality of American life. These achievements include higher wages for laborers, a shorter working day and week, the abolition of child labor, better working conditions, increased job security, a wide variety of fringe benefits, compensation policies, medical care, pension plans, equal opportunity, and sometimes even profit sharing among workers.

The Supervisor's Role in Labor Relations

The National Labor Relations Act defines a supervisor in this manner:

> The term supervisor means *any individual* having authority, in the interest of the employer, to hire, transfer, suspend, lay off, recall, promote, discharge, assign, reward, or discipline other employees, or responsibility to direct them, or to adjust their grievances, *or effectively to recommend such action;* if in connection with the foregoing, the exercise of such authority is not of a merely routine or clerical nature, but requires the use of independent judgment.

One of the functions of the National Labor Relations Board is to supervise employee elections in which the idea of union representation is accepted or rejected. If you are a "supervisor" in the eyes of the NLRB—anyone with responsibility for other employees—you must follow fairly strict rules when dealing with unions and your workers. This section will review some of these guidelines. You should realize that in the NLRB's opinion, your actions are to be as binding on the company as your company president's would be.

Most managers do not believe that their employees would benefit from unionization. In fact, they believe that workers who consider unionization have a lot to lose. Since supervisors are managers, any attempt by a supervisor to join a union or to encourage formation of a union may be grounds for dismissal. The supervisor is expected to report all matters of interest to management so that they may deal openly and fairly with union representatives.

The following list includes some specific guidelines for supervisory behavior while a union organization period is in progress. You should note especially that any threats or promises of benefit from a managerial employee are specifically forbidden by law and can be used against the company when the union begins to negotiate.

As a supervisor, you cannot do any of the following:

1. Spy on the union.
2. Encourage employees to spy on the union.
3. Go to a union meeting or near where a union meeting is being held.
4. State to anyone that the company knows about a membership in the union, or of union activity.
5. State to any employee that the company knows of another employee's union membership or union activity.
6. Make any threat, such as
   (a) Blacklisting employees for union activity.
   (b) Cutting out overtime.
   (c) Removing certain privileges.
   (d) Transferring the employee to more undesirable work.
   (e) Laying off an employee.
   (f) Discharging any worker.
   (g) Closing the plant.
   (h) Moving the plant.
7. Make any promises of benefits to discourage or encourage any employee in union activity.
8. Make any statements that could be interpreted as a threat or promise of benefit.
9. Question employees about their union activity or about the activity of any other employee.
10. Question employees about feelings toward or opinions of the union.

The following actions can safely be taken, as long as the statements are general in nature and cannot be interpreted as threats or coercion:

1. Express your views regarding labor unions generally.
2. Extol or justify wage policies or other company practices.
3. Answer union arguments or charges.
4. Explain that union membership is not a requirement for continued or future employment.
5. Discuss union dues and the check-off system.
6. Discuss union tactics and election results in other companies.

7. Express your desire that employees vote against the union.

8. Express your desire to deal with the employees personally and individually, without union interference.

9. Make statements about the history, background, and character of labor.

10. Advise employees as to some of their rights under the law without informing them of all such rights.

The supervisor must exercise extreme care in all activities during a union organization period. Anything you say can and will be used against you!

In a unionized plant, supervisors are often placed in a touchy situation. From management's viewpoint, they represent the workers and should be attuned to their needs, moods, and complaints. From the employees' and union's viewpoint, the supervisor is a representative of management. This is not an easy position to be in, and the supervisor must exercise caution in union dealings and treatment of employees.

Union Contracts

A company does not contract for labor with the union. Rather, it contracts with each individual employee, either verbally or in writing, regarding wages, hours, and working conditions. Through collective bargaining, the union negotiates, shapes the terms, and defines the company's offer that comprises each employee's work contract. Every individual worker has the freedom to accept or reject these terms. If accepted, the individual enters into a contract directly with the company.[3]

Some of the subjects covered and negotiated in a union contract include the following:

1. Management prerogatives.
2. Union recognition.
3. Hours of work.
4. Wages.
5. Vacations and holidays.
6. Seniority.
7. Working conditions.
8. Layoffs and rehirings.
9. Grievance procedures.
10. Arbitration and mediation.
11. Renewal clauses.

Detailed arrangements made in each of these categories will vary enormously from company to company and from union to union. In a sense, the union contract simply puts in writing what should be good personnel practices in all these areas.

[3] Edwin F. Beal, Edward D. Wickersham and Phillip Kienast, *The Practice of Collective Bargaining,* 4th ed. (Homewood, Ill.: Irwin, 1972), pp. 256–57.

Avoidance of Grief with Grievances

Though many of the items covered in a union contract are handled by those at or near the top of the management hierarchy, grievance procedures play an important role in the job of every first-line supervisor. A good supervisor should not require a formal grievance process to indicate that employee morale is down. Morale problems and a low level of satisfaction among employees can be resolved by an alert supervisor before they grow into major crises.

The astute supervisor is interested in any dissatisfaction that may disturb subordinates. Workers may be displeased because they must fill out unnecessary forms, or because they are underemployed, or because another worker is paid more. This dissatisfaction graduates to a complaint as soon as something is said or written about it to the superviser (or the shop steward if the firm is unionized).

Technically speaking, a *grievance* is a complaint presented in writing to a representative of management or a union. A typical labor contract might explain this term in the following manner:

> The term *employee grievance* shall mean any grievance of an employee arising out of the interpretation or application of any term in this agreement or any alleged breach or violation of the terms of this agreement. Such an employee grievance shall be filed within five working days from the date it was found to exist by an employee. The word *filed* shall mean the first discussion with the supervisor.

A typical procedure for dealing with grievances includes four steps. The first step occurs when an employee presents a complaint to an immediate supervisor or shop steward. Ideally, the complaint can be resolved at this point if the supervisor and employee are both willing to be reasonable. If their informal discussion is not productive, the complaint becomes an official grievance. Sometimes a written grievance is filed in the first stage. In unionized firms, a dissatisfied employee usually has the right to have the shop steward present when first mentioning the complaint to the supervisor. In these firms, the second stage involves appealing the written grievance to higher management—perhaps the plant manager. The third step represents the final stage of the process to take place within an organization. Here, an unsettled grievance is presented to the top level of local management. Almost 95 percent of all grievance procedures end in voluntary arbitration—the fourth step.[4] An impartial party will then make a decision that the parties agree in advance to accept as binding. The process we have described is illustrated in Figure 18-1. Note the points at which the union can take an unsettled grievance to higher management.

If the firm is not unionized, the right-hand portion of this chart would be missing. Even without unionization, many firms initiate formal grievance procedures in order to maintain the confidence of their employees. As you can see, if the supervisor is able to resolve a complaint adequately at its initial stage, the entire organization can save considerable time, money, and bad feelings.

---

[4] Paul Pigors and C. A. Myers, *Personnel Administration,* 8th ed. (New York: McGraw-Hill, 1976), p. 213.

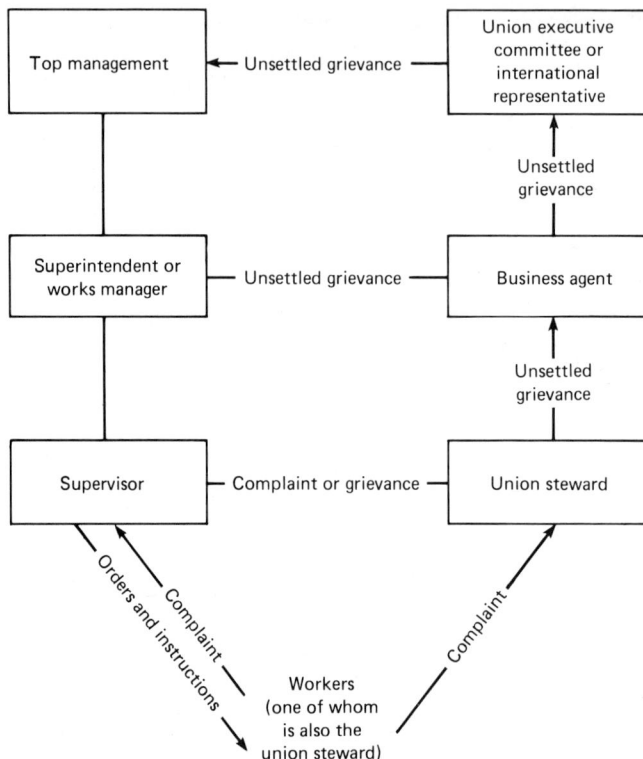

Figure 18-1. Role of Supervisor and Union Steward in the Complaint and Grievance Procedure.

Summary

Dealing with unions has become a fact of life for many supervisors. Business-union clashes can be seen as a conflict between "rights of property" and "rights of persons," although the issues are much more complex.

Labor unions gained power largely because of federal and state legislation in the last few decades. Several important federal acts include the Norris-La-Guardia Act, the Wagner Act, the Taft-Hartley Act, and the Landrum-Griffin Act. Several states have enacted "right-to-work" laws limiting the power of unions.

Unions may be organized at three levels: locals, nationals, and federations. Within these levels, there are major differences in the structures and functions of craft and industrial unions.

In union negotiations, the supervisor plays an important role for both management and employees by gathering information and keeping accurate records. Collective bargaining continues even if a strike occurs, and it does not end until the final contract is signed.

Businesses often criticize labor unions for their monopolistic power, make-work rules, interfering with management rights, and assuming that all productivity increases are due to labor. On the other hand, labor complains that management is too impersonal, too concerned with profit making, and that it too often ignores the achievements of unions.

Collective bargaining may decline as an effective method of meeting demands in the future. Several important reasons are public inconvenience during a strike, the wage-price spiral of inflation, and poor public opinion and support of union activities.

During a union organization period, the supervisor must be extremely careful in words and behavior. Anything that can be construed as a threat or a promise can be used against management in later negotiations.

Key Terms

AFL-CIO. The American Federation of Labor-Congress of Industrial Organizations, the largest and most powerful labor federation in the United States.

Arbitration. The process by which both parties to a grievance submit their complaints to an impartial third party and agree to abide by that person's decision.

Closed Shop. A practice that requires all workers to be union members and all new employees to present proof of union membership or to become union members at the time of hiring.

Collective Bargaining. The process of offers, counteroffers, and compromises by which union representatives and management reach an agreement on working conditions, wages, benefits, and other matters of importance to workers.

Cooling-Off Period. Under the Taft-Hartley Act of 1947, the President of the United States is empowered to call for a "cooling-off period" of up to eighty days whenever a labor dispute threatens to create a national emergency.

Cost-Push Inflation. The upward spiral created by higher wages leading to higher costs, higher prices, and thus higher wages again.

Craft Union. A union whose members are skilled in a particular craft.

Grievance. A complaint filed by labor against management, which is handled by grievance procedures specified in corporate policy or union contract, culminating in arbitration if necessary.

Industrial Union. A union whose members may come from a number of different industries and types of work.

Labor Agreement. A contract specifying working conditions, wages, and other factors in the work environment, reached through collective bargaining by labor and management.

Labor-Management Relations Act. Also known as the Taft-Hartley Act, this 1947 legislation modified the union rights gained in the Wagner Act by forbidding unfair labor practices by unions and forcing unions to police themselves internally.

Landrum-Griffin Act. Popular name of the Labor-Management Reporting and Disclosure Act of 1949 that outlined union members' rights and the union's duties toward its members. The act also revised portions of the Taft-Hartley Act.

Mediation. Submission of grievances to an impartial third party whose decision is not binding, but who seeks to formulate a compromise between the two parties.

National Labor Relations Act. Federal legislation passed in 1935 giving employees the right to organize and to engage in collective bargaining, and establishing a legal obligation for employers to bargain collectively with union representatives.

Norris-LaGuardia Act.   An act passed by Congress in 1932 that severely restricted the use of injunctions to halt union activities and outlawed yellow-dog contracts.

Right-to-Work Laws.   Section of the Taft-Hartley Act that permits employers in certain states to refrain from joining a union in order to obtain or keep a job.

Union Shop.   A business in which employees must join the union if they are to be hired or retained in their jobs.

Yellow-Dog Contract.   Agreement making it a condition of employment that new employees will not join a labor union. This type of contract was outlawed by the Norris-LaGuardia Act.

Review Questions

1. Distinguish between a local, national, and a federation. What is the major role of each?
2. List and describe the membership of the three largest unions in the United States.
3. Distinguish between a craft union and an industrial union.
4. Write a paragraph in which you demonstrate how federal legislation has affected the growth and development of unions.
5. What are the major complaints of business against labor? What are labor's complaints against business?
6. List and describe the features of a union contract.

Exercise

Will They Vote the Union In?

Read the case and answer the questions that follow.

Jason Hartfield was in a tricky position and he knew it. The vote was coming up next week in his plant for union representation, and he was afraid that his employees were going to vote the union in. As far as Jason was concerned, the union would only bring trouble. There were a few goof-offs working in the plant now, and they were going to be in like Flint if the employees decided to be represented by the union. Besides, he could just imagine the headaches that would be caused by handling complaints through grievance procedures instead of his usual method—trying to find the source of the problem and correcting it.

Jason had been warned by management that any interference on his part in union activities or any attempt to influence the vote would invalidate the whole process, and the National Labor Relations Board was watching closely to see that the rules were followed. He was having a very difficult time dealing with his workers, since he could not promise them anything or say anything to them about the company's future plans for improvements. Hostility was in the air, and workers he had formerly been friends with had turned cold and indifferent.

Jason had to think of a way to convince his workers—legally—that the union would do them no good. But how? And why was there going to be a vote anyway? His employees had always seemed relatively content with the way things were run.

What could possibly have gone wrong? And what was he going to do about it now?

1. Is it likely that the workers were happy with the way things had been run in Jason's shop?
2. Is it possible that a few "troublemakers" stirred up the rest of the employees to ask for a representation vote?
3. Within the limits of the law, what could Jason do to influence his workers to vote against the union?
4. Would having a union necessarily be such a bad thing? Whose side is Jason taking in displaying his feelings about the union? Why do you think he feels such a strong allegiance to that side?
5. What would you do if you were in Jason's position? How would you attempt to regain the confidence of your workers?

Case 18 • Sandy Hagy

Bill Fuller is plant manager for the Georgia Kuke Relish Company. He recently received a petition from the employees in one department indicating that they were interested in being represented by the International Bottlers Brotherhood. Fuller is radically opposed to the union and has called his bottling supervisor, Sandy Hagy, in to discuss the matter.

Fuller begins the conversation, "Sandy, as you might suspect, I am opposed to the unionization of this plant. One of the reasons the founder of the company, Muriel Kuke, settled the plant in this region was to avoid the dangers of a union shop. The election is less than a month away, so I want you to do everything you can to discourage your workers from voting for the union. At the same time, I want you to be careful not to violate any laws in the process. The NLRB will be keeping a close watch, so we don't want to get into any trouble.

"By next Monday, I would like to have your recommendations—things that you plan to do to present management's point of view. Personally, I am willing to explain my views about labor unions in general to the employees. You know, I was a member of two different unions in the past, and I think I have some real insight into them. Oh, and you want to use this—a copy of a *Times* article exposing corruption in the union."

Sandy has been a supervisor for only a short time and is anxious to make a good impression with her recommendations. She has worked all weekend on the report and on Monday morning presents Mr. Fuller with the following list of recommendations:

A. Schedule a meeting where Mr. Fuller can explain his feelings about labor unions to the employees, and re-emphasize the company's wage policies.
B. Distribute copies of the *Times* article to all employees at Georgia Kuke.
C. Interview each employee for his or her stand on the union and ascertain which employees appear to be the organizers of the effort.
D. Transfer the pro-union workers to the night shift.
E. Announce that the company plans a lavish picnic at company expense if the union is rejected.
F. Show how a company organized by the union in the past was forced into bankruptcy and no longer exists because of prohibitive labor costs.

1. Evaluate Mr. Fuller's approach to the union organization attempt.
2. Evaluate the proposal prepared by Sandy Hagy. If you were Mr. Fuller, which of her suggestions would you approve? Which of her suggestions are legal and which are illegal?

CHAPTER 19

Supervising Minorities

Art. 1. All human beings are born free and equal in dignity and rights.

United Nations, Declaration of Human Rights

Learning Objectives

• To understand the nature and extent of discrimination and prejudice in the work place.

• To become aware of the various minority groups in the work force and the types of discrimination they encounter.

• To identify and become familiar with legislation that attempts to resolve job discrimination.

• Assist employers and employees toward a deeper awareness of changing attitudes to work and occupational status today and how these are affecting day-to-day working relationships.

Throughout this book we have explored many profound changes occurring in the world of work through changing technology, increasing bureaucratization, and the shift from a production-oriented economy to what has been described as a "postindustrial society." Work is a powerful force within the lives of human beings, yet the inner lives of people are at work and the changing relationships occurring in the work place are still largely unexplored territory. As a social issue, work has been viewed primarily in economic terms—wages, fringe benefits, equal pay, and so on. With the advent of affirmative action, efforts have been made to establish ethnic balance and parity between men and women.

The problems arising out of equal employment opportunities and affirmative action policies that are hampering the best efforts of organizations are directly related to occupational habits and attitudes that are rooted in the belief systems of a previous era. These policies, posing challenges to both employers and employees, have opened up a Pandora's box of questions and dilemmas as people from varying backgrounds with differing values and social codes are brought together in job situations to work for common goals.

Racial and Ethnic Groups: The Underprivileged Minorities

Discrimination against racial minorities and first- or second-generation immigrants has characterized our history. Since these two groups share many cultural characteristics that often result in prejudice and job discrimination, they will be discussed together.

Several characteristics describe the racial and ethnic groups we call "underprivileged": (1) different skin color or clothes; (2) cultural values in conflict with the American value system (e.g., cheating on taxes and bribery are acceptable behavior in some cultures); (3) language differences; (4) inadequate education; (5) ignorance of life-styles, customs, and cultural traits of American society; (6) poverty, or a continual concern for providing physical, safety, and security needs; and (7) job discrimination.

Together these factors prevent the underprivileged from breaking out of the failure and poverty cycle. The following characteristics of minority individuals and families emphasize the detrimental effects on life-style, values, and attitudes:[1]

1. Pervasive feelings of insecurity.
2. Little or no experience of success in school, family life, work, and personal life.
3. Preoccupation with money for the scant security it provides.
4. Disruptive life experiences: violence, frequent arrests, or police harrassment; and high geographical mobility.
5. Strong support of "law and order," desire for strict authority to introduce some stability into life.
6. Inability to plan ahead, little awareness of the future, and concentration on the present.

---

[1] William F. Glueck, *Personnel: A Diagnostic Approach* (Dallas: Business Publications, Inc., 1974), pp. 539–40.

7. Avoidance of new situations because of insecurity, history of failure, and poor communications skills.

Discouragement and despair make minority problems self-perpetuating, void of hope, and open to manipulation or opportunism. The social tragedy of people without a chance for success is a drain on national resources, creates social problems, and leads to economic waste.

On the other hand, the social benefits to be derived from employing the underprivileged are numerous, immediate, and far-reaching:[2]

1. Creation of useful, contributing members of society.

2. Improvement in the individual's self-image and sense of worth.

3. Creation of productive taxpayers from former recipients of assistance.

4. Reduction of need for government control over the lives of individuals.

5. Improvement in the standard of living for large numbers of people.

6. Strengthening of the role of business in social and economic development.

7. Improvement of the social image of business.

Anything worth having is worth working for diligently. If these advantages are to be realized, supervisors must spend time, money, and effort on programs to hire underprivileged minority members and to train them effectively. Supervisors must educate themselves about the complexities of minority problems and must be fair and patient in dealing with all employees. Sporadic gestures will not work; the effort must be on-going and include attention to recruiting, training, and supervision of workers in special categories.

Recruiting Underprivileged Employees

Standard recruiting practices probably will not be effective because underprivileged workers are skeptical of traditional sources like newspaper advertisements, personnel agencies, or school placement offices. Previous experiences of failure will persuade them not to seek job opportunities in these channels. Therefore, a different strategy is required. *Community newspapers* are closely read in many racial neighborhood and ethnic communities, and can be a good source of minority employees. Similarly, *ethnic radio and television* can assist by announcing job opportunities as part of their public service responsibility. *State employment offices* are a good source for matching your employment needs with minority workers. Agency lists are quite extensive because businesses that receive over $10,000 in federal government business each year must list job opportunities with state employment agencies. Finally, *community agencies* and their leaders often know individuals who are looking for employment. A discussion of your company's needs with such leaders can make them allies with you in the recruitment process.

[2] Keith Davis, *Human Behavior at Work,* 5th ed. (New York: McGraw-Hill, 1977), p. 327.

Hiring and Training the Underprivileged

Managers, subordinates, and underprivileged employers all need training in communication and human relations so that they can understand each others' special problems and better handle interpersonal relations on the job. The critical issues today, transcending affirmative action per se, encompass the fundamental nature of people interacting with each other in their jobs. Thus, while a double standard for performance may be necessary initially, it must fade away quickly or resentment will build against minority employees and destroy the positive results of affirmative action.

Five essential elements for a minority employees' training program are[3]

1. Preparation of supervisors.

2. Attitude training for the new minority employees. Cultural habits and negative attitudes that prevent job success must be overcome.

3. Basic education. Disadvantaged workers are likely to be deficient in reading and writing skills, basic arithmetic, and problem-solving techniques.

4. On-the-job training. Many disadvantaged workers have no job skills at all and will require special training and close supervision for months.

5. Related services. To emphasize the new employee's importance to the company and to assist in solving personal problems that may hinder job performance, a number of services can be provided. These include financial counseling, medical checkups, assistance in finding child-care facilities, help in finding suitable transportation, counseling, and follow-up on absences.

Basically, it is hard work to train the underprivileged. Training supervisors to train, understand and be sensitive, and work effectively with them is also a difficult challenge. Patience is needed to wait for pay-offs, which are sometimes slow in coming.

Supervising the Underprivileged

There are several problems associated with the introduction of an affirmative action program for underprivileged workers. The following are some of the most common problems initially faced by supervisors:[4]

1. Low rates of production.

2. Poor production quality, often resulting in excessive production costs.

3. High rates of tardiness, absenteeism, and turnover.

4. Uncertainty or hostility about work regulations and supervisory practices.

5. Sloppy or inconsistent work habits, and inability to conform to a tight work schedule or to strict regulations.

6. Slow and sometimes unstable progress.

7. Fighting, loafing, and interference with another's work.

Most of these problems should disappear with experience on the job and strong, fair, and firm supervision. A manager may need to spend extra time

[3] Ibid, p. 328–29.
[4] Ibid, p. 328.

and effort with those needing special training or counseling, but must also be careful not to neglect responsibilities for regular workers and routine duties.

Another potentially dangerous result of an affirmative action program is tension between regular workers (usually white) and minorities (usually black or female). Regular workers must be assured through communication and demonstration that adherence to company policies, procedures, and rules will be required by all workers and that equal criteria will be used for pay raises, promotions, and vacations. The experience of working side-by-side in a productive relationship is usually the fastest and best solution for prejudice. Once again, strong supervisory leadership is required to set the proper tone for the entire work group by assuring that disputes and hostilities are handled quickly, honestly, and fairly.

The Majority Minority

Women are considered a minority group in America, even though they comprise 53 percent of the total population. In spite of the fact that women outnumber men, possess more wealth, are generally healthier and live longer, women are still consistently discriminated against in the job market. A brief look at how this came about and what pressures are forcing the system to change can assist the supervisor in preventing sex discrimination on the job.

History, Tradition, and the Feminine Mystique

Prior to the Industrial Revolution, women worked in the fields, cooked and stored food, made clothes, and provided medical care for their families. The growth of industrialism and urbanism saw women become a cheap source of labor, along with children. They worked as long and hard as men, but no one would consider paying them equal wages.

In the 1940s and 1950s, there was a massive movement of women from the workplace to the home. The role shifted from producer to that of consumer for household and parental functions.[5] Her position typically reflected her husband's occupational status. The myths of this "feminine mystique" in the 1950s included the view that women are emotional, irrational, dependent, and best suited to be wives and mothers.[6] This sterotype has held women back in business and industry and created discrimination against them in the labor market.

After College: Sex-Typing Jobs

Male and female children in America have been encouraged to attend college in large numbers. After college, male degree holders are usually absorbed into the job market. Promotion and success is assured for the hard working young male. But such has not been the case for women.

---

[5] Evelyn Sullerot, *Women, Society and Change* (New York: McGraw-Hill, 1971).
[6] See Betty Friedan, *The Feminine Mystique* (New York: Norton, 1963).

Companies have been reluctant to hire females for a variety of mythical reasons: they belong at home, they may move if their husband is transferred, they cannot hold up under pressure, and so on. Therefore, many females are channeled into routine jobs rather than careers. As mentioned earlier, 40 percent of the work force are women, yet they are relegated to the bottom 20 percent of jobs in terms of pay and prestige.

The myths of the feminine mystique have culminated in the *sex-typing* of jobs—the assumption that certain jobs are expected to be held by men and others by women. In spite of the fact that women hold college degrees, many people still believe that women are just not supposed to be managers, doctors, lawyers, or other high-ranking professionals.

Sex-typing breeds discrimination that in turn costs society in the form of economic power, frustration, and low self-esteem of a large segment of its population. Many women want to work at home, but many other capable, well-educated and trained women are desperate for outside employment and the opportunity to contribute to society from a higher-level position or by more challenging work. Affirmative action legislation for women is a first step in developing and reaping the benefits of female potential in the labor force.

Affirmative Action for Women

The Equal Pay Act of 1963 was the first federal legislation that specifically sought to correct discrimination against women in employment. This law prohibited employers from paying different wages to different sexes for essentially identical jobs. The Civil Rights Law of 1964 carried a provision forbidding sexual discrimination. The Civil Rights Act was subsequently amended by executive order and prevented sexual discrimination among federal contractors, allowed the government to sue companies discriminating against women, and required filing of affirmative action programs in firms not hiring women on their qualifications and accessibility.

Dealing with Differences

Psychological, physical, and behavioral differences do exist between men and women that can present problems in supervising female workers. Because of cultural roles women occasionally display more uneven work patterns and are likely to request more time off because of childbirth and childrearing. Many prefer part-time employment or irregular hours that accommodate their school-age children's schedules. Others prefer jobs that will not compete with their husband's status.

These role conflicts can be resolved by supervisors participating in affirmative action programs directed at changing traditional, more "comfortable" ways of doing things. Many jobs in our society can be performed on a part-time basis and on-site day-care facilities can be provided by large organizations to care for working parents' children. Many employees' schedules can be adjusted to accommodate children's needs. It is conceivable that if many females could be meaningfully employed on a part-time basis, overall production could increase enough to allow male employees more flexibility in their work schedule as well!

The Woman Supervisor: Dittos and Dissimilarities

Women managers have to plan, organize, communicate, make decisions, administer, control, suffer consequences, and operate under stress just like men. Many employees of both sexes resent any form of authority over them, but female authority, especially over males, can compound and reinforce resentment.

Myths of the feminine mystique contribute to the difficulties of female supervisors by having society insist on their dependency, insecurity, instability, cooperation, passivity, and willingness to take, not give, orders. Both sexes often resent a "tough" female supervisor, and the female manager should expect to pay the price of resentment, frustration, and anger directed toward her.

Supervisory and professional positions for women have increased in recent years due to governmental legislation promoting equal rights for all. This vanguard of women managers in prestigious positions of authority will have to accept the greater stress and more delicate situations until our society becomes more adjusted to dealing with them. Astute female leaders will convert these challenges to their advantage and to the advantage of all women.

The Aging Minority

People are having fewer babies and living longer. This means that more and more of our population will be composed of older people. Yet older workers are increasingly becoming the subject of job discrimination. Early retirement or firing of older workers to save money robs individuals of personal worth, accomplishment, direction, and meaning to life.

Justification for Age Discrimination?

Forty years of age is the formal classification of an "older worker." The following are reasons why workers have difficulty obtaining meaningful and rewarding jobs:[7]

1. With 80 percent of the labor force employed by someone else, there are increasingly fewer opportunities for self-employment among older workers.

2. Seniority and promotion-from-within regulations, especially in large organizations, make it difficult for the unemployed older worker to get a job worthy of his or her skills and experience.

3. With the decline of the extended family, more older workers are seeking jobs to support themselves.

4. Middle-aged women who have raised their children are entering the job market in larger numbers, often without the skills or experience to land a good job.

[7] Davis, pp. 322–23.

5. Technological advancement frequently renders skills learned in one's youth obsolete in today's job market.

6. Younger workers generally have more education and more current training than older workers.

7. Pension structures increase the cost of hiring older workers because they will not be able to contribute to the system for as many years as younger workers.

8. Mandatory retirement forces out many workers over sixty-five who are still competent and willing to work.

9. Older workers are more frequently laid off than younger workers in industries without seniority regulations because their costs to the company are greater, for example, in pension and insurance benefits.

10. Older workers often fail to keep up with changes in technology or resent policy changes, leaving themselves open to early dismissal. Companies that use these reasons for refusing to hire or retain older employees do themselves a great disservice.

Why Hire Older Workers?

Many myths surround older workers' inability to get along with co-workers and their poor job performance. These stereotypes, as with racial, religious, and ethnic groups, are mostly false and overlook the following reasons for hiring older people:[8]

1. Greater experience, more maturity.

2. Good quality and quantity of production.

3. No more likely than younger workers to be rigid or inflexible.

4. More careful and thus less accident-prone.

5. Stable rates of absenteeism (no greater than younger workers).

6. Less turnover.

7. More appreciative of jobs and consequently tend to show more loyalty or better performance.

8. Employee attitude equal to, or better than, younger workers.

The social costs of not using or underutilizing older employees are staggering. The Social Security system will face early bankruptcy if the work force continues to be reduced in size by early firing or forced retirement. National productivity is diminished and needs for social and welfare programs to benefit the elderly is increased. In short, loss of pride and accomplishment are converted to dependency upon others for sustenance.

Some Solutions

The solution to these problems goes beyond good supervision, communication, and understanding. Top management must implement clearly defined plans

[8] Robert M. Fulmer, *Practical Human Relations* (Homewood, Ill: Richard D. Irwin, 1977), p. 451.

and policies that will stimulate continued high performance from competent older men and women employees. In most companies, adjustments in working conditions and policies can be made easily that will encourage the retention and continued productivity of most older workers.

The recent raising of the forced retirement age from sixty-five to seventy is a step toward protecting older employees who choose to continue their contributions to society through work. There are several other options available for companies wishing to benefit from the human resources of older citizens.

Age requirements for retirement could be eliminated altogether so that an employee could retire at any time from age fifty to one hundred, depending on job performance and success in meeting work requirements. The forced retirement age could be raised to seventy-five and allow employees to retire at any time between seventy and seventy-five without any loss of retirement benefits. Annual extension contracts could be offered to capable employees over seventy, which would allow the employer greater flexibility in replacing the worker and provide the employee with more years of active work.

Part-time work arrangements after retirement could be made with many older employees for jobs that are not physically demanding, but are necessary for the smooth operations of the firm. Older employees who have not reached retirement age sometimes develop physical disabilities that will not hinder their performance if a little imagination and creative engineering is employed by management. A soft chair may be all that is needed, or a power tool or better lighting may alleviate the potential hinderance.

Most companies have a great investment in older employees. However, their experience, stability, and desire to contribute cannot be measured in just economic terms. Organizations severely harm *themselves* if they do not use human assets to their fullest.

Hiring the Handicapped

The Rehabilitation Act of 1973 provides that, "No otherwise qualified handicapped individual . . . solely by reason of his or her handicap be excluded from the participation in, be denied the benefits of, or be subjected to discrimination under any program of activity receiving federal assistance." Though this regulation applies specifically to recipients of all federal assistance, the same general guidelines are recognized by large corporate employers. In 1973, specific regulations were provided to describe specific acts of discrimination against qualified handicapped employees. Basically, these provided that employers should make reasonable accommodations for the handicaps of current or potential employees. Unless these accommodations would cause the employer undue hardships, it was expected that special facilities should be provided for individuals with physical handicaps. Employers are also expected to provide modifications in existing programs or facilities to make the same kind of opportunities available to handicapped employees as is provided for individuals without these limitations. When new facilities are to be constructed, they should be designed to be accessible by handicapped persons.

Because of these regulations, many organizations have begun to provide Braille lettering for elevator instructions, parking places for handicapped individuals, and special ramps as alternatives to stairs.

Performance Advantages

Like other minority groups, handicapped workers have much to offer. Management must, however, take the time and effort to determine where they can make their greatest contribution to the business and properly match the handicapped worker to the job.

Studies have revealed that about 66 percent of physically handicapped workers perform equally as well as able-bodied employees, 24 percent outperform regular workers, and only 10 percent produce at a lower rate. Absenteeism and turnover is usually lower among handicapped workers because jobs are better matched to their skills, and they possess more positive attitudes and a higher level of motivation toward work.[9]

A study in Pennsylvania revealed that less than 1 percent of handicapped workers experienced auto accidents, compared to nearly 5 percent for regular workers. Western Electric discovered that its handicapped employees (1) had 33 percent fewer accidents on the job than able-bodied workers, (2) resigned 7 percent less often, (3) were dismissed 5 percent less often, and (4) experienced 7 percent less absenteeism than able-bodied employees.[10] It is senseless to waste the skills, abilities, and motivation of the more than 7 million handicapped workers in America. Discrimination against them is a sign of near-sighted management that "can't see the forest for the trees."

Summary

Discrimination costs our country economically, socially, and individually. Smart supervisors can play a major role in preventing this destruction and loss.

Minority groups that experience consistent prejudice and discrimination include the poor, racial, religious and ethnic groups, women, older employees, special employment groups, and handicapped workers.

Discrimination against underprivileged racial and ethnic groups can be terminated only by an understanding of the historical and cultural complexities of this problem, affirmative action programs with special recruiting, hiring, and training techniques, close supervision, and the willingness to give people a chance to succeed.

Discrimination against women developed from the traditional role of women and has been prolonged by the acceptance of the domestic image of the feminine mystique. The sex-typing of jobs has discouraged women with college educations, relegating them to lower pay and prestige positions within business. Supervision can contribute toward eliminating sexual discrimination in hiring, wages, benefits, and promotions.

Job discrimination against older employees is a serious and persistent problem. With people living longer and mandatory retirement raised to seventy, supervisors need to be aware of the advantages of hiring these experienced employees. Possible solutions to this problem include variable retirement, part-time work, and creative job engineering.

Handicapped workers are discriminated against because organizations have

9 Glueck, p. 73.
10 Ibid.

stereotyped them as liabilities. Studies show they perform as well or better than 90 percent of able-bodied employees, incur fewer accidents, and have lower turnover and less absenteeism.

Top management planning and the creation of new policies is necessary for effectively eliminating discrimination against all minorities. But supervisors must deal with and control their own prejudices and eliminate discriminatory action with their employees for any plan or policy to work. Objectivity, sensitivity, understanding, fairness, and honesty in supervisory dealings with employees will provide any organization with benefits by utilizing the contributions of these valuable groups of people.

Key Terms

Affirmative Action Programs. Programs instituted by the federal government requiring those holding contracts with the government to guarantee equal job opportunities to minority group members.

Discrimination. Manifest behavior or actions favoring an individual or group over another without consideration of personal qualifications or job performance.

Equal Pay Act of 1963. The law prohibiting employers from paying different wages to different sexes for essentially identical jobs.

Feminine Mystique. The traditional American myth that a woman's place is in the home and that women are emotional, irrational, dependent, and most suited for roles as wives and mothers.

Minority Training Program. Development programs by businesses and government designed to prepare minority supervisors, instill positive attitudes in workers, provide basic remedial education, encourage on-the-job training, and assist workers in personal, financial, family, and child-care counseling.

Prejudice. The attitude or feeling that some other individual or group is strange or inferior.

Rehabilitation Act of 1973. The law forbidding discrimination against handicapped workers in any federally funded program.

Sex-Typing. The assumption that certain jobs are expected to be held by men and others by women.

Underprivileged Minorities. Racial or ethnic groups usually characterized by one or more of the following: differences in skin color; different cultural values and customs; language differences; inadequate education; poverty; and history of job discrimination.

Review Questions

1. It is said that prejudice is an attitude, and discrimination is a practice. How can they be harmful to an organization?
2. List and describe the various ways in which minority groups are classified.
3. List and describe the ways in which organizations can effectively recruit disadvantaged persons.
4. Why are older citizens and handicapped persons desirable employees?

5. List and describe the characteristics of an effective training program for disadvantaged employees.

6. What are the most common problems encountered by a supervisor in starting an affirmative action program?

7. What are the characteristics of an affirmative action program?

8. The "feminine mystique" describes conditions in America observed by its author in 1963 and before. Do the myths surrounding the mystique still exist, or have we overcome them?

9. List and describe the similarities and differences between male and female supervisors. Do the distinctions you list make you a prejudiced person? Why or why not?

Exercises

I. Hire the Handicapped

Interview the personnel manager of two or three large companies in your city and ask if they actively hire the handicapped, how they orient them to their jobs, and what kinds of on-going training programs they have for these employees. Ask to see the company figures on turnover, absenteeism, and performance and accident reports of handicapped versus nonhandicapped employees. Ask the personnel managers their personal opinions as to the value of employing handicapped workers.

II. Verbal Expressions of Prejudice

Often we are guilty of prejudicial feelings without recognizing them as such. These prejudices can be detected in the verbal expressions we use to stereotype individuals and groups. Give examples of expressions in common use to prejudicially describe:

Blacks.	Homosexuals.
Women.	College graduates.
Attractive women.	Jews.
Polish-Americans.	Blacks with large cars.
A single woman.	An old woman.
A mentally retarded child.	A person without a job.

Discuss with classmates how you can eliminate these expressions and the prejudices they reveal.

III. The Orientation Program

Develop a two-week orientation program, day-by-day, for a newly hired, disadvantaged employee. Select any particular disadvantage factors you wish.

Case 19 • Chris Trapnell

Chris Trapnell was born in Augusta, Georgia, and grew up in Jacksonville, Florida. His father was a successful physician, and Chris often accompanied his father to a special clinic on Saturdays where he would treat those who could not afford regular medical care. Most of these people were black, and some were white; they were all very poor. Chris enjoyed working with his father and he felt much sympathy and understanding for these people.

During the summers of his childhood, Chris spent one month with his grandparents in a small southern Georgia town. His grandfather owned three farms, and on each of them were numerous small dwellings in which black tenant farmers lived. Chris often picked cotton, rode the tractors, and participated in other farm experiences. He liked to fish with black children his age and generally enjoyed the summers of his youth.

Now, at thirty years of age, Chris has been hired as a supervisor for a medium-sized service firm in Atlanta. He "inherited" a black secretary, Elizabeth, who was hired two years ago by his predecessor. Elizabeth is twenty-six years old, a high school graduate, married, and the mother of two children.

The first week at his new job was very difficult for Chris and Elizabeth. Her typing skills were very poor; every letter she typed from dictation was full of errors. The second week, he gave her a fifteen-page report to type, which was returned three days later with so many typing mistakes that it was unreadable. As if this was not enough to concern Chris, he observed that Elizabeth never arrived at work on time, and at the end of the day would sit by her desk twenty minutes before quitting time just waiting for the clock to strike five o'clock. He also observed that she spent considerable time on the telephone talking to her family. In addition, she was absent from work at least one full day each week. Her reasons for being absent included dental and medical appointments, car trouble, children needing medical attention, and her own medical problems.

Recently, Elizabeth told Chris that she would be absent from work on Friday to attend her nephew's funeral. Chris approved her request. But, on Tuesday of the following week, another secretary in the office showed Chris the obituary column that showed that her nephew's funeral was held on Saturday.

1. With this information, what should Chris do?
2. What is your analysis of the problem facing Elizabeth? Facing Chris?
3. How might the general situation created by Elizabeth have been avoided?

CHAPTER 20

Coping with Change

Changing one thing for the better does more good than proving a dozen things are wrong.

Spanish proverb

Learning Objectives

- To compare the complexity and pervasiveness of change in the modern world with past eras.
- To identify the reasons for rapid change and the interrelationships affected by change.
- To learn how to overcome resistance to necessary change effectively and in the least disruptive manner.
- To learn to apply the steps in the change process to facilitate needed change and restore equilibrium.

Everyone has heard the phrases "age of transition" and "era of rapid change." Even though our ancestors have probably applied these phrases to every period of history from the Garden of Eden on, they have never been more appropriately applied than today. Change is one of the few permanent things in today's world.

Why is our age so different? Because the *rate* of change has altered. A few simple examples should make the point dramatically clear.[1] If the past 50,000 years of human existence were divided into lifetimes of about sixty-two years each, there have been about 800 lifetimes. Of these 800, approximately 650 were spent in caves. Only during the past six lifetimes have large numbers of people ever seen a printed word. Only during the past four has it been possible to measure time with any degree of precision. Only those who have lived in the past two lifetimes have used an electric motor. And the overwhelming majority of all the material goods we use today have been developed in the present—our 800th lifetime.

The speed at which we travel today is another example of the increasingly rapid rate of change. In 6000 B.C., camel caravans represented the fastest means of transportation, averaging eight miles an hour. Three thousand years later, the horse-drawn chariot pounded onto the scene, carrying drivers at the daredevil speed of twenty miles per hour. Less than 100 years have passed since the development of a locomotive capable of going 100 miles an hour. By 1931, people could travel at 400 miles an hour in airplanes. We doubled that speed within the next twenty years. In the 1960s, some planes approached speeds of 4000 miles an hour. Today, rockets can travel to the moon and beyond and orbit the earth at speeds over 18,000 miles an hour.

Over half the amount of energy consumed in the last 2000 years has been used in the past century. Of course, we have used more energy in recent years because today's population figures equal 25 percent of the world's total population since history began. Ninety percent of all physical scientists who ever existed are alive now, helping to double our technical information every decade.

Although change is a fact of life in any progressive culture, supervisors and workers faced with change oppose it almost universally. Many of our most trusted beliefs and practices were at one time outrageously new. Most were strongly resisted. We all should have learned by now to welcome the change that has brought us a higher quality of life, more leisure time, and more satisfying work. But most experienced supervisors would agree that resistance to change is one of their most troublesome problems.

What Is Change?

The word *change* refers to any alteration, substitution, new development, process, or difference from the way things once were. In one sense, a change is any difference in one part of an environment that alters the total environment, whether drastically or in a very minor way.

In a work situation, the entire organization is likely to be affected by a change in any part of it. Every organization is composed of separate parts that must work harmoniously together in a state of equilibrium, or balance.

---

[1] The illustrations that follow are based on Alvin Toffler, *Future Shock* (New York: Random House, 1970), pp. 11–26. Toffler continues his work on change in *The Third Wave* (New York: Knopf, 1980).

No department can effectively do its job without the cooperation and support of all other departments. This relationship among parts of a whole can be extended to any system, whether a corporation, a government agency, or a whole society.

When change occurs in an organization, it usually takes place at a particular point and with a particular group of people. Naturally, the change will be most drastic at the "point of pressure," or the primary location of the change. But any change will have repercussions throughout the organization and will affect all workers, whether or not they are directly involved. Technological change is a human problem, not just a technical problem.

When change occurs frequently at one point in an organization, it will probably weaken that point. When extensive changes are made often, workers must continually adjust to new situations, new relationships, and new ways of doing things. These adjustments are bound to cause anxiety and uncertainty. If change occurs too frequently, workers in an organization may become so frustrated that the organization is seriously damaged, ruptured, or destroyed.

When an organization has achieved equilibrium, the people involved know what to expect of each other and their work environment. They become familiar with their surroundings, their relationships with others, and what to expect tomorrow. It is much easier for individuals to remain well adjusted when their environment is in equilibrium. Change requires that adjustments be made to reach a new equilibrium. Naturally, most people resist alterations in their environment that require them to adjust. Thus the supervisor's job is (1) to get workers to accept necessary changes and then (2) to help restore the equilibrium of the work group and the individuals within it. The adjustments demanded by change are quite complicated, and the supervisor should study them in order to prepare the staff to adjust to change as smoothly as possible.

Resistance to Change

The supervisor faces a major challenge whenever subordinates have to accept new ideas or new ways of doing things. Why is this so? In this section, we shall consider some common reasons for human resistance to change.

Economic Reasons

When change threatens to disrupt the work environment so extensively that it appears that some workers are likely to lose their jobs, economic reasons play a major role in resistance to change. In recent years, automation has eliminated some jobs. Workers may undergo retraining or even enter entirely new lines of work. Once it seems certain that a change will cost workers their jobs, they are not soothed by arguments that automation in their plant will help the business run more efficiently. Their only concern is their own economic well-being and that of their families.

Supervisors, office workers, and craftsmen also have grounds to fear that new developments may make their employment less secure. A supervisor might, for example, worry about the impact on a chance for promotion or pay raise.

Inconvenience

Any change that makes life more difficult, even for a short time, is likely to be resisted. People naturally resist taking on extra duties. A worker already knows the ins and outs of an old job, but new duties call for new methods and new standards of performance. Learning a new job requires energy and concentration. It is much easier to continue old ways of doing things. "Keep the status quo" is the motto of those who stubbornly resist change.

Uncertainty

Even when change brings improvement, it still creates uncertainty and anxiety. Many people feel threatened when former ways of doing things no longer apply. Fear is often the major cause of hostility toward any change that threatens a person's security or status.

Frequently, the employees who are most afraid of change are those who have the least reason for uncertainty. They are often people with high rank, long service, or great ability—the very ones who should be least upset by change. Insecurity, however, is one of the most deeply rooted human emotions. The laws of human nature apply to the business world as well, and the weak usually have difficulty surviving. Even the strong often feel weak. Basic insecurity causes us to avoid the conflicts inherent whenever change occurs.

The average person has many fears and they are often justifiable. A seemingly insignificant change at the organizational level can spell serious consequences for an individual worker who is directly affected. For instance, when management decides to combine the jobs of janitor and maintenance in one position, that decision becomes the most important thing to the two people who hold those jobs. Which will be fired and which kept? How will the "winner" be able to reorganize activities and learn the new job's requirements?

The supervisor may also have to cope with change on a personal basis. If offered a new position, promotion, or transfer, he or she will ask several questions. How hard will the new job be? How long will it take to learn new duties? Will I be able to meet the challenge? Will I have new friends? Who will they be? Even though added responsibility often means more status and money, there is a tendency to leave well enough alone.

One reason that we fear new situations is that we lack factual information. When answers are provided, many of our fears will disappear. When uncertainty and anxiety are caused by the individual's fears about performing in a new position, there are no easy answers. Though facts alone will not remedy this situation, reassurance from friends and superiors may help dispel these feelings of uncertainty.

Threats to Social Relationships

As we learned in the chapter on groups, workers develop complex relationships within their work groups. Status arrangements, leadership and follower positions, task specialists, and other roles are determined within the group. These relationships are understood by group members and situations can be handled according to the group's informal rules.

When a change occurs in the work group, it will often alter the patterns of personal relationships. If a key worker is promoted to another position, the leadership role in the former work group must be assumed by someone else. If a new supervisor comes into a plant, old relationships are disrupted and new ones must be formed. Every new supervisor must undergo a lengthy period of orientation before being fully accepted by the new group of workers. One reason for this adaptation period is that workers are often afraid that the newcomer will not follow the predecessor's pattern of informal relationships. These are some of the social dimensions of change that the supervisor must be aware of within an employee group and in personal relationships with workers.

Resentment of Control

Change often means that workers will be supervised more closely for a while to insure that they are learning their new tasks and accomplishing them properly. When this happens, workers are constantly reminded that supervisors and management have greater authority, and this can increase their irritation before or during a change. Many people resent having to take orders. If they can perform their jobs without a great deal of supervision, they can largely forget the superior authority of management. But when new techniques and duties require increased supervision, workers sometimes become hostile to the change and the supervisor.

Any attempt on the part of management to increase control over workers will also increase resentment. People become used to a certain amount and type of control and will fight management efforts to strengthen that control. Greater control often means that workers lose some of their sense of autonomy and self-reliance, and this loss can represent a major factor in their resentment toward change.

Coping with Resistance to Change

Although change is a way of life in most organizations, the supervisor must be aware of the social dynamics of change. People's fears, resentments, and adjustments are very much involved in any process of change. The need to preserve their values must always be considered in trying to contend with resistance.

Ben Franklin once remarked:

> The way to convince another is to state your case moderately and accurately. Then scratch your head and say, "At least that's what it seems to me, but of course I may be wrong." This causes your listener to receive what you have to say, and, like as not, come about and try to convince *you* of it, since you are in doubt. But if you go to him in a tone of positiveness or arrogance, you only make an opponent of him.

Granted, Franklin's way of handling resistance to change is manipulative, but it is one workable solution to the problem. The following steps, however, would probably be more useful to the supervisor in efforts to cope with subordinates' resistance to change:

1. Recognize all the factors in a change situation.   Wouldn't your job be much simpler if people adjusted simply and directly to change! But the realities of change are far more complicated. Reactions to change depend upon each individual's attitude toward the change, the job, and the work environment. Feelings and attitudes will influence the response to change. In addition, synergy may operate within a work group to produce a group reaction to change and blend individual reactions.

A famous experiment shows the relationship between individual and group attitudes in dealing with change. Several researchers wanted to test the effects of different working conditions on performance—for example, they felt that better lighting would lead to greater productivity. A test group of female workers was chosen and moved to a special section of the Hawthorne plant of Western Electric. When the lighting in this area was increased, productivity increased, as was expected. Then the researchers decided to decrease illumination to illustrate that the reverse effect would reduce productivity. They were quite surprised when productivity actually increased again! Lighting was again decreased and the result was still higher productivity. Finally, lighting was decreased to not much more than the equivalent of moonlight. At this point there was an appreciable decline in output.[2]

The researchers had discovered an important principle of work organizations. Instead of direct cause-and-effect relationships between change and responses to change, they found that unanticipated influences upset the pattern of response to change. It turned out that morale was the factor influencing the change in productivity. The workers felt that the supervisors "cared," and worked harder, even under odd circumstances. The research also taught the researchers something about conducting experimental studies with humans.

2. Support can be gained through worker participation.   People who are involved in the decision-making processes will accept change more readily. During World War II, when whole milk was scarce, health authorities wanted housewives to use more dried milk. A group of researchers demonstrated that support could be gained by participation. In an experiment with Midwestern housewives, two different ways to increase dried milk consumption were tried.[3] First, lectures by experts in nutrition were given to homemakers explaining why they should use dried milk. A month later, only 15 percent of these women used more dried milk.

The health authorities then decided to try another method. Groups of about six women were brought together to talk over among themselves the benefits of using more dried milk. The leader of the discussion did very little talking, but kept the conversation on the subject of milk. These small groups of women decided they should use more dried milk. No outsider told them what to do—it was their own decision. A month later, 50 percent of these women were using more dried milk in their homes.

Another experiment was conducted in a textile mill plagued by low produc-

[2] F. J. Roethlisberger and W. J. Dickson, *Management and the Worker* (Cambridge, Mass.: Harvard U. P., 1939).

[3] Described in Donald Laird and Eleanor Laird, *Psychology: Human Relations and Motivation,* 5th ed. (New York: McGraw-Hill, 1975).

tion rates. Since the equipment could not be changed, the only course of action was to increase worker productivity. Since all employees were paid on the basis of piecework, an incentive program was already in operation. Yet production remained low. The experiment began with two similar groups of workers chosen for the study.

In one group, an industrial engineer was brought in to develop improved methods of production. These methods were explained to the workers and they were told that the new methods would make their jobs easier and more rewarding, and that management expected increased production. The workers could now make more money for themselves, but almost no one did. In fact, during the next few months, their average output dropped.

In the other situation, the workers were brought together in small groups to talk over what might be wrong with production. The workers did the talking, not the bosses. The discussion leader did not tell them how to turn out more work, but left it up to the workers to decide where improvements might be possible. After several discussions, conducted on their own time, these groups decided they could increase output and set a goal for themselves. Although their methods were not as "efficient" as those worked out by the professional engineer, their output jumped to a new high. During the next few months, it averaged 18 percent higher than it had been before they developed their own changes in procedures.

We will look at one final example of a positive response to a work change through participatory decision making. This experiment took place at Texas Instruments, Inc., and led to increases in productivity and significantly lower absenteeism rates.[4] A group of women had been assembling radar equipment according to methods suggested by the engineering department. For the study, the group was given an opportunity to supervise their own methods and goals. The women had full access to cost information and could request the assistance of staff specialists. After implementing their own system, the assembly time per unit dropped from 138 hours to eighty-six hours. At this point, a second goal-setting session was conducted. The women suggested that they did not need a supervisor. In their opinion, they were ready to practice self-control. They did agree to keep the supervisor informed but requested permission to direct their own activities. The assembly time for the unit was eventually reduced to thirty-six hours. Though this example is exceptional, it illustrates the positive response of people to change when they are allowed to help in the decision-making process.

3. The workers' trust in the supervisor's authority can affect their acceptance of change. If workers' past experience with change has not been good, it will be almost impossible to convince them that more changes will prove beneficial. Most workers require definite evidence of management's sincerity in turning over a new leaf before they will fully accept any change in their work environment. Because trust has not been created, a new supervisor will experience much greater difficulty initiating new techniques and procedures than will a familiar, trusted supervisor. The new supervisor must first establish a reputation for fairness among workers. For a supervisor beginning a new job, it may be good practice to "lie low" for a while, observing the relationships

---

[4] Charles L. Hughes, "Applying Behavioral Science in Manufacturing Supervision," *Proceedings of the Ninth Annual Midwest Management Conference* (Carbondale, Ill.: Bureau of Business Research, Southern Illinois University, 1966), pp. 85–89.

that exist and the degree of trust that workers have in management. Aggressive, rapid restructuring of work situations can build more hostility among workers than almost any other kind of action—especially if the supervisor doing the restructuring is new and unknown.

4. How to overcome resistance to change.   One researcher has identified two ways of gaining acceptance for a necessary change.[5] The first is to increase pressures for the change. This can be done by winning over the informal leader of the work group or by circulating information about the benefits of the change. Still another way is to get workers not directly affected by the change to approve the new idea. Peer pressure, if wisely encouraged, can be a very strong tool in speeding the acceptance of change.

Another way to win acceptance is to eliminate as many of the resisting factors as possible. If you can find out why your workers are opposing a particular change, you may be able to compromise or readjust so that negative attitudes are overcome. An example of this method occurred when a group of female factory workers objected to a new requirement that they wear hard hats on the job. Management set about discovering the workers' specific objections, then proceeded to overcome the resistance.

The first resistance factor was removed when it was found that lighter, more comfortable hats could be substituted at a cost of about five cents more. The employer was willing to make this additional expenditure in order to gain cooperation. Next, a contest was announced. Each woman was to decorate her hat in whatever way she thought appropriate. This not only made the hats more attractive, it gave each individual a chance for self-expression. When these resistance factors were removed, the wearing of protective hats gained positive support and negative pressure was overcome in a lasting and positive way.

5. Do not make changes unless they are necessary.   Changing something for the sake of change adds nothing but confusion and uncertainty in a work situation. Even though the benefits of change may be great, there is always a price to be paid in terms of workers' attitudes and the necessity of readjustment. Our society is changing so rapidly in many areas over which we have little or no control that it seems senseless to introduce change merely for variety. Unnecessary change can also cause workers to distrust their supervisor.

Figure 20-1 illustrates how each individual views and reacts to a change in environment.

It is the supervisor's responsibility to see that any changes made in the department are necessary and reasonable. Just as movement is not always progress, change is not necessarily an improvement.

Middle-aged supervisors and workers alike may often be heard to long for a return to "the good old days." In fact, those "good old days" may exist only in the imaginations of those who feel that the past outranks the present or the future.

Because you as a supervisor will share in creating change, you must take care that you do it effectively and with consideration for other people. The core of good supervision is the ability to find and maintain the correct balance of order and creativity, progress, and stability. In other words, "The art of progress is to preserve order amid change, and to preserve change amid order."

[5] Based on Kurt Lewin et al., *Field Theory in Social Science* (New York: Harper, 1951).

A major change is proposed.	The worker evaluated the impact as	and responds to the change by
	_____ destructive.	_____ opposing it.
	_____ threatening.	_____ tolerating it.
	_____ uncertain.	_____ accepting it.
	_____ good.	_____ joining in it.
	_____ very positive.	

Personal decision is affected

_____ extent of information about the change.

_____ extent of participation in the change decision.

_____ trust in the initiator of the change.

_____ past experience with change.

Figure 20-1. An Individual's Response to Change. [Adapted from Robert M. Fulmer, *The New Management,* 2nd ed. (New York: Macmillan Publishing Co., Inc., 1978), p. 367.]

The Three Steps of Change

It is common knowledge that people do not change easily. Nevertheless, people *do* change their attitudes and beliefs, their values, and their behavior. As we have already seen, the process is not easy, but it does follow a fairly regular pattern for each individual. The steps outlined below are the steps each individual must take in order to accept and implement a change. These stages can be briefly labeled as (1) *rejection* of the old attitude or behavior, (2) *transition* from the old to the new, and (3) full *acceptance* of the new behavior pattern or attitude.[6]

Rejection of the Old: Step One

Regardless of the subject, if people are willing to learn something new, they can. Though there are many kinds of learning, including acquiring new skills or changing behavior or attitudes, all learning depends on the learner's willingness and ability to *unlearn* something old in order to *learn* something new. Let us follow an example through these stages of change.

Ralph Cross is the supervisor of a quick-service chain restaurant with few patrons. Ralph has always believed in the power of negative thinking, the laziness of the average worker, and the superiority of himself. In other words, he follows the authoritarian approach to supervision. Ralph decides to sign up for a course in supervision at his local college, since passing the course may earn him a promotion and a raise. During the course, Ralph learns that many people believe ten lashes every Friday is not the best way to retain competent, cooperative workers, and he begins to realize why the turnover rate in his restaurant is so high and service so poor. Ralph begins to *unlearn* some of those things he has always believed about the proper way to supervise.

[6] Based on Edgar H. Schein, "Management Development as a Process of Influence," *Industrial Management Review,* 1968, pp. 56–76.

Transition: Step Two

Internalization is the process of trying, adopting, and using new attitudes or methods. In many cases, an individual will internalize new ideas because they seem to work for other people, or because someone else holds those ideas. If the person has begun to reject old ideas, he or she may be willing to consider the new and find out how it works. If the new idea or approach works, then that person will probably accept it and put it to use in daily activities.

In our example, Ralph learns about democratic and participatory leadership from his course. He also meets a fellow in his class who has been using that method for years with excellent results. Ralph becomes good friends with this classmate and learns to respect him. At this stage, Ralph decides that he will try this different method of handling employees. Cautiously at first, he begins to offer praise instead of criticism. He begins to let his workers have more responsibility in their own work areas and checks up on them less frequently. He begins to ask their opinions about improving service and working conditions. After the initial shock dies down among his employees, they begin making constructive suggestions, taking better care of their work areas, and greeting customers more cheerfully. Since Ralph has not been at all sure of himself in this new approach, he has watched carefully for any signs that his employees are slacking off or responding negatively to the "new" Ralph. To his surprise, his changed attitude brings about improvements throughout the restaurant.

Acceptance of the New: Step Three

The final stage of the change process is the acceptance of the new attitude or approach and implementation of that approach in the individual's daily life. The new idea becomes a part of the person, replacing the old. Acceptance takes time, and it is necessary that the individual have support from other people.

Ralph fully accepts his new supervisory style as the appropriate method only after the area supervisor comes by the restaurant for a spot check. He is amazed at the cleanliness, friendly service, and cooperative attitudes evident throughout the operation. At his recommendation, Ralph *does* receive a substantial raise—not for passing a course, but for increasing productivity and worker satisfaction. As time passes, Ralph completely changes his attitudes toward supervision and fully accepts a more democratic style of leadership. He must continue to learn, for the processes are new to him, but after the results of his trial, he is willing to relearn ways of doing things to fit his new beliefs. After several years, Ralph would probably not believe anyone who told him that his employees used to call him "The Dictator."

A Word of Warning

Although it probably took you only a few minutes to read this description of the process of change, remember that change occurs much more slowly in the real world. Each stage requires time, and more time is required for a major change than for a minor one. It is not easy to unlearn things we have done from childhood, then relearn and accept new methods.

From the time we are very small, all of us begin to internalize a certain set of attitudes, beliefs, and patterns of behavior. Though the time may come when change is so common and accepted that the relearning process is much less difficult, that time has not yet arrived. Supervisors should remember that change is not an easy task for most people, and that they should treat people gently when uprooting and replacing any cherished and comfortable beliefs, attitudes, and behavior patterns.

Summary

Our age is characterized by increasingly rapid change. In all phases of life, change occurs so dramatically and so fast that we are often bewildered. Basically, change may be thought of as any alteration, substitution, new development or process, or difference from the way things have been.

Equilibrium in a work organization means that people know what to expect of each other and of their work environment. Their relationships are steady and stable, and they are likely to oppose change which alters those relationships. The supervisor must (1) gain acceptance for necessary changes, and then (2) help restore the equilibrium, or balance, of the work group.

Some of the reasons for resistance to change are (1) economic, or the threat of losing one's job or earning ability, (2) inconvenience in having to learn something new, (3) uncertainty caused by fears of being inadequate or of being unprepared for a strange situation, (4) threats to social relationships, and (5) resentment at being reminded that management can impose powerful controls.

There are several guidelines that the supervisor may find helpful in coping with resistance to change among workers. They urge a supervisor to (1) recognize all the factors in a change situation, (2) gain support through worker participation, (3) gain workers' trust in supervisory authority, (4) overcome resistance by increasing the pressures for change or by eliminating the resisting factors, and (5) make changes only when absolutely necessary.

Change is a process and can be traced through (1) the rejection of the old, (2) the transition from the old to the new, and (3) the acceptance of the new. Each step takes time, for people do not change their attitudes or behavior patterns easily.

It is possible that some day people will learn to accept change eagerly. Until then, supervisors must remain aware of the dynamics of change and must be sensitive to the feelings of their workers when changes are initiated. We may be learning how to deal with change more effectively, but resistance to change is still very much with us.

Key Terms

Acceptance. The final stage in the process of change, in which a new idea, method, or procedure is fully accepted.

Change. Any alteration, substitution, or new development in organizational structure, personnel hierarchy, procedural requirements, or processing techniques that affects the nature of an individual's job or work environment.

Equilibrium. When the various factors that keep a business going are in a state of balance.

Point of Pressure. The spot in the total environment at which a change is taking place.

Rejection. The first stage in the change process, during which an old idea, method, or procedure is discarded as obsolete or inappropriate.

Transition. The middle phase of the change process, in which the new idea or procedure is tested before being fully accepted.

Review Questions

1. Why has the rate of change accelerated in this country?
2. It is said that a company can be in a state of equilibrium. How is this possible in a time of such rapid change?
3. Coping with change gives a supervisor considerable responsibilities to workers and the organization. List and describe the supervisor's responsibilities.
4. List and describe why both workers and management would resist change.
5. Describe a situation in which change in a work situation produces changes in the relationships among group members.
6. List and describe some practical rules for overcoming resistance to change.
7. Describe how participatory decision making can be used as a tool to facilitate the acceptance of change.
8. How can a supervisor build a work atmosphere that will be receptive to inevitable and necessary changes?
9. Is change for the sake of change a good idea? Why or why not?
10. Describe in detail the three stages of change.
11. Describe the role of learning in accepting change.

Exercises

I. Predicting Change

Take a look into the future and make a list of the changes likely to occur in your company in the next five years. Consider such areas as working conditions, wages, prices, available equipment and resources, the labor market, promotion opportunities, new products or services, and restructuring of the work environment. Then try to think of ways to put the changes into operation without creating major resistance. Finally, try to decide whether the change will be a simple or a difficult one, easily accepted or likely to be rejected. The following chart may serve as a guide for completing this exercise.

II. Getting Change Accepted

In your department, workers have always been fairly flexible in being able to change their tasks and shift from one job to another as the situation required. Now, however, management has decided that job descriptions and more rigid job control methods

Change Prediction Chart

Current Practice	Predicted Change	Method of Getting Change Accepted	Predicted Ease or Difficulty of Change

are needed. Although you fought their decision, you lost, and you must set up a system for developing specific job descriptions for your workers and getting them to accept certain specific job responsibilities. Develop and write a plan for guiding your workers through the stages of the change process, keeping in mind methods of restoring disrupted equilibrium and overcoming resistance.

Case 20 • Joanna A. Danna

Joanna A. Danna is a shift supervisor for the LaLetta Hosiery Manufacturing Co., Inc. The factory assigns each work group a production quota and measures progress on a weekly basis. Joanna's group has not met its quota for the last two weeks even though it has been working hard. Equipment failures have been frequent over the last six months, and after interruptions for repairs, the lost time appears to make it impossible to catch up with the schedule. This is a problem throughout the plant, which has largely antiquated machinery, badly in need of repair or replacement.

Today, at a meeting of shift supervisors, Joanna is told that the company is moving to a more modern facility located about ten miles from the existing factory. The move will begin in exactly three months, and for one month before the move, extraordinary shifts will be added, and require half the work force on Saturdays and Sundays. Joanna knows that this development will not be popular with her subordinates. She also expects some resistance to the move because of its distance from the city, the fact that that area of the county is not serviced by regional transportation buses, and that established patterns will be disrupted for many workers. She is especially concerned that child-care facilities will not be as accessible.

1. How can Joanna plan for this move and minimize worker resistance?

2. How can she handle the problem, which will take time, when time is already at a premium because of failure to meet quotas?

3. What kind of support can she expect from the company's management during the transition? From other shift supervisors?

CHAPTER 21

Supervisory Management and the Future

It is very difficult to prophesy. Especially about the future.

Chinese proverb

Learning Objectives

- To learn to plan for the future in order to make the most of the present.
- To develop objectivity and care in dealing with future predictions, whether continuations of present trends or major changes.
- To learn the difference between crystal ball gazing and making probable estimates of what the future will be like.
- To discover which business trends and changes are expected to occur in the next few decades.
- To investigate supervisory styles that prevailed in the past and predict some characteristics of tomorrow's supervisor.

Actually, it is very easy to prophesy about the future. The difficulty comes in being right.

341

If you could climb into science fiction's time machine and travel to the year 2000, what would you find? Would a look at that not-so-distant year make a difference in the way you do things now? Over the centuries, speculating on the future has held many people spellbound. Though they often ignored the present, they were captivated by imagining what could take place in a hundred, two hundred, or a thousand years.

What is the use in planning for a future so distant we can hardly comprehend it? Are those hours used to develop fifteen- and fifty-year plans wasted? Since it is obvious that the future cannot be known until it is the present, are we wasting valuable time and effort that could be better used to make the present more understandable and desirable?

If we do not plan, we lay our future in the hands of chance. Everybody—individuals, governments, small businesses, and giant corporations—must prepare for the future. And, though the future remains unpredictable, our ability to forecast future events may mean the difference between successful adaptation and failure to cope with change.

In spite of all our interest in the future, we cannot leave the present. We can never think big enough to anticipate all the future's possibilities. We can study the trends, try to overcome our preconceived ideas, gather our knowledge, and attempt reasonable predictions, but our forecasting powers remain severely limited. Many of the "facts" we know today will be tomorrow's myths, and we may be forced to build new foundations for our assumptions and procedures. In fact, the only tool we can build today that may help us conquer future challenges is an open mind.

Facts and Fantasies

One day it will be interesting to see how accurately today's predictors foresaw the changes ahead. Forecasts range all the way from continuations of current trends to wild science fiction fantasies. The real world of the future will probably lie somewhere between these two extremes. Recent years have exposed us all to so many fascinating and drastic changes that it is easy to believe the future will not resemble the present.

Time after time, science fiction has unerringly pointed to unusual inventions that seem commonplace today. Jules Verne wrote about submarines before they skulked the seas, Buck Rogers' spaceship has circled the moon, and George Orwell's *1984* threatens to emerge from just around the corner. At the same time, much science fiction is pure fantasy, with no basis in science or technology.

What are we to believe about the future? We may find that the truth will come close to the story of the investor who had himself frozen and returned to life one hundred years later. Upon awakening, he dashed to the phone and called the stock market. To his great delight, he found he could sell his IBM stock for $3 million per share, and his AT&T holdings had risen to $4 million a share. With visions of yachts and mansions dancing in his head, he was about to inquire about his other holdings. At that moment, the operator interrupted and requested another $50,000 for the next three minutes. For the investor, some figures had changed, but this future was much like the past.

On the other hand, any seer's wildest imaginings may turn from fiction to fact. One writer has described the business executive of the future as a person who shuttles back and forth between planets, speaks many languages, and conducts business from a computer terminal in the home or rocket.[1] The executive will have thousands of employees, support several families, and conduct worldwide business dealings from the comfort of a well-stocked command post. This super supervisor may be a regular user of pepper-uppers, intelligence vitamins, tension-reducing pills, and personality-modifying drugs.

After we have speculated and debated about what is to come, one fact remains—the future is not here yet. As there is no sure way to *know* what will happen in the future, we must remain open-minded, realize the possibilities, and try to chart the best course.

The Supervisor Faces the Future

You know that your day-to-day predictions and forecasts of the immediate future are very important. You can often sense developments as they are occurring and plan your actions around these forecasts. Because of the rapidly increasing rate of change and technological development, it is critical that the supervisor develop a feeling for the distant future. Although long-range predictions have a lower possibility of being accurate, they *can* help you plan effectively and foresee events before they happen.

Of course, no one is suggesting that we study a crystal ball. Relevant questions will provide a more efficient and predictable way of foretelling the future. What will consumer demand be like in five or ten years? What kinds of products will consumers be buying? What resources will be so scarce that substitutes must be found? What new demands will the labor force make? What will be the educational requirements for workers of the future? What kinds of equipment and processes are likely to be developed to make tasks easier? Though these questions cannot be answered definitely, it should be possible to spot those trends that are likely to continue and to identify new trends that may develop.

There is a danger, however, in predicting the future. Many people assume that the future will be much like the present: The status quo will remain basically the same, and the world will be conducting business as usual. With change taking place at the current pace, this is a dangerous assumption indeed. Many factors will interfere with "business as usual." Increasing consumer awareness, decreasing resource supplies, a shift to service rather than manufacturing industries, and many other developments will probably alter the course of many business practices. Planning on status quo assumptions is much like building a house on the beach at low tide. It is important to ask why certain changes have occurred in the past and why certain others are likely to occur. What has happened is less valuable in predicting the future than *why* it happened, because the "why's" may provide some of the answers we seek about future events.

Many people have attempted to predict the future of supervision and business in general. Articles about the future, frequently found in professional publications, discuss changes in organizational structure, automation, information tech-

<hr>

[1] Auren Uris, "Executives of the Future," *Nation's Business,* January 1969.

nology, labor relations, working conditions, and professional development. More recently, resource supplies and pollution controls have been added to the list of topics. Many of these writers are experts in their fields, but their opinions are still just that—opinions. The major value in reading and talking about the future is that it can stimulate each of us to think about what may happen and how we shall react. The opinions of experts make an excellent foundation on which to build, but each of us must construct a personal version of what is likely to happen.

Working More or Less

There is a belief that people of the future will not have much work to do. We hear stories about workers putting in ten-hour weeks and producing twice what they now do in forty hours. It is likely that automation and increased efficiency will reduce the work week, but it is unlikely that most of us will be without jobs. Current labor force trends indicate that the work week will remain much the same for the next twenty years.

Pleasant as it would be to reduce our work weeks, there is too much to be done. Machines can certainly take over many of the tedious, time-consuming, and boring jobs that have trapped us, but there can be no substitute for human creativity, skills, and intelligence. As productivity increases, consumer and industrial demands will probably keep pace. Service industries will mushroom to offset the loss of jobs to automation. We shall have increased discretionary income and more leisure time for the pursuit of satisfaction for higher-level human needs.

In 1900, the average working American spent about one-fourth of the day in leisure time. By 1950, workers were taking it easy about one-third of the time. If the trend had continued at the same rate, Americans would be spending almost half of their days in leisure pursuits by the year 2000. Unfortunately, economic pressures have affected this progress, and for many individuals, extra jobs have provided the only means of staying up with inflation. During the 1970s, the number of "moonlighters," people with more than one job, increased almost 20 percent and the number of women holding multiple jobs doubled. The average family today has 1.7 workers. About half of the families making above the median income do so because two members of the family work. At the same time, we can anticipate that the average work week will shorten. Holidays will be more frequent and vacations longer.

Changes in Population and the Work Force

Despite a decline in the birth rate and the overall rate of growth, total population in the United States will continue to grow. By the year 2000, the U.S. population will stand at approximately 262,494,000. The greatest amount of growth will take place among those who are middle-aged and elderly. However, the number of children under thirteen years of age will grow significantly in this period, to almost 13 percent. The number of teenagers will actually decline, while that of young adults will grow at a very negligible rate.

The U.S. Labor Department estimates that the work force will move from approximately 100 million workers in 1980 to approximately 117 million in 1999. Labor force participation by women will grow from 37 million in 1975 to almost 50 million in 1999. As for age composition, the labor force will grow primarily in the central age group. The number of people between the ages of sixteen and twenty-four in the labor force will actually decline between now and 1990. The same is true of workers who are fifty-five years of age and older.

There is certain to be a large increase in women working. Much of the increase will come from women aged forty-five and over. During the recent past, women workers in this category grew three times as fast as male employment in the same age bracket. But the number of younger workers will also increase dramatically. By 1990, they will amount to nearly 29 percent of the total labor force.

In the immediate future, labor specialists foresee a glut of qualified workers at the high and low ends of the occupational totem pole. Employment opportunities in jobs generally filled by college graduates and by people with only an elementary school education will not increase fast enough to fill the projected need. By 1985, white-collar employment will account for more than half the jobs in the country. The proportion of direct service workers—including people doing everything from emptying bed pans to providing police and fire protection—should increase and grow to about 14 percent of the total work force. Though the number of people involved in blue-collar jobs may rise, their share in total employment will probably drop to about 33 percent.

U.S. News and World Report has estimated that the United States faces the monumental challenge of creating an average of 72,110 jobs every week for the decade between 1976 and 1986. This means 3.75 million jobs per year, in addition to those that will open up because of retirement and death. That number of openings will be required to provide work for those seeking jobs for the first time, workers displaced by machines and new technology, and those unemployed. The challenge of creating so many jobs is staggering.

The Emerging Service Economy

Some fields will acquire more workers while other fields lose them. New jobs will be created and old jobs will become obsolete. The Council on Trends and Perspectives of the U.S. Chamber of Commerce predicts that the growth of service activities will continue. Already the United States is the only country in the world that employs more than one-half of its labor force in the production of services rather than goods. The fastest growing segment of the service industry is government employment, particularly state and local government. Among the slowest growing industries are mining and agriculture.

Those who study human society are cautious about making predictions, but it is possible, nevertheless, to perceive certain trends. Futurists—those who make a profession of studying such trends—use the term "postindustrial society" to mean the kind of society we are heading toward in the United States and other developed countries. Every age has its dominant institutions. As we have already seen, agriculture and industry have taken turns on the throne of our economy. But now, the scepter is likely to go to the quaternary sector. The quaternary sector includes some of the most rapidly expanding fields.

Table 21-1. Where the Jobs Will Be.

	Goods-Producing Industries	Service Industries
1976	26,800,000	60,700,000
1990	30,700,000	74,750,000
2000	32,200,000	82,260,000
Change 1976–2000	Up 20.1%	Up 35.5%

Table 21-1 indicates that the service (quaternary) sector of our economy will continue to grow at a much faster rate than the goods-producing portion of the economy.

The Value of Education

In the recent past, expenditures for a college education have been viewed as an investment in a better future. Several studies have shown that a college education pays off financially while helping an individual become a better-informed citizen. Today, some people are debating the desirability of advanced education for all citizens. Some studies indicate that the rate of return on a college education fell from 11–12 percent in 1979 to 7–8 percent at the present time. These figures are based on projected lifetime earnings for a college graduate minus tuition and other costs (such as lost income) incurred while in college. Naturally, the return on investment is higher for students who major in a "practical" discipline such as business or engineering.

Although there is a tendency to question the desirability of advanced education for everyone, the best jobs will still be available to people who are well trained. The length of time spent in formal education will continue to grow, although the rate of increase will not be as fast as it was during the 1960s.

Emerging Attitudes Toward Work

Workers have already begun to expect more from their jobs. This trend will continue in the future for several reasons: desire for an increased standard of living, more education, continuing automation at the workplace, and vast changes in the environment. To the problem of rising expectations will be added that of finding jobs for the hard-core unemployed. We have learned how to avoid mass unemployment of the kind the United States experienced in the 1930s. But though the right fiscal and monetary policies can keep the economy expanding, and provide jobs for perhaps 95 percent of the labor force, this still leaves several million workers who are unable to find employment. Many of them lack the necessary education or training, many have little motivation to work, and some happen to live in areas where few jobs are available. The problem of the hard-core unemployed will yield only to a cooperative effort on the part of business, government, and education. We may get some help in this effort from our experience in training workers during

World War II, when the labor force had to be greatly expanded, as well as from experience in employing the blind and other handicapped persons.

Why Work?

The changing value systems of workers and the changing demands of production are likely to create some unprecedented motivational problems. For companies interested in recruiting and keeping capable employees, paychecks and fringe benefits will probably come to mean less than job satisfaction. The help wanted ads of the future may include, along with the salary being offered, a description of the opportunities for education and self-development.

Another expected trend is the gradual disappearance of the wage-salary difference among workers. The growth of benefit programs (especially income security programs and short work week provisions) over the past twenty years has laid some groundwork for a shift to salaries for workers who are now paid by the hour. And regular workers in some industries may gradually get guarantees of annual earnings. Labor market conditions may make such guarantees of salaried status necessary in order to attract and hold skilled workers. Actually, the cost of substituting salaries for hourly wages in an economy with high employment and few layoffs may be negligible.

Income maintenance is another potential development. There will be proposals to raise and maintain the income level of employed workers who are not earning enough to keep their families out of the poverty ranks. These will probably be extended to unemployed workers as well. Income maintenance will be financed through some sort of negative income tax—that is, people below a certain level of income will receive payments from the government according to their income. As they rise out of the poverty ranks, the benefits they receive will taper off. It is generally expected that some form of income maintenance program will be enacted during the next decade although initial research indicates that such programs tend to reduce the desire to seek employment.

People are not going to retire much earlier than they do now. Truck drivers, airline pilots, and police officers may be exceptions to this. Many other workers will wait until after age sixty-five to retire in order to maintain their standard of living.

Crises in Cities

By the year 2000, approximately three-fourths of the U.S. population will be living in the thirty largest metropolitan areas. Almost certainly, the air will be dirtier, the slums even more unlivable, traffic more unmovable, and the psychological tolls of overcrowding greater. Financial crises in major cities will become more common. Services provided by cities are becoming much more expensive. At the same time, many of the larger cities are experiencing a declining tax base as property values fall when businesses and people move to the suburbs. In 1978, citizens across the country indicated that they were tired of paying higher taxes for deteriorating services.

The crises in the cities are complicated by the threatening shortages in the nation's power supply and raw materials. For years, warnings have been advanced that we are using up natural resources at too fast a rate. People finally started paying attention in 1974 and 1980 when they had to wait in long lines to buy gasoline and found the previous price doubled when they got to the tank. Once the lines disappeared, people adjusted to paying higher prices and stopped worrying. Prices everywhere were going up, and it was easy to assume that this was the way that things were going to be.

Since salaries are also increasing, people tend to assume that they are better off. Recently, however, incomes have not been increasing as quickly as prices. Many observers believe that the real purchasing power of the average worker increased almost 60 percent between 1940 and 1965. Between 1965 and the present, the income for middle-class families who have not supplemented their incomes by extra jobs, would have lost 20 to 30 percent of their purchasing power.

Social Problem Solvers

Supervisors and managers may be expected to become political experts in the future. Governmental and community problem-solving processes will play a greater role in business as the public begins to demand the business community pay more attention to the "quality of life." Areas that will require more attention include the continuing education and personal development of employees, the level of product and service quality, and business's contribution to solving urban problems such as transportation, pollution, education, and minority relations.

Historically, the American economy has developed from fulfilling subsistence needs to supplying luxury wants. We are now developing a market based on "human fulfillment" wants. Subsistence needs play a less important role for the American consumer than do social and psychological needs, and this trend can be expected to continue. The consumer will want to develop talents and interests, improve as a person, maintain an attractive and livable environment, reduce suffering and poverty for others, and attain a generally higher quality of life. People want increased opportunities for education, health care, and culture. They will demand cleaner, safer cities and improved environmental conditions. These new wants are creating a vast new market. It has been estimated that the market for these new wants and needs could total $100 billion per year for the rest of this century.

Most of these predictions sound encouraging, but there is no guarantee that they will come true. Indeed, the current economic paradox of spiraling prices and an erratic stock market suggests that we may be plagued by inflation and shortages into the indefinite future. If inflation does not subside, any wage and earning gains will be absorbed by rising prices. If we continue to squander our vital resources without providing for their replacement, they will not support our present rate of economic growth for long.

Supervisory Management: Past, Present, and Future

In a less liberated era, Bob Hope remarked that "women's styles may change, but their designs remain essentially the same." This may also hold true for supervisors. The supervisor's task has always been to achieve goals efficiently through the efforts of others, but styles of supervision change, and the supervisor of 1850 would be just as inappropriate today as a coach and four horses in the parking lot.

By examining model styles of supervision from the past, however, we may be able to identify appropriate styles of leadership for the present and predict future trends in supervisory management. In the first section of this book, we talked about the opportunities and challenges of supervision as a career. We then turned to the most difficult lesson of all—"Know thyself."

In the next section, we discussed the personal skills of communication and creativity that are invaluable to any supervisor and analyzed time management, legal challenges, and personal ethics. We then turned to the administrative skills so essential to managing others—planning, decision making, organization, personnel, control, and information.

The final section dealt with human relations skills: developing the ability to handle the job of supervision through working with groups, understanding labor relations and worker motivation, knowing how to be an effective leader, and being able to cope with change.

Throughout these chapters, we have emphasized principles to guide the supervisor's behavior in the practice of professional management. We have also attempted to relate basic concepts to the reader's own experience.

In this chapter, we turned our attention to probable and possible developments of the future. Our supervisory tasks in the present will be guided largely by what we expect of the future.

Tomorrow's Ideal Supervisor

Though supervisors of the future will not be superhuman by any means, they will probably possess certain sets of identifiable characteristics. The following five styles of supervision were all popular at one point in our history, and some survive today. By looking at these five, we may be able to summarize some of the major characteristics of tomorrow's ideal supervisor.

Turn-of-the-Century Tarzan

In the early 1900s, labor was the cheapest part of doing business. Supervisors and managers had no need to consider human relations, motivation, communication, job enrichment, or other "nonproductive" activities. The emphasis was on getting the highest production for the lowest wage. Upton Sinclair's famous novel, *The Jungle,* depicts the terrible conditions under which workers labored during this era. The scarcity of jobs created a veritable jungle. The supervisor could swing through the vines, holler and strut, and consign to the quicksand pits anyone who did not perform. Unfortunately, these prewar supervisory Tarzans were not on the side of right or humane working conditions. The common opinion was that if "good horses cost $200 but you can get a hire for 50 cents a day," then horses should be treated better.

Conditions improved slowly, but concern for employees was not in style. Though studies were conducted during this period that could have led to more humane supervision, business's concern for reversing the Depression kept the hard-nosed supervisory style popular until the 1940s.

The 1940s Happiness Crowd

In the postwar period, conditions improved considerably. Psychology and sociology were used as tools to force greater production from the labor force. Supervisors in these days practiced "country club management," based on something known as "cow psychology." The premise was that if contented cows gave more milk, contented workers would produce better also.

When Linus, in the "Peanuts" comic strip, heard someone say that people were placed on earth to make others happy, he said, "I guess I'd better start doing a better job . . . I'd hate to be shipped back." Supervisors in this period were not running the risk of being shipped back either. They enrolled in training courses by the thousands and studied behavioral and social sciences to learn the key to human behavior. Despite their useful and beneficial knowledge, most supervisors still had a tendency to manipulate rather than truly manage.

Management by Objectives—The 1950s

The second half of the twentieth century ushered profits to the fore in most companies. Management by objectives or results was the style of the day, and the objectives were almost always higher profits. Supervisors who could cut costs, increase production, keep their workers happy, and keep the accountant smiling stayed at the top of the heap. Some businesses learned, however, that short-term profits could cripple future developments when the importance of profits overwhelmed evaluation efforts.

The Generalists of the 1960s

In the 1960s, supervisors considered themselves generalists—people who knew a little bit of everything about managing employees. They were judged more by what their employees did than by their own actions because they worked through the organization to accomplish their goals, rather than rely solely on their personal efforts.

In the 1960s, under the full impact of rapid change, these supervisors faced the task of adapting to and dealing with complex and varied situations. Under these conditions, the generalist discovered that traditional guidelines to supervision were no longer useful, and in attempts to shift with the wind, became overly flexible.

The Systems Supervisor of the 1970s

The model supervisor of the 1970s was able to find a type of fixed flexibility. Although highly adaptive, he or she was more than a firefighter. Needing the ability to relate many activities to the overall objectives, they possessed a broad view of the "big picture." Even if responsible for a specific division or department, the systems supervisor saw this area as a subsystem of the corporate whole. When Charlie Brown was asked if he knew the mystery of life, he promptly responded, "Be kind, don't smoke, be prompt, smile a lot, eat sensibly, avoid cavities and mark your ballot carefully . . . avoid too much sun, send overseas packages early, insure your belongings, and try to keep the ball low." Although managers of the 1970s did not have the answer so well in hand, they did recognize the diversity of their responsibilities; they were decision makers and delegators.

The Contingency Coordinator of the 1980s

One of the earliest attributes of successful supervision was *coordination.* One of the most recent advances in management theory is the recognition of the importance of the *uniqueness* in each situation and the contingencies that apply. The model supervisor of the next decade will combine these two important characteristics. This approach also recognizes and builds upon the situational emphasis of the 1960s and the systems orientation of the 1970s.

Contingency coordinators recognize that every situation is unique. Thus they will not attempt to apply hard and fast rules; they will anticipate developments and be able to draw from past education and experience to keep things moving toward predetermined objectives. The watchwords of this type of supervisor are anticipatory, adaptive, and assertive. The contingency coordinator anticipates the uncertain and unpredictable nature of the future. Yet, he or she works to keep surprises at a minimum. Though vision into the future is seldom crystal-clear, this supervisor has a concern for what is about to happen.

Despite tremendous uncertainty in a period of rapid change, the contingency coordinator must be prepared to move assertively in order to cope with the internal demands of the organization and the external challenges to the organization. Management has never been a comfortable career for the recluse, and the future demands both courage and commitment.

The primary characteristics of the model supervisor of the next decade can be summarized as follows:

1. Supervisors will not stand alone. They will recognize the importance of the wide variety of interrelationships that connect their departments, the corporation, country, and the world. They will need to be generalists, knowledgeable in many areas. At the same time, they will be specialists in communications, leadership, and other essential supervisory skills.

2. They will be concerned with production, profits, professionalism, and people. Production levels formed the first basis for evaluating a supervisor's work; then the focus shifted to profits as guidelines for action. Later, employee morale was considered the foundation for evaluation. Today's supervisor understands that all three aspects are important, and understands that they must be balanced in order to meet objectives. Production will continue to be important because it provides a means for worker satisfaction and a base for continued profits. Profits will retain a place of honor because they keep our economic system operating and provide for the continued existence of the company. But people are now recognized as the most valuable resource of all, for they provide the means for reaching production objectives and insuring profits. This supervisor will be a true professional, dedicated to excellence in all aspects of life.

3. The formal education process will be continuous for them. Twenty years ago, college courses for supervisors were nonexistent. In these days of rapid change, however, professional managers and supervisors will become better educated and will take frequent refresher courses and retraining sessions to cope with changing practices and procedures. Successful supervisors will find that they can never stop learning. Continued education will be essential to keep the supervisor from becoming as obsolete as the last century's machinery.

In the 1980s, supervisors must be coordinators; they must make many things work together and draw upon many areas of knowledge and many previous experiences. The supervisors of tomorrow will use the best of the past to make the future better.

Summary

Tomorrow cannot be known until it becomes the present, but if we do not plan, we lay our future in the hands of chance. Our ability to foresee the future may mean the difference between successful adaptation and failure to cope with change.

Predictors of the future have foreseen developments ranging all the way from continuations of current trends to outrageous science fiction fantasies. Since the future is where we shall spend the rest of our lives, it is important to consider the opinions of experts in formulating our own opinions of what is to come.

It is important to ask why certain changes have occurred in the past and why certain others are likely to occur. What has happened is less valuable in predicting the future than finding out *why* it happened.

Some important areas in business's future include changes in organizational structure, automation, information technology, labor relations, working conditions, professional development, resource supplies, and pollution controls.

Several trends were identified that can be expected to continue in the future. Among these trends are (1) more work accomplished in fewer hours; (2) changes in the work force, especially in age and sex characteristics; (3) new types of work as service industries become dominant; (4) changing attitudes about work accompanied with increasing affluence; (5) new reasons for working; and (6) continued economic expansion.

We examined five styles of supervision from the past and characterized the supervisor of the future. The past leadership styles were (1) the turn-of-the-century Tarzan, (2) the 1940s happiness crowd, (3) management by objectives in the 1950s, (4) the generalists of the 1960s, and (5) the systems supervisor of the 1970s.

The contingency coordinators of the 1980s will be aware of the broad scope of personal activities and responsibilities, as well as interrelationships within the system. They will display supervisory characteristics that set them apart from former types: (1) they will not stand alone; (2) they will be concerned with production, profits, professionalism, and people; and (3) their education will not be an accomplished state in their lives, but a process.

Key Terms

Income Maintenance. Programs designed to sustain the income of workers near the poverty level and to raise their standard of living.

Limits to Growth. Restrictions on company expansion deriving from the complex interrelationships among the shifting levels of population, food supply, resources, industrial output, and pollution.

Negative Income Tax. A form of income maintenance that proposes to tax workers above a certain income level and make cash payments to those below this level, with taxes and benefits based on a sliding scale.

Service Industry. An industry composed of firms whose primary function is to provide services to consumers rather than produce raw materials, equipment, or consumer goods. Examples are education, dry cleaning, government, janitorial services, and advertising agencies.

Structural Unemployment. Unemployment that is "built into" the economic system, as opposed to unemployment caused by an actual shortage of jobs. Lack of education and training opportunities, a police record, physical and mental handicaps, and a history of job failures all combine to make certain individuals almost impossible to employ.

Trend. The general direction of events, economic, technical, and so on. Trends can be long- or short-term, but the patterns suggested by the trend can be traced over a period of time.

Review Questions

1. How is it possible to plan for the future when it is uncertain?
2. Writers of science fiction sometimes come very close to predicting the future. List and describe science fiction predictions you are aware of that have become reality in your lifetime.
3. Can you forecast any trends that might radically alter the way business is conducted in America?
4. It is said that workers will have increased amounts of leisure time over the next decades. How will this affect the worker-supervisor relationship?
5. What changes are likely to be made in compensation packages over the next few decades?
6. What is the impact of rapid population growth on industrial output?
7. American society has been called a "people of plenty." Will the time ever come when consumer needs and desires are fulfilled?

Exercise

The Twenty-Year Nap

Read the story and then answer the questions that follow.

You have supervised a small janitorial supply manufacturer for three years. During that time, you have seen many changes take place in worker and management attitudes, consumer demands, and production techniques and equipment. One morning when you arrive for work, you are startled to discover that the plant looks very different. There are many new faces and all sorts of strange activities going on. You begin to ask a few discreet questions and find, much to your surprise, that you—like Rip Van Winkle—have slept for twenty years! As you begin to explore the situation, you run into your former young assistant, now middle-aged and in charge of the plant. When he learns of your predicament, he agrees to spend the day showing you the plant.

1. Considering the areas listed below, imagine the changes you would find in your plant. Add any other areas you can think of.

Production techniques.   Types of goods or services produced.
Company organization.   Compensation packages.
Composition of your labor force.   Management attitudes.
Supervisor's responsibilities.   Communications equipment.
Government regulation.   Labor relations.

2. What changes in the business world as a whole might your friend tell you about?

Case 21 • Geoffrey Soma

Geoff Soma was hurtling home from his job as "people coordinator" at Laser Educational Products Corporation. His two-seat hover car, "Dragonfly," operated by remote control, would land him at his front door swiftly and safely in about ten minutes.

The training session that day at Laser had seemed endless. The three-dimensional Holotron television system—occupying one wall of the ultrasonic developmental facility—seemed like a good addition back in 1994, but it was still ominous and almost overpowering. Seven corporate vice-presidents from seven different countries had presented their plans for the coming year on one screen! The picture was so real that Geoff thought he could reach out and touch them; it made it difficult for him to grasp the implications of their plans.

Geoff pressed the digital communicator in his "Dragonfly," which connected him with the "black box" of his home computer. By pushing one button, the garage doors opened, the air conditioning unit was activated, his microwave oven started a soybean steak *a la romano con caperi,* his bath filled with water to his preferred temperature, and his automatic bar dispensed mineral water with ice.

At forty, Geoff was one of the old-timers at Laser. In a month, he was to make a presentation to the entire staff discussing changes in the business world he had observed in twenty years with the company. Using his cathode ray sketch pad while he soaked in the tub waiting for his dinner to be completed, Geoff began outlining his presentation. He reflects, "These kids were probably just born about the time I started with Laser. They won't believe the changes that have taken place over their lifetime and mine!"

1. How realistic is this picture of the future?
2. Outline the presentation you believe Geoff will make to the Laser staff.

Index

McClelland, David, 27 *n*
McCreary, E. A., 132 *n*
McGregor, Douglas M., 20 *n*, 271–72, 286 *n*
MacKenzie, R. Alec, 29 *n*, 68, 69–70, 76 *f*
Maier, Norman, R., 207 *t*
Maintenance characteristics, motivation and, 282–85
Make-work rules, 303
Management, union view of, 304
Management audits, 224–25
Management by objectives, 146, 147 *f*, 350
Managerial ethics, 93–98
  defined, 91
  influence of age on, 98–99
  public responsibilities and, 97–98
  responsibilities to associates and, 96
  responsibilities to employer and, 94
  responsibilities to immediate superior and, 96–97
  responsibility to self and, 93–94
  responsibility to workers and, 94–95
Managerial grid, 268, 269 *f*
Manipulation, motivation and, 279
Marconi, 136
Marketing information sources, 233
Maslow, Abraham H., 20 *n*, 21, 26, 27, 280 *n*, 283
Mayfield, Eugene C., 204 *n*
Mayo, Elton, 247 *n*
Media, recruitment of underprivileged minorities and, 315
Meditation, 39
Mental abilities, leadership and, 266
Merit rating programs
  purposes of, 204 *t*
  sample form of, 205, 206 *f*
Minorities
  federal training programs for, 122
  government regulations protecting, 115–23
  See also Underprivileged minorities
Money. *See* Compensation
Morale
  defined, 288–89
  and division of work, 163–64
  and informal work groups, 247
  isolation and, 249
  organizational structure and, 169
  productivity and, 288–90
Motivation
  childhood development of, 278
  comparative approaches to, 287 *f*
  compensation and, 199, 287–88
  definition of, 277–78
  of followers, 253
  in groups, 251
  human relations approach to, 281–82, 287 *f*
  morale and productivity and, 288–90
  relationship to personality and behavior, 278–79

two-factor approach to, 282–85, 287 *f*
Motivational characteristics, 282–85
Motivational needs, 27
Mouton, Jane F., 268–69
Murdick, Robert G., 221 *f*
Murphy, Dennis, 41 *n*, 232 *n*
Murphy, Edsel, 129
Murphy's Law, 129
Myers, C. A., 307 *n*
Myers, M. Scott, 283–84

National Industrial Conference Board, 171, 204 *t*
National Industrial Recovery Act, 298
National Institute of Certified Professional Managers, 23
National Labor Relations Act, 298
National Labor Relations Board (NLRB), 298
  on role of supervisors, 304–307, 308 *f*
National Management Association, 93
Needs. *See* Human needs
Noise, in communication process, 36, 37
Nominal group technique (NGT), 135
Norris-LaGuardia Act, 298

Observation, as communication, 39–40
Objectives
  communication of, 145–47
  crisis management and, 128–29
  See also Goals
Observation, for job evaluation, 195
Occupational Safety and Health Act (OSHA), 110–15
  employees' rights under, 114–15
  enforcement of, 110–11
  firms covered by, 111
  forms, 112 *f*, 113 *f*
  provisions of, 110
  record-keeping requirements of, 111–13
  supervisors and, 114–15
O'Donnell, Cyril, 166 *n*, 216 *n*
Older workers, 118
  See also Age discrimination; Retirement age
Optimizing in decision making, 134
Organization theory, 162–72
  and division of work, 162–65
  efficiency and, 161–62
  and scalar and functional processes, 165–67
  and span of management, 170–72
  and structure, 167–70
Organizational charts, 168 *f*, 169 *f*
Organizational goals, performance standards and, 202
Organizational size
  effectiveness of leadership and, 270–71
  employee morale and, 170
  interaction expansion and, 171 *f*

Organizational structure, 167–70
  departmentalization and, 167–68
  employee morale and, 169–70
  and levels of authority, 168–70
  and "tall" and "short" organizations, 171–72
Orientation, 182–84
Orwell, George, 342

Paperwork, 145
Parent role, 46, 47
Part-time work, retirement and, 321
Participation approach, 165
Pay grades, salaries based on, 196, 197 *f*
Peer performance ratings, 205
Performance evaluation, 184–85, 203–208
  appraisal interview for, 205–206, 207 *t*, 208
  and control process, 215–16
  and control standards, 215
  definition of, 203–204
  and management by objectives, 146
  and merit rating, 204
  performance standards and, 202–203
  promotion and, 187
  responsibility for, 204–205
  system for, 205, 206 *f*
Performance standards
  defined, 202
  determination of, 202–203
  job descriptions and, 201
  sample of, 203 *f*
Perkins, Frances, 137
Personal goals, decision making on, 136
Personal skills, 25
Personal values
  group control and, 256
  managerial success and, 94
Personalities
  components of, 278
  creativity and, 54–56
  of leader and group members, 271–72
  leadership and, 266
Personnel function
  compensation decisions and, 185–86
  components of, 180–88
  determination of needs, 180–81
  evaluation of performance, 184–85
  fringe benefits and, 186–87
  importance of, 179–80
  orientation, 182–84
  promotions, 187
  selection and recruitment, 181–82
  termination, 187–88
PERT technique, 222, 223 *f*
Phillips, Donald, 59–60
Phillips 66 buzz session, 59–60
Physical exertion, job evaluation and, 194
Physical traits, leadership and, 265

Skills assessment, 22–26
  comparison with average skills profile, 24
  and self-improvement techniques, 25–26
Skills Rating Chart, 22, 23 f
Sloane, Arthur A., 300 n, 301 n
Small businesses, supervisors in, 14
Smith, Adam, 162
Social accountability of corporations, 97–98
Social control. See Control process
Social needs, 249
  change in work group and, 330–31
Software, 237
Span of management, 170–72
Speaking, as communication, 40
Specialization requirements, in job evaluation, 194
Standards
  formulation of, 214–15
  job evaluation and, 215
State employment offices, 315
Status hierarchies, 252
Stogdill, Ralph, 266 n
Strauss, George, 195 n, 201 n
Strikes, management attitudes toward, 302–303
Sullerot, Evelyn, 317 n
Supervisor(s)
  attitudes toward workers, 8
  as catalyst, 8
  changes in styles of, 348–52
  communication styles of, 41–43
  compensation for, 185
  as contingency coordinators, 351–52
  as decision makers, 11, 127–28
  definition of, 6, 15, 304
  delegation and, 166
  employment opportunities for, 13–15
  female, 319
  and female workers, 318
  functions of, 11–12, 13
  human needs and, 20–22
  knowledge required of, 10–11, 15–16
  from minority groups, 122–23
  National Labor Relations Board guidelines for, 306–307, 308 f
  as overseers, 52
  of own business, 13–14
  and planning for future, 341–42
  and profit motive, 9
  role of, 7–8, 349–50
  self-rating, 22–26
  skills required of, 9–11
  span of management and, 170–72
  Theory X and Theory Y, 285–86
  time requirements of, 68
Synergy, 246–47, 253, 332
Synthesis, creativity and, 53
Systems approaches. See Forced relationship approaches
Systems supervisors, 350–51
Szymanski, Frankie, 28

Taft-Hartley Act, 298–99, 300, 303
Tariffs, 107
Task evaluation, situational approach and, 270
Task orientation, formal and informal leaders and, 252
Taylor, Charles, 26 n
Taylor, Frederick W., 68, 280 n
Termination, types of, 187–88
Texas Instruments, 122
Thinking, as communication method, 39
Time
  insufficiency of, 67–68
  as resource, 68
  supervisors' attitudes toward, 68
  See also Time management
Time budget, 29
Time Inventory Form, 76 f
Time log, use of, 75–77
Time management
  activity level and, 72–73
  importance of, 68
  time logs and, 75–77
  and time perception test, 74
  and time perspective test, 73–75
  time wasters and, 69–71, 77–78, 79 f, 80 f, 81 f
  work hours and, 72
  and workaholics, 71–72
Time perception test, 74
Time perspective test, 73–75
Timetables, development of, 153, 154 f
Toffler, Alvin, 328 n
Trade associations, 233
Training programs for disadvantaged employees, 120, 122, 316
Transactional analysis, 46–47
Transition stage of change, 336
Travis, J. W., 247 n
Tregoe, Benjamin, 132 n
Trusteeships, local unions and, 299
Two-factor approach to behavior motivation, 282–85, 287 f

Uncertainty, change and, 330
Underprivileged minorities
  benefits of employment of, 315
  characteristics of, 314–15
  hiring and training of, 316–17
  recruitment of, 315
Unethical action, illegal action compared with, 91–92
Uniform Commercial Code, 107
Union contracts, 306
  grievances and, 307
Union shop, 299
Unions
  achievements of, 304
  and avoidance of grievances, 307, 308 f
  federations of, 301–302
  historic background, 296–300
  locals, 300–301
  and management vs. labor rights, 296
  management views on, 302–303

membership in, 300, 301
  national, 301
  organizational forms of, 300–302
  performance standards and, 203
  promotion criteria and, 187
  purpose of, 295–96
  state labor laws and, 300
  trust funds of, 300
  See also Labor relations
Unity of command, 166–67
Uris, Auren, 343 n

Variable budget, 219
Verne, Jules, 342
Vroon, Victor H., 285 n

Wagner Act. See National Labor Relations Act
Walker, Charles R., 163
Watson, Hugh J., 237 n
Watson, Thomas J., Sr., 164
Webber, Ross A., 68 n, 136 n
Whyte, William F., 288 n
Wickersham, Edward D., 306 n
Wigdor, L. A., 283, 284 t
Williams, Ted, 39
Withdrawn communicator, 43
Witney, Fred, 300 n, 301 n
Women
  age discrimination and, 319
  job discrimination and, 119–20, 317–18
  as "minority" group, 317
  as supervisors, 319
Work, changes in, 313–14
  See also Division of work; Job evaluation; Work environment
Work environment
  elements of effectiveness of, 15
  job evaluation and, 194
  worker performance and, 7–8
Work hours, 72, 344
Work location, job evaluation and, 194
Work quality, morale and, 289–90
Workaholics, 71–72
Worker characteristics, job requirements and, 195 f
Worker performance, environment and, 7–8
Workers
  controlling supervisor and, 43
  and determination of performance standards, 203
  knowledge of company's objectives, 146–47
  needs of, 20–22
  protective legislation and, 109–15
  responsibilities to, 94–95
  role in goal setting, 147
  See also Black workers; Handicapped workers; Personnel function; Unions; Women
Worthy, James C., 170 n
Wright brothers, 136
Written communication, 40–41, 44

Zander, Alvin, 273 n
Ziegler, Ron, 90